Hegel's Political Philosophy

Hegel's Political Philosophy

On the Normative Significance of Method and System

EDITED BY
Thom Brooks
and Sebastian Stein

OXFORD
UNIVERSITY PRESS

Great Clarendon Street, Oxford, OX2 6DP,
United Kingdom

Oxford University Press is a department of the University of Oxford.
It furthers the University's objective of excellence in research, scholarship,
and education by publishing worldwide. Oxford is a registered trade mark of
Oxford University Press in the UK and in certain other countries

Published in the United States of America by Oxford University Press
198 Madison Avenue, New York, NY 10016, United States of America

British Library Cataloguing in Publication Data
Data available

Library of Congress Control Number: 2017932295

ISBN 978–0–19–877816–5

Printed and bound by
CPI Group (UK) Ltd, Croydon, CR0 4YY

Contents

Acknowledgements vii

Notes on Contributors ix

Introduction 1
Thom Brooks and Sebastian Stein

1. What Might it Mean to have a Systematic Idealist, but Anti-Platonist,
   Practical Philosophy? 25
   Paul Redding

2. Systematicity and Normative Justification: The Method of Hegel's
   Philosophical Science of Right 44
   Kevin Thompson

3. In What Sense is Hegel's *Philosophy of Right* "Based" on His
   Science of Logic? Remarks on the Logic of Justice 67
   Robert B. Pippin

4. Method and System in Hegel's *Philosophy of Right* 82
   Allen W. Wood

5. The Relevance of the Logical Method for Hegel's Practical Philosophy 103
   Angelica Nuzzo

6. The State as a System of Three Syllogisms: Hegel's Notion of the
   State and Its Logical Foundations 124
   Klaus Vieweg

7. Hegel's Shepherd's Way Out of the Thicket 142
   Terry Pinkard

8. To Know and Not Know Right: Hegel on Empirical Cognition
   and Philosophical Knowledge of Right 161
   Sebastian Stein

9. Individuals: The Revisionary Logic of Hegel's Politics 183
   Katerina Deligiorgi

10. Hegel on Crime and Punishment 202
    Thom Brooks

11. The Logic of Right 222
    Richard Dien Winfield

12. Hegel, Autonomy, and Community   239
    Liz Disley

13. Hegel's Natural Law Constructivism: Progress in Principle and
    in Practice   253
    Kenneth R. Westphal

Index   281

Acknowledgements

We have collected several debts leading up to the publication of this book. We must first thank our contributors for producing a diverse range of insights into the neglected topic of how Hegel's system informs his political philosophy. When Thom was a graduate student at the University of Sheffield and Sebastian was a graduate student at the University of Oxford, the importance of Hegel's system and method remained underappreciated in our view. This is a project we have wanted to produce for some time and we hope that this topic will feature more prominently in future work on Hegel's philosophy more generally, as a productive insight into his complex and wide-ranging works. Working together on this project has been as interesting as it has been enjoyable.

Thom extends his thanks to Sebastian for his considerable help in putting much of this book together, including producing an original translation of the chapter by Klaus Vieweg rendered in English for the first time here. This was a substantial task to undertake in addition to contributing his own original piece and sharing editorial duties— and this book is much richer for it. I owe many thanks to Brian O'Connor for being the first to help me realize the importance of Hegel's system and method for understanding his political philosophy. I am grateful to Michael Rosen whose work continues to exercise a profound influence on me explicitly and implicitly. Bhikhu Parekh developed my thinking on much of this material and my work benefits enormously from his critical interventions and scholarly example. Finally, Bob Stern deserves the most thanks of all for guiding much of my thought to where it is today.

Sebastian would like to thank Thom for conceiving of the project, taking him on board just at the right time, and for commenting on the contribution's main draft. It was nothing but joy to work with such a motivating mentor and learn about the intricacies of the editing process. I would also like to extend special thanks to Michael Inwood and Felix Stein for patiently commenting on two drafts of the contribution and to professors Anton Koch, Jens Halfwassen, Robert Pippin, Sebastian Ostritsch, and Ioannis Trisokkas for helping me shape its core ideas. Much was learned from the constructive criticism made by the participants at the Leuven University conference "Hegel, une pensée de l'objectivité" and Professor Koch's and Professor Halfwassen's research workshops at Heidelberg University. The works of Michael Inwood and Stephen Houlgate have been a source of great inspiration ever since my first encounter with Hegel's thought, as have been the exchanges with David Merrill, Lucia Ziglioli, Susanne Herrmann-Sinai, Lisa Herzog, Roberto Vinco, Carl O'Brien, Frank Chouraqui, Hermes Plevrakis, Christian Martin, Tobias Dangel, Giuseppe Blasotta, Lee Watkins, Resgar Beraderi, and Daniel Dragicevic amongst others. Their curiosity and passion for the truth keep me on the Way.

Notes on Contributors

THOM BROOKS is Professor of Law and Government, Dean of Durham Law School and Associate in Philosophy at Durham University.

KATERINA DELIGIORGI is Reader in Philosophy at the University of Sussex.

LIZ DISLEY is an Honorary Research Fellow in Philosophy at the University of St Andrews.

ANGELICA NUZZO is Professor of Philosophy at CUNY.

TERRY PINKARD is University Professor of Philosophy at Georgetown University.

ROBERT B. PIPPIN is the Evelyn Stefansson Nef Distinguished Service Professor in the Committee on Social Thought, the Department of Philosophy, and the College at the University of Chicago.

PAUL REDDING is Professor of Philosophy at the University of Sydney.

SEBASTIAN STEIN is Postdoctoral Researcher at Ruprecht-Karls-University in Heidelberg.

KLAUS VIEWEG is Chair for Civil Law, Law of Information Technology and Law of Technology and Business at the Law School of Erlangen University and Director of the Institute of Law and Technology.

KEVIN THOMPSON is Associate Professor of Philosophy at DePaul University.

KENNETH R. WESTPHAL is Professor of Philosophy at Bogazici University and Honorary Professorial Fellow at the University of East Anglia.

RICHARD DIEN WINFIELD is Distinguished Research Professor of Philosophy at the University of Georgia.

ALLEN W. WOOD is the Ward W. and Priscilla B. Woods Professor Emeritus at Stanford University.

Introduction

Thom Brooks and Sebastian Stein

I.1. A New Debate

Bertrand Russell called Hegel 'the hardest to understand of all the great philosophers'.[1] Hegel's philosophy has certainly attracted much debate—and the *Philosophy of Right* and his political philosophy have been at the heart of important controversies. The first concerned his ideology, where scholars were divided on whether he work supported a politically right or left interpretation. Shortly after its publication in 1821, Hegel's work was branded dangerously authoritarian.[2] Others agree, including Karl Popper who claimed Hegel is 'the father of modern historicism and totalitarianism'.[3] Such views are now widely rejected by virtually all commentators—and even Popper shifted his position.[4]

A second, more contemporary debate has focused on the role played by metaphysics in Hegel's philosophy. In the first section of the *Philosophy of Right*, Hegel says this work is primarily concerned with 'the concept of right [*Recht*] and its actualisation'.[5] For Hegel, 'right' does not merely exist, but it can exist in varying degrees—and so some manifestations of right are said to be more real or actual than others. Hegel's metaphysics of 'the Concept' have been challenged by many interpreters leading to the 'non-metaphysical' reading of the *Philosophy of Right* dominant today which attempt to separate out Hegel's ontological claims from his account of political thought.[6] In the words of Z. A. Pelczynski:

Hegel's political thought can be read, understood, and appreciated without having to come to terms with his metaphysics. Some of his assertions may seem less grounded than they might

---

[1] Bertrand Russell, *A History of Western Philosophy* (New York: Simon & Schuster, 1945): 730.

[2] See Rudolf Haym, *Hegel und seine Zeit* (Berlin, 1857).

[3] Karl Popper, *The Open Society and Its Enemies, Vol. II: The High Tide of Prophecy: Hegel, Marx and the Aftermath*, 5th edition (London: Routledge & Kegan Paul, 1966): 22.

[4] Popper later admitted 'factual mistakes' in his interpretation of Hegel's political philosophy and said that 'I looked upon my book as my war effort: believing as I did in the responsibility of Hegel and the Hegelians for much of what happened in Germany'. See Popper, *The Open Society and Its Enemies*, 393–4.

[5] G. W. F. Hegel, *Elements of the Philosophy of Right*, trans H. B. Nisbet (Cambridge: Cambridge University Press, 1991): §1.

[6] See Thom Brooks, *Hegel's Political Philosophy: A Systematic Reading of the Philosophy of Right*, 2nd edition (Edinburgh: Edinburgh University Press, 2013): 2–3.

otherwise have been; some of his statements and beliefs may puzzle one; some intellectual curiosity may be unsatisfied when metaphysics is left out; a solid volume of political theory and political thinking will still remain.[7]

Comments like these raise serious questions about the importance of Hegel's philosophical foundations and whether they are more than 'some intellectual curiosity' of a few Hegel scholars—or whether there is something of greater interest to be found in taking a much closer look.

We believe such an examination is needed urgently. The topic of this book is a new issue that emerges from this debate between the non-metaphysical readings that isolate the *Philosophy of Right* from its systematic context and metaphysical readings that take the *Science of Logic* and the wider system into account when they interpret the *Philosophy of Right*. This difference entails a profound interpretative change concerning *the philosophical foundations of Hegel's political thought*. Hegel famously argues that the system-informing speculative method that he details in his *Logic* grounds his claims about socio-political reality and is the inevitable and superior alternative to all other ways of philosophical thinking. We argue that it is only in the light of this method and the system it begets that Hegel's claims about socio-political reality can be rationally evaluated in his own terms.

Until recently, however, Hegel scholars have paid generally insufficient serious attention to the importance of his philosophical *method* and *system* in explaining his philosophy. It has become commonplace for studies of his texts to focus on a specific aspect of his system and overlook the importance of his method for our understanding of his ideas. These readings can be considered 'non-systematic' because most commentators neglect the systematic structure of Hegel's arguments and overall philosophical enterprise. Instead, scholars have chosen to 'buckle down to the study of the *Philosophy of Right* for example and try to work out the context of his arguments as he elaborates in that text'—and ignore its connections to his philosophical system.[8]

A systematic reading of Hegel's work takes more seriously these features of method and system.[9] It is clear that Hegel intended his ideas about socio-political normativity to be understood in a particular way. The opening lines of his *Philosophy of Right* state that it:

is a more extensive, and in particular a more systematic exposition of the same basic concepts which, in relation to this part of philosophy, are already contained in a previous work designed to accompany my lectures, namely my *Encyclopaedia of the Philosophical Sciences*.[10]

This passages raises two key points. The first is that the *Philosophy of Right*—and his political philosophy more generally—was not meant to be understood separately from

---

[7] Z. A. Pelczynski, 'An Introductory Essay', in G. W. F. Hegel, *Hegel's Political Writings*, trans. T. M. Knox (Oxford: Clarendon, 1964): 136–7.

[8] See Dudley Knowles, *Hegel and the Philosophy of Right* (London: Routledge, 2002): 21.

[9] The distinction of a systematic reading versus a non-systematic reading of Hegel's philosophy is presented in Brooks, *Hegel's Political Philosophy*, especially 1–28 and 161–77.

[10] Hegel, *Elements of the Philosophy of Right*, 9.

his wider philosophical system that is outlined in the *Encyclopaedia*, with the *Philosophy of Right* being an elaboration of the *Encyclopaedia*'s section 'Objective Spirit'.[11] There is nothing controversial then about how Hegel intended his audiences to understand his work—although it is a topic of debate whether Hegel's method and system play the important role he assigned them.

The second key point is that if the *Philosophy of Right* and its political philosophy is to be considered part of the system then its claims should be understood in a systematic way. This means more than just locating the text within a wider philosophical enterprise outlined in his three-volume *Encyclopaedia*, but also demands becoming more attentive to the distinctive form of dialectical argumentation that informs the *Philosophy of Right* as much as they do his wider system.

Whether or not his method and system matter for his political philosophy has usually been dismissed. Examples abound. Frederick Neuhouser argues:

[E]ven though Hegel's social theory is undeniably embedded within a more comprehensive philosophical vision—one that includes views about the nature of ultimate reality and the meaning of human history—it is possible, to a surprisingly large extent, to understand his account of what makes the rational social order rational and to appreciate its force even while abstracting from those more fundamental doctrines.[12]

Similar comments about the relation of Hegel's philosophical system to his political thought are made by Allen Wood:

Because Hegel regards speculative logic as the foundation of his system, we might conclude from its failure that nothing in his philosophy could any longer be deserving of our interest. But that would be quite wrong. The fact is rather that Hegel's great positive achievements as a philosopher do not lie where he thought they did, in his system of speculative logic, but in a quite different realm, in his reflections on the social and spiritual predicament of modern Western European culture.[13]

Serious criticisms like these raise questions about Hegel's systematic project. Was he wrong in tying the notion of philosophical truth to systematic thinking and the speculative method? Is it possible to criticize or appreciate some of his claims without endorsing or rejecting the entire system and its method? Was Hegel deceived about the importance of his method and system for his political philosophy? Are his claims about the rationality of political institutions—like monarchy, unequal gender relations, and a corporation-based economy—beyond non-speculative revision or even reconstruction? Since Hegel's method is supposed to save him from both dogmatism and relativism, is there anything about his criticism of previous philosophies that could make his approach attractive to contemporary thinkers? Or is it preferable

---

[11] See G. W. F. Hegel, *Philosophy of Mind* (Oxford: Oxford University Press, 1971): §§483–552.

[12] Frederick Neuhouser, *Foundations of Hegel's Social Theory: Actualising Freedom* (Cambridge: Harvard University Press, 2000): 4.

[13] Allen W. Wood, *Hegel's Ethical Thought* (Cambridge: Cambridge University Press, 1990): 5.

to focus on Hegel's conclusions only, disregard his method, and interpret him non-systematically?

There is clearly a debate to be had about the importance of Hegel's method and system for his political philosophy and wider thought—and we think that there is too little substantive work that explicitly explores this issue. We thus see an urgent need for greater reflection on these foundational ideas and for a new wave of research into Hegel's systematic thought in general and the *Philosophy of Right* in particular.

I.2. An Overview

This collection of new essays is dedicated to the questions that surround Hegel's philosophical method and its relationship to the conclusions of his political philosophy. It contributes to the ongoing debate about the importance of a systematic context for political philosophy and the relationship between theoretical and practical philosophy. It also engages with contemporary discussions about the shape of a rational social order and gauges the timeliness of Hegel's way of thinking.

In Chapter 1, Paul Redding uses a discussion of Rorty's endorsement of Hegel to analyse the nature of Hegel's 'new' metaphysics.[14] Rejecting the old metaphysics' Platonic project of talking about the world in 'God's own language', Rorty finds a brother in arms in Hegel and his method of 'redescription': in the *Phenomenology*, so Rorty argues, Hegel 'out-redescribes' the major philosophers of the Platonic-metaphysical tradition and thereby enables an emancipation from their objectivist aspirations.

The freedom from classical metaphysics that Hegel thereby makes possible, so Redding's Rorty, is more important than Hegel's own attempt at providing a new objectivist point of view with his account of 'absolute knowing'. While the practical goals of freedom and justice remain accessible through the empirical world's truths, the metaphysical master narrative, i.e. 'Truth' and its claim to necessity, is undermined. Inspired by Hegel's method of redescription, the (post)modern philosopher is to adopt a point of view from which previous thinkers are undermined but unlike Hegel remains 'ironic' about this perspective.

While Redding agrees with Rorty that Hegel is anti-Platonic in his aspirations, he rejects Rorty's sacrifice of 'Truth' for freedom: Redding's Hegel is able to have both. How so? Drawing on the notion of 'struggle for recognition', Redding describes Hegel's notion of 'the will' as overcoming Kant's and Fichte's rejection of desire's object: Hegel's rational will accommodates a positive as well as a negative dimension—it is a will *to* something as well as a negation of a given object of desire.

Drawing on the *Logic*'s section of the syllogisms of 'existence' and 'reflection', Redding suggests that the content of Hegel's 'free willing' sublates the 'de re' ('freedom') and 'de dicto' ('Truth') dichotomy. While the validity of 'de re' ('existence') beliefs

---

[14] All quotations in discussion about Chapter 1 are from that chapter unless otherwise stated.

depends on contextual background information, 'de dicto' (reflective) validity is supposed to be timeless. Both existence and reflection are necessary but on its own, neither is sufficient for describing rational intentionality: To be properly rational actors, we must reflectively adopt a contextually defined content to our willing. The choices we make take place 'in the world', and by conceptually redetermining the content of our willing, we ever more adequately 'bring out the structure of the *actual* world for a subject who *belongs* to that world'.

This means that there is no essentially (e.g. Aristotelian) right way of acting. Instead, what has to be done is to be judged in the context of a world with particular, specific features and contexts. For Redding, this makes Hegel a 'modal actualist'—the object of our metaphysical knowledge is the actual world we inhabit: it is knowledge of the actual world, known from 'a reflectively mediated position within it'.

So freedom is to be gained 'by grasping real possibilities that exist within the actual, possibilities that can thereby be realized to create a new actuality'. This happens 'via participation in a socialized cognition in which others are, in the style of Kant, recognized as free minds and not as objects of nature'.

In Chapter 2, Kevin Thompson argues that Hegel's notion of normative justification in general and of the state in particular has to be able to withstand the three sceptic challenges: (A) a claim is grounded in unwarranted assumptions, (B) the claim's foundation is itself in need of justification, and (C) the claim presupposes what it seeks to establish.[15]

According to Thompson's Hegel, 'representational thinking' is unable to answer these challenges because it 'employs preconceived notions or makes use of ungrounded assumptions' and while both rationalism and empiricism fall prey to the shortcomings of representational thought, Hegel proposes thinking in terms of 'concepts' as an alternative to representational thought. Unlike representations, so Thompson argues, Hegel's 'concepts' are independent from representational and (rational) intuition-informed content because they (a) track conceptual, immanent development, (b) establish necessary entailment of their determinations, (c) engage in 'retrogressive grounding', and (d) begin without presuppositions (i.e. they assume neither rules of procedure nor their subject matter). The only fundamental precondition of Hegelian 'concepts' is the 'justification of the systematic [i.e. concepts-mapping] standpoint itself'. By connecting all conceptual determinations, Thompson's Hegel sets out 'to establish the oneness of thought and being so that the concepts and relations out of which the system is to be fashioned already had their ontological credentials secured'.

This enables Hegel to undermine the notion of a standard of truth that is external to thought/being and so Hegel 'is [...] able to capture the core of foundationalism's concern with grasping the nature and truth of reality itself and coherentism's insistence on constitutive relational dependence in a way that avoids the dogmatism of the former and the relativism of the latter'. Thompson's Hegel's 'true way of knowing [...] is

---

[15] All quotations in discussion about Chapter 2 are from that chapter unless otherwise stated.

nothing other than the process of development that is proper to being itself and this is to grasp the rationality, the dialectic of the concept, within all that is'.

What does this mean for the *Philosophy of Right*'s concern with 'right', itself a conceptual determination and thus part of the conceptual system? Also here, so Thompson argues, philosophical thought has to 'observe the immanent development of the pure concept of right into its interdependent whole, [i.e.] its complete actualization'. So it is by sticking to the requirements of systematic, concept-mapping justification that Hegel 'is able to show that right is not only one of the essential determinations discovered in the unfolding of freedom, it is the concrete existence, the necessary embodiment, through which human striving is able to be genuinely free.'

In Chapter 3, Robert B. Pippin connects the project of the *Science of Logic* with the *Philosophy of Right* via the notion of actuality: in virtue of its status as logic, transcendental logic, *and* metaphysics, the *Science of Logic* tells us about those categories in the light of which simultaneous sense-making about thought and world takes place.[16]

Beyond Kant's restriction of the question of intelligibility to the concerns of the finite representatives of a 'species' and its sense-making practices, Pippin's Hegel is concerned with 'general intelligibility' and argues that any notion of 'objects "outside" something like the limits of the thinkable is a non-thought, a *sinnloser Gedanke*'. To Pippin's Hegel, 'to be *is* to be intelligible; the founding principle of Greek metaphysics and philosophy itself'.

In going beyond Kant's limitations, so Pippin argues, Hegel approximates Aristotle. To him, '[e]ntities are the determinate entities they are "in terms of" or "because of" their concept or substantial form. Such entities embody some measure of what it is truly to be *such* a thing, and instantiate such an essence to a greater or lesser degree'. This leads Pippin to describe Hegel's 'actuality' as the result of Aristotle-style 'dynamis' (potential, *Möglichkeit*) that actualizes itself and takes on the form of an actualized potential (energeia, *Wirklichkeit*). This actuality—rather than mere existence or appearance—is the concern of the philosopher: 'The suggestion is that Hegel thinks of anything's principle of intelligibility, its conceptual form, as an *actualization* in the Aristotelian sense, the being-at-work or *energeia* of the thing's distinct mode of being'.

This also applies to the *Philosophy of Right*. Its concern, the actuality of freedom, 'is neither an analysis of the mere concept of right, nor an empirical account of existing systems of right'. Instead, it is 'the concept together with its "actuality," where the latter is distinguished from "external contingency, untruth, deception, etc."'. So on Pippin's reading, Hegel's philosopher wants to know whether what he is historically confronted with is *actually* a freedom-actualizing socio-political institutional framework, whether it truly is 'the determination by the power of thought of its own norm for a free life?'

Pippin notes that in Hegel's philosophical description of the forms of 'actualized freedom' in the *Philosophy of Right*, the *Logic*'s categories of being, essence, and the

---

[16] All quotations in discussion about Chapter 3 are from that chapter unless otherwise stated.

concept correspond to the abstract right, morality, and ethical life. Each form leads into another due to the previous one's incoherence: e.g. thinking of each other only as abstract right's persons does not allow us properly to understand the motivations behind our actions and so morality is needed to fill that sense-making void.

According to Pippin's Hegel, the actuality of someone's rational activity is thus not just the sum total of their externally observable actions or their inner motivations. It has to consider both of these: 'We need to understand *how* "what shows," "what manifests itself" [*Schein*] can be said to reflect their essence when they do (if they do, then as appearance [*Erscheinung*]), even if, as appearances, no one deed is ever a manifestation or simple representation of essence as such'. While Pippin admits that 'Hegel's *Logic* does not provide any ground rules for how to do this', he argues it is enough to know that this is how sense-making of actions ought to proceed.

So although the *Logic* does not furnish a 'blueprint' for understanding the *Philosophy of Right*, it describes what people *actually* are, and how they can lead free, norm-governed lives. The rational norms in question constitute Hegel's notion of 'right' and they can 'be understood only in terms of our ways of understanding anything', i.e. logically. However, so Pippin maintains, 'Hegel freely admits and insists on the fact that these modalities of righteous lives can be, must be, inflected in different historical ways'. While Hegel might be correct in arguing that the rational state enables and controls civil society's pursuit of self-interest, the concrete way in which this historically happens is not necessarily for Hegel to grasp.

Rejecting attempts to read Hegel as deducing everything that socio-politically exists from the concept of right (e.g. down to 'Krug's fountain pen'), Pippin is also open to criticisms of Hegel: just because Hegel knew *that* right is the essence of socio-political reality does not mean that he necessarily knew *what* right is. Analysing our contemporary political landscapes, Pippin dismisses Marx's critique of Hegel that the latter tried to fit history into the concept rather than the other way around, but Pippin allows that Hegel might have been wrong about how civil society and state can be reconciled. With liberals and conservatives both rejecting the state without giving an alternative, it seems that civil society has freed itself from the state's embrace. And while we do not need to understand the *Logic* and its intricacies to understand what is wrong with contemporary political life, so Pippin concludes, it remains important to understand the *logic* of Hegel's project in the *Philosophy of Right*.

In Chapter 4, Allen W. Wood argues that labelling him as a 'non-systematic' interpreter of Hegel's practical philosophy amounts to misunderstanding his stance.[17] Maintaining that 'we still have much to learn from past philosophers, by asking them our questions and reading their texts as answers to them', Wood rejects that this amounts to 'reading your own thoughts into the philosopher': 'In appropriating a past philosopher, you need to be self-aware of your own act of appropriation, and you must devise an approach that lets you get the most philosophically out of the encounter.'

---

[17] All quotations in discussion about Chapter 4 are from that chapter unless otherwise stated.

With regard to Hegel, Wood argues that appropriating him implies understanding him which in turn implies 'understanding the system and method through which he thought'. This, so Wood deduces, entails that '[t]here is no choice between reading Hegel "systematically" and reading him in response to our questions. There are only different ways of doing both at once.' Although Hegel's 'speculative logic' is no 'replacement for traditional logic' and that one need not 'see Hegel's ethical insights as *grounded* in (hence sharing the same fate as) his now clearly outdated speculative-logical system', Wood also maintains that 'one's understanding of Hegel's ethical thought [is] greatly enhanced if one approached it with an appreciation of the way it is shaped by his method and his systematic concerns'.

Wood then traces Hegel's method back to the post-Kantian period during which Kant was criticized for drawing his categories rather 'mechanically from the tradition of scholastic formal logic' and called for a more 'rigorous kind of derivation' of philosophical concepts. Second, so Wood, the post-Kantians accused Kant of separating 'sensible intuition from the thought of understanding' and asked for 'a transcendental explanation not merely of the forms of thinking but also of the matter'.

It was Fichte who took the 'first great creative step' beyond Kant on Wood's reading and 'sought a method by which the categories of thought might be successively introduced'. Simultaneously deducing 'I' and its object ('non-I'), Fichte attempted to justify the categories of thought by exposing their contradictions. For Wood's Fichte, the most basic contradiction between 'I' and 'non-I' can be avoided if 'we introduce a new concept—that of limited, partial or divisible activity or negation'. It implies that each negation is 'compatible' with the other and '[t]his compatibility constitutes the common *ground* for their synthesis or reciprocal dependency'. Fichte's method is 'synthetic', so Wood, insofar as he seeks to unite opposing propositions in higher-order categories that avoid the lower-level contradiction.

For Wood, '[i]t seems self-evident that the synthetic method was the model for Hegel's dialectical method' since 'Hegel also proceeds by showing how every limited thought-determination leads us into contradictions, which can then be resolved by introducing a new thought-determination. Hegel calls this process the "proof" of the new thought-determination.' Unlike Fichte, so Wood,

Hegel did complete the systematic development of such a system of thought determinations. This was his *Science of Logic*. He then developed the 'real' parts of his encyclopaedic philosophical system by going through a similar process with the thought-determinations through which those regions of reality are grasped: the philosophy of nature, and the philosophy of spirit. Hegel's *Elements of the Philosophy of Right* is a yet more detailed execution of this dialectical process within one part of the philosophy of spirit, namely the sphere of objective spirit (or social life).

Wood rejects the idea that Hegel's project *as undertaken by him* has 'continuing philosophical value' but asserts that 'understanding the details of Hegel's systematic [is] indispensable to the appropriation of his living philosophical contributions'. Wood then gives examples for why he thinks Hegel is still of philosophical interest today: He argues that 'Hegel anticipated some of the problems philosophers now have relating [...] the sciences to one another, arguing that Hegel developed an approach to such problems that 'is worthy of serious consideration'. According to Wood, Hegel's 'conceptual pluralism' can teach us something about the limits of naturalism's tendency to reduce all phenomena to natural ones instead of acknowledging each domain's limitations. While Hegel would be more systematic about the different concepts' relationships than contemporary thinkers, so Wood claims, he would also argue that the spiritual is privileged over the natural and that the 'highest spiritual cognitions' such as art, religion, and philosophy enable access to the 'highest truth'.

While sympathetic to conceptual pluralism in general, Wood does 'not think we can accept Hegel's version of conceptual pluralism in its original form' and that 'Hegel belongs to an earlier stage of the history of science and philosophy than the one where we are now. We cannot simply look at Hegel's own writings and doctrines for the right answers to our questions'. Still, Wood maintains that Hegel's spiritual categories 'deserve to be seriously considered as options in dealing with the issues to which naturalists think they have [...] all the answers'. Since Hegel's own thoughts can only be understood in the context of method and system, so Wood argues, he resists the idea to '"quarantine" [Hegel's] philosophy of right from his system' and does not 'refuse to take his system into account when understanding his ethics'.

Wood also finds Hegel's 'hierarchical version of conceptual pluralism' at play in the 'philosophy of objective spirit—his philosophy of right': 'Social life and the norms that belong to it form a plurality of different systems and subsystems, whose limitations are signalled by the fact that a way of thinking, when pushed beyond its limits, falls into contradiction and becomes self-undermining.' In differentiating between abstract right, morality, and ethical life, Wood thinks Hegel 'captures the distinctness and independence of right and morality that he inherited from Kant and Fichte' and even in the face of Hegel's differentiations within ethical life, morality and abstract right 'retain their validity'.

To show that not all the problems of Hegel's account of right have solutions, Wood cites Hegel's treatment of peasants, women, day labourers, 'rabble', and 'poverty', all of which seem unavoidable features of Hegel's 'just' state. For Wood, this points to the problem that 'it is not at all clear that people's rights or aspirations to subjective freedom were even close to being properly actualized in the European state of 1820, or in the society in which we live today': 'As Hegel presents things, the benefits of both right and morality are enjoyed only by a minority of the members of society—in effect, by the male bourgeoisie and civil servants—the young men, and their fathers, whose social position was like that of Hegel himself and of those to whom he lectured. The inadequacy of that society, as Hegel portrays it, even by the standards of his own theory of freedom, is all too clear today.'

Citing Fichte, Wood counters that '[i]f we can be reconciled with existing social reality at all, it must be only conditionally and provisionally; we cannot rationally be content with the world as it actually is' and states that '[i]f Hegel's philosophy really aims at reconciling us with the modern world, we must reject it. For the modern world is not reconcilable to itself.'

In Chapter 5, Angelica Nuzzo argues that the *Philosophy of Right* and the *Science of Logic* are systematically united by their concern with what Hegel calls 'the idea'.[18] And it is this common concern that enables a reading of the *Philosophy of Right* in the light of the *Logic* and vice versa.

Arguing that 'the fruitfulness and vitality of Hegel's practical philosophy [...] depend both on its being conceived as a part of the system of philosophy' and 'on its being based on and articulated according to the dialectical-speculative method developed in the *Logic* as the first and foundational part of the system', Nuzzo relies on the notion of 'action' as common denominator between *Logic* and *Philosophy of Right*: while the *Logic* discusses action as such, the *Philosophy of Right* discusses action in the forms of right, morality, ethical life, politics, and history.

With regards to systematicity, Nuzzo suggests that 'the "system" (or systematic "whole") is the form that [freedom as truth, i.e. the "discrete, dynamic, ongoing process of self-production and self-actualization"] takes as it acquires objective reality—in knowledge, in action, in history'. The same freedom that informs the determinations of the *Logic*, so Nuzzo argues, defines and structures the *Philosophy of Right*. This freedom is the concept (or world-immanent 'soul' or 'consciousness') that gives itself actuality (or the idea) and so *Logic* as well as the 'philosophical science of right' are both 'complementary investigations on the actuality of the idea': The *Logic* describes the idea's ontological structure, the *Philosophy of Right* describes the idea's 'historical actualization'.

Nuzzo parallels the 'retrospective character' mentioned in the *Logic*'s final discussion of 'absolute method' with the *Philosophy of Right*'s philosophical look on to the world once actuality has manifested itself, and she argues that Hegel's speculative method performs the very 'dynamic flux' of thought's movement that also determines the world: 'By bringing change to bear directly on pure thinking, by making thinking one with the movement it accounts for, Hegel's logic *does* the very thing that it purports to understand and describe.' For Nuzzo, this means that the question of intelligibility becomes one of theory as much as one of praxis.

On her reading, logic *is* action and it is this action that informs the *Philosophy of Right*'s determinations: the logic of action is actualized by 'different spiritual agents—alternatively, individual, collective, institutional, economic, political agents—under the specific conditions dictated by a changing historical actuality'. Focusing on the *Logic*'s absolute method's notion of 'beginning', Nuzzo compares how the *Logic*'s moments of 'being', 'essence', and 'concept' deal with this notion in different ways. While the logic of being defines beginning as pure immediacy and nothing, the logic of

---

[18] All quotations in discussion about Chapter 5 are from that chapter unless otherwise stated.

essence begins in opposition to being as something 'other' while the concept is always already with itself from the beginning.

This, so Nuzzo argues, parallels the *Philosophy of Right*'s discussions of different forms of violence: being's beginning's emptiness is the absolute freedom of destruction and revolutionary violence. Meanwhile, essence is violence against being, as manifested in revenge and Unrecht's 'shine' that enables right to reassert itself. The logical concept's constructive freedom parallels the determination of ethical life. Here, violence is turned on itself, and constructive formation and creation in the form of 'ethical powers' 'rule over the life of individuals in a non-violent way as the citizens identify with them, trust them, and see in them the source of their self-conscious activity within the ethical whole'.

In Chapter 6, Klaus Vieweg examines the syllogistic architecture of the *Outlines'* account of the state in order to find a more rational rendering than the one Hegel provides.[19] For Vieweg, Hegel's whole argument for the modern state 'rests on the logical spirit' and it takes the 'speculative mode of cognition' to grasp properly the argument's philosophical nature.

Vieweg's focus on logical form leads him to argue that the state's 'inner constitution is a whole consisting of three syllogisms' whose mutual connection takes place within the idea of right's totality. After analysing the role of syllogistic structure in the realm of inter-state relations, Vieweg turns to the notion that 'the state is a system of three syllogisms'. These are: '(1) the singular (the person) con-cludes himself through his particularity [...] with the universal [...]. (2) The will or the activity of the individuals is the mediating [term] that gives satisfaction to their needs in the context of society, right, etc., and provides fulfilment and actualization to society, right, etc. (3) [T]he universal (State, government, right) is the substantial middle term within which the individuals and their satisfaction have and preserve their full reality, mediation, and subsistence.'

Vieweg maintains that the 'syllogisms of quality' and of 'reflexion' fail adequately to describe the interconnections between the particular, universal, and individual moments and only the syllogism of necessity succeeds because it explicates that 'Concrete freedom consists in the fact that personal individuality (I) and its particular interests (P) find their complete development and the recognition of their specific right within the state (the universal of the constitution).'

For Vieweg, this means that it is only as 'citizen' that the acting subject 'achieves the *highest form of recognition* within an individual community' and is able to unite all the 'dimensions of subjectivity'. These are: 'Personality, moral subjectivity, membership in a family and in civil society'. As a citizen, the subject grasps its individuality 'also as an universality' and proves its freedom by, for example, 'respecting reasonable laws as something universal'. Of the three available necessary syllogisms (categorical,

---

[19] All quotations in discussion about Chapter 6 are from that chapter unless otherwise stated. This essay appears for the first time in this collection translated into English by Sebastian Stein.

hypothetical, and disjunctive), it is the disjunctive syllogism that 'exposes the moments of the concept in their *speculative unity*' and explicates that each of the moments 'represents the whole and contains the respective others within itself'. For Vieweg, this means that '[o]nly a citizen (Citoyen) that is logically-speculatively thought of in this way can serve as the foundation of a political state that is truly free.' According to the disjunctive syllogism of the state, '*every* moment of the concept's determination (I, P, U) *is itself the whole* and the *mediating ground*—the citizens, civil society, and the political state as community of the citizens (Citoyens)'.

After identifying the necessary, disjunctive syllogism as most adequate description of inter-state and intra-state relations, Vieweg applies the same analysis to the state's constitution's separation of powers. In so doing, he follows Hegel and identifies the power of the crown with individuality (I), government with particularity (P), and the legislative power with universality (U), but argues that Hegel's own descriptions of their relation 'fail sufficiently to develop the *entirely developed concept and the transition into the idea*'. Vieweg is surprised 'that the brilliant logician Hegel does not properly demonstrate the connectedness ('con-clusion') of the three syllogisms and fails to explicate the moment of the systematic whole, i.e. of the three syllogisms' unity, in sufficient detail.' For Vieweg, it is not the monarch as final decider but the legislative power that 'must be associated with the highest function of finalization'.

One reason for Hegel's failure to employ the disjunctive syllogism in the context of the division of powers and to establish the ideal nature of the constitution, so Vieweg suspects, 'can be found in Hegel's debt to his time': His contemporaries' 'debates surrounding constitutional theory' led him 'to find a guarantee of stability and order in constitutional monarchy and motivate him clearly to delineate this notion of monarchy from other versions and varieties of state constitutions'. Still, since the application of the disjunctive syllogism's requirements would place the legislative power at the centre of the state—and Hegel was aware of this—Vieweg suspects that Hegel 'fooled the Prussian censors with considerable finesse and chutzpa and placed his faith in his subsequent interpreters to realize a *reconstruction and correction in accordance with the requirements of Hegel's Logic* especially'. Applying Hegel's own syllogistic reasoning to the state's constitution, Vieweg argues that it is the legislative power, which is the only one capable of truly tying the three conceptual moments together and bringing them into the unity of the *universal reasonable will*: 'The constitution and the constitutional laws, the constitution itself and the legislative power' are the true foundation of the state's structure.

On Vieweg's reading, placing the legislative power at the deserved middle position of the syllogism reveals that it is 'the true syllogism of state-life, in which all powers originate in the people as such'. This makes the people themselves the 'sole purpose of the state' and the legislative power 'has the special function of *cognizing* and *determining* the specific purposes of the state'. Since the citizens elect the legislature, the disjunctive syllogism's application reveals 'their function as justifying instance of state power'. For Vieweg, this is '*universal reasonable will*, which manifests itself as constitution and as legislative assembly' and this entails that '[e]very citoyen must be enabled to equally participate in the creation of the universal—be it by way of membership in political parties and societies, by way of direct (plebiscitary) democracy, or by indirect, representative institutions'.

For Vieweg, '[a]pplying the logic correctly entails the *theoretical legitimization of a republican, democratic constitution* and of the fundamental meaning of the legislative assembly as expression of a representational-democratic structure.' This means that 'the *political trinity* has its ground in the "holy spirit" of the universal reasonable will of the citizen, the educated Citoyenneté as lawmaker and sovereign'. Ultimately, so Vieweg, the application of the disjunctive syllogism to the state's constitution shows that in the most rational state, the institutional set-up 'is the subject's *syllogizing with itself*, which, strictly speaking, is no syllogizing anymore' and so 'enables the citizen and citizenship in general to be autonomous, i.e. free, *within* the reasonably structured, legislative power in which universality, particularity, and individuality are united'. The truly rational state, so Vieweg argues, 'is the structure that satisfies the needs of the citizens as much as it is the product of the free activity and unification of the legal subjects'.

In Chapter 7, Terry Pinkard asks how Hegel combines 'his appeal to sociality and history with his otherwise timeless conceptions at work in his *Logic*'?[20] Pinkard's search for an answer leads him through a discussion of Hegel's notion of the idea to observations about Kant's and Fichte's notions of rational action, and finally, to a history-focused, social interpretation of Hegel's account of rational willing.

According to Pinkard, Hegel's 'idea' is 'the phenomenal world as comprehended in thought, and in practical contexts, Hegel expresses this by saying that the Idea is the warp and the passions are the weft of world history'. As 'unity of the phenomenal world and the noumenal world', the idea is actualized against the 'infinitely extending' background of the phenomenal world that escapes perception and intuition to some degree. Insofar as it does not, it forms part of the Idea, whose '"infinity" can be grasped not, as it were, as one thing after another but in the boundlessness of the conceptual'.

Some ways in which the idea is manifest and grasped are abstract right and the moral standing of persons. Asking why such reasons-motivated persons have moral rights, Pinkard suggests that part of the answer 'lies in the philosophy of history that comes at the end of the book and is therefore supposed to be the "ground" for all that has come before it. History has led us to the conclusion that we are required to think of all subjects that they are free', i.e. that 'there is no overarching natural authority among persons'. For Pinkard, both history and philosophy thus converge in their defence of the necessity of the modern conception of rights.

Arguing that 'there is something in people which does historically come to demand respect for itself', Pinkard's Hegel thinks of the intra-subjective seeming conflict between the demands of 'reason' and 'the drives' as reason 'shadowboxing' with itself.

---

[20] All quotations in discussion about Chapter 7 are from that chapter unless otherwise stated.

This is because Pinkard sees Hegel as subscribing to the 'incorporation thesis', according to which both reason and emotions are aspects of a historically realized reality of moral subjectivity that has self-consciousness about itself and its inner moral conflicts—the 'I think' is its constant companion. For Pinkard's Hegel, the subject's knowledge of what he is doing is essential to the action: '[T]he subject gives the "form of self-consciousness" to his life'.

This also means that self-conscious agents 'bring themselves' under the concept of leading an apperceptive life. They know this non-empirically because it is a feature of their subjectivity that they are subjects that bring themselves 'under the concept of "subject"': '[W]e are concept-mongering creatures because we make ourselves into concept mongering creatures'. To Hegel, being a spiritual being, so Pinkard argues, means just that: to self-consciously engage in progressively unfolding actions.

This reading relies to the Aristotelian notion of actuality: 'To understand a concept fully, we must understand how it may be actualized in use, and in the case of a practical concept, how, in Hegel's way of putting it, it must be able to "actualize itself" if it is to count as a practical concept at all.' So that a 'purportedly practical concept that could not be made real (be "actualized") would in fact not be a practical concept at all'.

For Pinkard, it is finite subjects who actualize practical concepts by taking them up and putting them into practice, thereby translating them from possibility to actuality. When they choose to actualize the human good, self-determining subjects can come into conflict about how and what to actualize. Such conflicts can be dissolved only in a social space that is structured by some kind of authority that motivates the subjects mutually to recognize and treat each other as ends, also. Each of these structured social contexts is 'historically indexed' so that all human action and enacting takes place in the context of world history that defines what is possible for the agents.

Pinkard adds that Hegel's rationally acting subjectivity 'takes its own concept, its concept of itself, to be the truth to which the world should measure up, not the other way around' and expresses the significance of its own concept of human life in art, religion, and philosophy. These describe 'shapes of life' and '[w]hen a shape of life cannot comprehend what it is doing, it begins to lose its normative allegiance among people living in terms of it'. This leads to alienation among the agents that are supposed to live in accordance with it. Once a form of life has 'broken' the agents have to pick up what still works in a new, hopefully viable socio-political arrangement. To Pinkard, 'Hegel has a view of history such that people have under many different conditions lived through such breakdowns of meanings in a way that has compelled them to a conclusion about human life such that nobody by nature has authority over anybody else, and therefore "all are free"'.

Finally, Pinkard identifies another feature of Hegel's rational agents: the two interests of (1) insuring that one's 'judgments about what a human life has subjective validity' by thinking '"This is what those of us would do in this case"' and (2) that the maxims of actions be objectively valid. The agent wants to know if her maxims are 'true' and she acts wondering 'whether "What we do" is true, that is, is what a true human being would do'.

One of Hegel's objective truths about modern agency, so Pinkard, is the notion that modern moral rights

demand a moral point of view, a reasoning from the standpoint of what any rational human would do; and a conception of those social goods that make it good for any individual subject to think of his concept as good—that means that it is good to be a rights-bearing, moral agent, in the sense that one is doing what ultimately matters in a human life—so that even when the world fails to conform to this concept, it has the means to right itself.

What this actually means, so Pinkard argues, is what Hegel attempts to capture with the triad of 'rights, morality, and ethical life', moving on from there into 'not yet adequately charted thickets'.

In Chapter 8, Sebastian Stein investigates the relationship between empirical cognition and philosophical knowledge in the context of Hegel's practical philosophy.[21] Against interpretations of Hegel that suggest empirical experience and historical circumstance condition philosophical knowledge, Stein differentiates between unconditioned philosophical knowledge ('PK'), conditioned empirical knowledge ('EK'), and potentially conditioned philosophical knowledge ('PCPK'). While PK is true by definition, EK is always opinion and PCPK is how finite, potentially mistaken thinkers relate to PK.

According to Stein, Hegel defines the conceptual structure of EK as 'the unconditioned concept as Geist that knows about the unconditioned concept in form of a presupposed reality'. In contrast, PK is the unconditioned concept as free Geist that knows the unconditioned concept as free Geist: it is unconditioned, self-thinking, absolute Geist. From PCPK's perspective, so Stein's Hegel, 'we' as cognizing subjects aim for PK when we attempt to replace 'representations with concepts'. Instead of the conditioned, externally informed representations of EK, 'we' want to think PK in the form of determinations of the very unconditioned concept that informs and enables our existence, thinking in general and reality.

Crucially, so Stein's Hegel, PK grounds EK and PCPK. 'We' can err and entertain doubt about PK because there is PK in the first place. If PCPK were more fundamental than PK, it could not guarantee the universal validity it automatically appeals to when posited as fundamental. Furthermore, if PCPK were everything there was, there would be no criterion for distinguishing PK from error: unless 'we' as finite thinkers always already know PK, we could not recognize it when we encounter it.

Unlike other interpretations of Hegel's notion of philosophy that focus on the conditioned or potentially conditioned perspective of finite thinkers only, so Stein maintains, his reading addresses Hegel's explicit concern with the ultimate unconditionality of PK *and* is able to explain how 'we' and 'Hegel' as historically positioned, finite thinkers

---

[21] All quotations in discussion about Chapter 8 are from that chapter unless otherwise stated.

can err about PK. From 'our', PCPK-style perspective, there remains the possibility that the 'always already present', all-informing unconditioned truth of PK is explicated inadequately. The same applies to Hegel: as a historically situated, finite thinker, it is possible that he erred about PK and that his account of right is partially or totally mistaken. However, 'our' alternative account of right can only successfully substitute 'his' insofar as 'we'—rather than 'him'—correctly channel unconditioned Geist's self-thinking. The only adequate standard for PK's truth is neither 'Hegel's' thinking nor 'ours' but the truth itself.

In Chapter 9, Katerina Deligiorgi connects the *Logic* and the *Philosophy of Right* by investigating the conceptual role that 'individuality' plays in both contexts.[22] In so doing, she aims to make sense of Hegel's 'criticism of the politics of individualism [...] and his recognition of the positive, liberating function of modern individualism'.

Looking at the *Logic*, Deligiorgi finds two meanings of 'individual', one that Hegel wants to preserve, the other, he wants to undermine: Deligiorgi's Hegel rejects the idea that an 'individual' is 'something that counts as one by virtue of not being reducible to something else', i.e. a 'simple'. Instead, so Deligiorgi argues, Hegel thinks of an 'individual' as something 'incomplete': 'in order to fully characterize what makes someone an individual, further information must be adduced'.

More precisely, Deligiorgi locates Hegel's discussion of individuality in the *Logic*'s Kant-inspired discussion of 'the notion': unlike Spinoza's 'just given' unity, 'the notion'—Hegel's shorthand for Kant's 'transcendental unity of apperception'—there becomes a placeholder for the concept of 'individuality'. Arguing that the notion has 'the determination of negativity', Deligiorgi's Hegel follows Kant in thinking that the notion 'is known only through the thoughts that are its predicates' and that individuation takes place in the individual's 'opposing itself to all that is other and excluding it'. For Hegel, so Deligiorgi, an individual is an individual because it is not one or more other individual(s) and because it assumes certain predicates in a negativity-driven manner.

Via a discussion of Geach's reconstruction of Aquinas' conception of 'form', Deligiorgi suggests that Hegel thinks of individuality in the same way Geach argues that Aquinas thought of 'form': for Geach's Aquinas, 'form' is the 'that' in propositions of the kind 'that by which X is y'. This 'that' is not a 'thing' like a universal Platonic 'form' but only makes sense in connection to the thing it is the form of: without something that has the form, there is no form.

In the same way, so Deligiorgi argues, for Hegel there is no 'individual' unless it is an individual determined as something. How then are individuals determined in the context of political philosophy? Hegel's concept of 'ethical life' gives us a clue, so Deligiorgi: 'members of ethical life are very finely characterized as family members, members of particular estates, classes, and so on. These contents have normative weight: to be a son, a citizen, and a farmer is to be under certain obligations, there are certain things you have to do, they are marked out as the "rules of his own situation"'.

---

[22] All quotations in discussion about Chapter 9 are from that chapter unless otherwise stated.

For Deligiorgi's Hegel, individuals are individuals because of 'the multi-layered spiritual being that defines them'.

Deligiorgi then suggests supplementing 'moderate collectivist' readings of Hegel's notion of political individuality with 'methodological atomism' to ensure the 'normative dimension' of Hegel's conception by enabling reference to 'interests at the atomic level' that do not stand in the way of 'formation of shared interests', since they allow for 'non-instrumental participation in a social whole'. Despite this progress with regards to an analysis of Hegel's notion of (political) individuality, Deligiorgi maintains that there is need for further discussion how the desiderata of an 'ongoing redefinition of political, social, cultural identities' and 'friction among competing models' can be reconciled with the demand for the possibility that 'someone [...] reflectively accepts her world and finds in it simply what is her own and nothing else'.

In Chapter 10, Thom Brooks evaluates the common perception of Hegel as a retributivist regarding punishment who 'justified punishing deserving criminals in order to "annul" their crimes'.[23] Although 'Hegel is clear that punishment is only justified where it is deserved by an offender for committing a crime', the orthodox reading of Hegel as a 'genuine retributivist' 'rests on a mistake', so Brooks, because such labelling fails 'to take sufficient account of Hegel's distinctive form of [systematic] argumentation': while the conventional readings focus almost exclusively on the *Philosophy of Right*'s section on 'abstract right', the passages in 'ethical life' also need to be considered in order to make systematic sense of Hegel's complete notion of punishment.

'Abstract right' suggests that a crime is 'an infringement of a right as a right' that makes it necessary to reassert the violated right and 'cancel the crime' by 'punishing the criminal'. Brooks argues that '[p]unishing offenders is a way to protect and maintain the rights of individuals. This includes offenders, too.' By arguing that the criminal has a right to punishment, Brooks' Hegel reasserts 'the rights of all—including the offender's rights' by means of punishment: 'Punishment is not about damaging an offender's rights, but maintaining them.' Rejecting deterrence and the 'eye for an eye' doctrine, so Brooks, Hegel argues that proportional, not equal 'punishment is merely a manifestation of the crime'.

While Hegel's remarks in 'abstract right' seem to support the retributivist interpretation, so Brooks suggests, they do not do so unequivocally nor is this all Hegel says on the topic. Undermining the retributivist reading of punishment in 'abstract right', Hegel argues that a crime is the failure to recognize what is right by appealing to a 'particular point of view' alone. When right's universal validity is undermined and agreed contracts are broken; a crime is committed.

Punishment, so Brooks' Hegel, 'is merely the negation of the negation' (*PR*, §97A). Its purpose is to nullify the crime by reaffirming the right that illegality contravened and restore right to its proper recognition'. Since Hegel says nothing about moral

---

[23] All quotations in discussion about Chapter 10 are from that chapter unless otherwise stated.

responsibility for wrongdoing or 'how much punishment is deserved', his view is not an example of classical retributivism.

Against the notion that Hegel's theory of punishment is close to Kant's, Brooks argues that Hegel considers 'additional factors' in defining punishment and does not argue that 'there is some ideal value—provided to us by way of retribution—that we can use to set deterrent or rehabilitative punishments to'. Rather than a moral retributivist, Hegel shows himself to be a legal retributivist in abstract right: 'offenders deserve punishment on the more narrow and limited justification that the offender commits a crime. It is this act or omission resulting in a public wrong like illegality that is what any offender must possess to be held deserving of punishment.'

Crucially, if one goes beyond the claims of abstract right into ethical life, Hegel's notion of punishment turns out to be even less retributivist for Brooks. Taking seriously Hegel's claim that 'his work should be read in a systematic way where concepts, including crime and punishment, are developed and fleshed out as we proceed through a dialectical process', the responsible commentator must consult Hegel's remarks in ethical life on the matter.

Hegel claims that 'the distribution and amount of punishment is *not* determined by an individual's state of mind alone, but external factors like a crime's potential "danger to society" (*PR*, §218)'. This means, according to Brooks, that the affirmation of right that is punishment 'transpires within a wider context—and Hegel takes this context seriously. All thefts may share specific features in general as attempts permanently to deprive another of her possessions. Hegel's point is that the damage done to this right to own property, in this example, and reaffirm it can shift in value due to external factors.'

Such factors include the 'stability of society'—'[a] stable society that is self-confident and relatively harmonious is less threatened by crime; offences do not pose as chilling a threat to it'. Furthermore, '[f]or Hegel, a theft during peacetime is the same offence-type as a theft committed during civil war. But the thieves are not the same all the way down because the circumstances surrounding their thefts can be different. It is this difference in circumstances that is substantively important for informing how we should punish offenders.'

This motivates Brooks to argue that '[i]nterpreters that claim context has no substantive part to play fail to grasp the fact that punishment is an institutional practice *in the world* and not apart from it. Only in some heavenly, unreal beyond are all crimes to be the same independently of their becoming *real*. Punishment is a practice in human community and the wider circumstances pertaining to justice are relevant to the just administration and distribution of any criminal justice system.' However, for Brooks, Hegel's remarks on punishment leave opaque 'how we should make judgements about when and how to punish' and that '[t]he orthodox consensus has not caught on to this problem'.

Citing the *Science of Logic*, Brooks ends his argument by showing that Hegel is the first to provide a 'unified theory' of punishment, combining retributive, preventative, and reformative characteristics:

Punishment must be deserved, but its distribution is determined by the relevant circumstances affecting the crime's impact on the stability of a particular civil society. The restoration of right may call for more deterrence, rehabilitation or other penal factor depending on these circumstances. In setting the value of punishment, we seek to restore the violated right and the form that punishment might take is justified where it best approximates what is required for the restoration of right.

In Chapter 11, Richard Dien Winfield traces both logical truth and ethical freedom back to the common root of 'self-determination'.[24] According to Winfield's Hegel, logical enquiry must be based on 'autonomous reason' that is independent from presuppositions and that determines 'its own method and subject matter': in the *Logic*, philosophy is informed by the concept's self-determining universality that unites with its self-posited particularity to form individuality. Similarly, so Winfield argues, the *Philosophy of Right*'s concern, i.e. 'free conduct', must be liberated from external domination and at once embody the creation and possession of legitimacy. This entails that ethics is philosophy that describes the reality of self-determination, i.e. the 'actuality of freedom'.

Despite their shared interest in self-determination, logic and ethics also differ for Winfield. This is due to ethics' more concrete concern with 'action' rather than logic's abstract thought. Both *Logic* and 'objective spirit' have different conceptual positions within the philosophical system that is organized in light of the idea's three different forms of logic, nature, and spirit: while the logical concept presupposes the logics of being and essence, so ethics conceptually presupposes nature and subjective spirit.

Winfield notes a further difference in the fact that the architecture of the *Logic*'s 'logic of the concept' (judgement, syllogism, objectivity, etc.) cannot be easily mapped on to the *Philosophy of Right*'s concern with abstract right, morality, and ethical life and unlike the concept, Hegel's notion of 'the will' involves the interrelationship of individuals: while the logic of the concept develops its moments 'without reference to any plurality of individuals', free willing always implies interaction and interdependence with the self-determination of others.

For Winfield, this means that independent, 'monological' willing is unable to determine the identity of its own agency as it relies on a 'given' faculty of choice and on a given content. The individual agent may decide which goal to pursue but the faculty of choice 'does not supply the options'. This motivates Winfield to wonder 'How can willing be autonomous if it fails to supply everything, faculty and content, by itself?' According to Winfield, it is the interaction with 'one another' that supplies willing's faculty and content: because we recognize each other as willing agents, we *are* such agents and our willing has content: '[the agents'] interaction establishes an agency whose identity is defined by the recognized embodiment it gives itself rather than by any features given independently of their willing'. And 'what each individual thereby wills is an embodiment of that agency, which, as its self-determination, is defined not

---

[24] All quotations in discussion about Chapter 11 are from that chapter unless otherwise stated.

by any given features of that embodying factor, but by the recognition that it actualizes the self-determination agency that wills it as its own realization. Since each participant can determine itself only by facilitating in its counterparts the same type of willing that it itself engages in, each partakes in a universal, lawful willing.'

At first instance, so Winfield suggests, such mutual practices of inter-recognition take abstract right's forms of self-ownership and ownership of external objects. Since the recognition of these is unstable because people can always dispute property claims, there is need for a higher adjudicating institution that according to Winfield's Hegel comes in the form of morality and then ethical life.

While Hegel's division into abstract right, morality, and ethical life 'fit the logical demands of systematic unity', so Winfield, the same can be said about ethical life's division into family, civil society, and state although Hegel did commit several mistakes in describing these as he did: 'Unable to free his conception of holdovers of the pre-modern arrangements of his day' so Winfield, Hegel 'leaves key features of each ethical sphere structured by factors extraneous to self-determination'.

According to Winfield, these are: (1) Hegel's limitation of 'marriage to a monogamous heterosexual relation in which the male spouse lords over the female spouse as household manager and exclusive representative of the family in civil society and the state'. (2) Hegel's substitution of estates for economic classes and corporations for social interest groups in civil society. (3) Hegel's failure to conceive of the legislature 'as a representative assembly in which all citizens have equal political opportunity'. (4) His endorsement of the 'hereditary reign of a constitutional monarch'. And (5) Hegel's insistence that a state can only exist in negative differentiation from other states.

Luckily, so Winfield, these errors can be corrected without violating the basic purpose of each aspect of ethical life: while the family is defined by the co-determined joint private good of the household, civil society is defined by the pursuit of particular, individual ends and 'political association aims at the universal end of freely ordering the totality of freedom over which it presides'. Furthermore, so Winfield, '[a]lthough the state can be one among others, there is nothing about political unity that requires that it be a particular state confronting others in international relations. [...] In principle, the state could be global or a solitary body politic with no relations to any other.'

In Chapter 12, Liz Disley investigates whether Hegel offers a solution to the apparent contradiction between two notions.[25] On the one hand, Hegel's 'ethical community rests on a picture of the human agent as incomplete, vulnerable, and constantly changing' and on the other 'Sittlichkeit and civil society in general [seem] to rest much more on a concept of the individual as fully formed and with a far greater degree of autonomy'.

For Disley, the notions of 'intersubjectivity and interdependence' point in the direction of the contradiction's resolution. For Disley, '[r]ecognition [...] is a condition of possibility for [...] subjectivity, [i.e.] selfhood or agency' as '[i]t is only within a civil context that our (ethical) actions become meaningful'. Since 'the self, by itself, is

---

[25] All quotations in discussion about Chapter 12 are from that chapter unless otherwise stated.

incapable of sustaining projects' and 'is constantly reaching out to the others purely in order to continue to be, to sustain itself', so Disley argues, notions of self-sufficient autonomy are 'guilty of both an empirical neglect of human independence and a more theoretical neglect of genuine human intersubjectivity'. Since 'the subject is not complete by itself, but must always include the social context in which it finds itself— the subject is always already embedded', 'recognizing the extent to which the self is socially constituted during the narrative of its life is a pre-condition for honest moral judgement'. 'True autonomy', so Disley suggests, 'is mediated autonomy' and 'autonomous freedom is intersubjectively mediated'.

How does this sit with Hegel's claims about state and civil society? For Disley, common practical concerns of society's members, practices of mutual recognition, shared 'dialog, debate[,] cultural creativity' that is fuelled by dialectical and 'combative interaction' enable successful intersubjectivity. Since the state enables these phenomena, it is 'not some external apparatus acting heteronomously to restrict freedom, but is in fact the context in which freedom is possible'.

Disley finds the most fundamental pointer towards a resolution of the seeming contradiction at the foundations of Hegel's notion of what a philosophical system is. Like the self, so the system is defined by a tension between the system's closedness and simultaneous openness, between 'the finite and the infinite or [...] between totality and infinity'. For Disley, the self is a part of the system's 'metaphysical totality' that is incapable of enclosing infinity within it and so both system and self are 'always itself looking for a completion that can never come': 'Just like the human subject or self, the totality, that which is covered by any systematic approach, is incomplete and looking beyond itself.'

According to Disley, it is thus our finitude and incompleteness that motivates us to 'seek actual encounters with others' and which 'aims at transcending, our finite and incomplete natures'. This 'does not interfere with our capacity for self-legislation or self-determination, since the encounter is not forced and is not aimed at serving some heteronomously dictated goal. We can determine our own actions, but that does not mean that we are capable of seeing every meaningful project to completion without encounters with other (autonomous, rational) agents'.

In Chapter 13, Kenneth Westphal rejects approaches that want to make sense of Hegel's practical-philosophical claims by 'inexorable dialectical logical deduction' or that suggest that according to Hegel we must simply endorse whatever 'the *Weltgeist*' does next.[26] Instead, Westphal identifies a Hegelian method that constructs 'regressive proofs' by means of 'immanent analysis of the phenomena pertaining to practical philosophy'. Such proofs ought to exhibit 'the kinds of structures and relations Hegel analyses abstractly in the *Science of Logic* or *Encyclopaedia*'.

Westphal's Hegel thinks of reasoning in public terms: '[W]e can each *be* maximally rational and actually *justify* our best judgments rationally, only insofar as we recognize

---

[26] All quotations in discussion about Chapter 13 are from that chapter unless otherwise stated.

our mutual interdependence for the critical assessment of our own best judgments and their grounds and principles.' As rational agents who justify their actions in a way that shows that they all can be 'understood by and assessed and adopted in thought or in action by all concerned (i.e. all affected) parties, consistently with one's own judgment and action on that, and on all relevant such occasions; this is the ultimate, fundamental thesis demonstrated by Hegel's analysis of mutual recognition'.

This social, recognition-based reasoning process includes critical self-assessment and implies that 'justifying one's assessment on grounds, evidence and principles which *all* others can understand, assess, adopt, and use consistently in thought and in action—including consistently with one's own thoughts, judgments, and actions on that occasion, and on all such occasions'. This, so Westphal, is Hegel's social '*conditio sine qua non*' of rational justification.

Arguing that Hegel 'adopted Kant's fallibilism about rational justification' and 'is still one of the very most sophisticated pragmatic realists' because he advocates 'conceptual explication, *within* actual contexts of use, responsible philosophy must be both systematic and historical' because 'the relevant issues are so easily obscured or distorted. [W]e must carefully consider how the many and the wise have discussed and formulated these issues, in order better to understand and assess our own and others' formulations presently, and in the future.' Westphal's Hegel's public reasoning is thus of 'pragmatic, social, and historical character' and therefore profoundly 'fallibilist'.

How does this fit Hegel's claims about 'self-actualizing concepts'? According to Westphal, 'to "realize" (*realisieren*) a concept is to show that some actual instances of it can be located and identified by us. This task is crucial to show that any *a priori* concepts we might possess, we can accurately and justifiedly *use* in actual or humanly possible judgments *about* relevant particular instances we have located, identified, and individuated.' However, so Westphal argues, Hegel's fallibilism does not make him anti-realist. To the contrary, it 'is consistent with, and ultimately justifies, realism about the objects of empirical knowledge, and strict objectivity about basic moral norms'. This is due to Hegel's 'insight that comprehending what something is, what it can be and what it ought to be, are mutually interdependent, integral cognitive achievements'.

In the realm of moral philosophy, so Westphal suggests, this makes Hegel a 'functionalist': his analysis of social practices and institutions 'allow us to argue that a form of institution he did not consider may equally well, or perhaps better, fulfil the function(s) Hegel ascribed to those historical institutions he considered'. In continuation of Kant's project in the *Metaphysics of Morals*, Hegel's account of 'ethical life' is the result of the application of 'metaphysical principles' of morals to the 'human condition'.

Continuing a tradition of 'natural law constructivism' commenced by Hume and passed from Rousseau to Kant, Westphal's Hegel argues for those institutions of socio-political life, which embody 'publicly acknowledged principles and titles to acquire, possess, use and exchange things and promised actions together with sufficient social institutions to make known these principles and titles, to monitor compliance with them, and to make proper and no more than sufficient redress of infractions'.[27] Hegel combines this with 'Rousseau's non-domination principle' according to which '[n]o one is entitled to acquire the kind or extent of power or wealth so as to command unilaterally the decision of another person to do one's bidding'.

According to Westphal, Hegel combines Kant's demand for universality with the real manifestation of universal principles: When he 'anthropologizes' practical normativity, he finds the rational within customs understood as 'intelligent activities': 'The development and the individual adoption of social customs literally *customizes* whatever needs, ends, desires, or motives we have due simply to our human psycho-physiology'. So whenever we consider how to act, so Westphal's Hegel, 'we avail ourselves of conceptual and material resources, together with a variety of procedures, permissions, entitlements, and prohibitions. All of these are socially constituted, as is our knowledge and understanding of these provisions and how and when to use them (or not)'.

However, this does not make Hegel a social determinist or holist, so Westphal. For him, '[s]ocial practices exist only in and through individuals who participate in, perpetuate, or *modify* them as occasion, need, and inventiveness allow and require'. The people who realize Hegel's normative institutions 'can in practice revise its legal, social, and political institutions to achieve significant and progressive constitutional reform over generations'. This, so Westphal, also explains Hegel's own shortcomings in the description of ethical life: rejecting Hegel's views on women, Westphal proposes to revise Hegel's account of the family and think of it 'based fundamentally as it is on deep love and commitment between two adults, to the well-functioning of their joint household and to their children's upbringing, education, and well-being'.

Defending Hegel's historically conditioned critique of plebiscites, Westphal emphasizes the advantages of representative systems and supports Hegel's concern that 'all sectors of society and all branches of the economy are represented within public political deliberations'. Once 'political education and participation of *all* citizens' is achieved, so Westphal suggests, Hegel's system 'can easily be made fully democratic by introducing universal suffrage via corporate membership'.

Methodologically, Westphal's Hegel's focus thus remains with the temporal present: 'Hegel's focus upon comprehending the present is itself justified by his recognition that only by comprehending and conscientiously assessing the present can we correctly identify and enjoy our individual and collective achievements in matters moral, *and* also correctly identify those aspects of our individual and collective lives wherein we ought and can improve morally, and how best to do so'.

---

[27] On Hegel's distinctive understanding of natural law, see also Thom Brooks, 'Hegel's Ambiguous Contributions to Legal Theory', *Res Publica* 11 (2005): 85–94; Thom Brooks, 'Between Natural Law and Legal Positivism: Dworkin and Hegel on Legal Theory', *Georgia State University Law Review* 23 (2007): 513–60; Thom Brooks, 'Natural Law Internalism', in (ed.), *Hegel's Philosophy of Right* (Oxford: Blackwell, 2012): 167–79 and Brooks, 'Law', in *Hegel's Political Philosophy*, 82–95.

Together, these thirteen chapters do not approach the topic of the relationship between Hegel's method and system with his political philosophy from the same perspective—nor do they reach the same conclusions. But they suggest that greater attention can and should be paid to how Hegel's political philosophy relates to his larger philosophical enterprise.

We hope this volume enlivens a wider debate about the importance of Hegel's system for understanding his philosophy—the *Philosophy of Right* and other works—as a potentially fruitful site for future research. And we look forward to the Owl of Minerva beginning its flight once again.

1

What Might it Mean to have a Systematic Idealist, but Anti-Platonist, Practical Philosophy?

Paul Redding

1.1. Richard Rorty: Modern "Ironist" Hegelian

In an essay, "Trotsky and the Wild Orchids", the controversial American neo-pragmatist philosopher Richard Rorty describes a phase of his intellectual life in which he regarded as "the two greatest achievements of the species to which I belonged", Hegel's *Phenomenology of Spirit* and Proust's *Remembrance of Things Past*.[1] This can seem a strange endorsement on the part of someone who might otherwise be taken to represent a cluster of attitudes not unusual in a western liberal intellectual who had come to philosophical maturity in the aftermath of World War II. In terms of his actual first-order, *non*-philosophical beliefs, Rorty probably had more in common with the majority of the analytic philosophers with whom he worked in the early parts of his career in the 1960s and 1970s. He believed in science and rejected the claims of religion, seeking and finding in a God-free aesthetic experience the sorts of satisfaction that others sought in institutional religion. One of his early teachers had been the logical positivist Rudolf Carnap, and like such earlier positivists Rorty was critical of traditional metaphysical pursuits with their Platonic aspirations. Indeed, among the writings that brought him first to philosophical attention had been ones staking out a radical *eliminativist* form of naturalism in philosophy of mind.[2] Moreover, he was likewise wary of political ideologies that, he thought, dressed up a kind of moral–religious commitment in scientific garb and portrayed moral choices as somehow metaphysically necessitated.

Rorty was later to become known for his ruthless use of analytic philosophical tools to deflate the types of claims made by his fellow analysts. His motivations here might

---

[1] Richard Rorty, "Trotsky and the Wild Orchids", in *Philosophy and Social Hope* (London: Penguin Books, 1999), p. 11.
[2] For example, Richard Rorty, "In Defense of Eliminative Materialism", *Review of Metaphysics*, 24 (1970), pp. 112–21.

be seen as continuous with those directed against the claims of traditional metaphysics. Philosophy was clearly not an empirical science like the type of physics on the basis of which one could intervene into nature and bring it to bear on human needs and purposes. Nevertheless, in breaking with the religious culture with which it had been more intimately tied up in the nineteenth century, philosophy, especially in relation to the "analytic revolution", had increasingly portrayed itself as an objective science—if not empirical, then "formal".

That is, Rorty had come to think of much of what was emerging as the institution of analytic philosophy as both motivated by and as feeding a desire that was closer to a religious than a scientific one—a desire, as he describes it, to hold "reality and justice in a single vision", the pursuit of which "had been precisely what led Plato astray".[3] Expressed in linguistic terms, this aspiration might be described in terms of the idea of speaking about the world in *God's own* language or vocabulary, a view Rorty countered with his critique of the idea of language as *representing* an independent world.

This anti-Platonic insight he had found strongly conveyed in a variety of sources: early American pragmatists such as John Dewey, those within the analytic tradition such as Carnap, the later Wittgenstein and Wilfrid Sellars, and philosophers from the rival "continental" tradition, such as Martin Heidegger and Jean-Paul Sartre. From Rorty's own point of view, I take it, what separated him from his typical analytic colleagues was that he was simply more consistent in his anti-Platonism, as analysts too often exempted their own commitment to analytic methods and doctrines from the sceptical scrutiny to which they subjected other claims. In particular, they too eagerly acquiesced in the aspiration that had traditionally been understood in terms of the goal of seeing from the God's-eye view, or representing the world in God's language. Reference to "God" may have been dropped, but the idea of finding logico-linguistic forms thought to "limn" reality simply expressed this theological desire in a different way. But if this crude sketch of Rorty *qua* philosopher and general intellectual is at all along the right lines, then the puzzle becomes: why would such a person take a work of G. W. F. *Hegel* as one of "the two greatest achievements of the species to which I belonged"? Hegel is widely regarded as perhaps the nineteenth century's *most* extravagant metaphysical-cum-religious thinker. Moreover, he is also considered to have contributed centrally to the infrastructure to Marx's scientific socialism, Marx supposedly having "inverted" Hegel's God-soaked idealism into a materialist vision of a world driven by the iron-clad laws of science towards an inevitable *telos*—a kind of heaven on earth in which the class divisions generated by a particular phase of economic history would be overcome. Perhaps, then, Hegel is capable of being read in other ways than those that fed the traditional picture?

What had attracted Rorty to Hegel was exactly what attracted him to Proust: both had created masterpieces of "redescription"—a use of language that was in the service of human freedom. But the project of redescription has surely been a part of modern

---

[3] Rorty, "Trotsky and the Wild Orchids", p. 12.

analytic philosophy. As Michael Beaney has stressed,[4] "analysis" had meant different things at different times in analytic philosophy, but a central dimension of the notion from the time of Russell had been that of translation into a different logical form, in other words, redescription.[5] Early in his career Rorty had devoted himself to the idea of analytic philosophy as having a type of redescriptive methodology, editing a volume entitled *The Linguistic Turn: Essays in Philosophical Method*.[6] But for the later Rorty, sceptical of any claims of philosophy to "getting things right", that is, to *truth*, the activity of redescription could only be understood as in the service of freedom *rather than* truth, for the latter brings with it connotations of an aspiration to speak in the resources of God's own vocabulary and so represent the world as it "really is" in abstraction from the epistemic resources *humans* bring to it. In the case of Proust, Rorty makes this connection apparent. For Proust, freedom was conceived as freedom from the constraints that originate in descriptions of Proust himself given by others. As he puts it elsewhere, Proust had wanted:

to free himself from the descriptions of himself offered by the people he had met. He wanted not to be merely the person these other people thought they knew him to be, not to be frozen in the frame of a photograph shot from another person's perspective. He dreaded being, in Sartre's phrase, turned into a thing by the eye of the other...His method of freeing himself from those people—of becoming autonomous—was to redescribe the people who had described him....Proust became autonomous by explaining to himself why the others were not authorities, but simply fellow contingencies. He redescribed them as being as much a product of others' attitudes toward them as Proust himself was a product of their attitudes toward him.[7]

Rorty could link Proust to Hegel in that the *Phenomenology of Spirit* could be read as a case of Hegel "out-redescribing" virtually all the major philosophers of the tradition.[8] For Rorty, Hegel's philosophical genius consisted in his capacity of taking philosophical positions found in the history of philosophy and transposing them into new categories—a new "vocabulary"—that suited his own philosophical purposes. Partly, the goal of this was, in becoming freed of the grip of the categories or vocabulary underlying the arguments of earlier philosophers, to see these building blocks of language and thought as products of their historical culture and so to see philosophy as "its time raised to thought". And the way to do this was to describe them *differently*.[9]

---

[4] Michael Beaney, "The Analytic Turn in Early Twentieth-Century Philosophy", in Michael Beaney (ed.) *The Analytic Turn: Analysis in Early Analytic Philosophy and Phenomenology* (London: Routledge, 2007).

[5] Thus Russell famously redescribed *intensionally* understood categorical judgments as *extensionally* understood conditionals ("All Greeks are wise" becomes "If something is a Greek, then it's wise"), and *specific* judgments about non-existing objects as general qualitative judgments about *existence* (thus, "The present King of France—is he bald?" becomes "Does existence contain anything both present-King-of-France-ish, and bald?").

[6] Richard Rorty (ed.), *The Linguistic Turn: Essays in Philosophical Method* (Chicago: University of Chicago Press, 1967).

[7] Richard Rorty, "Proust, Nietzsche, and Heidegger", in *Contingency, Irony and Solidarity* (Cambridge: Cambridge University Press, 1989), p. 102.

[8] Rorty, "Trotsky and the Wild Orchids", p. 11.

[9] This was the approach of Nietzsche, another of Rorty's philosophical heroes.

Hegel's exemplification of this activity of redescription was so compelling that it could, for Rorty, outweigh contrary tendencies, such as the fact that the *Phenomenology*, in ending in "Absolute Knowing" seemed not only to aspire to the God's-eye view, but to the claim that it had *already been achieved*. Hegel thus becomes a powerful exemplification of how the activity of redescription undermines any quasi-theological initial desire motivating it.

Rorty's strategy for recuperating Hegel thus aimed at allowing the modern disillusioned Hegelian to have the benefits of the *practical goals* aimed at by metaphysics, such as freedom or justice, without the burden of any metaphysical "Truth" over and above the lower-case "truths" of the empirical world—a metaphysical Truth which could externally constrain our choice of vocabulary in which we express all our first-order theoretical and practical commitments. This, of course, had to be achieved at the expense (although Rorty seemingly didn't see it *as* an expense) of a definite "ironism" with respect to the commitment to one's *own* vocabulary—presumably that of Hegel's "absolute knowing". The redescriber needs to *endorse* some new vocabulary in order to disendorse the old, but also grasp that she is thereby opening up her own vocabulary to subsequent disendorsement by subsequent radical redescribers. In this sense, any individual's endorsement of her own vocabulary must be freed from any sense of its *necessity*.[10] Absolute knowing has to be expressed in a decidedly ironic tone.

Rorty has not been alone in his efforts to divest Hegel of "metaphysics" meant in any traditional, Platonic sense. Since the late 1980s and 1990s, accounts of Hegel from the likes of Robert Pippin and Terry Pinkard have attempted to give to Hegel's philosophy a form that could be believed by those who might be said broadly to share Rorty's secular, largely liberal and generally "post-Kantian" anti-Platonic outlook.[11] This chapter is written from the perspective of a fellow-traveller of this broadly "post-Kantian" party. Its goal is to understand how one might maintain those aspects of the readings of Rorty and other post-Kantians that aim at construing Hegelianism as an *anti-Platonist* philosophy, *critical* of the aspiration to speak in God's vocabulary, while at the same time being wary of the abandonment of philosophical "truth" in the name of "freedom", a separation that Hegel himself would clearly have never endorsed. Such a reading, I suggest, will need to incorporate *some* sense of the necessity of one's vocabulary and, given Hegel's undoubted association of truth with "the whole", a commitment to some idea of philosophy as a systematic doctrine. Furthermore, I suggest this effort is properly linked to exactly that aspect of Hegel's method that attracted Rorty as so important— the practice of "redescription" or conceptual "redetermination". Our question thus becomes: How might one approach the centrality of redescription to Hegel's philosophy without embracing the alternatives of conceptual triumphalism or conceptual

[10] C.f., especially, Richard Rorty, "The Contingency of Language", in *Contingency, Irony, and Solidarity* (Cambridge: Cambridge University Press, 1989), pp. 3–22.

[11] See especially, Robert Pippin, *Hegel's Practical Philosophy: Rational Agency as Ethical Life* (Cambridge: Cambridge University Press, 2008); Terry Pinkard, *Hegel's Naturalism: Mind, Nature, and the Final Ends of Life* (Oxford: Oxford University Press, 2012).

"ironism"? To this end I'll be suggesting a picture of Hegel as a *modal actualist* in contrast to Rorty's *ironic naturalist*.[12] The strategy will be to draw parallels between assumptions underlying Rorty's thought and ones informing an approach to which Hegel stood as both follower and critic—that of Kant and Fichte. In short, Hegel's critical appropriation of Kant and Fichte will, hopefully, point the way towards a critical appropriation of *Rorty's* Hegel. Hegel, I will suggest following Rorty, employed redescription *not* in the service of an attempt to speak of the world in the vocabulary of a being who was not of the world: the goal was not to speak God's own language. And yet to abandon this goal should not be seen as abandoning the goal of philosophical truth. Redescription can still be employed for the purpose of finding an adequate language for a *true* account of the actual world *for* a speaker who essentially *belongs* to that world and whose knowledge is conditioned by it.[13]

1.2. Kant, Fichte, Sartre, Rorty, and the Struggle for Recognition

The reference to Sartre in Rorty's account of what is going on in Proust's redescriptive activity provides an explicit link to Hegel, and in particular to the famous dialectic of "master and slave" in chapter 4 of Hegel's *Phenomenology of Spirit*. Sartre had read Hegel in the light of Alexandre Kojève's account of the "struggle for recognition"—a struggle motivated by a purported "desire for recognition" meant to be fundamental to the human species. In Rorty's hands this struggle becomes a cultural one, a struggle between attempts to *impose* a vocabulary on others—to become the creator of the categorical framework within which claims to "getting it right" will be assessed. But if "getting it right" consists of adherence to the norms of a vocabulary, then the imposition of a new vocabulary cannot be seen as an act that can be assessed in terms of correctness—a lesson Rorty had learnt from his teacher Carnap. The transition to a new vocabulary can only be based on pragmatic considerations that have weight for *particular* agents. In the context of Hegel, this is the Proustian struggle of redescription that Rorty sees as carried out by philosophers with respect to their forebears. Philosophy as activity then needs to be detached from the goal of "getting it right", the goal of truth, a goal that aims at speaking God's language.

While widely influential throughout the second half of the twentieth century, this portrait of the "struggle for recognition" as described by Kojève and adapted by Sartre had not been free from criticism as an interpretation of Hegel's actual views. Kojève had

---

[12] In the context of recent modal metaphysics, Arthur Prior employed the term "actualism" to contrast the "possibilist" position espoused by David Lewis who, like Leibniz, considered the actual world as just one of an array of equally real different possible worlds.

[13] Robert Stalnaker makes a similar point about the actualist position vis-à-vis language: "Since we are actualists, we have only the resources that the actual world provides for representing possibilities." Robert Stalnaker, *Mere Possibilities: Metaphysical Foundations of Modal Semantics* (Princeton: Princeton University Press, 2012), p. 13.

drawn on both Heidegger and Marx, and numerous Hegel interpreters have at various times complained that Kojève's reading was at best a simplification and at worst a serious misrepresentation. A stronger criticism of the Kojève–Sartre–Rorty rendering of the "struggle for recognition", however, would be that it reduces Hegel's account to a view that is not only *not* his own but is one of which he was explicitly critical, and critical *for good reasons*. Elsewhere, I have argued that Hegel's account of the master–slave dialectic in *Phenomenology of Spirit* chapter 4 is in fact directed against *Fichte's* treatment of recognition.[14] In short: Fichte had introduced the conception of "recognition" (*Anerkennen*) in his 1796-7 work *Foundations of Natural Right*, and while this was a notion that Hegel was going to incorporate into his own philosophy as the basic medium of spirit (*Geist*), doing this required a much broader treatment of recognition than the narrowly legalistic and abstract, *rights-centred* notion found in Fichte. For Hegel, one shortcoming of Fichte's approach was its link to an account of self-consciousness that, consonant with Kojève's focus on the "desire for recognition", had its basis in *desire*.

Seemingly anticipating a certain *pragmatist* turn within later philosophy,[15] Fichte had conceived the basic orientation of the mind to the world as a type of striving or endeavouring, although this could not be reduced to any naturalistic conception of striving for satisfaction of desire as in, say, Hobbes or Hume. Following Kant, Fichte had conceived of the finite but rational ego as striving against anything beyond itself that limited or determined it. The model here was Kant's idea of moral action stemming from the rational agent's capacity to both *will* and *to hold itself to* the moral law, which had its basis in that agent's own rational capacities. From this perspective, an agent's own *natural* inclinations and appetites would come to be counted among the "external" sources of determination against which it strived, and so here we might think of "morality" as conceived by Kant as the "new vocabulary" within which the contents of desire could be redescribed in the service of freedom. Thus the contents of one's arbitrary desire-based willing, one's *Willkür*, must now answer to the moral law as expressed in the Categorical Imperative understood as the expression of a rationally self-legislating will—*der Wille*. Hegel had characterized Fichte's conception of this commanding will as *desire or appetite generalized* (*Begierde überhaupt*), seemingly intending to portray the practical stance of morality as in fact analogous to the type of *natural* inclinations against which it was directed. That is, this new *moral* desire was formally like the one being replaced. It aimed to *negate* its object *as* a desire in a way analogous to *that* desire aimed at negating the object to which *it* was directed. This precluded the rational will from *having* any particular content (characteristic of Kant's

---

[14] Paul Redding, "The Independence and Dependence of Self-Consciousness: The Dialectic of Lord and Bondsman in Hegel's Phenomenology of Spirit", in F. Beiser (ed.), *The New Cambridge Companion to Hegel and Nineteenth Century Philosophy* (Cambridge: Cambridge University Press, 2008), pp. 94–110.

[15] C.f., Fichte's comments in J. G. Fichte, *Foundations of the Entire Science of Knowledge in the Science of Knowledge*, trans. and ed. P. Heath and J. Lachs (Cambridge: Cambridge University Press, 1982), that "all reflection is based on the striving and in the absence of striving there can be no reflection" (p. 258) and "it is not in fact the theoretical faculty which makes possible the practical, but on the contrary the practical which makes possible the theoretical" (p. 123).

moral philosophy), and had opened up the gates to the return of arbitrary, non-rational content in the context of *morality* (a characteristic of Fichte's development of Kant).

Fichte's idea of the rational will as a negating "*Begierde überhaupt*", I suggest, might be understood as anticipating current ways of thinking about the will employing Frankfurt's well-known distinction between first- and second-order desires.[16] Take the example of having a first-order desire to, say, smoke a cigarette, and the second-order desire to be a person *without* that desire. From the perspective of the agent *in the grip* of such first-order desires, the practical intention to embrace the second-order desire looks like a withdrawal from something determinate and existent—the brute fact of one's desire. Fichte had taken over Kant's distinction between *der Wille* and *die Willkür*, with *der Wille* conceived as a type of legislative function of pure practical reason commanding the lower faculty of *desire-driven choice* (*Willkür*) by addressing it in the form of an imperative.[17] From the point of view of me as a rational will, my attempt to disinvest myself from some particular first-order desire just *is* the attempt to show it as *unnecessary*, un-lawlike and arbitrary—*willkürlich*—and this lower desire will be perceived as *willkürlich* precisely to the extent that it is *not* supported by *reasons*: the sorts of reasons that are ultimately articulated by *der Wille*, the rational law-giving authority on all that is good and thereby rationally desirable. In the capacity for moral judgment so conceived we might therefore see something of the precursor of the capacity of Rorty's Hegel for "redescription". Prior to reflection and generalization, desire, *qua* the voice of *inclination*, seems to address its bearer as a necessary demand; post-reflection, this necessity has been transformed, what inclination had demanded of me is now grasped as contingent and negatable. Why *should* I listen to the commands of my own desires? When I grasp them from the point of view of a rationality that *commands*, I come to see their inessential nature. My liberation from them has come from adopting a God's-eye point of view *on them*.

Hegel's method of "redescription" should, I suggest, be seen as a critical appropriation of the Kant–Fichte position, with Hegel being nevertheless critical of the way in which Kant and Fichte had conceived of this redetermining power of *der Wille*, and its relation to *Willkür*. These issues can be seen as addressed in Hegel's sketch of the logic of *der Wille* in a few short paragraphs from the "Introduction" to his *Elements of the Philosophy of Right*.

1.3. Hegel on the Logic of the Will

In a series of sections in the "Introduction" to his *Philosophy of Right*, Hegel expands on the claim made in §4 that the spiritual, "*das Geistige*", is "the ground (*Boden*)" of "right",

---

[16] See especially, Harry Frankfurt, "Freedom of the Will and the Concept of a Person", in Gary Watson (ed.), *Free Will* (Oxford: Oxford University Press, 1982), pp. 96–110.

[17] The distinction is first explicitly made in Immanuel Kant, *The Metaphysics of Morals*, trans. Mary Gregor (Cambridge: Cambridge University Press, 1991), pp. 41–2 and p. 52, but is implicit in earlier works. On the distinction see Henry Allison, *Kant's Theory of Freedom* (Cambridge: Cambridge University Press, 1990), pp. 129–36.

and that the point of origin of right is "the will", *der Wille*. Principle α, stated in §5, tells us that will contains "the element of pure indeterminacy, or of the 'I's pure reflection into itself, in which every limitation, every content, whether present immediately through nature, through needs, desires and drives, or given and determined in some other way, is dissolved (*aufgelöst*)". This is, he goes on, "the limitless infinity of *absolute abstraction* or *universality*, the pure thinking of oneself".[18] This clearly is the dimension of the will that can be thought of along the lines of Frankfurt's higher-order desire/object desire distinction and Fichte's related conception of the will as "*Begierde überhaupt*". Considered in isolation it appears to instantiate the God's-eye view. But Hegel was concerned with this exclusively *negative* characterization being carried over into the higher-order desire itself. For Hegel, as for Schiller before him and Nietzsche after him, this had produced a defective moral psychology. One needs to somehow maintain a *positive* determination of an affirmed *particular* content of the will in addition to this negative "dissolving" moment, and the failure of the Kant–Fichte conception here is its failure to provide for some affirmed particular content. In order to *live* good lives, communities and individuals need to be able to represent the types of lives *worthy* of being led. As Nietzsche was later to elaborate, Kant's categorical imperative looks to have the "thou shalt not" character of the Ten Commandments, portraying moral life in terms of a set of prohibitions against a determinate set of *evils*, with no associated picture of any type of *good life*, as found in ancient ethics, for example.[19]

The need to embrace a *positive* conception of some particular willed content is stated by Hegel as principle β in §6. It asserts that the "I" must also involve the transition from undifferentiated indeterminacy and immediate self-identity to "differentiation, determination and positing of a determinacy as a content and object", and that this content "may further be given *by nature*, or generated by the concept of the spirit".[20] For Hegel the task will be to show how these apparently antithetical principles, α and β, are to be resolved—to show how *der Wille* can actually be "the unity of both these moments— *particularity* reflected *into itself* and thereby restored to *universality*".[21] While a similar structure can be observed in Fichte,[22] the difference of Hegel's approach in conceiving

[18] G. W. F. Hegel, *Elements of the Philosophy of Right*, ed. Allen W. Wood, trans. H. B. Nisbet (Cambridge: Cambridge University Press, 1991), §5.

[19] Friedrich Nietzsche, "On the Genealogy of Morals", in *On the Genealogy of Morals and Ecce Homo*, edited with commentary by Walter Kaufmann (New York: Vintage Books, 1969), books 1 and 2.

[20] Hegel, *Elements*, §6. C.f., Hegel's declaration in the *Encyclopedia Philosophy of Spirit* that "consciousness is finite in so far as it has an object". G. W. F. Hegel, *Hegel's Philosophy of Mind: Part Three of the Encyclopaedia of the Philosophical Sciences*, trans. W. Wallace and A. V. Miller (Oxford: Oxford University Press, 2007), §441.

[21] Fichte's third principle is needed to reconcile the apparent contradiction between the first two, a principle which has the "I" positing *both* itself *and* the not-"I" *as* somehow opposed. The second and third parts of this version of the *Wissenschaftslehre* are now devoted to developing the third principle into a system with parts covering both theoretical and practical knowledge that allows us to understand how the first two principles can coexist.

[22] In Fichte's first principle, the "I" is portrayed as immediately *self-positing* and *self-determining*—a self-identical "I=I" resistant to any determination from any source other than itself. However, if we conceive of "I" as a consciousness, then we must also conceive of it as confronted by an object *other* than itself, *of which*

the logic of these relations will be one of the defining marks of his practical philosophy. There must be another way of conceiving of the situation, and the relation of *Wille* to *Willkür*.

Fichte had conceived of the higher-order *Wille* as an essentially *negating* desire; following Frankfurt, we might think of the will as issuing a command *not* to act on the lower-order desire—a command, for example, to refrain from smoking. But might this *higher-order* desire not be reconceived as involving a desire with a *positive* content— for example, a desire *to be a non-smoker*, conceived in way such that this is a contentful desire? After all, to picture oneself *as* a non-smoker might be to picture oneself as having capacities for which *not* smoking is necessary—say, as living a life capable of a greater range of activities, let's say becoming a competitive cyclist. Non-smoking ceases to be a matter of *refraining* from acting in a certain way and becomes an *objective condition* of acting in other certain ways. This involves just that feature of Hegel's approach that Rorty points to: his use of "redescription". The life of the non-smoker is no longer to be described in privative terms from the perspective of *the smoker*, but from the new perspective of an agent who conceives of his or her non-smoking self differently—that of being a serious cyclist. But this new perspective is just as "worldly" as the old: it only makes sense for an agent engaged in activities in the actual world. Living as a competitive cyclist must *actually* exclude the possibility of living as a smoker. From the perspective of one's new identity one doesn't purport to issue commands to oneself from some position outside it. Rorty's exemption of any comparison here from all considerations of truth, seems to lean on Hume's point that competing *desires* can never *per se* be subject to evaluation on the basis of *truth*, but this assumption will not find a place in Hegel's alternative logic framework. We can see more details of this from his account of judgment given in book 3 of the *Science of Logic*.

1.4. The Typology of Judgment Forms in Hegel's *Science of Logic*

In the *Science of Logic* Hegel treats judging as an act in which the "concept"—which we are to think of as the concept *qua* judging subject, the "I", and not simply some general representation *said* of an object—is "realized" by "stepping into existence as determinate being [*das Treten ins Dasein als bestimmtes Sein*]"[23]—a form of words close to what Hegel uses in principle β in §6 of *Philosophy of Right*, where it is said that the I "steps into existence" through positing *itself* as determined (*Durch dies Setzen seiner selbst als eines bestimmten tritt Ich in das Dasein überhaupt*). Here we might, following Robert

it is conscious—a condition expressed in Fichte's second principle, "the principle of opposition". As for Hegel, the task for Fichte will be to show how these apparently antithetical principles are to be resolved, but for Hegel this resolution could simply not be achieved within the Kant–Fichte framework, restricted as it was to the "the understanding".

[23] G. W. F. Hegel, *Science of Logic*, edited and translated by George di Giovanni (Cambridge: Cambridge University Press, 2010), p. 550, translation altered.

Brandom, think of such theoretical and practical judgments as acts in which the I "steps into determinate existence" in the sense of taking on particular theoretical and practical, publically assessable *commitments*—that is, those commitments concerning ways the world *is* or *should be* that essentially make up the agent's concrete identity as an intentional being.[24] Brandom captures the rationality implicit in such acts as residing in the pragmatic norm that any agent's *entitlement* to such commitments are always questionable by others, and asked for justification. In turn, he treats the inferential linkages between the judgments involved as determining the very *content* of the commitments themselves. This capacity for any judgment to be brought into question and potentially given up, we might think, recapitulates Hegel's principle α, but might we have suspicions as to whether Brandom's approach can do justice to Hegel's principle β?[25] In this section, I will use Hegel's treatment of judgment forms in the *Science of Logic* to confirm what we can see in relation to Hegel's principle β concerning willing: we must understand *de re* attitudes as irreducible to *de dicto* ones, such that they are both "*aufgehoben*" in a content that can offer a redescription that is responsive to considerations of *both* freedom and truth.

In book 3 of the *Science of Logic*, Hegel explores a variety of conceptual forms that the content of a judgment may take,[26] putting them in a series that leads to a judgment form—the "judgment of the concept"—that can equally be treated as a complex judgment or as an inferential relation between two judgments, and showing the syllogism to be "the truth" of the judgment.[27] Here, however, I want to focus on an earlier distinction between two judgment forms differentiated by the different conceptions of predication involved. Drawing on a distinction from Aristotle, Hegel distinguishes a predicate understood as *inhering in* a subject, as typically found in "judgments of determinate existence [*Dasein*]",[28] and a predicate that *subsumes* its subject, as found in "judgments of reflection".[29] I will treat these as judgments that express *de re* and *de dicto* attitudes respectively, and the difference between these two ways of conceiving of predication, I'll suggest, corresponds to the difference between the "moments" of the will from §§6 and 5 from the *Philosophy of Right*.[30] In short, we should think of the logical form in which a *particular willed content* becomes determinate *for* an agent as being

---

[24] Brandom's normative pragmatic theory is most fully developed in his *opus magnum*, Robert B. Brandom, *Making It Explicit* (Cambridge, Mass.: Harvard University Press, 1994). As an example of its application to Hegel's idealism see Robert B. Brandom, "Some Hegelian Ideas of Note for Contemporary Analytic Philosophy", *Hegel Bulletin*, 35 (2014), pp. 1–15.

[25] Elsewhere I have questioned the purported "Hegelian" nature of Brandom's assumption that the judgment's inferential relations are not only necessary but also *sufficient* for the determination of the judgment's meaning. See my "An Hegelian Solution to a Tangle of Problems Facing Brandom's Analytic Pragmatism" *British Journal for the History of Philosophy*, 23, 4 (2015), pp. 657–80.

[26] Hegel describes the determinations into which a concept may divide as singularity, particularity, and universality, and any judgment will typically divide into two of these determinations, resulting in a taxonomy of various particular judgment forms depending on which of the three determinations occupy grammatical positions of subject and predicate in their expressions.

[27] Hegel, *Science of Logic*, p. 593.   [28] Ibid., pp. 557–68.   [29] Ibid., pp. 568–75.

[30] This also corresponds to the conceptions of objecthood (as that to which predications can be applied) represented in the "Perception" and "Understanding" chapters of the *Phenomenology of Spirit*. I have developed

analogous to the subject of a judgment of *existence*, and that in which a willed content becomes available for evaluation and possible negation by its being put in inferential relations to other contents, as analogous to the subject of a judgment of *reflection*.

With the idea of judgments of existence Hegel has in mind the type of judgments in which *certain particular perceivable objects* are singled out with the use of definite description such as "the rose"—that is, judgments that express intentional attitudes directed to specific perceivable things or "re"s in the judge's immediate environment— particular objects a judge can be said to "have in mind" and that might be identified, handled, picked out with demonstratives, and so on.[31] Moreover, what is said *about* such an object via the *predicate* of these judgments is conversely thought of as the property found *instantiated, in the particular way that it is, in* that particular object as perceptually available to that agent. Thus, when saying "the rose is *fragrant*", for example, the predicate term "fragrant", Hegel tells us, is meant to refer to the *particular* fragrance belonging to *that particular rose*—that is, the quality that Kant would presumably have thought of as the content of a "singular" (*Einzeln*) intuition.[32] Phenomenal properties commonly have strongly motivational dimensions: in Bernard Williams's terms, they are commonly "action-guiding", experienced as attracting or repelling:[33] we are typic- ally attracted by fragrant things, repulsed by sour, malodorous ones. But as Diotima had pointed out in Plato's *Symposium*, the generalization associated with conceptual thought can loosen the compelling quality of such specific instances: when reflected upon and generalized, earlier intense desires can seem but "small" things to be *des- pised*.[34] Such "reflection", I suggest, might reflect other contexts in which terms such as "rose" and "fragrant" function differently and are taken to express *de dicto* intentional attitudes with a *different* logical form in which the predicate is understood as *subsuming* the subject along with many other actual or possible items.

Hegel analyses the subsumptive judgments of reflection in ways that are closer to the analyses of analytic philosophy. These judgments explicitly take quantifiers, for example, and it is clear that in using a universally quantified judgment such as "*all roses are fragrant*" I need have no *particular* instance of a rose or particular fragrance in mind. Indeed, in the use of "all roses" I could be referring to roses that I'm not and never will be familiar with—possible roses that do not as yet exist, or perhaps ones that will never exist, and clearly, I cannot have *their* particular fragrances in mind. I am "reflected" out

this approach in "Hegel's Anticipation of the Early History of Analytic Philosophy", *The Owl of Minerva: Journal of the Hegel Society of North America*, 42, 1–2 (2010–11), pp. 18–40.

[31] Here I largely follow the approach of Tyler Burge. See Tyler Burge, "Belief De Re" and "Postscript to Belief De Re", both in his *Foundations of Mind: Philosophical Essays, Volume 2* (Oxford: Clarendon Press, 2007).

[32] "The predicate is determined in the subject, for it is not a determination in general but the determin- ation rather of the subject. 'The rose is fragrant.' This fragrance is not some indeterminate fragrance or other, but the fragrance of the rose. The predicate is therefore a singular." Hegel, *Science of Logic*, p. 560.

[33] See, for example, Bernard Williams, *Ethics and the Limits of Philosophy* (London: William Collins, 1985), chapter 6.

[34] Plato, "Symposium", trans. Alexander Nehamas and Paul Woodruff, in *Plato: Complete Works* (Indianapolis: Hackett, 1997), p. 492.

of any *particular* relation to any *particular* rose—seemingly suspended in some conceptual space leaving me equidistant to *all* the roses that fall under the scope of my general description. Not surprisingly, the negation of the reflective judgment "it is not the case that all roses are fragrant" does *not* explicitly posit the existence of malodorous ones. The roses referred to may simply be without odour. The mutually *excluding* features of properties required for the pair *being a smoker* and *being a competitive cyclist* here go missing.

In short, what is important in the case of reflective judgments is that the content expressed has a determinate "truth value" conventionally understood—its being either true or false *timelessly*. That is, what is essential to the "dictum" negated in the negated *de dicto reflective* judgment is a property conceived in such a way that allows a judgment to stand in inferential relations. In contrast, in the case of a *de re* judgment like "this rose is fragrant" or a contrary such as "this rose smells sour", it is explicit that questions of truth or falsity are context specific. Tomorrow *this* rose might have changed, its initial fresh fragrance having been replaced by a different, sickly one.[35] In contemporary ways of putting it, *de re* beliefs do *not* have fully propositional contents—to understand *what* proposition is expressed in an utterance of the sentence "the rose is fragrant" requires background information: for example, information as to the time and place of the utterance, so as to determine *what* rose is being referred to, and so to understand *what* propositional content is being expressed. To understand *what* was said one *had to be there*! But while such judgments may be incomplete from the point of view of a disembodied God, why should we think this to be necessarily the case for subjects in the actual world? After all, *everyone has to be somewhere.*

This distinction, while typically applied to "theoretical" attitudes, can be applied to practical attitudes as well. We commonly think of agency as the capacity to *change* the states of some object. My phone rings and I lift the receiver, making a judgment that was formerly true—that the receiver is sitting in its cradle—now *false*. This coheres with the "*de re*" nature of my practical intention to answer *the phone*—that is, *that particular phone* that is in my immediate environment, the one with which I *can* interact. Just as the *physical* properties of such objects can be in causally relevant relations to our perceptual states, we can similarly bear such relations to the *properties* of those objects.[36] From a practical point of view, the fact of a phone's ringing is perceived as action-guiding. It "says", as it were, "answer me!", just as for the smoker, the alluring

---

[35] Furthermore, without this timeless quality, they cannot be candidates for standing in what we *normally* think of inferential relations. In the history of logic, Aristotle's subject–predicate way of thinking of judgments typically express such *de re* attitudes, while Stoic and modern, *proposition-first*, conceptions of judgments better express *de dicto* ones. See my "Hegel, Aristotle and the Conception of Free Agency", in Gunnar Hindrichs and Axel Honneth (eds), *Freiheit: Stuttgarter Hegelkongress 2011* (Frankfurt am Main: Vittorio Klostermann, 2013), pp. 389–404, and "The Role of Logic 'Commonly So Called' in Hegel's *Science of Logic*", *British Journal for the History of Philosophy*, 22, 2 (2014), pp. 281–301.

[36] I address this issue in relation to the structure of the practical intentional attitude of the slave in Hegel's "master–slave dialectic" in the *Phenomenology of Spirit* in "The Role of Work within the Processes of Recognition in Hegel's Idealism", in Nicholas H. Smith and Jean-Philippe Deranty (eds), *New Philosophies of Labour: Work and the Social Bond* (Leiden and Boston: Brill, 2012), pp. 41–62.

cigarette can say "smoke me!". Reflection can, in some sense, counter this. When con-strued as a mere *instance* of a class, ringing phones, I can question the norm involved: should ringing phones necessarily be answered? Similarly when I reflect on *this* allur-ing cigarette, I can raise the question: Should cigarettes be smoked? Should immediate desires be acted upon? Kant was well aware of how thinking of the consequences of acting in a certain manner could impact on the original desire that motivated that par-ticular action. This is a type of redescription, but it is *not* one that produces a desire that motivates a contrary action. Hegel was attuned to the need to take redescription to this further level—to replace one action-guiding description by another, but one that reflecting reason has had *some* hand in choosing such that it better fits into a realistic conception of what it is to live a reasonably coherent life and actualize a reasonably coherent self.

1.5. The Dynamics of *De Re* and *De Dicto* Judgments

In Hegel's presentation of *de re* judgments of existence and *de dicto* judgments of reflec-tion in the *Science of Logic*, with their conceptions of predication as "inherence" and "subsumption" respectively, both are "*aufgehoben*" within further, more complex, explicitly modal judgment forms, and, further on, more encompassing *syllogistic* forms. I interpret this as reflecting on a series of *further conditions* required for any subject to possess and exercise the capacity to reason with such judgment forms, such as belonging to a community of agents in which each can mediate their located experi-ence with that of differently located others. But at this point I am interested simply in the relation between these two initial capacities, and whether we talk of this in terms of the notion of "*Aufheben*" or, as in §7 in the *Philosophy of Right*, in terms of the "unity" of both these moments, it is clear that Hegel thinks that these two capacities, with their distinct content-acquiring and form-conferring dimensions, must be both somehow integrated into the succeeding capacity for the self rationally to determine itself. The failure to do justice to the particular *de re* contents of principle β is precisely the prob-lem of the Kant–Fichte approach. It cannot be that *de dicto* forms simply unilaterally supersede *de re* ones without loss, as this is just the assumption found in Kant's con-ception of the unilateral *subsumption* of the objects of *die Willkür* under principles of *der Wille*.

To bring this issue of the relation of *de re* and *de dicto* forms more clearly into focus we may look to a difference within contemporary approaches to the relations between these forms. Typically within analytic philosophy, following the approach of Quine, the *de dicto* form of intentionality is treated as primitive, and *de re* forms are treated as derivative from *de dicto* ones.[37] In contrast, Tyler Burge has argued against Quine that while such analyses may hold for the *ascription* or *attribution* of intentional states to

[37] W. V. O. Quine, "Quantifiers and Propositional Attitudes", *The Journal of Philosophy*, 53 (1956), pp. 177–87; reprinted in his *The Ways of Paradox* (New York: Random House, 1966).

others, they do not go to the nature of the actual psychological states *themselves* that such ascriptions are meant to capture.[38] When one considers the states themselves, he argues—and in particular, think here of *perceptual states* as the paradigms of *de re* attitudes—the natural tendency will be to treat *de re* states as *primitive* rather than derivable from *de dicto* ones. *De re* contents should be thought of as typically involving a *demonstrative* element that ties the agent to some particular worldly context. *De re* contents are thus not fully conceptual in the conventional sense, not elements of standard "propositions" thought of as having an eternal truth value. Moreover, he goes on to argue for the stronger thesis that the capacity to have and exercise *de dicto* intentional states, in fact any intentional states at all, *presupposes* the capacity to have these not-fully-conceptualized *de re* ones.

To refuse the reducibility of located *de re* attitudes to abstracted *de dicto* ones in this way need not, of course, commit one to the opposing thesis that reduces *de dicto* attitudes to *de re* ones. Rather, the non-reducibility of *de re* attitudes is compatible with the idea that each is necessary, but not sufficient, for rational intentionality, and that they must somehow work together. In the *Science of Logic*, the non-reducibility of the *de re* dimension of judgment is apparent when we follow the passage from the judgment of reflection to the superseding "judgment of necessity", as the *de re* features of the surpassed judgment of existence now *reappear* in that the *subject* term comes to designate some particular *genus*.[39] While the earlier *subsumptive* judgment of reflection had expressed nomological regularity in the form of universally quantified judgments about "all plants" or "all men", for example, the judgment of necessity expresses judgments about "the plant *as such*" or "man *as such*"—that is, it grasps the particular *genus* in terms of its essential properties.[40] In the following judgment of *the concept*, the role of the *genus* characterizing the particular is preserved, but now in a different way that appears explicitly to hold on to the dimension of singularity of the experienced object that exemplifies the genus.

This circular pattern manifested by the transitions in Hegel's *Science of Logic* stands in obvious contrast to the type of Platonic "ascent" characteristic of Plato's *Symposium*, or, closer to Hegel's time, of Leibniz's idea of a step-wise progression from clear and confused ideas to ones that are increasingly "clear and distinct", a progression that is set on a path towards God's knowledge which is pictured as *entirely* clear and distinct. But even from a theological point of view Hegel thought this to be a misleading *Vorstellung*. The modern (Protestant) Christian God, for Hegel, *had* to become part of the actual world to live up to its own concept *as* God. Even God did not have the unmediated "God's-eye" point of view, or speak the type of language that Leibniz pictured as that befitting a being liberated from all particular corporeal and located existence. The circular pattern of conceptual redetermination for Hegel is meant to bring out more adequately

---

[38] Burge, "Belief *De Re*".   [39] Hegel, *Science of Logic*, p. 575.

[40] G. W. F. Hegel, *The Encyclopaedia Logic: Part I of the Encyclopaedia of Philosophical Sciences with the Zusätze*, a new translation with introduction and notes by T. F. Geraets, W. A. Suchting, and H. S. Harris (Indianapolis: Hackett, 1991), § 176, addition.

the structure of the *actual* world for a subject who *belongs* to that world. Divine representation is not abandoned in the name of a freedom that is disengaged from truth.

In the first sub-type of the judgment of the concept that succeeds the judgment of necessity—the assertoric judgment—one once again finds an immediate perceivable object analogous to the judgment of existence. But in contrast to that earlier simple qualitative judgment, the predicate of the new judgment form is an evaluative rather than a descriptive one—"an *ought* [*ein Sollen*] to which reality may or may not conform."[41] Thus in judgments such as "this house is *bad*, this action is *good*",[42] the subject is posited as "a concrete singular, [*ein konkretes Einzelnes*]",[43] and it is this determination of *singularity* which distinguishes this judgment form from the preceding judgment of necessity. *There*, the universal had "obtained completion itself *in its particularization* [*Besonderung*]",[44] but had failed to achieve the determination of "singularity, [*Einzelheit*]" that is present in the more developed assertoric judgment. In short, the judgment of necessity was a general *de dicto* judgment of which the subject was any mere instance of a house *as such*. What distinguishes the *judgment of the concept* is that it has returned to *de re* form, the subject of which is a *specific* thing—*this* house, not simply any house.

Qua singular, the thing is thus not conceived simply as a "particular" exemplification of a kind: when one makes an evaluative judgment about a house, say, one cannot simply subsume that house under some determinate concept that can be understood in abstraction from the particular objects experienced. As in Kant's aesthetic judgments, it is the particular way in which the more general determinants of "goodness" are exemplified in *this house* that is crucial, and like Kant, Hegel portrays the initial manifestations of these evaluative judgments as *subjective* and without truth. They are *problematic* because based on some bare subjective assurance (*Versicherung*), which is able to be "confronted by an opposing one [*entgegengesetzte*]".[45] But this confrontation leads the judges to attempts to justify their judgments, and say *why* the particular house is good or bad. We see this in the transition from the second sub-type of the judgment of the concept (the problematic judgment) to the final sub-type (the apodictic judgment), for which Hegel gives the example, "the house, as so and so constituted, is *good*",[46] or, as he labels the structure in the *Encyclopaedia Logic*, "*this*—the immediate singularity (*Einzelheit*)—*house*—the genus—*being constituted thus and so*—particularity—is good or bad".[47] Such a judgment whose mediating term gives its justifying *grounds*, making explicit *why* the house is good, appeals to some rule or principle (the thing's normative essence) and could thus be set out as a syllogism:

Rule: Houses are essentially constituted thus and so.

Case: This house is (is not) constituted thus and so.

Result: This house is good (or bad).

---

[41] Hegel, *Science of Logic*, p. 582.   [42] Ibid., p. 583.
[43] Ibid. That is, this is Hegel's equivalent to the type of judgment that Frege considers the fundamental atomic judgment in which the concept applies to an individual object.
[44] Ibid., p. 582.   [45] Ibid., p. 584.   [46] Ibid., p. 585.
[47] Hegel, *The Encyclopaedia Logic*, §179.

While the appearance of conceptual structures such as these is sometimes taken to signal Hegel's espousal of a type of Aristotelian essentialist realism about *kinds*, such a metaphysical reading is, I suggest, mistaken. As the example of the judgment of the house brings out, the judge must be a worldly one, in proximity to a *particular* house, by which it can be affected. The Aristotelian realist position on essences conceives of the essential form of the "house as such" as shining through *any* exemplar. But for Hegel it requires a *specific* house that can serve as a normative model for the good house—a specific house by which one can be affected. I take this as all evidence for a reading of Hegel as a "modal actualist" for whom the scope of metaphysical knowledge is the actual world to which the subject him or herself belongs.[48] Of course the actual, to be understood *as* actual, must be able to be contrasted with the *possible*, but for the actualist, the possible cannot exist "outside" the actual for the actual is all there is. The possible must be, therefore, as Hegel says in the *Encyclopaedia Logic*, the "reflection-into-itself" *of* the actual, giving the actual a "concrete unity" that contrasts with the "*abstract* and *unessential* essentiality" of the possible.[49] Actuality must be understood as "the more comprehensive, because it is the concrete thought which includes possibility as an abstract element".[50]

Such a conception of the actual as the object of philosophical knowledge must, I suggest, be understood as contrasting with the traditional Aristotelian goal of metaphysics as knowledge of the *necessary* or *essential* that, as Hegel pictures it, is understood as "shining through" the merely contingent, *non-essential* appearance. Philosophical knowledge is knowledge of the actual world *as actual*, and as such has to be understood as always had from a reflectively mediated perspective within it. In this sense it is committed to *truth* about the actual, in contrast with the mere "correctness" of claims that coincide with isolated *facts* within the actual.[51] Rorty, in his reading of Hegel, shows himself to be committed ultimately to a form of *amodal naturalism*, but the Hegelian *actualist* is not restricted to the natural in this way. The actualist is free to conceive of the non-reducible existence of actual minds without any commitment to their being *necessary* components of reality in the traditional sense. Hegel's *recognitive account* of mindedness, the account that Rorty attempts to reduce to a quasi-natural "struggle for recognition", I take to be central to his actualism.[52]

---

[48] For a recent account of Hegel's logic that takes it in the direction of an actualist metaphysics, see Rocío Zambrana, *Hegel's Theory of Intelligibility* (Chicago: University of Chicago Press, 2015). I expand on this theme in my review, "Rocío Zambrana, *Hegel's Theory of Intelligibility*" in *Notre Dame Philosophical Reviews*, (2016).

[49] Hegel, *The Encyclopaedia Logic*, §143. So, possibilities belong *essentially* to the actual world but, of course, each particular possibility is not itself essential, only possible.

[50] Ibid., §143, addition. For a good account of Hegel's treatment of the category actuality see Karen Ng, "Hegel's Logic of Actuality", *Review of Metaphysics*, 63 (2009), pp. 139–72.

[51] Hegel, *Science of Logic*, p. 562.

[52] Hegel's actualist metaphysics is still a type of *idealism* in the sense that the existence of *abstracta*, such as possibilities, requires the existence of actual minds, conceived as having the capacity of conceiving and acting on such *abstracta*. Similarly, such minds are themselves only conceivable in relation to *abstracta*, as it is those capacities that define them as minds.

1.6. Recognition Underlying Any "*Struggle for Recognition*"

In chapter 4 of the *Phenomenology of Spirit*, Hegel's argument had unfolded against a conception of self-consciousness on the model of how one immediately finds oneself in the phenomenal states thought of as appetitive ones and that one takes as defining one's identity—a stance he calls "self-certainty", and that parallels the "sense-certainty" of theoretical intentionality explored in chapter 1. There *is* a compelling sense in which one is aware of oneself in one's appetitive states, but there is a definite "content externalism" implicit in Hegel's approach that brings different desirers into conflict over common objects. Thus we are given a glimpse of the type of Hobbesian life-and-death struggle found in the realm of nature understood as a struggle for survival. Against this picture, however, we are shown a possibility for a resolution of such struggles seemingly unlike *any* found in nature—in this case the establishment of an institutionalized social relation of a master to a slave who has capitulated in the struggle, trading particular objects of desire for life itself. So it is not any desired *object* (marked, as it is, by a type of essentially *negative* existence) that conveys back to the original desirer a conception of itself—it is the other *agent*: the master understands himself as master *of* this slave, the slave as slave *of* this master. As such, this relation can no longer be thought of as a natural one but as a crude and primitive version of a *spiritual* (*geistig*) one in which agents hold themselves to rules mediated by the role of the other. Moreover, measured against the reciprocity that is part of the essence of the recognitive relation, the master–slave relation will be grasped as self-contradicting and thereby self-undermining. The resolution of this contradiction will be a transformation of this crude social form into some other "higher" form, which can somehow mediate the contradiction unleashed in the former, but it in turn will be beset by similar contradictions and will be subject to the same dynamic.

That is, the sequence of scenarios of recognition that we now trace through the forms of life in Hegel's *Phenomenology* provide contexts in which an "I" struggles to achieve unity with itself—to be "*bei sich*"—in an other. Thus the proper relata of a rational will that allows this must be *another will*, and it is in this sense that it is "*das Geistige*"—the realm of human recognitive interactions that is "the spiritual"—that is the "ground" of normative human relations, the ground of "right". Such a conception of recognition at the heart of "*das Geistige*" can therefore no longer be *reduced* to Rorty's Kojèvean *struggle* for recognition in which agents attempt to achieve freedom by imposing their normative criteria on each other. Moreover, such a Rortarian struggle must itself be recognized as an *inadequate* and *limited* instance of the recognitive interaction that for Hegel is the ground of the normative. Hegel expresses this in terms of the self-contradictory nature of the struggle between master and slave, a contradiction between a concrete instance of a recognitive relation and the "universal" it expresses. But I suggest that we now have a way of understanding the framework alluded to here in a way that could be free from the worry of Platonic metaphysics.

Hegel appeals to what he sees as the inherent logic of our actual rational practices, a logic in which the pragmatic functions served are reflected in the categories of the language employed. It is a logic that cannot be independently cognized in the manner of Kant's "transcendental logic"; it must be discoverable in our practices and their history. So rather than assume that Hegel's path is that of a retreat from Kant's critique of traditional metaphysics to such metaphysics itself, we might see him as developing Kant's implicit account of the power of "redescription" in the effort to free it from the problems that impede it. Hegel may be a master of redescription, but in relation to Kant's his redescription is meant to capture what is valuable in Kant's and so taken as the essential core of Kant's Copernican revolution, freeing it from the residual pre-revolutionary metaphysical assumptions that accompany it. This is not simply to impose a "new vocabulary" that disendorses the old; rather it *endorses* the essential *function* of the older thought by attempting to capture it in a vocabulary that better captures this function. In this it aims at *truth*.

Hegel is of course critical of the emptiness of Kant's formal *practical* solution to an unrealizable metaphysics, and of his account of a theoretical knowledge of the world's systematic *appearances*, and Rorty is right in thinking this does not lead back to the traditional metaphysical aspiration of "absolute knowing" *qua* seeing from the "God's-eye view" or speaking in God's vocabulary. The alternative Rorty misses, however, is a systematic view of the actual world in which the subject, while finding itself subject to the conditions of its worldly location, is capable of *local*, but not *global*, "transcendence" of those conditions. This can be thought of as an appropriation of Kant's critique of metaphysics, but now translated from Kant's *epistemological* register to what we might think of as a *modal* one. In adopting a sceptical attitude to metaphysical knowledge Kant had remained in the thrall of a traditional conception of metaphysical knowledge as knowledge of the necessary, but Hegel, the master redescriber, has recast metaphysics as a knowledge not of the necessary as opposed to the contingent, but of an actual that necessarily contains possibility with it. Freedom is to be gained not by the mere victory of a vocabulary that disarms the objectifying vocabulary of some other, in the manner of Proust, but by the victory of a vocabulary that the victor must regard in an ironic, naturalistic mode. Freedom is rather to be gained by grasping *real* possibilities that exist within the actual, possibilities that can thereby be realized to create a new actuality, via participation in a socialized cognition in which others are, in the style of Kant, recognized as free minds and not as objects of nature. In short, on a properly *Hegelian* reading of the inadequacies of Kant, we might see Rorty's own critique of Kantian formalism as relying on the same general *formal* assumptions that underlie the Kant–Fichte approach to the will.

I have argued that tracing the general outlines of Hegel's alternative to Kant allows us to understand how the more *substantive claims* about the structures underlying and enabling freedom can be understood without the sort of traditional metaphysical commitment that Rorty fears. Read as a "modal actualist" in the way I have suggested, Hegel presents us with a mode of philosophizing that is not out of step with the general attitudes that Rorty had brought to his reading of Hegel, nor, I take it, out of step with the basic outlook, with its suspicion of the tradition of "metaphysics", that has been characteristic of much of the history of analytic philosophy over the last century. While Hegel's can be thought of as the re-establishment of a type of metaphysics that replaces Kant's metaphysical scepticism, it is a metaphysics of the *actual*, and not an instance of the type of metaphysics of which Kant had been critical.

2

Systematicity and Normative Justification

The Method of Hegel's Philosophical Science of Right

Kevin Thompson

The aim of what follows is to set out an interpretation of the method of normative justification that Hegel employs in his political philosophy. By this I mean the form of argumentation by which the validity and soundness of the central doctrines of the *Elements of the Philosophy of Right* are established. But perhaps no other aspect of Hegel's political theory has been more controversial than the relationship between its core doctrines and what Hegel called its scientific or speculative method or, to put the issue more broadly, the relationship between the substantive normative claims of Hegel's political philosophy and the metaphysical doctrines of his broader philosophical system.[1]

The current field of studies of Hegel's political philosophy can be divided into four main tendencies defined by two distinct axes: systematic vs. non-systematic and metaphysical vs. non-metaphysical. The first tendency holds that the systematic order of Hegel's thought is essentially tied to the metaphysical claims that it makes about the nature of reality and that both of these together provide the foundation for his political theory.[2] The second agrees that the systematic structure of Hegel's work is significant

---

[1] For a useful review of this issue, see Hans-Friedrich Fulda, "Zum Theorietypus der Hegelschen Rechtsphilosophie," in *Hegels Philosophie des Rechts: Die Theorie der Rechtsformen*, ed. Dieter Henrich and Rolf-Peter Horstmann (Stuttgart: Klett-Cotta, 1982): 393–427, and for an excellent overview and more recent assessment of the broader terms of the debate, see Jean-François Kervégan, *L'effectif et le rationnel: Hegel et l'esprit objectif* (Paris: Vrin, 2007): 7–15.

[2] Major representatives of the systematic-metaphysical tendency include: Hugh Reyburn, *Hegel's Ethical Theory* (Oxford: Clarendon Press, 1967); Manfred Riedel, *Studien zu Hegels Rechtsphilosophie* (Frankfurt am Main: Suhrkamp, 1969); Emil Angehrn, *Freiheit und System bei Hegel* (Berlin: de Gruyter, 1977); Dieter Henrich, "Vernunft in Verwirklichung," in Georg Friedrich Wilhelm [sic] Hegel, *Philosophie des Rechts. Die Vorlesung von 1819/20 in einer Nachschrift*, ed. Dieter Henrich (Frankfurt am Main: Suhrkamp, 1982): 9–39; and Adriaan T. Peperzak, *Modern Freedom: Hegel's Legal, Moral, and Political Philosophy* (Dordrecht: Kluwer Academic Publishers, 2001).

for its normative claims, but believes this can be detached from its metaphysical core.[3] The third tendency attributes little significance to the systematic form of Hegel's work, holding, instead, that its real significance lies in its core metaphysical commitments.[4] Finally, though it acknowledges Hegel's systematic and metaphysical ambitions, the fourth tendency finds both to be dismal failures and, instead, seeks to isolate what remains philosophically valuable and coherent amidst the rubble.[5] As noted in the Introduction, I will be offering an interpretation that takes the systematic character of Hegel's thought and the metaphysical commitments that issue from it to be absolutely essential not only to understanding the core claims of his political philosophy, but, more importantly, to assessing their philosophical merits. As such, the present study stands clearly in the wake of the first tendency. However, the interpretation of the relationship between the organizing structure and metaphysical doctrines of Hegel's philosophical system and the normative theses of his political philosophy that I begin to develop in this chapter has been enriched by all four of the tendencies in varying ways. Moreover, I believe that the debate over this issue has demonstrated that understanding the link between systematic structure and normative justification must stand as a litmus test for any reading that hopes to do justice to Hegel's thought in a way that will also allow it to speak beyond its own historical context.

We must acknowledge that Hegel himself is partly responsible for the debates in the literature. He tells us quite clearly and quite adamantly that his political philosophy is to be judged solely in terms of its "philosophical manner of progressing from one matter to another and of conducting a scientific proof, the speculative way of knowing in general" (GW 14,1, 5/Werke 7, 12/Nisbet, 10). But rather than including an exposition of this methodology in the work itself, Hegel notoriously takes a "familiarity with scientific method" (GW 14,1, 5/Werke 7, 12/Nisbet, 10) for granted: "As for

---

[3] Excellent statements of what has come to be called the "non-metaphysical" reading of Hegel can be found in its originator, Klaus Hartmann, "Ideen zu einem neuen systematischen Verständnis der Hegelschen Rechtsphilosophie," *Perspektiven der Philosophie* 2 (1976): 167–200; in the early work of his student, Terry Pinkard, "Freedom and Social Categories," *Philosophy and Phenomenological Research* 47 (1986): 209–32; and, more recently and in a more developed form, in the work of Robert Pippin, *Hegel's Practical Philosophy: Rational Agency as Ethical Life* (Cambridge: Cambridge University Press, 2008).

[4] Influential versions of this now somewhat neglected view are to be found in Joachim Ritter, *Metaphysik und Politik: Studien zu Aristoteles und Hegel* (Frankfurt am Main: Suhrkamp, 1969) and Charles Taylor, *Hegel and Modern Society* (Cambridge: Cambridge University Press, 1979).

[5] The most prominent and substantive representative of the non-systematic, non-metaphysical view is Allen W. Wood, *Hegel's Ethical Thought* (Cambridge: Cambridge University Press, 1990). However, there have been and continue to be important variants of this approach. Some scholars favor replacing the systematic and metaphysical foundations of Hegel's political philosophy with a version of the phenomenological approach found in Hegel's Jena period: see, for instance, Karl-Heinz Ilting, "Rechtsphilosophie als Phänomenologie des Bewusstseins der Freiheit," in *Hegels Philosophie des Rechts: Die Theorie der Rechtsformen*, ed. Dieter Henrich and Rolf-Peter Horstmann (Stuttgart: Klett-Cotta, 1982): 225–54; and Mark Tunick, "Hegel's Nonfoundationalism: A Phenomenological Account of the Structure of the *Philosophy of Right*," *History of Philosophy Quarterly* 11 (1994): 317–37. While others have argued for a more broadly social scientific reading: Michael O. Hardimon, *Hegel's Social Philosophy: The Project of Reconciliation* (Cambridge: Cambridge University Press, 1994); and Frederick Neuhouser, *Foundations of Hegel's Social Theory: Actualizing Freedom* (Cambridge, MA: Harvard University Press, 2000).

what constitutes the scientific procedure of philosophy, that is presupposed here on the basis of philosophical logic" (GPR §2A). As a result, the exact nature and status of the work's core claims were left ill defined. Accordingly, the task of the present chapter is to begin to rectify this situation. To do so, it considers two fundamental questions: (1) what exactly is speculative method?; and (2) how does this method serve as a form of normative justification?

The strategy I will follow in addressing these questions will be to set out a comparison between Hegel's systematic conception of normative justification, what he calls the "philosophical science of right," and the rationalist and empiricist forms of demonstration that have defined the Western tradition of political theory and, particularly, as these shaped late eighteenth-century and early nineteenth-century German political thought. The chapter's principal thesis is that the distinctiveness of Hegel's methodology lies in the fact that, unlike the traditional approaches, it holds the justification of a normative claim to require showing that it is necessarily entailed as a moment in the immanent unfolding of the concept of freedom within a general systematic order of knowledge. The normative standing of a concept, principle, institution, or practice, for Hegel, on this reading, thus flows from its being established as a necessary moment in an arrangement of knowledge that is itself immune to skeptical challenge precisely by virtue of its systematic form. Normativity, in short, is a product of the systematic structure of the science of right.

The key to this view is Hegel's contention that the traditional forms of normative argumentation fail to establish the authoritativeness of their claims because they are rooted in the dogmatism of what Hegel calls "representation." Hegel argues that representation renders any normative claims vulnerable to the challenges posed by skepticism and this motivates his commitment to a distinctly presuppositionless form of systematic justification. Accordingly, I begin by setting out an account of normativity and the traditional forms of justification that have been developed to secure the authoritativeness of fundamental norms. I show how these, on Hegel's analysis, fail because they take for granted the epistemic certainty both of their object and of their methodology. I then, in turn, use this critique to construct an interpretation of systematicity as a general form of epistemic argumentation and, from this, develop, by means of a reading of the opening paragraphs of the *Elements of the Philosophy of Right*, an account of systematicity as a unique form of distinctly normative justification.

2.1. Normativity and the Traditional Representational Forms of Justification

Hegel's political philosophy aspires to establish what is arguably the most fundamental norm of the political domain: state sovereignty. Now a concept, standard, institution, or practice is said to be normative to the extent that it makes a claim to authority. And it does this insofar as it asserts not just that it possesses a binding hold with regard to someone or something as to what is good, permissible, forbidden, or obligatory, but that it is rightfully entitled to possess such a hold. In the case of sovereignty, the claim at issue is that the state possesses supreme authority, the right to rule, over its citizenry. As a claimed status, though, normativity requires demonstration of its warrant to this standing. That is to say, it stands in need of justification.

Now for a method of justification to succeed in establishing a genuine grounding for a norm such as sovereignty, it must do so in a way that overcomes the challenge classically posed by skepticism. For any justification offered for a norm, the skeptic undertakes to show that this grounding is either an unwarranted assertion (that the grounding is arbitrary, merely a hypothesis), a foundation that itself stands in need of justification (that the grounding opens on to an infinite regress), or an account that presupposes what it seeks to establish (that the grounding is actually viciously circular). This challenge—what has been termed the "Agrippan trilemma"—has set the agenda for all the various forms of justification since their inception.[6] In the normative domain, this has meant that the task has been to develop a mode of argumentation that successfully outflanks the Agrippan challenge, while grounding the authority of some principle or concept with respect to the activities and dispositions of an agent or group of agents.

The central methodological question that any attempt to ground the norm of sovereignty confronts, then, is how can it justify the supreme authority of the state in such a way that it is safeguarded against falling prey to the challenges posed by skepticism. Hegel's answer to this challenge is systematic normative justification, the "philosophical science of right". Systematicity is thus properly seen, in Hegel, not simply as an exercise in constructing an order of interdependent claims and concepts, nor as an expression of some abstruse desire for totalization, but rather as a distinctive method of establishing warrant, in the present case, normative warrant.

Now I shall argue that the key to the success of Hegel's conception of systematicity in avoiding the threats of skepticism is its distinctive epistemic commitment to presuppositionlessness.[7] Put simply, this means that systematic justification is dedicated to taking nothing for granted, assuming neither rules of procedure, nor even the subject matter it is to examine. Instead, this form of argumentation derives its mode of demonstration wholly from observation of the immanent unfolding of its most basic concept: in the case of political philosophy, the concept of right (*Recht*).

The radicality of Hegel's political philosophy, like that of his philosophical enterprise as a whole, thus flows, as Hegel himself often reminded us, not primarily from the principles, concepts, or even the doctrines that it propounds, but from the systematic method it employs, "the only true one, the one identical to its contents" (Enz. [1817] 5/46)

---

[6] On the decisive role of skepticism, and the "Agrippan Trilemma", in particular, in German Idealism, see Paul W. Franks, *All or Nothing: Systematicity, Transcendental Arguments, and Skepticism in German Idealism* (Cambridge, MA: Harvard University Press, 2005).

[7] Cf. Enz. [1817]: §36. The centrality of presuppositionlessness to Hegel's philosophical enterprise has been most forcefully articulated and defended by Stephen Houlgate, *The Opening of Hegel's Logic: From Being to Infinity* (West Lafayette, IN: Purdue University Press, 2006): chapter 2.

or what he also calls "the resolve *to will to think purely*" (Enz. [1817] §36A). But what exactly does a presuppositionless science of right mean and how is this approach able to overcome the skeptical threats of arbitrariness, regressivity, and vicious circularity?

Hegel's central contention is that all other competing methods of normative justification fail because they are fundamentally dogmatic modes of argumentation and, as such, are vulnerable to the skeptic's challenges. The nerve of his argument for this admittedly dramatic and perplexing claim is the idea that the dogmatism of traditional forms of justification flows from their being what he calls representational forms of justification. A form of argumentation is representational, for Hegel, just insofar as it employs any preconceived notions or makes use of ungrounded assumptions, all of these presuppositions deriving from a common source, representation (*Vorstellung*), the mental power by which we create images, symbols, and signs and construct narratives. Thus, what defines a truly philosophical science of right as a presuppositionless form of normative justification and what separates it from the traditional methods of demonstration is its ability to generate both its method and its object independent of the resources of representation.

Now, obviously, this crucial claim requires further explication. It will suffice, for our present purposes, however, simply to note that Hegel took systematic and representational modes of normative justification to be mutually exclusive and exhaustive philosophical enterprises and, as such, they also constitute, for him, the only conceptually viable strategies for grounding norms. Thus, in order for us to see the motives, methodological imperatives, and fundamental structure of Hegel's distinctive approach, it will be useful to begin by developing an account of what he meant by the dependency of the traditional forms of normative justification upon representation. We can then use this analysis to construct an interpretation of the presuppositionless form of normative demonstration that constitutes the philosophical science of right.

2.1.1. *The Traditional Forms of Normative Justification: Rationalism and Empiricism*

In what are admittedly broad terms, rationalism and empiricism have been the two principal methods for establishing the authoritativeness of the ultimate grounds of conduct and character in the Western tradition of practical philosophy. Rationalism seeks to derive normative principles from properties it holds to be necessary features of the fundamental order of things, while empiricism claims that such standards derive their standing from various kinds of facts such as sentiment, inclination, tradition, language, and culture. The fundamental difference between these strands can be said to lie in their antithetical conceptions of rationality.[8] For rationalism, reason is

---

[8] For this characterization of the distinction between rationalist and empiricist conceptions of rationality, see Frederick C. Beiser, "Two Concepts of Reason in German Idealism," in *Internationales Jahrbuch des Deutschen Idealismus (2003)/International Yearbook of German Idealism (2003): Konzepte der Rationalität/ Concepts of Rationality* (Berlin: Walter de Gruyter, 2002): 13–27.

principally an intuitive power. It is able not only to engage in discursive thought—such as conceiving, judging, and inferring—it is also capable of perceiving or grasping the fundamental structure of being, the providential order of reality. For empiricism, reason is nothing more than its discursive ability. It simply conceives, judges, and infers things about the data it receives from the senses. The former contemplates the order of things, while the latter produces order out of random contingency. Each method can thus be said to be rooted in a different form of intuition. For rationalism, it is reason's own intellectual intuition that has insight into the fundamental order of being, while, for empiricism, it is sensible intuition that is the root of reason's creations. These different conceptions in turn lead to different understandings of normativity and correspondingly different forms of justification.

To justify a norm for rationalism is to do nothing less than to see that the principle, concept, institution, or practice making a claim to binding authority is itself specified by or determinable within the providential order of nature, the fundamental structure of reality. For instance, that crimes require punishment may be grasped as part and parcel of the objective moral order. This principle is normative, that is, it is vested with obligatory moral force, however, because it is itself the ground or it is grounded in the law of nature. Normative justification, on this view, establishes the authoritativeness of something by showing that the claim in question possesses the requisite status within the totality of the moral order of the world or that it is deducible from a claim that does. It follows that, for rationalism, one acts rightly or one's disposition is virtuous when one is in accord with the laws of being discoverable by reason through intellectual intuition.

On the empiricist construal, a principle, concept, institution, or practice is normative to the extent that it is endorsed or is laid down as binding by some individual or corporate willing. Crime requires punishment, on this view, not because some fundamental moral order dictates this, but because an authoritative person or group holds to this principle, concept, institution, or practice as necessary, required, for instance, for the maintenance of social order. Justification is here thus a matter of there being an appropriate desiring of something to be normative and this alone being sufficient to make it so. For empiricism, then, one acts rightly only when one follows one's own conventions; reason here is subservient to the demands of what is found in and though sensible intuition.

Now the rationalist and empiricist forms of justification and normativity defined the conceptual space of German political thought in the late eighteenth and early nineteenth centuries and they thus provided the foundations for quite specific doctrines and movements concerning the nature and purpose of the state and of social order. And it was on this determinate and contested terrain that Hegel sought to establish the radicality of the systematic method.

Rationalism's insight into the natural moral order was taken, by theorists of Enlightened Absolutism, such as Seckendorff, Pufendorf, Wolff, Garve, Eberhard, and the Cameralists (Justi and Sonnenfels), to support the notion that the authority of the ruler lies in his commitment to providing and promoting the material and spiritual welfare of his citizenry and that these goals were to be achieved through the strict and centralized regulation of industry and trade, price controls, public education, and censorship of the press.[9] State paternalism was thus thought to be the means to secure the principles and attendant blessings of the providential order.

Empiricism, on the other hand, bore a more complex lineage in this period of German political thought as it was the root of both Conservatism and Romanticism. For Conservatives, such as Möser, Rehberg, Gentz, and Wieland, the reliance upon empirical warrant was taken to mean that the authority to rule is properly derived from historical sanction and that the well-being of society was to be ensured by the establishment and support of the ties of tradition afforded by religion, culture, language, and the public rituals whereby a people are bound to one another as a cohesive community.[10] However, for Romantics, such as Herder, the Schlegels, Schleiermacher, Novalis, Fries, and Savigny, the purpose of the state was to promote and provide for the rights and freedoms of its citizens to form communal associations and the requisite principles for creating this social order were freedom of the press, religious tolerance, and equality of opportunity.[11] For them, the authority of the sovereign lay in the devotion of the citizenry spurred by the majestic aura that true artists and tradition create around him.

Hegel's decisive insight was to recognize that these divergent strands of political rationality could all be traced back, in differing ways, to the traditional forms of normative justification. He was thereby able to cut through their ideological and programmatic differences and unearth their underlying fundamental methodological orientations. Following from this, he was able to see that these traditional forms of normative justification took their respective subject matters and procedures for granted because they shared a common reliance upon representation and it was this, he argued, that rendered them all vulnerable to the charges of arbitrariness, regressivity, and vicious circularity: the skeptical trilemma.

2.1.2. Normativity and the Problem of Representation

Hegel's critique of rationalism and empiricism as forms of normative justification develops in three distinct stages: he first sets out a basic critique of representationalism

---

[9] On the theory and policies of Enlightened Absolutism in Germany, see Karl Otmar Freiherr von Aretin, ed., *Der Aufgeklärte Absolutismus* (Köln: Kiepenheuer and Witsch, 1974); Leonard Krieger, *An Essay on the Theory of Enlightened Despotism* (Chicago: The University of Chicago Press, 1975); and Franklin Kopitzsch, ed., *Aufklärung. Absolutismus und Bürgertum in Deutschland* (München: Nymphenburger Verlagshandlung, 1976).

[10] On the development of Conservatism in Germany, see Klaus Epstein, *The Genesis of German Conservatism* (Princeton, NJ: Princeton University Press, 1966).

[11] For discussions of the political philosophy of German Romanticism, see Jakob Baxa, *Einführung in die romantische Staatswissenschaft* (Jena: Fischer, 1923); Jacques Droz, *Le romantisme allemand et l'état* (Paris: Payot, 1966); Theodore Ziolkowski, *German Romanticism and Its Institutions* (Princeton, NJ: Princeton University Press, 1990): chapter 3; and Frederick C. Beiser, *Enlightenment, Revolution, and Romanticism: The Genesis of Modern German Political Thought, 1790–1800* (Cambridge, MA: Harvard University Press, 1992): part II.

as a form of philosophical knowledge; from this analysis, he then proposes general criticisms of rationalism and empiricism as distinct kinds of representational knowledge; and then, based on this, he derives specific objections to each as accounts of distinctly normative justification.

In the opening paragraph of the *Encyclopedia of the Philosophical Sciences in Outline* (1817) Hegel draws a sharp distinction between representation and genuine forms of knowledge:

All sciences other than philosophy have objects that are given (*zugegeben*) as immediate from representation (*Vorstellung*), and they are thus presupposed (*vorausgesetzt*) as assumed (*angenommen*) from the *beginning* of science, so that in the course of further development, requisite and needed determinations are taken from representation.   (Enz. [1817] §1)

Hegel employs the term representation here, as he does throughout his mature writings, to refer not only to a specific sort of mental content but, more fundamentally, to a distinctive kind of human capacity: the mental power by which images, symbols, and signs are created (cf. Enz. [1817] §§373–83). Representation, in this sense, is an ability set over against both empirical intuition (*Anschauung*), in that the content it creates is not dependent on the immediate presence of its object, and against thought (*Denken*), in that its content is nonetheless inseparable from its figurative presentation. Images, symbols, and signs, Hegel claims, are generic enough to be separated or abstracted from that to which they refer—be it an individual object, a concept, or a more complex state of affairs—yet they still remain tied to their sensuous origin in that their particular configuration is still set by this source. In other words, representations as created by our representative capacity are, at once, particular and general figures that serve to denote other, more concrete, mental or physical objects.

The distinction that Hegel wishes to draw in this passage is thus between bodies of knowledge that are composed of or, at least, rooted in these sorts of images and philosophical forms of knowledge, which take concepts rather than representations as their resource and object. A concept, for Hegel, is distinctive in that it comprehends the fundamental essence of a thing without recourse to any kind of symbolic or figurative elements derived from sensible intuition. It is a setting forth of the fundamental structure of a thing purely in terms of its essential properties, where the relationship between these is a matter of logical necessity. Whereas representational forms of knowledge draw their objects ready made from the power of representation; they thus take over their objects from sensible intuition and thus presuppose, rather than deduce, both the subject matter of their inquiry and the relations between its various objects.

Hegel offers examples of representations as they function as the subject matter or object of inquiry in various sciences: magnitude is taken to be the object of mathematics, space is the object of geometry, number is the object of arithmetic, disease is the object of medicine, animals are the objects of zoology, and plants are the objects of botany (Enz. [1817] §1A). He contends that, despite the rather wide array of objects and sciences invoked here, each of these is nothing other than a generic conception that has been forged through generalization and comparison from the raw material of sensible experience. The details of how this works in each case need not concern us here. What is important to note is that all these objects possess a necessarily indeterminate epistemic, and as we shall see, normative, status. As representations, each of these objects of inquiry stand between the spatio-temporal individuals of empirical intuition and the unbounded universalities of conceptual thought. And this means that these objects are necessarily defined by an admixture of contingent and arbitrary associations, ones either produced in the formative process itself or already present as a feature of the existing empirical source from which they were derived. Hegel's argument is that this intermediate status is what renders not just the objects, but the methods of representational argumentation that draw upon them, impotent before the skeptical trilemma.

Consider first the objects. Representational forms of knowledge take the objects they wish to investigate for granted since representation, as a faculty, continually makes them available, literally it places (*stellen*) them before (*vor*) us for investigation. Accordingly, these objects are always on hand, ready to be explored. But this means that in accepting these objects as they are, their existence is never called into question. They simply are, and, as such, they can be presupposed: "Such a science does not have to justify the necessity of the objects that it treats…because they [its objects] are assumed to be existent from representation" (Enz. [1817] §1A). But if an account of the very existence of some object is not required, then its warrant to be a valid subject matter for rational explanation is left outstanding and any concepts, inferences, and claims derived from or about this object are necessarily open to the accusation of being mere assumptions rather than genuine knowledge.

If we turn now to the methodologies of such forms of knowledge, we find that the examination of a representational object amounts to nothing more than unpacking the determinations it already contains. With the givenness of the object comes the givenness of its properties. The methodological task, then, is simply to extract these determinations and, by doing so, claim to have derived genuine knowledge about the subject matter. Hegel provides a succinct description of this process: "At first, such an object is given its *familiar name*. This is fixed, yet it initially gives only the representation of the matter. But more determinations of the matter must be given. These can, certainly, be taken (*aufgenommen*) from the immediate representation" (Enz. [1817] §1A). The procedure Hegel describes here is a mix of analysis and observation that, in the end, produces a set of features that can only be contingent generalities, instead of the necessary and essential properties that genuine knowledge requires.

Accordingly, representation renders the method and objects of representational forms of knowledge necessarily arbitrary, unwarranted, and presupposed, the core charges of the skeptic. But how does this general critique of representationalism apply to rationalist and empiricist forms of epistemic justification?

Hegel examines the representational underpinnings of rationalism as the rubric common to the projects of classical, medieval, and modern metaphysics. He argues that this form of knowledge takes its object, the structure of reality, from the empirical world by abstracting from it all that it deems to be in conflict with the universality of natural law. This order's existence as well as its intellectual intuitability are thus both taken for granted and, as such, the supposedly natural order of being—defined by its principal objects: the soul, the world, and God—is a foundation lacking a warrant to be what it purports to be. Hegel makes this point quite precisely:

> Its *objects* are certainly totalities, which in and for themselves belong to reason—*soul, world, God*—but metaphysics took them from representation, establishing itself on them as *complete, given* subjects by applying the determinations of the understanding and had only its representation for its criterion as to whether the predicates fitted and were satisfactory or not.   (Enz. [1817] §20)

Similarly, rationalism's methodology seeks to produce genuine knowledge by taking various properties—such as existence, finitude, and simplicity—all of which have been abstracted from experience, and ascribing them to the natural order, what Hegel calls trying "to determine the absolute through the attribution of predicates" (Enz. [1817] §19). In this sense, rationalism strives to construct an account of the in-itself, the unconditioned, with the finite determinations of representation. It thereby substitutes the contingent for the necessary, the transient for the essential. The result is a rigid, exclusionary conception of truth where only one side of opposed attributes can be true, a position Hegel designates as the very epitome of dogmatism (Enz. [1817] §21).

Empiricism, for Hegel, also takes its object as well as its method from representation, but unlike rationalistic metaphysics, it seeks to preserve the full breadth and density of this sensuous domain through its appeal to the immediacy of experience. Empiricism thus begins as a rejection of the abstractions of rationalism, searching for a new concrete and sure foundation in sensible, rather than intellectual, intuition. But in doing so, it falls prey to the very same strand of dogmatism because it simply takes the content of perception, feeling, tradition, and sentiment and tries to elevate these contextually bound, particular experiences to the status of universal, eternal principles and concepts, the content of genuine philosophical knowledge. To do this, empiricism has to disentangle the concrete nexus presented by these facets of experience and distill a supposedly essential set of properties. The result is precisely the kind of abstractions that empiricism had sought to reject. Hegel sums up this aspiration and its failure in a rather succinct formulation:

> [Empiricism] takes not only the entire content of representation but also all the content and determination of thought as it is found in sensory perception, with feeling and intuition as an external or internal fact of consciousness, or as it believes it can derive it, and it takes these empirical facts in general and their analysis for the source of truth, but either denies the supersensory altogether or at any rate all knowledge of it, and makes only the form of abstraction, identical positing, available for thought.   (Enz. [1817] §26)

Now if Hegel is correct in this assessment and the objects and methods of rationalism and empiricism are indeed taken from representation, then they must be either wholly arbitrary, infinitely regressive, or viciously circular. As a consequence, each approach vitiates its own work because the insufficiency of their respective foundations and modes of demonstration must necessarily flow to all the concepts, claims, and inferences that are derivable from them. This means, of course, that not only is the epistemic status of the knowledge each purports to derive in question, but their normative standing is in jeopardy as well. If the moral order or the empirical world serve as nothing more than covert assumptions or brute assertions, and if rationalist attribution and empiricist analysis amount simply to means for portraying the ephemeral as the eternal, then the authoritativeness of the principles, concepts, and institutions derived from them can make no validly binding claim on the conduct or character of agents.

Hegel draws the implications of this critique of rationalism and empiricism as forms of knowledge for their corresponding concrete species of normative justification in the introduction to the *Elements of the Philosophy of Right*. In the domain of practical philosophy, he contends, rationalist metaphysics, which he calls the "formal" method, takes its principal task to be the formulation of the definition of right itself as opposed to the determination of the rightfulness of specific acts or claims. To define right, in this sense, is thus to grasp it as a principle endemic to the natural moral order. Now, as we shall see, Hegel will agree that the main charge of a genuine science of right is to set out what right itself is, that it must begin from a proper deduction of right. The problem with rationalism as a form of normative justification, for Hegel, is thus not with its aim, but with the way in which it seeks to ground the concept of right. Rationalist normative projects purport to derive the concept of right by way of intellectual intuition. But this is really nothing more than abstraction and attribution from representation: "But [in this way] the deduction of the definition becomes something reached by etymology, by abstraction from particular cases, so that it is grounded in the feelings and representations of human beings. The correctness of the definition is therefore posited in its agreement with prevailing representations" (GPR §2A). As such, right itself is rendered nothing more than a generic conception and, as such, it is filled with all the contingencies and arbitrariness of the empirical fount from which it is fashioned. Rationalist metaphysics therefore makes of right an unwarranted posit: arbitrary, open to infinite regress, and vicious circularity.

Hegel considers empiricism as a form of normative justification under the guise of two distinct kinds of Romanticism: subjectivism and historicism.[12] Both seek to root the concept of right in sensible intuition because only here, they contend, can it have the kind of concreteness that such principles require in order to move those under their authority to act. As with rationalism, Hegel will affirm the basic intent of this approach: right must be concrete in order to compel action. But subjectivism and historicism seek determinacy in representation, the only difference between them is whether the "source of right" from which its warrant is drawn is personal (subjective) or communal (historical).

---

[12] Hegel does not explicitly address the theories of the Conservatives. He, instead, analyzes the methodological weaknesses that they share with their empiricist brethren among the Romantics.

For subjectivism, Hegel argues, the idea of right and its further determinations "are immediately taken up and asserted as *facts of consciousness*, and our natural or intensified feelings, our *own heart* and *enthusiasm*, are made the source of right" (GPR §2A), whereas in historicism "the emergence and development of determinations of rights as *they appear in time*," what Hegel also terms, "development from historical grounds," "is confused with development from the concept," a confusion that illegitimately extends "the significance of historical explanation and justification" into "justification which is *valid in and for itself*" (GPR §3A). Empiricism, like rationalism, thus constructs right as a problematically determinate figure drawn from the well of representation, rather than as a genuinely rational, grounded concept. And in so doing, empiricism, like the rationalism it seeks to oppose, deprives right of any basis for its claim to possess binding authority over human conduct and character.

Hegel viewed the contested conceptual space of late eighteenth- and early nineteenth-century German political theories through the lens of representationalism and found it rife with openings to skepticism. Though Enlightened Absolutism, rooted in rationalist metaphysics, with its "formal definitions, inferences, proofs, and the like," had, he believed, "more or less disappeared" (GPR §2A), Conservatism and Romanticism, both tied ultimately to empiricist forms of justification, were, particularly in their subjectivist and historicist forms, ascendant and their identification of right with personal or communal conviction, he contended, promoted nothing less than a "hatred of law (*Gesetz*)" (GW 14,1, 10/Werke 7, 20/Nisbet, 17). He therefore saw the terrain within which he sought to establish the need for his own method of normative justification as a pitched battle to ground right itself. Because it merely presupposes right, rather than providing it with valid justification, representationalism, in all its forms, threatened to reduce political authority to a dogmatic "shackle" opposed to any sense of freedom. In so doing, it threatened to render the very core of right itself, its legitimate hold or bindingness over conduct and character, invalid. Hegel thus saw the very concept of right as endangered by the traditional forms of normative justification and their attendant political theories. He thus conceived his own project as a contribution to working out what he called the appropriate "rational form" for the deeply rational content of right because it is only when right possesses this proper form, he argued, that it will be firmly and finally established, that is, it will only then be "justified to free thinking":

For such thinking does not stop at what is *given*, whether the latter is supported by the external positive authority of the state or of mutual agreement among human beings, or by the authority of inner feeling and the heart and by the testimony of the spirit which immediately concurs with this, but starts out from itself and thereby demands to know itself as united in its innermost being with the truth (GW 14,1, 7/ Werke 7, 14/Nisbet, 11).

A genuine science of right is thus demanded, as Hegel understands it, by the fundamental principle of critical thought itself—that we must have the courage to think for ourselves—what Kant proclaimed to be the core dictum of the Enlightenment.

To take the given as the standard of right—and this, as we have seen, is precisely what stands at the core of the project of representationalism—is to cede the very ground of normativity itself.

2.1.3. From Representation to Systematicity

When we reviewed the objects of inquiry of the representational forms of knowledge that Hegel lists in the opening paragraph of the *Encyclopedia*, we left one aside—*Recht*—right, the traditional subject matter, Hegel tells us, of jurisprudence, in German, *Rechtswissenschaft*, the science of right. We can already see that the line of argument that Hegel has mounted against representational forms of knowledge, in general, and the representational forms of traditional normative justification, in particular, requires a profound rethinking of this object and of the methodology that seeks to found it. The pivotal question, then, for Hegel, is what would constitute a non-representational form of *Recht* and, correlatively, what would be a genuine science of right? We have seen that the central problem of representational forms of knowledge in general is that they presuppose both their object and their methodology. We have also seen that, although he rejects their basic justificatory strategies, Hegel affirms the fundamental goals of rationalism and empiricism, namely that the concept of right must be defined and that it must be conceived concretely. What would it mean, then, to begin in political philosophy without taking the nature or the existence of what one was investigating, namely *Recht*, for granted and without a justificatory procedure already in place by which to consider the matter? What would it mean to understand right in a conceptually precise, yet determinate fashion?

Hegel has already shown that to justify the authoritativeness of right requires a type of argumentation that is not beholden to representation, one that, out of fidelity to the principle of critique itself, abjures all presuppositions. Such a science would have to be, in a word, systematic. Of course, with this, we have in hand what amounts to the negative criterion for Hegel's project, and we can now clearly see the methodological imperative that motivated this enterprise, but the question still remains: what would a genuine system of right such as this look like? What would be its distinctive form of normative argumentation?

2.2. Systematic Normative Justification

As we noted at the beginning of this chapter, it is precisely on this issue that Hegel leaves us with a dilemma: he repeatedly proclaims that what is ultimately distinctive about his science of right is its systematic method, and that it ought to be judged by this standard alone, yet he also acknowledges that, throughout the *Elements of the Philosophy of Right*, he presupposes a familiarity with this kind of scientific procedure and even admits to omitting the precise derivation of each and every detail involved in this project. The dilemma is certainly ironic since, as we have seen, the science of right clearly presupposes a method that is itself committed to taking nothing for granted. Yet, despite this, Hegel does offer students of the *Elements of the Philosophy of Right* several methodological statements that, although brief, we can take, together with his rejection of representationalism, as guiding clues to develop an account of systematic normative justification. In this section, then, I use these passages to work out a basic sketch of Hegel's general philosophical methodology and I then show how this method serves him as a distinctly non-representationalist form of normative justification.

2.2.1. Systematicity and Justification

Hegel's remarks regarding philosophical method define systematic justification in terms of three fundamental and interrelated principles—(1) immanent development, (2) necessary entailment, and (3) retrogressive grounding—and one fundamental precondition: the justification of the systematic standpoint itself. Let us consider each of these elements in turn.

The cornerstone of the systematic form of justification is its commitment to presuppositionlessness. As we have seen, in distinction from representationalism, this means that systematic justification cannot presuppose its object, its content, nor can it presuppose its method, its form. But if neither the subject matter of the science, nor its mode of demonstration can be taken as given, then the justification of each can only be established together. Object and method, content and form, must be inseparably one. The content cannot be taken over and simply unpacked, nor can the method be presupposed and applied to whatever the subject of investigation may be. The epistemic credentials of both must be established together. In philosophical science, Hegel says in the famous preface to the *Elements of the Philosophy of Right*, "the content is essentially bound up with the *form*" (GW 14,1, 6/Werke 7, 13/Nisbet, 10).

Systematic justification's commitment to set aside all assumptions thus entails methodological immanence. Its basic task is to suspend all that might serve as preconceptions about both the nature of the object it seeks to examine and the procedures to be employed in justifying it and, instead, faithfully to observe the way in which the matter at issue develops wholly of itself and thus how it itself demands to be thought. Systematic justification, as a general philosophical enterprise, therefore seeks to do nothing other than attend to the immanent conceptual unfolding of its object for it is only in abiding by this stipulation that dogmatism and skepticism can be avoided— because nothing is taken for granted, nothing is open to the skeptic's trilemma—and, concordantly, form and content can truly be one. As Hegel puts it in the *Elements of the Philosophy of Right*, a science of right must "observe (*zuzusehen*) the matter at issue's own immanent development" (GPR §2) and this is the "method whereby the concept, in science, develops itself out of itself and is merely an *immanent* progression and production of its own determinations" (GPR §31).

But if, as Hegel argues, the task of philosophical science is to grasp the immanent development of its subject matter, then this development must be intrinsic to the matter itself. It cannot be produced by extrinsic associations. That is to say, for the development of an object to be genuinely immanent, it must be the whole and complete unfolding of the nature of the matter itself; it must be the articulation of its essence. The immanent development of an object is thus the unfolding of the set of properties that make an object what it is; the features that demarcate it from all other things, its "determinations (*Bestimmungen*)". But since these determinations are the essential predicates of the object, their unfolding must correspond to their inherent relationality. Given that these determinations mutually constitute the object, their relations to one another must be that of necessity. That is, since these determinations are mutually and exhaustively implicative, each property must, of necessity, entail the other. The modality of the development thus follows from its immanence. The conceptual elaboration of a matter is the development of one concept into another where the former necessarily entails the latter. As Hegel puts it, the principal concern of philosophical knowledge is "the *necessity* of the concept" (GPR §2A).

The commitment to immanent development leads to that of necessary entailment and this to what is arguably the most innovative and distinctive feature of Hegel's theory of systematic justification: retrogressive grounding. The idea follows out the central implication of presuppositionlessness. Hegel recognizes that to suspend all presuppositions disallows taking the veracity of the object from which one starts for granted, and since observing the immanent unfolding of the object is setting out the complex of properties that makes the object what it is, the line of argumentation involved in this kind of justificatory enterprise cannot follow that of traditional linear derivation. Specifically, the beginning cannot serve, as in conventional forms of justification, as a foundational or non-inferential axiom from which further premises or conclusions are to be deduced. Systematic justification, for Hegel, is thus not a conventional foundationalist form of argumentation. But its rejection of classical foundations and the epistemology of intuition does not lead Hegel to affirm that justification is a function solely of the relationships that are able to be established between various claims or concepts, the central tenet of coherentism. Instead, Hegel's method cuts a clear path between these conventional alternatives.

As we have seen, the hallmark of systematic justification is that it sets forth the immanent and necessary unfolding of its object. What this kind of analysis shows is that the object with which the inquiry begins is comprised of a set of necessary relations between concepts. As mutually necessary and exhaustively implicative, these relations constitute the object in question as what it is. These relations, then, are the ground of the object that they together comprise. Accordingly, the linear progression from the object to the conceptual relations that constitute it is a retrogression into its ground, the origin, and truth upon which the object with which we begin depends and from which it arises. In systematic justification, then, to move forward is, in a sense, to move back and to move back is to secure the non-arbitrary status and veracity of what precedes. Hegel thus refers to the object of science as the "result (*Resultat*)" of that which precedes it: "In philosophical cognition…the chief concern is the *necessity* of a concept, and the path by which it has become, as result, [is] its proof and deduction" (GPR §2A). The proof structure of speculative demonstration therefore moves from what is in need of justification back into the set of conceptual relations that form the foundation from which its object originates and upon which it continually depends.

But an important problem obviously remains here. As it stands, the construction of a system, for Hegel, seems to be little more than the fashioning of a "seamless web" of interdependence. But this model does not, of itself at least, ensure that its members and their interrelations are in any way truth preserving. That is to say, it looks as though Hegel has advanced a holistic account of knowledge that is open to the classical objection that coherence is not itself a sufficient indicator of truth. A body of knowledge that holds together does not, by virtue of that fact alone, entail that it properly articulates the joints and junctures of reality.

Hegel recognized this crucial problem and, throughout his career, maintained that the standpoint from which the system of reason is to be constructed, the standpoint of systematic knowledge, itself stands in need of justification. He devised several distinct epistemic strategies by which to address this issue, the specifics of which cannot be examined here,[13] but they all had the same mission: to establish the oneness of thought and being so that the concepts and relations out of which the system is to be fashioned already had their ontological credentials secured, that, as he put it, the "determinations of thinking" have the "value and significance of being in and for themselves the ground of everything" (Enz. [1817] §17).

Systematic justification thus stands on the terrain cleared and vindicated by this preparatory investigation and, by so doing, its observing of the immanent and necessary unfolding of a subject matter back into its ground is, at its core, a form of what can

---

[13] In the period under investigation here, Hegel marked out two distinct approaches to the issue of establishing the veracity of the systematic standpoint: (1) the phenomenological investigation of the forms of consciousness to show that absolute knowing is the condition for the possibility of all more elementary kinds of knowledge, the project he had undertaken in the *Phenomenology of Spirit* (1807); and (2) the decision simply to think purely, that is, to abstract from anything and everything and for thought thereby to grasp itself in its own simplicity (cf. Enz. [1817] §36A).

The first route is obviously well known, though its exact significance is disputed. The second is less so, so a word about it is in order: to think purely, to think abstractly, has a twofold sense.

Firstly, it is a disengaging of thought from its entanglement with all that it takes for granted; in this sense, it is a suspension of thought's commitments, whether tacit or explicit, to any and all preconceptions about itself and the world it inhabits.

Secondly, though it is a withdrawal, it is not an escape into nothing, it not only "abstracts from everything", but rather, having done this, it "grasps its pure abstraction", namely itself, the activity of thinking, in its "simplicity". Now, given that such thought has set aside the core assumptions of representation, and the centerpiece of these is the presupposition that the knowing subject stands over against the object it seeks to know, Hegel claims that to think purely is not, strictly speaking, a form of knowledge at all. In grasping itself, it does not know itself, rather it withdraws into itself and exists as nothing other than the mere activity of withdrawal. It is not known, nor conceived of, it simply and immediately is.

Hegel therefore concludes that to think purely and abstractly is to think pure being, being in general. A truly presuppositionless system must begin then with the "objective thought" of being, free from any specificity or concreteness of any kind; in other words, a genuine system must begin with the sheer indeterminacy of being.

be called ontological justification, an establishing of the fundamental orders and constitutive processes of being. Hegel is thus able to capture the core of foundationalism's concern with grasping the nature and truth of reality itself and coherentism's insistence on constitutive relational dependence in a way that avoids the dogmatism of the former and the relativism of the latter.

Taken together, then, the principles of systematic justification and the vindication of the systematic standpoint mean that the warrant of a concept, claim, or belief to be what it purports to be is vindicated if and only if it is shown to be a moment that is either itself the result of a conceptual unfolding of some object or is a moment in a differential relation included in such a progression. The construction of this kind of system is therefore, at the same time, the justification of its constitutive parts.

2.2.2. Systematic Method

To complete our sketch of Hegel's model of systematic justification, we need briefly to turn from its metaphilosophical underpinnings to the actual system itself. We do so not in order to set out its shape and structure, but solely to note the special role that its first part, the *Science of Logic*, plays in the system as a whole. As we have seen, in order for systematic justification to avoid the threats of dogmatism and skepticism inherent in representational forms of knowledge, it is entitled to assume neither its content, nor any form of argumentation. This means that Hegel's appeals to the necessity of assessing his work in terms of its speculative methodology must refer to the distinctive method that the system itself establishes from within itself. This is one of the fundamental tasks of the first part of the system, the *Science of Logic*.

Hegel there sets forth, following the principles of immanence, necessity, and retrogressive grounding, a fundamental ontology, a genuinely critical metaphysics, that has, as its culmination, an account of the basic structure of systematic method. The placement of the discussion is itself telling. Method is the culmination of the project of the *Science of Logic*. Its epistemic standing is thus a matter of the way in which it follows from the ontological analyses that precede it. Justification stands or falls not just on its systematic form, but with its metaphysical content.

The line of argument that Hegel develops in the *Logic* begins with the emptiness of the concept of pure being, for only this is left when all presuppositions have been laid aside. Hegel shows that, if the immanent developmental structure of being is followed, it proves to be nothing other than what he calls "actuality (*Wirklichkeit*)," the set of all entities that are constituted in and their complete necessary and reciprocal causal interaction with one another. Crucially, he then argues that this thoroughgoing relationality is itself produced by an immanent generative process. This process is the movement of self-differentiation. All objects come to be what they are through self-negation, that is to say, all entities attain their own self-identity by othering themselves, and, in and through this negation, come finally to be themselves. Hegel calls this movement the concept (*Begriff*), well aware that he is diverging from its traditional usage to denote that which is common to several objects. When this logical process is fully and exhaustively differentiated, that is, when it is no longer just a process, but when its complete conceptual structure has been explicated, and thus fully actualized, it is, he says, the idea (*Idee*), again moving away from its received definition as an unchanging, universal exemplar. Hegel's central claim in the *Logic*, and the core of his system as a whole, is thus that the actualized movement of self-differentiation, the idea, is the absolute ground and truth of being, the foundation of all objects and relations.

Now, having demonstrated this thesis about the fundamental nature of reality, Hegel turns, in the final chapter of the work, to the issue of method (cf. Enz. [1817] §§183–91, esp. 185–90). There he argues that since the pattern that the constitutive process exhibits—its movement from immediate identity to immanent differentiation and, from this, this negation necessarily negating itself, to its deeper, more concrete fulfillment—shows itself to be the fundamental ontological structure of being, this structure is not only the governing form in and through which all things come to be what they are, but it must at the same time be the method, the way of knowing, that is true to the process of determination inherent within being itself. Hegel thus concludes that the proper method of philosophical argumentation—if it is not to be, as it is in representational forms of knowledge, a ready-made procedure applied to each and every object from without—must be this form of immanent development. To be, then, is to be a moment in the process of immanent differentiation; it is to be part of the process of becoming-other whereby all things come to be determinate. Showing something to be such a moment is thus to give it its proper justification, the demonstration of its true standing, of its standing in the movement of actualization that is the concept. This process, of course, is the infamous "higher dialectic of the concept," which consists, Hegel tells us, "in producing and seizing the determination not merely as an opposite and restriction, but as the *positive* content and result that it [the dialectic of the concept] contains as that whereby it is alone a *development* and immanent progression" (GPR §31A).

Obviously much more would need to be said in order to offer a full interpretation and defense of Hegel's account of method here, but this much suffices to show that the distinctive concern of the *Science of Logic* is not just ontological, but, ultimately, epistemological, for what the first part of the system establishes is that the true way of knowing, the way of knowing things in their truth, is nothing other than the process of development that is proper to being itself and this is to grasp the rationality, the dialectic of the concept, within all that is. It follows that the other parts of the system, the Philosophies of Nature and of Spirit, the latter of which the *Philosophy of Right* is a part, are properly subordinate to the *Science of Logic* since it is only insofar as they discern the movement of the concept, the movement set out and established by the *Logic*, as the process constitutive of their own distinct domains that their claims and concepts are able to stand vindicated.[14] The fundamental task of philosophical knowledge, for

---

[14] My claim here is simply that insofar as the *Logic* sets forth and establishes the method by which the rest of the system argues, its account plays a controlling role in all the subsequent analyses. In support of

Hegel, is thus to grasp the movement of the dialectic as the immanent process whereby any and all objects come to be determinate, and that is, as Hegel puts it, "to bring to consciousness the matter's own work of reason" (GPR §31A).

2.2.3. Systematicity and Normativity

With this account of systematic justification in hand, we can now come to the second of our original questions: how is the systematic method of argumentation able to serve as a form of normative justification?

As we have seen, the hallmark of systematic justification is its rejection of representationalism and the commitment to the principles of immanence, necessity, and retrogressive grounding that this entails. Furthermore, we saw Hegel argue that the pattern that the process of immanent development exhibits is that of the self-differentiating movement of the concept as it actualizes itself into the idea. Systematic justification, then, is attending to the immanent and necessary unfolding of an object back into its ground where this development proves to be fundamentally dialectical. The question now before us is thus how this unique method is able to vindicate the authoritativeness of a claim with respect to action or a form of life. That is to say, how can the dialectic of the concept establish normative warrant?

The core of Hegel's answer to this question is the necessary relationship that he contends exists between the concepts of freedom and right. Now we cannot, of course, treat both of these concepts in the detail that they deserve here, but we do need to note that Hegel's examination of the concept of right takes the concept of freedom as its starting point because it is seeking to set forth a justification of right itself, and insofar as right is claimed to be authoritative with respect to the conduct and character of free agents, then the dictates of the systematic method require that right be shown to follow—immanently, of necessity, and as the ground of—the concept of freedom. The basic shape of Hegel's broader argument regarding this relationship becomes clear by examining the first two paragraphs of the *Philosophy of Right*. To do so, we begin by returning, once again, to the problem of representation.

this approach, I appeal to Hegel's articulation of the relationship between Logic, Nature, and Spirit at Enz. [1817] §477 where Logic, in the properly philosophical way of construing the syllogistic structure of the system, is said to play the role of mediating middle term between the extremes of Spirit and Nature.

On the vexed problem of the exact relationship between the *Logic* and the *Philosophy of Right*, see Herbert Schnädelbach, "Zum Verhältnis von Logik und Gesellschaftstheorie bei Hegel," in *Aktualität und Folgen der Philosophie Hegels*, ed. Oskar Negt (Frankfurt am Main: Suhrkamp, 1970): 58–80; Kenley Royce Dove, "Logik und Recht bei Hegel," *Neue Hefte für Philosophie* 17 (1979): 89–108; Manfred Hanisch, *Dialektische Logik und politisches Argument: Untersuchungen zu den methodischen Grundlagen der Hegelschen Staatsphilosophie* (Königstein: Forum Academicum, 1981); Heinz Kimmerle, "'Wissenschaft der Logik' als Grundlegung seines Systems der Philosophie: Über das Verhältnis von 'Logik' und 'Realphilosophie,'" in *Die Logik des Wissens und das Problem der Erziehung*, ed. Wilhelm Raimund Beyer (Hamburg: Felix Meiner, 1982): 52–60; Henning Ottmann, "Hegelsche Logik und Rechtsphilosophie: Unzulängliche Bemerkungen zu einem ungelösten Problem," *Hegels Philosophie des Rechts: Die Theorie der Rechtsformen*, ed. Dieter Henrich and Rolf-Peter Horstmann (Stuttgart: Klett-Cotta, 1982): 382–91; and Denis L. Rosenfield, *Politique et liberté: Une étude sur la structure logique de la Philosophie du droit de Hegel* (Paris: Aubier, 1984).

Representational forms of knowledge, we recall, take the object of their inquiry—an image borne originally from intuition, but generalized by the power of representation—for granted. To treat right as a representational object would be to take it either as the natural law of rationalism or the feeling, sentiment, or tradition of empiricism. Down both of these paths, as we have seen, lie dogmatism and the skeptic's trilemma. A truly critical account of right must be presuppositionless. It must set aside the conceptions offered by intellectual and sensible intuition and, instead, begin with nothing other than the pure concept of right itself. But what exactly is this?

Hegel begins the *Philosophy of Right* with a decisive, though stark, statement that responds to this fundamental question:

> The philosophical science of right has the idea (*Idee*) of right, the concept of right and its actualization (*Verwirklichung*), for its object. (GPR §1)

Now if we were to read this proposition by employing the standard definitions of its principal terms, we would conclude that the kind of philosophical inquiry being proposed here is concerned with the ultimate exemplar of right, that which is common to all individual rightful acts, dispositions, and states of affairs, and with the instantiations of this generality in particular cases. Such an interpretation would construe Hegel's project as a form of classical natural law, presupposing right as a transcendent moral order. But this, of course, is not what the idea of right is. But neither is it merely an empirical representation, an expression of subjective desire. Both of these readings would fall prey to representationalism. Hegel is instead employing the central terms here in the technical sense that we saw him develop in the *Science of Logic*, and that means that what is properly at stake in the science of right, for him, is something quite different than either of these ready-made conceptions.

Idea, for Hegel, we recall, denotes the fully differentiated concrete realization of the concept. Accordingly, the idea of right refers to the culmination of a process whereby the complete relational actuality of right—a world of authoritative social institutions and practices—is set forth. The proper object of the science of right is thus not a pregiven transcendent moral order, nor ready made feeling, sentiment, or tradition, but a set of interrelated normative social and political structures. The substance of the work to follow, then, that is the substance of the *Philosophy of Right* itself, is to unfold the immanent and necessary moments of this object. The "concept of right and its actualization" thus designates the generative movement of self-differentiation, the "higher dialectic," whereby the interdependent domain of right is constituted and its standing as ground of all that precedes it is vindicated. The object of the science of right, then, is not simply the result of this process, the constituted domain of normativity, but the conceptual progression of which this normative whole proves to be the result. In other words, the object of the science of right is the unfolding of the concept of right from its abstract immediacy through its immanent self-negation whereby it comes into its own as a concrete whole.

Hegel notes the special sense in which the notions of concept and idea are being employed here in the Remark to this opening paragraph:

Philosophy has to do with ideas and therefore not with what are commonly called *mere concepts*. On the contrary, it exposes the latter as one-sided and untruthful, and that it is the concept alone (not what is so often called by that name, but which is merely an abstract determination of the understanding) that has actuality, and in such a way that it gives actuality to itself.   (GPR §1A)

The task of the science of right is thus rigorously to observe the immanent development of the pure concept of right into its interdependent whole, which is to say, its complete actualization, the concept becoming actualized as idea, the way that "it gives actuality to itself." But how does this in any way establish the authoritativeness of right itself?

Hegel's answer to this question comes in the second paragraph of the work. "The science of right," he reminds us, "is a *part of philosophy*" (GPR §2). From this simple proposition, he draws two implications that stand at the very core of the project of the *Philosophy of Right*. The *first*, as we have already noted, is that for the science of right to be a genuinely philosophical, as opposed to a representational, form of inquiry, it must commit itself, as he puts it here, "to observe the matter at issue's own immanent development" (GPR §2). The method of a philosophical science of right must be immanent, necessary, and retrogressive; in a word, systematic.

The *second* implication is the more relevant for our present purposes:

As a part, it [the science of right] has a determinate *starting point*, which is the *result* and truth of what *preceded* it, and what preceded it constitutes the so-called *proof* of that result. Hence, the concept of right, so far as its *becoming* is concerned, falls outside the science of right; its deduction is presupposed here and is to be taken as *given*.   (GPR §2)

Like the first paragraph, the passage initially appears deeply puzzling, if not simply misleading. It seems to suggest that the science of right presupposes its object, the concept of right. We, of course, know that this can't be the case, but what exactly does it mean to say that the "proof [*Beweis*]" of the core concept of the science "falls outside" the science itself? How can a science where the justification of right is not itself a part of the science be a form of systematic normative justification?

The key here is the term "part [*Teil*]." Hegel's claim is that the science of right is a distinctly philosophical endeavor and, as such, it must abide by the systematic principles of immanence, necessity, and retrogressive grounding. But, as a part, it is not itself the whole of philosophical science. It is a distinct science within a broader system. This means that the justification of the object whose immanent development the philosophical science of right seeks to observe must necessarily precede this specific science. The "becoming [*Werden*]" of the concept of right—by which Hegel means its genesis as a moment within the immanent and necessary unfolding of a more basic concept— "falls outside" the science of right. But since this development of right from a more basic concept is, in systematic justification, as we have seen, the proof of its ontological and epistemological standing, then the justification of right itself is, strictly speaking, not what is at issue in the science of right proper. How then are we to understand the science of right in relation to the justification of its object?

Hegel's crucial thesis, the one upon which the entire normative character of the argument of the *Philosophy of Right* hinges, is that the justification of the concept of right consists in its being shown to be the immanent and necessary ground—the result or truth, as Hegel will say—of the more basic, and thus less determinate, concept of freedom. That is to say, unfolding the essential determinations of freedom shows that it is what it is only by virtue of the concept of right. Right, then, is the condition of the possibility of freedom. The content of these claims, of course, needs to be unpacked, but the issue at present is the fundamental structure of this kind of argumentation: how is it able to establish the authoritativeness of right itself and how can this authoritativeness, in turn, be said to flow to the more concrete determinations of right, its actualization?

The systematic method proves decisive precisely here for it is only by following its strictures that the normative standing of right and its concrete determinations can be justified in a way that avoids the dangers of skepticism. The nerve of Hegel's systematic justification of the concept of right is that it is the result of the immanent and necessary unfolding of the essential determinations of freedom and thus is its ground. As such, right is not only essential to being free, it has binding authority over all forms of free acting. Under representational forms of knowledge, it is simply taken for granted that right—whether it is conceived as a transcendent moral order, as in rationalist Enlightened Absolutism, or as the weight of tradition and desire, as in empiricist Conservatism and Romanticism—possesses legitimate authority over conduct and character. Such approaches thereby render the relationship that stands at the very core of the problem of normativity vulnerable to arbitrariness, regressivity, or vicious circularity. Systematic justification, to the contrary, is able to show that right is not only one of the essential determinations discovered in the unfolding of freedom, it is the concrete existence, the necessary embodiment, through which human striving is able to be genuinely free. But if being free is made possible by right itself, then this concept and its further, more concrete, determinations possess legitimate binding authority with respect to free actions and forms of life because they have proved to be the retrogressive ground of freedom itself. The normativity that is right thus flows from its being the necessary enabling condition of freedom: "the system of right is the realm of actualized freedom" (GPR §4).

Given this interpretation of Hegel's project, the philosophical science of right is thus indeed defined by its distinctive systematic methodology, its "philosophical manner of progressing from one matter to another and of conducting a scientific proof, the speculative way of knowing in general" (GW 14,1, 5/Werke 7, 12/Nisbet, 10). And we have seen that this is nothing less than its commitment, negatively, to presuppositionlessness, the rejection of representationalism, and positively, to immanence, necessity, and retrogressive grounding, to the "higher dialectic of the concept." The critique of representationalism allowed Hegel to move beyond the confines of the conceptual space of late eighteenth- and early nineteenth-century German political thought and its traditional forms of justification, and to outflank the Agrippan challenge that lurked behind these boundaries. But it was by bringing the demands of immanence, necessity, and retrogressive grounding to bear on the concept of freedom that he was able to open a decisively new pathway for thinking and justifying normativity itself. The object of the science of right is the "concept of right and its actualization," the idea of right, and this is nothing other than the immanent and necessary unfolding of right as the enabling institutional embodiment of freedom. The normative standing of a concept, principle, institution, or practice thus derives, on Hegel's account, from its being shown to be a necessary determination, and this means a necessary actualization, of freedom. In this way, one can claim that the fundamental thesis of Hegel's philosophical science of right is that systematicity is the only form of argumentation that is truly capable of fulfilling the task of normative justification. This method, in turn, places the essential relationship between freedom and right at the very heart of political philosophy in a truly unique fashion, where the nature of the latter flows directly from the nature of the former.

3

In What Sense is Hegel's *Philosophy of Right* "Based" on His *Science of Logic?*

Remarks on the Logic of Justice

Robert B. Pippin

3.1.

Hegel famously says in the "Preface" to *The Philosophy of Right* that that outline or *Grundriss* presupposes "the speculative mode of cognition." This is to be contrasted with what he calls "the old logic" and "the knowledge of the understanding" (*Verstandeserkenntnis*), a term he also uses to characterize all of metaphysics prior to his own.[1] He makes explicit that he is referring to his book, *The Science of Logic.*[2] In fact, Hegel repeatedly says in many different contexts that the core of his entire philosophy, what everything else depends on, is to be found in that two-volume, three-part book that he wrote while teaching Gymnasium students in Nürnberg between 1812 and 1816. The first volume is called an "Objective Logic" and it contains a "logic of being," and a "logic of essence." The third part, the second volume, is called the "Subjective Logic" and it consists of a "logic of the concept."

Now *The Philosophy of Right* has three striking characteristics that distinguish it from almost all prior work in political philosophy. In the first place, it does not appear to be a consideration of the simply best possible regime, but rather an unusual consideration of specific modern institutions like private property, moral individualism, the bourgeois or romantic family, a market economy and a representative state.

---

[1] G.W.F. Hegel, *Elements of the Philosophy of Right*, ed. A. Wood, trans. H.B. Nisbet (Cambridge: Cambridge University Press, 1991), hereafter cited in the text as PR.

[2] G.W.F. Hegel, *The Science of Logic*, trans. George Di Giovanni (Cambridge: Cambridge University Press, 2010); *Wissenschaft der Logik. Erster Band. Die objective Logik*, in Gesammelte Werke, ed. F. Hogemann and W. Jaeschke, Bd. 21 (Hamburg: Felix Meiner, 1984). (Hereafter SL. The translator has listed the German pages cited in the margins of his translation, so reference may now be made to the German pagination alone, in the manner of references to the Akadamie Ausgabe of Kant, and its A/B German page numbers.)

Secondly, the form of analysis itself is unusual. It involves considering something like the self-understanding of participants in each of these institutions (what Hegel will call the concept at issue in each), and a demonstration of sorts that there are insufficiencies or an incompleteness in such a self-understanding. (This is sometimes put by saying that the concept "does not agree with itself.") The realization of such a self-understanding in the actual institutional life at issue is shown to be incoherent or more generally irrational without appeal to a norm that is unavailable within the self-understanding of such a position. When the position is modified to reflect and correct such a deficiency, we ultimately end up with a different (but related) *kind* of self-understanding altogether.

This can sound like the demonstration typical of Hegel's Jena *Phenomenology of Spirit* of 1807, and there are similarities. But the core of the case Hegel wants to make does not concern an appeal to the "experience" of such a participant, but concerns the basic concept or norm at issue, and an analysis of the norm when measured against its own claims for adequacy and authority. This could be called an analysis of the "logic" of the concept, its role and the limitations of that role, in possible justifications among persons whose actions affect what others would otherwise be able to do (the realm of "objective spirit"). That kind of analysis of that sort of logic is what he says requires the "speculative mode of cognition."

Third, while Hegel is clearly a rationalist in political philosophy, this reliance on the logic of the concept in defending the rightfulness of the modern *Rechtsstaat* as he sees it clearly does not rely on what rational individuals would will or contract. In that sense the central problem for him is not the legitimacy of the state's monopoly on coercive violence, and so he stands outside the dominant tradition in liberal political philosophy. The claims of abstract right, the claims of moral duty, and the social order he calls *Sittlichkeit* or ethical life are all as they ought be, in themselves and in relation to each other, because the domain of right can be shown to have a rational structure and that structure is the logical articulation of the concept of right or justice.

My goal in the following is to show that we understand better why *The Philosophy of Right* has these unusual characteristics if we understand better what Hegel means by directing us to the speculative mode of cognition and so the *Science of Logic*. There is so little consensus among Hegel scholars about the *Logic*, even about what it is essentially about, that such a goal can only be in this context a sketch or a suggestion, well short of a full treatment of the many alternative readings.[3]

3.2.

So what is the *Logic*? It is surely some sort of study of concepts, but what sort? Clearly an a priori understanding of relations among basic concepts, not empirical concepts,

---

[3] The following summary derives in part from more elaborate presentations of the issue in two other papers. "The Significance of Self-Consciousness in Idealist Theories of Logic," in *The Proceedings of the Aristotelian Society*, vol. CXIV, part 2, 2014: 145–66; and "Logic and Metaphysics: Hegel's Realm of Shadows," in *A Handbook to Hegel's Science of Logic*, ed. Dean Moyar (Oxford: Oxford University Press, forthcoming).

but what sort of relations? Hegel's comments about these issues are of some initial help, although they are extraordinarily ambitious.

First, he says this, something he repeats in a number of ways:

> Thus *logic* coincides with *metaphysics*, with the science of <u>things</u> grasped in <u>thoughts</u>, which used to be taken to express the <u>essentialities of the things</u>. (T) [Die *Logik* fällt daher mit der *Metaphysik* zusammen, der Wissenschaft der *Dinge* in *Gedanken* gefaßt, welche dafür galten, die *Wesenheiten der Dinge* auszudrücken]. (All of these emphases are Hegel's)[4] (EL §24)

But what does Hegel mean by "metaphysics," both the sort that used to hold ("*galten*") and what is possible now? Adrian Moore, in a comprehensive survey of the history of metaphysics, has recently suggested that, given the variety of metaphysical projects, we define the subject matter as capaciously as possible, and he suggests, as a working definition of metaphysics: "the most general attempt to make sense of things."[5] He rightly notes that this is the way Hegel also describes his enterprise. For example: "metaphysics is nothing but the range of universal thought-determinations, and as it were, the net [*das diamantene Netz*] into which we bring everything to make it intelligible [*verständlich*]."[6]

Moore appropriately notes that the notion of making sense can range widely (as it does in Hegel, especially given the three different "logics" and their different assumptions) over "the meaning of something, the purpose of something, or the explanation for something,"[7] or in Hegel's most ambitious version, it can include an account of, a way of making sense of, the determinate identifiability of anything as just what it is and not anything else. In other words, to be is to be a determinate something. But how do we make sense of the stability and identifiability of such determinateness? Understood in this way, it is clear that metaphysics, while it has adequacy or satisfaction conditions, does not have the kind of truth-conditions that a matter of fact assertion has. Determining *when sense has truly been made* is not of the same order of tasks as "what caused the fire to start" or "why does water freeze."[8] For example, making sense of why there is a practice like art making, what it means that there is, what sense could

---

[4] G.W.F. Hegel, *The Encyclopedia Logic*, trans. T.F. Geraets, W.A. Suchting, and H.S. Harris (Indianapolis: Hackett Publishing, 1991) (hereafter EL); *Enzyklopädie der philosophischen Wissenschaften, Erster Teil, Die Wissenchaft der Logik*, in *Werke*, Bd. 8, ed. E. Moldenhauer and K. Michel (Frankfurt: Suhrkamp, 1970–1). Reference by paragraph numbers. "T" indicates an alteration in the translation.

[5] A.N. Moore, *The Evolution of Modern Metaphysics: Making Sense of Things* (Cambridge: Cambridge University Press, 2012), 6.

[6] *Hegel's Philosophy of Nature*, vol. I, ed. and trans. M.J. Petry (New York: Humanities Press, 1970), §246A.

[7] Moore, *The Evolution of Modern Metaphysics*, 5.

[8] In Kant's terms, both general logic and transcendental logic, if they can be clearly distinguished, would be canons, not organons; they both specify necessary conditions of possible truth, not sufficient conditions. In Hegel's terms, the strict differentiation of the two should be called into question. In Hegel's case, even a philosophy of nature and a philosophy of spirit specify such necessary conditions with respect to two special domains, the concept "outside itself" (nature) and "returned to itself" (spirit). These are substantive claims, not formal, but they are not first-order claims about God or nature or spirit. This is the characterization most objected to by, let us say, traditional Hegelians and which I will try to defend throughout. See Michael Wolff, "Der Begriff des Widerspruchs in der 'Kritik der reinen Vernunft," in Burkhart Tuschling, *Probleme der Kritik der reinen Vernunft* (Berlin: de Gruyter 1984), 188ff. on this point.

there be in it, involves a question that immediately becomes impoverished if we think the question can only mean "what causes human beings to take a distinct pleasure in artifacts?" The question rather invites a speculation on something like a "satisfying" account, rather than a factually true one.[9]

For our purposes, what is interesting is that Moore goes on to distinguish between making sense of things (rendering them intelligible, something we have to work at in any of the modalities described) from *making sense of sense*, which he ascribes to logic and the philosophy of logic. And this fits Hegel's "logic" to some degree on this reading. He is also making sense of how we make sense of things. The *Logic's* subject matter, what it is trying to make sense of, are the modalities of sense-makings. But, given that he does not think of such modalities of sense-making as a species-specific "subjective" capacity, but as constitutive of any possible sense, he would not say that this can be distinguished from "making sense of things." Logic emerged in Kant as something much more than the study of valid forms of inference, but much less than an account of the laws that thinking does or ought to obey (as in the Port Royale Logic), or as categorizing a basic ontological structure (as in Wolffian accounts of logic). For Kant, logic states the conditions of any possible sense, the distinctions and relations without which sense would not be possible, and so covers more than truth-functional assertions, but also imperatives and aesthetic judgments. For Hegel this ambition already represents a task of great philosophical substance, but he insists that Kant dealt inadequately with the questions it raises: how we determine what those conditions are and whether they can be rightly confined to what the avoidance of logical contradiction will allow, whether the "emptiness" that Kant ascribes to these forms can be maintained. Stated in Kant's terms, Hegel's claim is that general logic, properly understood, is already transcendental logic, properly understood, and transcendental logic, properly understood, is already metaphysics. (And finally, obviously, not every attempt to make sense of something is metaphysics. We must be talking about ways of making sense at the highest level of generality, without which nothing else would make sense: the sense of identity through change, individuality within common class membership, the relation of discrete moments to their continuum, and so forth.)

That is, general logic as Kant formulated it is for Hegel a logic of *general* intelligibility, not just of truth bearers; so failing to observe the "norms of thinking" is not mistakenly thinking, making an error in thinking; it is not thinking at all, not making any sense. The prospect of objects "outside" something like the limits of the thinkable is a non-thought, a *sinnlose Gedanke*.[10] But just because it is, the strict distinction between

---

[9] Hegel's own speculations on the question occur in the section on Ground in the Logic of Essence. In *The Encyclopedia Logic* discussion of that topic he uses as an example a theft of property, and raises the question of what are the grounds for calling it theft, rather than a justifiable expropriation of ill-used property, or the satisfaction of the thief's wants, and then moves on to a consideration of what counts as a "sufficient" ground (EL §121Z).

[10] See here Clinton Tolley, "Kant on the Nature of Logical Laws," *Philosophical Topics*, vol. 34, no. 1–2, 2006: 371–407. For more on the same point, see Wolff, "Der Begriff des Widerspruchs", 186. And on the

a priori, content-free general logic, and an a priori transcendental logic, the forms of possible thoughts about objects, can hardly be as hard and fast as Kant wants to make it out to be. Most controversially, the distinction depends on a quite contestable strict separation between the spontaneity of thought (as providing formal unity) and the deliverances of sensibility in experience (as the sole "provider of content").[11] If that is not sustainable, and there is reason to think even Kant did not hold it to be a matter of strict separability, then neither can the distinction between forms of thought and forms of the thought of objects be a matter of strict separability.[12] To consider beings in their intelligibility (what Hegel called "the science of things in thought") is not to consider them in terms of some species-specific subjective capacity, any more than considering truth-functional relations between sentences in a logic is a consideration of how we happen to go on with sentences. To be *is* to be intelligible; the founding principle of Greek metaphysics and philosophy itself. (Entertaining the idea of an unintelligible being is not thinking of something strange and limiting; it is not thinking at all.)

Now, this all places enormous pressure on what amounts to a kind of operator in Hegel's *Logic* on which all the crucial transitions depend; something like: "would not be fully intelligible, would not be coherently thinkable without..." What follows the "without" is some more comprehensive concept, a different distinction, and so forth. Excluding logical contradictions would be one obvious instantiation of the operator. But—and here everything in the possibility of Hegel's logical enterprise depends on this point—*the range of the logically possible is obviously far more extensive than the range of what Kant called the "really possible."* The latter is what we need if we are to have a logic of the real. And Hegel cannot avail himself of Kant's non-conceptual forms of intuition to establish a priori the sensible conditions that set the boundaries of "the really possible." However, to pick a strange ally at this point, Strawson demonstrated, in *The Bounds of Sense*, that the really possible *can* be determined without what he considered Kant's subjective idealism (the subjective forms of intuition), and this— revealingly for our purposes—by a reflection on whether a candidate notion of experience *could be said to make sense.* Moreover, the key issue in Hegel's account is not logical contradiction and logical possibility, but the possibility of the intelligible determinacy of non-empirical conceptual content. He would also point out that it is already the case in Kant that he seems to assume that he is showing how the minimal intelligibility of judgment could not be possible without his version of the necessary logical

---

mere "Schein" of sense, see James Conant, "The Search for Logically Alien Thought: Descartes, Kant, Frege, and the *Tractatus*," *Philosophical Topics*, vol. 20, no. 1, 1991: 115–80.

[11] I hasten to note that the denial of strict separability is not a denial of distinguishability, as if Hegel thought *there was no sensible receptivity*, no intuitions, that there were infima species or "concepts" of individuals. See my "Concept and Intuition: On Distinguishability and Separability," *Hegel-Studien*, vol. 40, 2005: 25–39.

[12] Wolff suggests that we think, with Hegel, of the relation between formal or general logic and transcendental logic not as "*vorgeordnete*" but as "*beigeordnete*" and that seems wise. Wolff, "Der Begriff des Widerspruchs", 196. He also suggests that the general-logical formulation of "the law" of non-contradiction means it cannot have unconditional, but only conditional validity.

moments, the twelve moments of the Table of Pure Concepts. That is already a kind of determination of the really possible. Kant, however, does not provide the arguments for such a deduction.

So to sum up, *this*—the inseparability of the questions, the fact that we cannot *make sense of sense-making* without it being the case that ways of making sense have actually made sense of things as they are, of *what things are, such that sense can be made of them*—is, I want to propose, what Hegel means by saying that logic *is* metaphysics, or that "being in and for itself" *is* the concept.[13] Once we understand the role of, say, essence and appearance as ways of making sense, we have *thereby made sense* of essences and appearances, and therewith, the world in which they are indispensable. (We have not made sense of some species-specific feature of human sense-makers, but of the sense *the world could make*.)[14]

Here is another formulation of the identity of logic and metaphysics:

> As science, truth is pure self-consciousness as it develops itself and has the shape of the self, so that that which exists in and for itself is the known [*gewußte*] concept and the concept as such is that which exists in and for itself. (SL, 21.33, my emphasis)[15]

Part of Hegel's huge debt to Aristotle emerges here.[16] Entities are the determinate entities they are "in terms of" or "because of" their concept or substantial form. That is,

---

[13] There are any number of ways to put this: we cannot be said to be making sense of our making sense of things, unless we actually are making sense of things, otherwise we would be making sense of how we fail to make sense, a possible project but one that is parasitic on the former. Cf. the similarity with Terry Pinkard, *Hegel's Dialectic: The Explanation of Possibility* (Philadelphia: Temple University Press, 1988), although I think the notion of the "explanation of possibility" in Hegel is more capacious than he acknowledges. An account of the categorical determination of possible content is not for Hegel, a determination of "thought-content," but of "actuality." This bears on the General/Transcendental Logic relation discussed here. So, if a Hegelian categorical analysis can show that the concept of freedom necessary to establish responsibility is compatible with a concept of determinism consistent with modern natural science, this does not just establish that the two concepts need not be incompatible, but that they are compatible; that "things are such" that the true assertion of both is possible and also unavoidable. For an example of such a disagreement, see p. 75. The precise statement of the modality issue is a topic in itself, however.

[14] This is obviously all a variation of the principle of sufficient reason, as Hegel was well aware: "Anything which is, is to be considered to exist not as an immediate, but as a posited; there is no stopping at immediate existence but a return must rather be made from it back into its ground" (SL, 11.293).

[15] There are passages like this from the *Philosophy of Spirit*: "was *gedacht* ist, *ist*; und daß, was *ist*, nur *ist*, insofern es Gedanke ist." G.W.F. Hegel, *Enzyklopädie der philosophischen Wissenschaften, Dritter Teil, Die Philosophie des Geistes*, in *Werke*, Bd. 10, ed. E. Moldenhauer and K. Michel (Frankfurt: Suhrkamp, 1970–1). *Hegel's Philosophy of Subjective Spirit*, trans. M.J. Petry (Dordrecht: Riedel, 1978), §465. But it is clear that by this point in the *Encyclopedia*, Hegel is not talking about what merely exists, and suddenly turning into Bishop Berkeley by claiming *esse est percipi*. What a think truly is, is its concept, and a concept is not a self-standing "thought" but a moment in a network of mutually inter-defining rules of determination.

[16] Paul Redding, *Analytic Philosophy and the Return of Hegelian Thought* (Cambridge: Cambridge University Press, 2007) has noted the oddity of Hegel using Aristotle's realism "to counter Kantian subjectivism" (222), even while still being indebted to Kant. Redding's general formulation states the (apparently) paradoxical position in all its glory. With respect to the relation of categories to being: "The categories, or thought determinations, do not reflect an independent determinate realm of objects, but nor do objects reflect an independently structured realm of determinations of thought. Rather we must be able *somehow* to think of these two realms as *one*" (Ibid.). See also the apt formulation on the last page of 232. I think we

such a form (or kind) accounts for such determinacy. Such entities embody some measure of what it is truly to be *such* a thing, and instantiate such an essence to a greater or lesser degree. A wolf is not simply, in itself, a wolf (we could also say: is not fully intelligible as what it is; this is part of the identity claim), but to some degree or other a better or worse exemplification of such a concept "for itself." The object is not just "as it is"; it is "for" (here, in some sense of, "for the sake of") its concept and hereby itself. A merely "existing" wolf is thus not an "actual" wolf. The latter would involve truly being for itself, the realization of wolfness. Hegel will tell us later that the subject matter of *The Science of Logic* is "actuality," not existence, about which more in a moment.[17] This is all in keeping with Hegel's general tendency to gloss himself his use of for-itself with Aristotle's notion of an actualized potential, an *energeia, actus,* or, in Hegel, *Wirklichkeit,* and "in itself" as *dynamis, potentia,* or, in Hegel, *Möglichkeit.*[18] To say that an object is "for its form" is just to say that there is an intelligible dynamic in its development. Various aspects or elements or moments make sense in terms of the concept of the thing. This intelligible dynamic is its concept and is not something that "exists" separate from or supervening on some physical attributes and efficient causation. It just is the intelligible way a development develops; there is nothing "over and above" the development.[19]

3.3.

But make sense *of what*? Everything? Hegel says these sorts of things about this:

When thinking is taken as active with regard to objects as the thinking over [*Nachdenken*] of something—then the universal, as the product of this activity—contains the value of the matter [*Wert der Sache*], what is essential [*das Wesentliche*], inner, true.   (E, §21, 77; Enl, 52)

Throughout passages like this, Hegel is distinguishing the question of actuality, the proper subject matter of the *Logic*, from questions about existence, and we see that distinction at work often. In *The Encyclopedia Logic* §6, he defines the content of philosophy proper as "actuality," and distinguishes it from the merely apparent, transient, and insignificant. In the *Philosophy of Right*, he begins with a reminder he repeats often, that his treatment of the issue is neither an analysis of the mere concept of right, nor an empirical account of existing systems of right, but of the concept together with its

---

need to go deeper into Kant to find the Hegelian position on logic than Redding intimates, and to say more about what one means by "being," but I agree with this formulation.

[17] The unity of concept and "*Realität*" is what Hegel means by *Wirklichkeit,* actuality. See EL, §215 and for its bearing on the famous "*Doppelsatz*" on the *Phlosophy of Right,* see EL §6. See also EL §121Z on the "ground" of the plant's growth being ultimately "nothing but the concept of the plant itself."

[18] For the relevant passage and a longer discussion see Kern's invaluable article W. Kern, "Die Aristotelsdeutung Hegels," *Philosophisches Jahrbuch,* vol. 78, 1971: 237–59.

[19] See Lear on Aristotle here, Jonathan Lear, *Aristotle: The Desire to Understand* (Cambridge: Cambridge University Press, 1988), 41–2.

"actuality," where the latter is distinguished from "external contingency, untruth, deception, etc." (PR §1).

It is the kind of issue that arises when we ask, for example, if some practice is "really" or "in truth" religious; peyote smoking, say; or scientology. We don't doubt that the practice exists; we want to know its "essentiality," *Wert, Sache an sich selbst*, and so forth.[20] We don't doubt that animals exist; we want to know if they are actually rights-bearers. We know computers can play chess and win, perhaps one day could even pass Turing tests, but we want to know not whether these facts are true, but whether they show that the computer is actually thinking. A gallery opens and objects are displayed; pieces of clothing thrown about the floor. Are they actually art? Or: is this institutional arrangement really a state?[21]

The suggestion is that Hegel thinks of anything's principle of intelligibility, its conceptual form, as an *actualization* in the Aristotelian sense, the being-at-work or *energeia* of the thing's distinct mode of being, not a separable immaterial metaphysical object. And "in us" as well it is the actualization of a conceptual power, an actualization that is not literally the same as, the being-at-work in the thing (the thing is not trying to make itself intelligible) but that, in the right understanding of that being-at-work, its actualization in thought, it is the same "it" that is actualized in being, the principle of its intelligibility. This can be understood in the same way that, according to Aristotle, in sense perception there can be a single "actualization" of two distinct potentialities, in the perceptible and in the perceiver.

3.4.

We have just barely enough in view now to say something about *what freedom actually is*; that is about the actuality of Right, the determination by the power of thought of its own norm for a free life. Let us say that in the *Logic*, Hegel examines three different sorts of sense-making. Summarized very crudely as forms of predication, these "kinds" of determinacy are expressed in qualitative assertions like, first, "Socrates is white," or "Rosie is a dog," or "copper is an electricity conductor"; second, in assertions like, "Such a plant is curative," "that punishment is effective," or "wolves hunt in packs"; and third, in what Hegel takes to be proper "judgments," like "that is a good house," or "that

---

[20] Why Hegel adds to this list, which is reminiscent of such Greek notions of *to alēthes, to ontōs on*, and the like, the notion of value (*Wert*) must await treatment of the logic of the concept. But we can note, with Mure (R.G.R. Mure, *An Introduction to Hegel* (Oxford: Clarendon Press, 1940), who tries to show that Hegel was committed to the identity of the ultimately real, the intelligible and the good), Hegel's reanimation of the Platonic and Aristotelian view that the world was, in actuality, *good*; good in that it was intelligible, allowed our demand for intelligibility to be met, and good in that that intelligibility was the manifestation of a kind of "genuineness," or even perfection, a thing fully intelligible if fully what it was to be that thing. See also Lear, *Aristotle*, chapters 1, 2, and 6.

[21] The ancient distinction is the one Hegel is after; not an account of *to on*, inseparable as it is from *me on* (*Schein*); we want rather *to ontos on*. And in this context, that will require that we understand the logic of the truth-seeming relationship, not at all the same problem as understanding the relation between nature's and spirit's seemings and their truth.

is bad for horses," and "that action is good." These are, respectively, paradigmatic of the Logic of Being, the Logic of Essence, and the Logic of the Concept.

These parallel, we can now say, the logic of abstract right, or relations of exclusion and possession based wholly on external relations of right (property and contract); secondly a form of account-giving that requires a differentiation between what is immediately accessible, what seems to be the case or externally, and what is manifest in such seemings but not itself directly graspable, only posited by reflection; the logic of the external as the manifestation of the inner (Morality and intentional action generally); and, third, some sort of relation between interiority or inner life and external relations to others in social roles that can fulfill the true form of spirit's actuality, being-with-self-in-others. (Or, said another way, an individual, being fully an individual but also fully instantiating its concept, the universal.)

And accordingly the crucial arguments in the book about the transitions will not be fully defensible on their own, but will require attention to this logical structure for its full justification. For example: the claim that one way of making sense of Right, Abstract Right, is limited to the point of inconsistency; say by the need to distinguish punishment from revenge that cannot be made within that modality of that sense-making, without reference to a person's inner intention, or without the way a moral point of view makes sense of right.

The bearing of this understanding of this problem of making sense of an appeal to the "logic" of "inner" or inner intention in practical matters is clear from an example Hegel gives in *The Encyclopedia Logic* in an addition to §112, brought out in order to explain the basic issue in a logic of essence. It is, as he describes it, the relation between a person's character, "essence" in that sense, and her deeds. It would be a mistake, he notes, to sum a person up, attempt to "understand" them in the distinct way persons should be understood, simply by adding up or listing everything they did; from what kind of pajamas she bought, to what she had for breakfast, to her volunteering for a dangerous mission. A person would not be properly understood by attention to such "immediacy" alone (or her qualitative/quantitative/measured appearances, as in the Logic of Being). We need to understand her deeds as "mediated" by what Hegel calls her "inwardness" (*sein Inneres*), something (and now in the most important difference with the Logic of Being) we cannot see, does not simply present itself.

For example, we can't really understand what she did except by some attention to her own formulation of the act description and her avowed motive (her "intention"). Sometimes what happens should not count as a deed because there is not the proper connection between inner and outer. An accident happens. Something prevents her from realizing the intention. On the other hand, as Hegel states the central claim of the entire Logic of Essence in a phrase, we must concede that any such inner self-construal can only "prove itself" (*sich bewähren*) in what manifests that inner outwardly, in the deeds. Too radical a separation and we have someone trying to disown what she in fact did, to fabricate excuses. ("Mistakes were made," "it was never my intention to deceive anyone," etc.) We need this distinction, but we can't establish *what* deeds are true manifestations of essence and which are mere aberrations by any statistical analysis of frequency, any simple inspection of what happens. We need to understand *how* "what shows," "what manifests itself" (*Schein*) can be said to reflect their essence when they do (if they do, then as *Erscheinung*, appearance), even if, as appearances, no one deed is ever a manifestation or simple representation of essence as such.[22]

But this issue of the proper or "true" expression of the inner should not be understood to be one just of honesty alone. As at the end of the Morality section, fanatical claims of conscience can be very honest, sincere. They are not any less evil for that. In a phrase, whether the inner can be reflected in the outer, a consideration that is central to the transition between Morality and Ethical Life, depends on what institutions are available, depends on the character of the outer at a time and place. It is also quite important that someone could be quite convinced of this, and could be sensitive to the nuances of the position, but still find it extremely difficult to make these distinctions properly in practice. Hegel's *Logic* does not provide any ground rules for how to do this; just the argument that these must be the terms in which the content of act descriptions can be fixed. This limitation of what a *Logic* will be able to provide is signaled in an extraordinary way by Hegel when he calls the Logic merely the "realm of shadows." This will be crucial for understanding the results of the *Philosophy of Right* as well, as I want now to show.

3.5.

This approach will make possible an appreciation of the limitations of the *Philosophy of Right*, as understood in Hegel's own speculative sense. It is a problem that can be posed in terms of the Aristotelian notion of actuality that I have been suggesting helps illuminate Hegel on actuality as central to any sense-making. If we assimilate Hegel and Aristotle on this point, and say that an object's intelligibility is primarily a matter of its substantial form, and if that form is to be understood as the distinct being-at-work of the thing, its distinct realization of itself, then this has obvious implications for epistemology. We can be said to know the "what it was to be" of a thing, neither by a direct intellectual intuition (it's being-at-work is a process, a way of being, not graspable as itself some noetic object) nor by just observing, say, the life of a living thing or the uses of an artifact. We would already have to be able to distinguish essential from inessential in order to track the *relevant* "realizations."[23]

[22] This could all be understood in the way that looking at someone by looking at their "reflection" in a mirror could seem to be looking at something "less real" than the thing itself. But, if, say, that allowed us to observe the person when he thought he was unobserved, the reflection would tell us more than the presentation of the subject himself. Film makers and artists, especially because it is a self-reflecting exercise as well, a commentary on art, play with this theme in many different contexts.

[23] Cf. my *Hegel's Practical Philosophy: Rational Agency as Ethical Life* (Cambridge: Cambridge University Press, 2008), chapter 6. With such examples, we are also introduced to the major logical problem in the Logic of Essence: a substrate or essence can only be identified determinately by its appearances; but we only know which appearances are genuine manifestations of essence and which incidental if we already have

But the actuality of *Geist*, or what it is actually to be such a being, is always treated by Hegel as distinctive. That is, that actuality is not its biological life cycle. *Geist* may be said to have a distinctive life form: it is a free being. But the actualization of that life form occurs in historical time, linked to institutions that are themselves self-transforming over time. It may be that, according to Hegel, we have to understand *Geist* in the modalities of understanding available for understanding or making sense of anything at all. So persons in their external relations to other persons, the realm of objective spirit, realize what they actually are, free beings, by living norm-governed lives. Those socially regulative norms amount to the notion of *Right*, and again, *Right* can be understood only in terms of our ways of understanding anything. But Hegel freely admits and insists on the fact that these modalities of righteous lives can be, must be, inflected in different historical ways.

One can see this in Hegel's impatience with those who think that his project aims to demonstrate that everything that exists, everything historically or ontologically contingent, is really necessary, deducible from the Concept. It boils over in §6 of the "Introduction" to the *Encyclopedia*. He refers to his famous "*Doppelsatz*" in the "Preface" to the *Philosophy of Right* (which clearly intersects our theme, that what is rational is actual and what is actual is rational), and he notes explicitly that what exists, certainly exists contingently and "*can just as well not be*," and he refers us to the *Logic* for the right explication of what is, by contrast with what merely exists, "actual." That is the task I have been trying to accomplish in this chapter. He adds, "Who is not smart enough to be able to see around him quite a lot that is not, in fact, how it ought to be?" Yet despite Hegel waving this huge bright flag, inscribed "I believe in contingency!", one still hears often (even from scholars of German philosophy) that his philosophy is an attempt to deduce the necessity of everything, from the Prussian state to Krug's fountain pen.[24]

In the simplest sense, this means that that domain of the actualization of freedom Hegel calls civil society, the realm of economic and civic activity, may, let us assume, be shown to be incomplete and self-undermining in the way we have been discussing, and that we could make sense of those limitations in terms of what would supplement and transform the essentially economic and locally and divided civic activities of civil society: genuinely political relations among citizens in the state. If this were so it would mean that relations among citizens would not be some sort of reflection of what still remain strategic forms of cooperation based ultimately on "the system of needs."

The most famous expression of what Hegel means by the status of the state comes in the Remark to Paragraph §258 in the *Philosophy of Right*:

If the state is confused with civil society and its determination is equated with the security and protection of property and personal freedom, the intent of individuals as such becomes the

identified essence and can make use of that identification in such separation. Besides Mure's treatment, this is a feature of Rosen's account of the section. Stanley Rosen, *The Idea of Hegel's Science of Logic* (Chicago: University of Chicago Press, 2014).

[24] For a good account of the issue and the legions of misinterpretations, see Klaus Vieweg, *Das Denken der Freiheit: Hegels Grundlinien der Philosophie des Rechts* (Munich: Fink Verlag, 2012).

ultimate end for which they are united…But the relation of the state to the individual is of quite a different kind. Since the State is objective spirit, it is only through being a member of the state that the individual himself has objectivity, truth, and ethical life. Union as such is the true content and end, and the destiny of individuals is to live a universal life…Considered in the abstract, rationality consists in general in the unity and interpenetration of universality and individuality.   (PR §258R)

Hegel is saying several things at once here. One is that if looked at as an extension of civil society, participation in the state would look optional, and thereby no real ethical relation. Another is that, looked at this way, persons would be offering others reasons to do or forebear from doing something that could not be reasons ultimately and genuinely shared (where this means with all persons as such), or as he says, would not amount *to a unity*, not a "universal life," not addressed to each other as free and equal beings. This all sounds Kantian, but Hegel is also saying that this universal life must have an institutional form, where that means "immediate existence" in custom (§257), and mediate existence in self-conscious allegiance to a state. And the most controversial thing he is implying here and saying explicitly elsewhere is that the state is the "ground" of the possibility of civil society, that were not businessmen and lawyers and police to understand themselves also as fellow citizens, the reasons they could offer each other and accept or reject in civil society, would be insufficient to function as actual reasons, and even the thin unity of civil society would not be possible (could not be coherent "to itself").

All of this is controversial, but none of it guarantees that Hegel has identified *the actual elements of the modern state* that could do this, and, what is more important, there is nothing about the overall project of the *Philosophy of Right* that requires that he be able to give such guarantees. (That would be like saying: because Hegel has defended the necessity of an essence–appearance distinction in any successful account of determinate being, he has to be able to tell us what all the essences are.) He is explicit that "the philosophical approach deals only with the internal aspect (*Inwendigen*) of all this, with the concept as thought (*dem gedachten Begriff*)" (§258R, 276). This demurral does not mean that Hegel can avoid trying to give this ideal a concrete historical form, but the ideal and the desiderata are two different desiderata, as he, in effect, admitted in the *Encyclopedia Logic* §6 passage quoted earlier.

I don't mean to suggest that providing the details of this historical inflection is a minor issue, a dispensable, marginal one; it is just a different one. If it is right to say that Hegel has not identified what in a modern state could be said to be responsive to the insufficiencies of a modern civil society, then his account is seriously defective. (And it is defective, in just this sense.) We are trying to understand the being at work, the actualization of an historical being, one whose life form is not fixed by nature. It is one thing to suggest that Hegel's speculative logic, which could be called a logic of the change or self-transformation in norms essential for a free or self-directing life, is uniquely suited to such an attempt to understand such a realization, and that understanding this part of his *Realphilosophie* requires attention to that mode of analysis. But if Hegel has not thought through correctly this aspect of "the real," "objective spirit," in terms of that idea of "making sense," then the question of whether he has understood the actual "logic" of *Geist*'s self-transformations is subject to serious criticism.

The criticism would be worse if it could be shown that there is *no* possible formulation of a possible state-concept, or any element of "ethical life," that could accomplish the transformation Hegel has argued to be necessary in any one instance that was not tied to the specific historical realization offered by Hegel. A frequently discussed example is Hegel's account of the bourgeois family, with its gender-based division of labor and its exclusion of women from public roles. The question then would be *what is essential to Hegel's account*: the individual choice of marriage partners based on the ideal of romantic love, and the education of children with the goal in mind of eventual independence, and so the nuclear and not extended family (goals that could obviously be fulfilled by gay marriage); or these gender divisions? I would argue for the former, not the latter, were there space enough to do so here.

In this context consider the most famous objections to Hegel's account of the State, those of the young Karl Marx. His most important questions concern the *Philosophy of Right*'s theory of political representation. Again, Hegel, in his attempt at a synthesis of ancient and modern views of politics, had argued that the enlightened self-interest and civic communality of civil society was an insufficiently integrative universal. He even thought that life in civil society itself would ultimately even make this manifest to its participants, "educate" them about it. The domain of true universality (and so, ultimately, genuinely mutual justifiability) could only be the state. As suggested, let us assume this is true. Still, by what right do we—could we—*now* expect, given what is taken to be "politics" in the twenty-first century, that the representatives in a contemporary political assembly are actually representative of their constituency in the original sense of the republican ideal? Forget Hegel and theory for a moment: who among us really believes that modern democratic representatives represent anything other than their own interests in prospering and in being re-elected, interests that tie them to the "special interests" of wealth and power in civil society? Because we believe in the moral anarchy otherwise known as the plurality of the good, we even prefer things this way, do not believe in an objective common good, and simply tolerate happily the fractured, competitive, inegalitarian relations of domination and submission that Hegel thought counted as the self-cancelling of the concept of civil society.

Hence, Marx's claim that the Hegelian State is a mere "mystification."[25] Is not any *bourgeois* state claiming to be a representative assembly anything other than such a mystification, a theatrical display, complete with all the Romanesque props of the American regime and transparently phony rhetoric? But Marx thought this would be true of *any* Hegelian theory that proposed some transcendence of the material relations of civil society. Hegel thought this, Marx charged, because he tried to fit historical

---

[25] Karl Marx, *Frühe Schriften: Erster Band*, ed. H.-J. Lieber and Peter Furth (Stuutgart: Cotta Verlag, 1962), 272.

reality to what he already thought the Concept required, rather than basing the Concept on historical actuality.

The charge is somewhat mindlessly repeated in his *Kritik des hegelschen Staatrechts*, but the heart of it is:

> The rationale [*Vernunft*] of the constitution of the state [*Verfassung*] is therefore abstract logic and not the concept of the state. Instead of the concept of the constitution, we have the constitution of the concept. Thought orients itself not from the nature of the state, but orients the state from an already completed thought.[26]

We have already seen that no one can approach the topic of the idea of the state or the idea of a constitution without some view of what it is to give an account of such an actuality, and that view must be part of a view about what it is to give an account of anything. So there is nothing suspicious or avoidable about Hegel's reliance on his *Logic*. Secondly, the argument that the concept of civil society cannot adequately account for "what civil society actually is" without relations among persons that are not based on civil society assumptions, but are genuinely political relations, is not in any way undermined if *we cannot see* in what is now politically actual any chance for such a realization, or if we now see that Hegel was too optimistic about the traces of reason he thought he detected in Corporations, the administration of justice, the role of the monarch, and so forth. But who could have anticipated mass consumer societies, global finance capitalism, and the transformation of the public sphere into the clash of the technocrats? Even Hegel's view that wars between states would at least revivify the patriotic feelings necessary for a national community (a rather casual view of the horrors of war that he is rightly often criticized for) has become much less relevant with the growing corporatization and privatization of war, the possibility of wholly unprecedented types of warfare, like cyber warfare, and the increasing reliance on what can only be called "abstract" weaponry, like drone attacks on civilians. What Hegel has "deduced from the idea" is the conceptual insufficiency of "civil society's idea of itself" and the historical realization of the idea, and therewith the lack of an embodiment of genuinely universal reason in the social relations based on need. (A state of need is experienced as nothing but contingent struggle for supremacy or domination without an actualization in the political realm.) That argument, the one based on the speculative mode of cognition, must have some historical inflection, but the logical argument is not affected by Hegel's mistaken view of contemporary possibilities. It is not even affected if Marx is right in Hegelian terms, and the insufficiencies of civil society cannot be resolved or "sublated" (*aufgehoben*) by merely "also" occupying the role of citizen, that viewing civil society from the perspective of demands of genuine universality requires significant structural transformations *in civil society* to make the roles of *burgher* and *citoyen* compatible. But for Marx to rule out of court *the very idea of the political* is to beg the question, not respond to it (as well as being based on a

---

[26] Ibid., 278.

metaphysical view of the relation between "material" and "ideal" that is even farther removed from actuality than Hegel's is supposed to be).

In fact, one could argue that the Hegelian framework gives us the right interpretation of the contemporary poverty of political life: (i) the complete subordination of the political by the interests of civil society, (ii) a great dissatisfaction with this situation (one based on the very concept of idea of civil society), with liberals complaining about the legalized bribery that now finances political campaigns, and conservatives complaining about the unwarranted intrusions of the regulatory state into the domains of the private.[27] Both are complaining about the transformation of the state into the steering mechanism of civil society, and both are able to produce evidence and argument for why that usurpation does not correspond with the true actuality of human freedom. Yet neither side evinces any serious ideas about the "restoration" of the genuinely political. This is not because they lack imagination or will, but because any such possible restoration has been objectively eliminated by the victory of civil society.

The claim that we will not have the right idea of the "mode of cognition" necessary to understand this situation unless we understand what it is to understand anything, unless we know how to address the question of the actuality of freedom for a historical being, or especially unless we know the difference between a *Wesenslogik* and a *Begriffslogik*, remains, no doubt implausible when stated in that form. I have, though, tried to suggest here that there is nevertheless much to be learned by trying to understand the comprehensive "logic" of Hegel's project in the *Philosophy of Right*.

---

[27] See Michael Theunissen, 1980, *Sein und Schein: Die kritische Funktion der Hegelschen Logik* (Frankfurt am Main: Suhrkamp, 1980), 481ff. for some useful remarks about Hegel's relevance to this situation.

4

Method and System in Hegel's *Philosophy of Right*

Allen W. Wood

4.1. The "Controversy"

There is supposed to be a controversy in the scholarship on Hegel's ethical thought between those who base their account on Hegel's "system" and "method", and those who reject this approach (see Houlgate, 1992, Brooks, 2007, Goodfield, 2014). I am supposed to be one of the latter. I have never been able to understand this. I utterly reject this characterization of me; it is false, unfair, and dismally uncomprehending. (I've tried to say so before, but no one seemed to be listening.) Those who describe me in this way should be ashamed, or else I should be, for letting them so badly misunderstand me. But I won't try to assign responsibility: there's already too much blame out there in the world. I just want to set the record straight.

As to the supposed controversy: there's nothing to argue about. As Gertrude Stein said of Oakland, CA: "There is no there there." Perhaps my utter bafflement disqualifies me from discussing the topic at all. But I do have some thoughts about the proper use of Hegel's system and method in understanding his philosophy of right. And I was, after all, invited to contribute a chapter about this. So here goes.

Frederick Beiser has represented the alleged controversy in the form of a frightful dilemma: either we approach Hegel by way of his "system" or we do not. If we do, then we are stuck with his antiquated speculative logic, and cannot hope to draw anything from Hegel that is of interest to present-day philosophy. If we try to read Hegel in light of insights from more recent philosophy, this is even worse: "We make Hegel alive and relevant, a useful contributor to our concerns; but that is only because we put our own views into his mouth. What we learn from Hegel is then only what we have read into him" (Beiser, 2005, p. 10). (I guess this last is supposed to be me.) Beiser's conclusion is that the only defensible Hegel scholarship is unashamedly antiquarian, exploring Hegel's relationship to his own contemporaries—especially to those minor figures whom only the most intimidatingly well-read scholars (perhaps only Beiser himself) have even heard of. Faced with Beiser's bleak options, one has to wonder how Hegel (or any other past philosopher) could ever be worth reading at all.

One reason I think there is no issue anywhere in this vicinity is that Beiser's dilemma is obviously a false one. The thought of every important historical philosopher is embedded in a tradition and a past age. It is no longer a real option for us, and disingenuous, as well as irresponsibly dogmatic to pretend that it is. This is as true of Hegel as it is of other past philosophers. Nevertheless, we still have much to learn from past philosophers, by asking them *our* questions and reading their texts as possible answers to them. We learn a lot by doing this not only about Hegel but also about our current philosophy. (For two examples of it done very successfully regarding Hegel, see Quante (2004) and Redding (2007).)

Philosophy itself would be impossible without this connection to its past. Those who think otherwise are connected to past philosophers every bit as much, only they do not know it. Of them we can say what Keynes famously said about so-called "practical men":

The ideas of economists and political philosophers, both when they are right and when they are wrong are more powerful than is commonly understood. Indeed, the world is ruled by little else. Practical men, who believe themselves to be quite exempt from any intellectual influences, are usually slaves of some defunct economist.   (Keynes, 2007, p. 164)

Present-day philosophers who think that the history of philosophy is nothing but a record of silly errors by dead white men would be wiser if they at least knew on which dead white men's silly errors their own philosophy is based. They might be in a better position to decide critically what to accept from the past and what to leave there.

Appropriating Hegel—or any past philosopher—always involves asking him *our* questions and finding out what *his* texts have to say in reply. This is *not* a process of reading your own thoughts into the philosopher. It is the only possible way to engage *philosophically* with past thinkers. The most self-deceptive approach of all is that of the "pure antiquarian" who claims to report simply "the facts" about the past, free of all interpretation or appropriation. This is no doubt a good way to do intellectual history, but it is worthless as a way of studying, for philosophical purposes, the history of philosophy. (Beiser has written a whole book about the nineteenth-century tradition of historiographers and philosophers of history who rejected philosophy in this way. See Beiser, 2011). In appropriating a past philosopher, you need to be *first*, self-aware of your own act of appropriation, and then *second*, you must devise an approach that lets you get the most *philosophically* out of the encounter.

To appropriate Hegel, you have to understand *Hegel*: that means, *of course*, understanding the system and method through which he thought. To try to understand *Hegel* without these would be like trying to understand arithmetic without understanding numbers or addition and subtraction. At the same time, you truly *appropriate* Hegel only if you ask him our questions and get answers to them that are relevant to our own time. There is no choice between reading Hegel "systematically" and reading him in response to our questions. There are only different ways of doing both at once.

4.2. Superstar or Anti-Hero?

In the invitation to contribute to this volume, I was described as "the non-systematic superstar." This label was no doubt applied with benevolent and flattering intentions, since it was intended to induce me to write something. But frankly, it makes no sense at all. To think of philosophers as "stars," or celebrities of any sort, involves a conception of the world so out of touch with reality as to rival the beliefs of American evangelical religion. The "non-systematic" part rests on total misunderstanding. Maybe for some Hegel-scholars I have in common with Voltaire's God that if I did not exist I would need to be invented—in order that they might refute me. So that's what they did: that is, invent me, then refute me. But their invention has nothing to do with me, and their refutation even less so.

I began *Hegel's Ethical Thought* (1990) with the aim of making Hegel available to moral and political philosophers who had long neglected or even despised him. I saw my project as in the same vein as Charles Taylor's *Hegel* (1975). Taylor's book exemplified, and also greatly advanced, the appropriation of Hegel by analytical philosophers, most of whom had been carefully trained to think Hegel a hopeless obscurantist, a charlatan like Georges Gurdjieff or L. Ron Hubbard. I devoted the opening pages of my book to telling this audience that there is a lot in Hegel's ethical thought that *should* interest them, even though Hegel's attempt to rethink traditional logic is nothing to which a present-day philosopher can be expected to subscribe in its original form. I was trying make Hegel's ethical thought appeal to an audience beyond what I contemptuously referred to as "an isolated and dwindling tradition of incorrigible enthusiasts" (Wood, 1990, p. 5).

No doubt, despite my earlier disparaging remarks about the concept of the "philosophical celebrity," I was suffering from delusions of grandeur. Perhaps I still do, comparing myself to Voltaire's God and now casting myself as a Sophoclean hero: the distortion of the book's claims is perhaps the *nemesis* that inevitably follows upon all human *hubris*. For the book was, all too predictably, read not by the wider audience I hoped for, but only by mere Hegel scholars, such as myself. (The right sort of drama for the portrayal of both myself and my critics was probably Aristophanes rather than Sophocles.) These scholars took immediate offense at my insulting description of them. In retaliation, they charged me with advocating that we study Hegel's philosophy by ignoring his whole system. They accused me of ripping out of context whatever I arrogantly decided were Hegel's few scattered insights and ignoring, or contemptuously dismissing, the larger philosophy of which they were a part. I stand in the dock, accused of trying to "quarantine" Hegel's political philosophy from the rest of his thought; alleged "counter-movements" in Hegel scholarship opposing my heresy have met with unqualified approval.

Had the people who said those things read anything beyond the first half dozen pages of the book? They gave little sign of it. Had they understood even those? I have to doubt it. I can interpret such gross distortions only as a symptom of the common philosophical vice (probably even more common among analytical philosophers than among Hegel scholars) of maliciously misinterpreting whatever other philosophers say in whatever way makes it easiest to ridicule and dismiss it.

It is a sad fact that people tend to form their impression of books from what is written at the beginning of them—often enough, from serious misunderstandings of those things. (I sometimes think most philosophy books are never read beyond the opening pages by most of those who later claim to have read them.) This is how people get the false impression that Locke is an empiricist; that Descartes leaves us doubting everything; that Kant hates the emotions; that Marx is a difficult thinker and an obscure writer. It is also why we still have with us the common caricature of Hegel as "conservative" and "quietist," based on his Preface to the *Philosophy of Right*, ignoring what he said in the rest of that work. I suppose I should feel honored that my book about Hegel has been treated with the same kind of unfairness as Hegel himself has been treated.

My presentation of Hegel's ethical thought followed Hegel's own order of presentation in the *Philosophy of Right*. I also made use, wherever possible, of the method of exposition Hegel used in that work, since no responsible account of Hegel's thoughts could have done otherwise. Hegel himself tells us right away (PR §§1–2) that philosophy's only contribution to understanding right is its appropriation through thought—in other words, through the method and system Hegel had developed. Clearly the movement from the immediate personhood of abstract right through the separation of morality to the reconciliation of ethical life, and again, from the immediacy of the family through the externalization of civil society to the unity of the state—these parallel the movement from Being through Essence to the Concept in Hegel's logic. This much is obvious, and governed the entire structure of *Hegel's Ethical Thought*. What matters, however, is not merely to assert these parallels like a Hegelian parrot, but to see what they mean for Hegel's ethical thought, as we can appropriate it today. That was my aim. Especially crucial to Hegel's way of understanding the dialectical developments in the system of right is the repeated use of the triadic "moments of the concept": universality, particularity, individuality. His use of this triad is indispensable to the exposition of Hegel's arguments. (See Wood, 1990, pp. 18, 23–8, 69–70, 88–92, 170–3, 179–80, 205–6, 210, 216, 238.) I wish those who attack my "anti-systematic" reading of Hegel would pay as much attention to these "systematic" matters as I did.

4.3. So Please, Let's Make a New Start

Let me try, even at this late date, to correct the whole wretched misunderstanding by asking (and answering) two distinct (and largely rhetorical) questions:

1. Is Hegel's speculative logic a replacement for traditional logic? Does one need to subscribe to Hegel's entire system and method, in their original form, in order to find things of great interest and value in his philosophy of object- ive spirit (his philosophy of right, morality and ethical life)? Must we see

Hegel's ethical insights as *grounded* in (hence sharing the same fate as) his now clearly outdated speculative-logical system?

Answer: Certainly not! Anyone who thinks so belongs to the isolated and dwindling tradition of incorrigible enthusiasts to which I disparagingly referred. Logic, such as we have it now, went through a major revolution in the nineteenth and early twentieth centuries, whose history involves such names as Bolzano, Frege, Russell and Whitehead, and Wittgenstein. Hegel belongs to an early phase of this process, but the philosophical contributions—which were significant—of what *he* called 'logic' were made to other areas of philosophy from the one where he located them—or at least where we now locate the subject of "logic." Later in this chapter I'll have some suggestions about what these contributions were.

2. Would one's understanding of Hegel's ethical thought be greatly enhanced if one approached it with an appreciation of the way it is shaped by his method and his systematic concerns? Is such an appreciation even indispensable to understanding Hegel's ethical thought and social philosophy?

Answer: Of course! This is all self-evident, too obvious to need stating, and in no need of defense. Anyone who thinks I meant to deny it has not understood anything of what I was saying. I can only believe that those who criticized my book on the ground that it is "anti-systematic" took my (obviously correct) negative answer to question (1) to be instead an (obviously incorrect) negative answer to question (2). Perhaps some people cannot distinguish the two questions, or think that a negative answer to the first question commits you to a negative answer to the second. Once these two questions are distinguished, however, and the obviously correct answer to each is supplied, then I see nothing left for intelligent people to debate. There might indeed be a debate about how best to defend an (obviously correct) affirmative answer to (2) without committing yourself to an (obviously incorrect) affirmative answer to (1). Maybe those who criticized me were trying to simplify (or even duck) that difficult task.

Here is yet a third question (or set of questions) whose answer might conceivably separate "systematic" from "anti-systematic" readers of Hegel:

3. Are there philosophically interesting ideas contained in Hegel's conception of a philosophical system itself, developed as he does it in the *Science of Logic*, the *Encyclopedia*, and *Philosophy of Right*? Are these ideas still relevant to the philosophical issues we face? Do they also have implications for our philosophical appropriation of Hegel's *Philosophy of Right*?

If an affirmative answer to all these questions makes one a "systematic" reader of Hegel, then the aim of the remainder of the present chapter is precisely to *defend* a "systematic" reading of Hegel. I do not regard anything I am about to say as either contradicting or retracting anything I said in 1990, but I will be developing some themes that were not present in that book (since I hope I have learned something more about Hegel during the past quarter century). I begin by discussing Hegel's method and system itself, in abstraction from its use in the *Philosophy of Right*. I start with a brief account of its historical origins and then discuss something that its approach still may have to contribute to philosophy. I of course do not claim that what I am going to say exhausts the interest Hegel's system and method may have for us today, but only that these would be among the philosophical benefits to be obtained by the study of Hegel. Only at the end of the chapter will I try to apply these lessons to the *Philosophy of Right*.

4.4. Hegel's System as the *Telos* of Post-Kantian German Idealism

Hegel's system was widely seen as the outcome of a movement in philosophy that had been initiated by Kant. More accurately, it was the movement created by a generation of philosophers who accepted Kant's revolution in philosophy but then attempted to "go beyond" Kant. This movement began with Reinhold, and then was spurred by the criticisms of Schulze and Maimon. Its first major representative was Fichte, and his project of creating a systematic Doctrine of Science (*Wissenschaftslehre*). But Fichte began his system over again from scratch more times than can be counted, without ever completing it. His follower Schelling, on the other hand, completed an entirely new system almost every year for nearly a decade, and then at the end of his life repudiated the entire post-Kantian movement itself—after Hegel's system had come to be seen as its *telos*.

We make a mistake—we disagree with Hegel himself as well as with his contemporaries and immediate followers—if we understand Hegel as aiming at great philosophical *originality*. Hegel's aim was instead to appropriate and summarize all of Western philosophy (from the Greeks onward), using the resources provided by the Kantian revolution, and the achievements of those who sought to perfect what Kant had begun. His system was intended to be encyclopedic, in that sense, as well as in others. You have to be pretty inattentive, for instance, not to notice that the first volume of Hegel's *Science of Logic* is drawn directly from Kant's table of categories: the Doctrine of Being from the mathematical categories of Quality and Quantity, and the Doctrine of Essence from the dynamical categories of Relation and Modality. The second volume, the Doctrine of the Concept, also follows the logic of the period which also guided Kant in the first Critique: concepts, judgments, and syllogisms. Of course Hegel nearly always enriches the Kantian determinations by seeing them in a broader and deeper historical context, drawn from pre-Socratic, Platonic, and Aristotelian sources, as well as from the science and philosophy of his own day. But the elements of the plan were already a familiar, and drawn directly from Kant. In this there was the reverse of any attempt at originality.

One common complaint against Kant raised by the first generation of his followers was that he had drawn his categories rather mechanically from the tradition of scholastic formal logic. But this logic itself, according to these philosophers, needed refounding as much as the rest of philosophy. (This disquiet with the Aristotelian-scholastic tradition in logic can be seen as the pre-history of the revolution in logic that actually occurred nearly a century later.) Kant's procedure needs therefore to be transcended by one in which the basic concepts of philosophy are given a more fundamental and rigorous kind of derivation than Kant's metaphysical deduction. A second complaint was that Kant had separated sensible intuition from the thought of understanding. The new philosophical method ought to provide a transcendental explanation not merely of the forms of thinking but also of the matter. This involved also a challenge to the entire a priori/a posteriori distinction, as understood by Kant. These two complaints determined the ways Kant's followers were determined to "go beyond" him.

4.5. Fichte's Synthetic Method

The great creative step that was taken on both fronts was found in Fichte's Jena Doctrine of Science (*Wissenschaftslehre*). Fichte began with the self-positing of the I (in effect, with Kant's transcendental unity of apperception), and sought a method by which the categories of thought might be successively introduced. His aims were quite Kantian, and can even be presented in straightforwardly Kantian terms. Each concept needs, namely:

(1) a *metaphysical deduction*, establishing its *transcendental origin*;
(2) a *transcendental deduction*—establishing its *applicability to objects*; and
(3) a *schematism*—a way of *recognizing instances* of it.

These aims were to be achieved simultaneously with a deduction of the *material* of experience—the not-I, to which the free activity of the I, both practical and theoretical, is directed.

Fichte's aims were also *transcendental* in the Kantian sense: he did *not* claim that the world's existence in itself was produced by the activity of the I (a notion Fichte dismissed as "insane"). This absurd metaphysical proposition, still attributed to Fichte in many bowdlerizations of his philosophy, was repudiated by him repeatedly and emphatically. The idealistic derivation of all reality from the I in Fichte's system is to occur only from the standpoint of transcendental philosophy, which is strictly distinguished by Fichte from the realism of common sense, which, he declares, it is the aim of philosophy *not* to reject or replace with some metaphysical system, but only to understand and to justify. He insisted downright fanatically on this point in his two Introductions to his system (1797), and then even more desperately in his garishly titled: *A Sun-Clear Report: An Attempt to Force the Reader to Understand* (1801). These protestations often sound paranoid, except that it is hard to dismiss them as delusions in light of the way Fichte was treated personally and professionally—by Charles

Augustus, by Goethe, Reinhard, Lavater, Kant, Jacobi, Schelling—as well as by over two centuries of misunderstanding.

For our purposes here, the most important part of Fichte's method was the new way he proposed to provide the necessary justifications of categories of thought. Fichte drew his transcendental method from a creative extension of Kant's Antinomies of Pure Reason in the Transcendental Dialectic. Kant saw that if certain concepts—the cosmological ideas regarding time, space, divisibility, causality, necessity, are pressed too far, they threaten us with contradictions. His aim was to reveal these as illusory. Fichte saw that apparent contradictions are easily generated if one is working with too few concepts. Conceptual impoverishment forces us to choose between false alternatives; we seem to have no way out of contradictions. For instance, Fichte thinks we face an apparent contradiction when we recognize that forming a determinate conception of the I requires us to posit a not-I negating its activity:

1. Insofar as the not-I is posited, the I is not posited; for the not-I completely nullifies the I.... Thus the I is not posited in the I insofar as the not-I is posited in it.
2. But the not-I can be posited only insofar as an I *is* posited in the I (in one identical consciousness) to which the not-I can be opposed... Thus insofar as the not-I is to be posited in this consciousness, the I must also be posited in it.
3. The two conclusions are opposed to each other... Hence [our] principle is opposed to itself and nullifies itself. (SW 1:106)

The apparent contradiction can be avoided if we introduce a new concept—that of limited, partial, or divisible activity or negation (SW 1:105–10). Each negation is therefore partly compatible with the other. This compatibility constitutes the common *ground* for their synthesis or reciprocal dependency (SW 1:110–22).

Borrowing Kant's own terminology, Fichte often calls the propositions apparently opposed one another the "thesis" and the "antithesis." The new concept needed to avoid the contradiction—to show it to be merely apparent—he then calls the "synthesis." This procedure provides a *metaphysical deduction* and also a *transcendental deduction* of the new concept, since in the fact that it is needed to avoid a contradiction we see both its philosophical origin and its necessary application. We acquire a *schematism* for the concept, which in Fichte's presentations often first itself appears paradoxical to us, by recognizing it, from the philosophical point of view, as the transcendental significance of a familiar concept we need to employ all the time—in this case, the concept "ground." Thus through Fichte's method we come to understand the true philosophical meaning and more precise determination of this already familiar concept.

This generation and validation of categories of thought Fichte calls the "synthetic method." Fichte's program in transcendental philosophy was to begin by deliberately abstracting from ordinary experience a self-evident first principle—that of the self-positing I—and then working our way back, by means of the synthetic method, to the completeness of experience from which we began by abstracting. But Fichte never completed his system as a Doctrine of Science. He did claim to have completed parts of it—those dealing with natural right and ethics.

It seems self-evident that the synthetic method was the model for Hegel's dialectical method. Hegel also proceeds by showing how every limited thought-determination leads us into contradictions, which can then be resolved by introducing a new thought-determination. Hegel calls this process the "proof" of the new thought-determination (PR §2). Like Fichte, he began by abstracting from experience: the concept of Being is for him the most abstract concept, and therefore the starting-point for logical development. Unlike Fichte, Hegel did complete the systematic development of such a system of thought-determinations. This was his *Science of Logic*. Then he developed the "real" parts of his encyclopedic philosophical system by going through a similar process with the thought-determinations through which those regions of reality are grasped: the philosophy of nature, and the philosophy of spirit. Hegel's *Elements of the Philosophy of Right* is a yet more detailed execution of this dialectical process within one part of the philosophy of spirit, namely the sphere of objective spirit (or social life).

Hegel took over Fichte's synthetic method, but not without basic revisions. He did not begin with a transcendental subject (the unity of apperception or the I), but instead with the thought-determinations themselves, which (he argued) can be regarded equally as acts of a subject or as determinations of objects. It is questionable (I won't try to decide the question here) whether Hegel's project should be called "transcendental philosophy" at all. It is also controversial (a controversy I also won't take up) how far Hegel intended his system to be a "metaphysics," and what else it is if it is not that. Hegel also studiously avoided Fichte's terminology "thesis-antithesis-synthesis." (All those philosophers, intellectual historians, political theorists, literary theorists, or other sophisticated know-it-alls who expound Hegel in these terms are telling you something very important—though usually without intending to. They are telling you that they probably have not read Hegel, and that in expounding his philosophy they simply do not know what they are talking about.) Hegel never directly addressed the question why he eschewed this particular jargon. I have sometimes been challenged to say why I make "such a big deal" out of scolding and disparaging those who use it in presenting Hegel. The following is a brief attempt to explain.

4.6.   What is a "System" of Concepts?

Beginning with Leibniz, and basic to the philosophy of Christian Wolff, was the idea of a *mathesis universalis* or a single canonical system of concepts which might be used to give a complete account of all reality. Wolff hoped to provide a definition, or an "enlightened" (*aufgeklärt*) account, spelling out the contents of each concept, and then base philosophical demonstrations on these analyses, using these concepts to offer us as complete an account as possible of whatever subject matter comes before us. Our actual account of the world may be incomplete, but a minimal condition for it to be acceptable is that it should be logically consistent. Concepts that are too unclear (or unenlightened) for us to see their applications as consistent are for this reason unsatisfactory, and to fall into contradiction would be a sign that something in your system is in need of at least local revision so that the contradiction can be clearly seen to be only apparent.

Kant thinks that in our system of empirical concepts we aspire to something like the complete conceptual system Wolff had in mind. He thinks our empirical concepts are necessarily at best only an approximation to such a system, because they are drawn from sensible intuition, and the limited information about things offered to us by the senses never permits us to grasp reality completely in conceptual terms. But if we are threatened by contradictions in our philosophy, as we seem to be in the cosmological antinomies, then our first task as philosophers is to understand the threat and show that the contradictions are only apparent.

Fichte's synthetic method has these same presuppositions. A complete Doctrine of Science would be a self-consistent system of concepts in the Leibnizian–Wolffian–Kantian sense, transcendentally generated out of a series of threats of contradiction, but the result in each case must be a new concept that displays the threatened contradiction as only apparent. Each newly generated concept is a "synthesis" in the sense that it allegedly unites the apparently opposed thesis and antithesis, saving us from the contradiction that would, if not avoided, destroy systematic understanding.

Hegel's dialectical method radically revises this project. Hegel agrees with the traditional view that to allow contradictions among the concepts we use would be to admit philosophical defeat. But from this it was also inferred by the tradition that our concepts must constitute a *single* self-consistent system. This last conclusion, however, is one Hegel rejects, along with the traditional notion of what a "system" of concepts, or thought-determinations, would have to be. Hegel's name for the traditional way of viewing concepts is that it is the "metaphysics of the understanding" (EL §§26–36, 80). The understanding is that faculty that keeps concepts separate and tries to avoid contradiction at all costs. Hegel views this as a one-sided and blinkered conception of what a true system of concepts can and should be.

Hegel devises a new conception of a system of concepts. He does so by borrowing yet another idea from Kant's cosmological antinomies, and from his Transcendental Dialectic more generally. This is the idea that our concepts, or thought-determinations, are *limited in their application*. This is implicit in Hegel's choice of the term "thought-determinations" (*Denkbestimmungen*) to refer to the items belonging to the system. Each thought-determination has an application that is determinate, that is, limited. If we attempt to employ it beyond its proper boundaries, we pay an unacceptable price: we fall into contradiction. The properly *dialectical* stage of reason's method is the one in which we expose the limitations in each thought-determination, the way that each thought-determination transcends the boundaries the understanding would set for it and thereby falls into contradiction (EL §81).

Kant of course thought that all our concepts have the *same* boundary: they are limited to the world of appearance, to what can be sensibly intuited. Kant holds that we misemploy any concept if we try to apply it cognitively beyond this boundary. Hegel rejects that conception of the boundedness of concepts because he thinks that any employment of a concept is already in some way cognitive. Even thought-determinations that refer to infinite realities—freedom, spirit, God—can be applied cognitively in a variety of ways, through aesthetic intuition, religious representation, and finally the conceptual cognition of philosophy (EL §§45–9). Hegel thinks instead that the limitedness of each thought-determination is peculiar to itself, or at least to the cluster of related thought-determinations to which it belongs. Every thought-determination has its legitimate place in a logical system, but none is cognitively applicable outside its properly limited sphere.

One way to contrast Hegel's position with the traditional one is to say that Hegel holds that contradictions in thinking can be both real and unavoidable. But this way invites multiple misunderstandings and common caricatures. Hegel is *not* a proponent of a dialethic logic (see Priest, 2006). Nor does he think that contradictions are simply "OK." He does not think that self-contradictory objects exist. The appearance of a contradiction in our thinking shows, just as the traditional view held, that something is wrong. But Hegel does not diagnose what is wrong in the same way as the understanding. The understanding thinks that if we run into a contradiction, we must back off. We must simply stop saying something that contradicts something else we have said. We must simply not go there.

Hegel, by contrast, thinks that the role of contradiction in our thinking should be different and more positive. Hegel holds that every thought-determination, if we explore its implications completely, will force us into contradictions. (The possible exception is the thought-determination Hegel calls the Absolute Idea, EL §§236–43; but this determination too forces thought beyond itself, to the reality in which thought necessarily acquires Being. This is Hegel's new way of endorsing the ontological proof of God's existence.)

When we come upon the kind of contradiction that indicates the limits of a thought-determination, we should do two things. First, we should recognize that the way the thought-determination has fallen into contradiction reveals its limits. We should conclude that the kind of application we were trying to make of the thought-determination is one that exceeds those limits; the thought-determination does not have unlimited application in our cognitions. Second, we should do something analogous to what Fichte's synthetic method did, namely, seek out a further thought-determination that enables us to understand the limits of the thought-determination that has fallen into contradiction, but is not encumbered with the same limits. This last project is what Hegel contrasts with the "dialectical" (or "negative") stage of reason, calling it the "speculative" (or "positive") stage (EL §82). (But sometimes Hegel uses the term "dialectic" in a way that encompasses both stages.) To represent the positive outcome of this process as a "synthesis" of the contradictories from which it emerges, as Fichte did, would be to imply (as Kant and Fichte intended) that it shows the contradiction to be only apparent and that the newly proven thought-determination belongs to the same self-consistent system. But that is just what Hegel denies: this is why he never used the "thesis-antithesis-synthesis" terminology to describe his dialectical method.

I think this is worth making a big deal over. What is generated (or "proven") by the dialectical-speculative process is a new thought-determination, a new level of thinking. It *aufhebt* (transcends or "sublates") the previous one. This thought-determination too, however, will have only its own limited application, which is established by seeing the way in which rational thought discovers further contradictions into which it must fall. It is the dialectical process of reason—including the grasping of each thought-determination in its limited and determined content, the cognition of its limitations by way of dialectic and contradiction, and then the speculative resolution of the contradiction in a new thought-determination—that replaces the Fichtean "synthetic method" of philosophy. In the process, it generates a new kind of systematic unity among concepts. This is not the unity of a single, self-consistent system of thoughts, but a unity composed of a hierarchical plurality of such systems, each generated from the limitations of the one preceding it in the system, and giving way to the one that follows it because that new thought-determination resolves the contradictions into which it inevitably falls.

In my opinion, a proper reading of Hegel's method does not in fact yield the result that every single thought-determination itself directly falls into contradiction. Rather, it presents us with certain localized systems of thought-determinations which comprehend parts, moments, or levels of reality within a limited sphere. It is really these sub-systems that fall into contradiction, and whose limits must be surpassed. For example, the first three thought-determinations Hegel discusses in the *Logic*—Being, Nothing, Becoming—constitute a single coherent (though highly abstract) way of conceptualizing reality in the most general sense (EL §§84–8). This soon passes over into a second system, whose central thought-determination is that of a determinate being or existence (*Dasein*), some entity that may be contrasted with other entities using concepts such as quality, limit, and the distinction between ideality and reality (EL §§89–98). Quality then passes over into Quantity (EL §§99–111). The Doctrine of Being views reality in one way, the Doctrine of Essence in another, and the Doctrine of the Concept in a third way. It would take a detailed exposition of Hegel's logic to develop all this properly.

How do we know that thought-determinations, when each is revealed in its limitedness, do yield a single complete system? This is not self-evident; it can be proven only by constructing such a system, which Hegel claims to have done in the *Science of Logic* and more briefly in the first volume of the *Encyclopedia*. He makes analogous claims for the stages of comprehension of nature and of spirit in the second and third volumes of the *Encyclopedia*. The sphere dealt with in the *Philosophy of Right* is a stage or level of the latter: it is Objective Spirit.

Is there something of continuing philosophical value in this project? Not, I believe, in its original form. We can't simply become 1830 Hegelians, any more than we can go back to 350 BCE and become Platonists. That is the import of my negative answer to question (1). But is understanding the details of Hegel's systematic indispensable to the appropriation of his living philosophical contributions—in particular, to ethics and political philosophy? Of course. It never occurred to me to deny it. That's my affirmative answer to question (2).

4.7. Conceptual Pluralism

But I have said that I would try to say something further about the continuing philosophical interest of Hegel's project: question (3). This involves drawing a philosophical thesis from Hegel's general conception of the systematic relation of thought-determinations to reality, Hegel's conception of how we should think about combining our thoughts about the world into a single system. Perhaps someone will say that I am ripping Hegelian doctrines out of their systematic connection, or even foisting on Hegel thoughts of my own. All I can say to this is that I deny I am doing any such thing. I am appropriating Hegel's own thoughts in a way that addresses some of our questions. As I have already argued, this is the only way that Hegel (or any past philosopher) could ever be of *philosophical* interest to us. More specifically, I think Hegel anticipated some of the problems philosophers now have relating—for example—the sciences to one another, and certain scientific studies to our common sense experience. I think he developed an approach to these which, whether or not we accept it in the end, is worthy of serious consideration.

Different empirical sciences approach their subject matters through different methods and different systems of concepts. It is often difficult to see how the laws they propose to establish relate to one another, or how to combine their results into a consistent picture of the world. One rather old-fashioned way of doing this was "reductionism," in which the laws of chemistry, biology, psychology, and anything else we want to honor with the title of a "science" would be reduced to (even translated into) the laws of physics, even of the most elementary physics. Nowadays, however, there are deep controversies even within elementary physics, and the reductionist project looks to most people pretty hopeless.

Certainly alive and well, however, is the idea that scientists, or perhaps philosophers allied with them and pretending to be their spokespersons, might produce a single self-consistent and theoretically coherent "naturalistic" conception the physical world, and every aspect of it, including our relation to it as knowers and agents. We will never answer all our questions about the world, of course, but philosophical naturalists think we can at least offer a determinate, self-consistent, and totalizing scientific picture that shows everything to be explainable in terms of our science, more or less in its current form. Whatever we can't explain in this way must be eliminated, deflated, or, if we can't help talking about it as if it were real, we must invent fictionalized, expressivist, or quasi-realist modes of discourse through which we can say the same superstitious-sounding things but without having to mean any of them. This is the only way to keep at bay pernicious relics of the past: religion, metaphysics, and witchcraft.

The intended totalizing naturalistic picture is often reminiscent of the system of understanding whose limits Hegel meant to expose. It is a direct descendant, in fact. Perhaps for just this reason, many of them might include Hegel among the Picts, Mongolians, or other barbarians against whose incursions they mean to build their Great Wall, whose uncouth ways they would keep outside the gates of civilization.

The question Hegel's method and system raises is: Why should we suppose that the different sciences must relate to one another in this way? What if instead they represent distinct approaches to investigating the world, or parts of it, that do not, and never will, yield a single comprehensive and self-consistent picture? Nancy Cartwright, for example, offers us quite a different picture of what science gives us—a "dappled world," in which different methods, research projects, systems of conceptualization, and modeling are to be found. Each succeeds in telling us something important about reality, but what we get is not a single picture but a heterogeneous collage (Cartwright, 1999; a similar view was anticipated by Miller, 1988). Cartwright even suggests that the problems reconciling classical physics and quantum physics may have no consistent resolution (Cartwright, 1999, pp. 216–33).

A whole host of problems arise in the philosophy of mind and its relation to biology and neuroscience. Is there a prospect that neuroscience will give us a complete and convincing account of consciousness, or rational decision making, or semantic meaning and content? Many seem to think so, and regard those who are skeptical about this, and resistant to their attempts to offer such accounts, as obscurantists and disseminators of superstition. But what if the problems addressed by neuroscience are not compatible with our everyday mental concepts? Neuroscience may understand the workings of the brain and nervous system without ever offering us a replacement for our everyday conceptions of experience, or the conceptual systems through which we think about choice or communication. (For two examples of the latter approach, see McGinn, 1991, and Searle, 1992). The same might be true of morality or value-talk more generally, which naturalists often feel they have to reject, and then, if they prove indispensable, replicate and mimic.

But why suppose these scientistic projects are necessary? Common sense, and even old-fashioned philosophical theories (of mind, reason, morality), might be perfectly all right just as they are. They are not primitive folk-superstitions, like the notion that infectious diseases are caused by evil spirits rather than bacteria and viruses. They are simply our human way of understanding our lives as humanly meaningful. We may never have any way of uniting everything we know, in science or in everyday life, into a single coherent "naturalistic" picture of the world. Each domain of inquiry and theorizing may simply have its limits. I suggest that Hegel's conception of distinct thought-determinations, or systems of these, offers us a conception of how there might be a coherent view we could take of such a "dappled world" in the sciences, and in the relation of science to both old-fashioned philosophy and to everyday life. Let me call such a view "conceptual pluralism."

I am not suggesting, however, that conceptual pluralism as such, or the present-day philosophers I have cited, or others who might take the views I have just described, are "Hegelians." That would be false, even absurd. Hegel combined conceptual pluralism with a systematic philosophical theory about what the thought-determinations are, how they fit together in a hierarchy, and how we might even put them altogether into a single logical system. Hegel would give more order and system to our concepts than more recent philosophers would allow. Hegel's world is not 'dappled'; it is systematically ordered, because he thinks he has a way of systematizing the plurality of thought-determinations through which reality is to be grasped. Hegel also seems to represent the systematic ordering relations between thought-determinations as something discoverable merely by *thought*, which is not the intent of the more recent philosophers.

Some more recent philosophers might argue that conceptual pluralism does not preclude naturalism. The "dappled world," they might say, is still a natural world, the one studied by the empirical sciences. I think it is important to appreciate that Hegel would not disagree with that. But he would dissent from the view that this precludes recognizing the spiritual, or even precludes privileging the spiritual over the natural. This is because Hegel also had yet another suggestion I think is also worth taking seriously. He argues that the truer or higher conceptual systems are the more concrete and complex ones. The plurality of our conceptualizations can be systematized through a hierarchy that gives the more complex and concrete a higher place in our scheme of things than the simpler and more abstract. Hegel offers reinterpretation rather than elimination; Hegel's approach would puncture deflationism, leaving the spiritual puffed up at its original full volume.

To state the Hegelian position harshly and bluntly: the subject matters and methods of the arts and humanities—the cognitions afforded us by art, religion, and philosophy— are compatible with, but also superior to, those of what we now call the "natural sciences." The more spiritual subject matters are the truth of things; so the methods suited to them do a better job of getting at the truth of things. The philosophy of spirit supersedes the philosophy of nature. The study of objective spirit (society) is truer than subjective spirit (anthropology and psychology). The highest truth is gotten at by the highest spiritual activities of all, which are for Hegel (in ascending order), those of art, religion, and philosophy. Naturalists of course don't like to hear that sort of thing. It's just what they are in business to oppose. But I submit that in some form it is still a serious alternative to their dehumanizing scientistic program.

Hegel's view does reject the modern ideal of science that was born in the seventeenth century, which proposed to understand the complex by reducing it to the simple. Hegel's system, by contrast, privileges the complex, the more organized, over the elements of which the early modern conception of science would say it must be composed.

Hegel's view would imply, for instance, that elementary physics is not the key to all reality, but rather a highly abstract investigation of one way of looking pervasively at the material world. It has no privilege over chemistry, biology, psychology, or the study of society. Our ordinary concepts of consciousness, action, and meaning deal with realities of greater complexity than those studied by neurophysiology. They get at a higher truth. Neuroscience may eventually tell us a lot about how our brains and nervous systems operate. But it will not "explain" living consciousness; it will not take away or reduce rational choice or linguistic communication to something simpler, or transform moral value into something less real—such as a mere expression of emotions. We should not expect them to, since these humanly meaningful domains are higher and truer, and more truly grasped from a philosophical standpoint, than the simpler, more abstract truths about neurons, synapses, signaling mechanisms in the brain, and so on. It betrays a basic and pernicious misconception of our entire human existence for someone even to hope that art, religion, and philosophy will ever be explained (or explained away) by natural science.

As my answer to question 1 implies, I do not think we can accept Hegel's version of conceptual pluralism in its original form. Further, let's be clear: I am not saying the controversial views I have just drawn from Hegel are necessarily the right views. But I think they deserve to be seriously considered as options in dealing with the issues to which naturalists think they have (or *soon will have*) all the answers. We need to entertain the thought that neither neuroscience nor any other such empirical discipline provides any privileged key to what people do in the arts and humanities, or even to their actions in ordinary life, as these are experienced by the agents themselves and investigated by historians and philosophers. The Hegelian position, as just sketched, is at least a possible tentative conclusion, based on what naturalistic or scientistic programs have been like so far. It should always be open-minded and receptive to new evidence.

Of course Hegel belongs to an earlier stage of the history of science and philosophy than the one where we are now. We cannot simply look at Hegel's own writings and doctrines for the right answers to our questions. That's my negative answer to question (1) again. But when we study Hegel, we have to understand his thoughts in the context of the system and method he formulated. That's why I don't want to "quarantine" his philosophy of right from his system, or refuse to take his system into account when understanding his ethics. I never did intend any such thing. It's why I answer question (2) in the affirmative: I am not a "non-systematic" or "anti-systematic" *reader of Hegel*. I never was.

4.8. Implications for Hegel's Philosophy of Right

Now at last I turn to Hegel's philosophy of right and ethics. Hegel's hierarchical version of conceptual pluralism is to be found in his philosophy of objective spirit—his philosophy of right—just as it is found elsewhere. Social life and the norms that belong to it form a plurality of different systems and subsystems, whose limitations are signaled by the fact that a way of thinking, when pushed beyond its limits, falls into contradiction and becomes self-undermining. Objective spirit involves three distinct and hierarchically ordered ways of looking at the rational norms that apply to us as social beings. These are abstract right, morality, and ethical life. Within each, there are also distinct phases or levels: abstract right begins with persons and property (PR §§34–70), passes over into contractual relationships between persons (PR §§71–80), and ends with wrong or injustice (PR §§81–103). Morality involves the free agency of the individual subject (PR §§105–28) passes into the pursuit of the good (PR §§129–38), and ends with evil (PR §§139–40). Ethical life, the highest and most concrete sphere of objective spirit, combines abstract right and morality and gives each its place within a more complex and concrete conception of modern social life. But the three spheres of right are each in its own way self-contained and incommensurable. To look at things from the perspective of persons and their rights is a way of looking at them that is separate from looking at them from the perspective of moral subjects. In this way, Hegel captures the distinctness and independence of right and morality that he inherited from Kant and Fichte. Even within ethical life, right and morality each retain their validity. Morality is a higher sphere than abstract right, but this shows itself only at the margins, where the totality of the subject's life gives rise to a right of necessity that overrides the abstract right of property (PR §§127–8); this is the point at which morality itself passes over from imputability to pursuit of the good (PR §129).

Ethical life too has its distinct spheres: family (PR §§158–80), civil society (PR §§182–256), and the state (PR §§257–320). These spheres are separate, like distinct conceptualizations, and can come into conflict. In the ancient world, Hegel thinks that the tragic conflict between the family and the state was dramatized in Sophocles' *Antigone* (PhG ¶¶471–5). In the modern world, these two phases of ethical life are mediated by a third institution—civil society—which also realizes the distinctively modern conceptions of personality (in abstract right) and subjective freedom (in morality). Civil society has its own distinct phases: the economic system (PR §§189–208), the legal system (PR §§209–29), and the social system (PR §§230–56). Each sphere of social life has its limitations: the family is limited by the death of its head and the maturation of children, who leave it to form families of their own (PR §§177–80); civil society is limited by the fact that its highest social institution, the corporation, has only limited and not universal ends (PR §256), which are found only in the state. (The problem of *poverty* is not for Hegel this limit. Hegel has no way of accommodating the problem of poverty within his system, and he knew it. We will return to this point later.) The state is limited by its relation to other states (PR §§330–40) and by the transitoriness of the shape of spirit it actualizes, which is exhibited as its place in world history (PR §§341–60).

An important part of Hegel's philosophical message in the *Philosophy of Right* is that there are inevitable tensions between the different conceptualizations of social life.

The ethical sphere itself is of limited validity, and not all its problems have solutions—matters I explored in *Hegel's Ethical Thought* (especially chapters 13 and 14, but also elsewhere, in treating the limits of abstract right and morality). To appreciate these tensions, one must understand them as Hegel derives them systematically. To the extent that Hegel's systematic program offers a solution to them, it does so by trying to locate the limited or abstract spheres harmoniously within the higher and more concrete ones. The legal system of civil society, for example, is the concrete form assumed by the abstract rights of persons (PR §§208–9). In the educative value of labor (PR §§194–7), in the contingent actions of people responding to one another's needs (PR §207) and in the social phase of civil society, both through state action (PR §230) and in the activity of one's calling or profession (PR §§251–3), moral subjectivity finds its proper place. Throughout Hegel's system, there is an attempt to acknowledge the distinctness and even the incommensurability of the different phases of right, or objective freedom (PR §29).

There are two ways to look at Hegel's project here. First, we can see it as an insistence that rational standards of right and morality should receive concrete expression in an entire social way of life. But also, second, insofar as Hegel is trying to demonstrate the rationality of the actual in the modern state, we can see it as an attempt to show that modern social institutions, more or less as they exist, do fulfill the more abstract demands of right and morality. This second way of looking at Hegel's project displays its most problematic features. For it is not at all clear that people's rights or aspirations to subjective freedom were even close to being properly actualized in the European state of 1820, or in the society in which we live today. To the extent that Hegel is offering a defense of the way his society treats women, or peasants, or wage laborers, we can see the clear limitations of his theory of modern society. As Hegel presents things, the benefits of both right and morality are enjoyed only by a minority of the members of society—in effect, by the male bourgeoisie and civil servants—the young men, and their fathers, whose social position was like that of Hegel himself and of those to whom he lectured. The inadequacy of that society, as Hegel portrays it, even by the standards of his own theory of freedom, is all too clear today.

The one area in which Hegel seems to have been painfully aware of this is in his treatment of poverty in civil society (PR §§240–6). He recognizes that modern civil society systematically produces a "rabble"—as it was later described by Marx: a class *in* civil society that is not *of* civil society. These are people whose abstract rights are violated by their condition of life, and who are excluded from the spiritual achievements of modernity (morality, ethical life, art, religion, philosophy). They therefore reject the only world that can have actuality for anyone. Marx optimistically hoped that they could be formed into a revolutionary class that abolishes class society and realizes our humanity. Hegel was not optimistic. He saw the rabble as a terrible danger to everything we regard as rational in modern society. I think that on this point, the horrific appeal to alienated groups of twentieth century movements like fascism and Nazism, and twenty-first century movements like jihadist terrorism and white supremacist political nihilism show that Hegel's pessimism was more likely correct.

The rabble in modern society is a class of people who are systematically produced by the economic relations of civil society, are not eligible for corporation membership (PR §243), and whose plight the "police" function of the state has no adequate means of addressing (PR §245). Its very existence constitute a wrong or injustice done by one class to another (PR §244R). Hegel uses poverty to explain colonization, but he does not see it as a solution (PR §§246–8). He even sees that there is no solution. Hegel's final word on the topic (in an Addition from his lectures of 1824–5) is this: "One can claim no right against nature, but within the conditions of society, hardship at once assumes the form of a wrong inflicted on this or that class (*Klasse*). The important question of how poverty can be remedied is one which agitates and torments modern societies especially" (PR §244A). This is still just as true two centuries later.

It is a tribute to Hegel's intellectual honesty that he did not shrink from identifying a social problem to which his own system has no solution. If such an admission is "anti-systematic," then Hegel himself was anti-systematic when the facts required it. I think we can now see that this problem is only one of many problems to which modern society has no solution. So there is also no solution within the framework of the concepts and institutions Hegel presents in the *Philosophy of Right*. We should be "anti-systematic" readers of Hegel too, at least in that sense, when we apply his philosophy to the real world. Hegel does not have the answer to the problems of modernity. Nobody does.

Hegel scorns Fichte's philosophy of an "ought to be" that stands over against the actual world and threatens our capacity to become intellectually reconciled with it (PR Preface, §57, EL §§6, 234). But it is difficult for any honest person to avoid Fichte's conclusion—if we can be reconciled with existing social reality at all, it must be only conditionally and provisionally; we cannot rationally be content with the world as it actually is: "Any constitution of the state is in accord with right which does not make it impossible to progress toward something better…Only that constitution is completely contrary to right which has the end of preserving everything as it presently is" (SW 4: 361). If Hegel's philosophy really aims at reconciling us with the modern world, we must reject it. For the modern world is not reconcilable to itself.

Any appropriation of Hegel's philosophy, therefore, must depend *both* on understanding it in its own systematic connections, and also on reading Hegel (as we should read any philosopher) critically, with a recognition of the historical limits of the philosopher's vision. We can never take over any past philosopher's system without critique and modification. All the real and interesting questions are about how best to do these two things in tandem. There is no choice between reading Hegel "systematically" and reading him "anti-systematically." We have to do both at once. To which of our questions does Hegel offer us interesting approaches? And which aspects of his philosophy—in the case of a thoroughly systematic philosopher like Hegel, which aspects of his method and system—should we use in discovering and explicating those approaches? Those are questions that must always be answered in detail. They are trivialized, and even treated with contempt, if we pose them as if we faced an "either/or" of accepting the whole of Hegel's system uncritically or else trying to read his ethics and political philosophy entirely apart from the context of his system.

Abbreviations
Writings of Hegel

EL   *Enzyklopädie der philosophischen Wissenschaften: Logik, Werke* 8. Cited by paragraph (§) number.

PhG   *Phänomenologie des Geistes, Werke* 3. Cited by paragraph (¶) number in the A.V. Miller translation. Oxford: Oxford Press, 1977.

PR   *Grundlinien der Philosophie des Rechts, Werke* 7. Cited by paragraph (§) number; "R" means "Remark"; "A" means "Addition."

Werke   *Hegel: Werke: Theoriewerkausgabe.* Frankfurt: Suhrkamp, 1970. Cited by volume:page number.

Writings of Fichte

SW   (1970) *Fichtes Sammtliche Werke*, edited by I. H. Fichte. Berlin: deGruyter. Cited by volume: page number.

References

Beiser, Frederick (2005). *Hegel*. London: Routledge.

Beiser, Frederick (2011). *The German Historicist Tradition*. Oxford: Oxford University Press.

Brooks, Thom (2007). *Hegel's Political Philosophy: A Systematic Reading of the Philosophy of Right*. Edinburgh: Edinburgh University Press.

Cartwright, Nancy (1999). *The Dappled World: A Study of the Boundaries of Science*. Cambridge: Cambridge University Press.

Goodfield, Eric Lee (2014). *Hegel and the Metaphysical Frontiers of Political Theory*. London: Routledge.

Houlgate, Stephen (1992). "Hegel's Ethical Thought," *Bulletin of the Hegel Society of Great Britain*, 13, 1: 1–17.

Keynes, John Maynard (2007). *The General Theory of Employment, Interest and Money*. London: Macmillan.

McGinn, Colin (1991). *The Problem of Consciousness*. Oxford: Blackwell.

Miller, Richard W. (1988). *Fact and Method: Confirmation and Reality in the Natural and Social Sciences*. Princeton: Princeton University Press.

Priest, Graham (2006). *In Contradiction*, 2nd edition. Oxford: Oxford University Press.

Quante, Michael (2004). *Hegel's Concept of Action*, tr. Dean Moyar. Cambridge: Cambridge University Press.

Redding, Paul (2007). *Analytic Philosophy and the Return of Hegelian Thought*. Cambridge: Cambridge University Press.

Searle, John (1992). *The Rediscovery of the Mind*. Cambridge, MA: MIT Press.

Taylor, Charles (1975). *Hegel*. Cambridge: Cambridge University Press.

Wood, Allen (1990). *Hegel's Ethical Thought*. New York: Cambridge University Press.

Wood, Allen (2016). *Fichte's Ethical Thought*. Oxford: Oxford University Press.

5

The Relevance of the Logical Method for Hegel's Practical Philosophy

Angelica Nuzzo

Of the entire outline of the system of philosophy that Hegel sketches out in the three editions of the *Encyclopedia of the Philosophical Sciences* (1817, 1827, 1830), the only two parts to which he has accorded a separate and more extensive treatment in independent book form are the logic and the political philosophy, which famously have been published respectively as the two volumes of the *Science of Logic* (1812–16) and the *Groundwork of the Philosophy of Right* (1820). If we take even a cursory look at the history of the interpretations of Hegel's philosophy, we can easily ascertain that these two works have at least one significant general trait in common. Considering these books in their own right, interpreters have often used their apparent self-enclosed independency as a tacit authorization to read and appraise them apart from the overarching systematic structure offered by the *Encyclopedia*. Significantly, this choice has generally been made in conjunction with the interpretive rejection (differently motivated and justified) of Hegel's philosophical system, which has often been considered a forceful, totalizing constraint on the work of philosophy. At the same time, however, interpreters have manifested a pervasive uneasiness as to the clear disciplinary qualification of both works, again taken in their isolation from each other and from the overarching philosophical system. The *Science of Logic* is obviously and explicitly declared a logic but, interpreters do not tire to ask, what kind of logic is this? And is it really or properly a "logic" or is it rather a metaphysics or maybe even something else (maybe a hidden theology or an anticipation or repetition of the *Realphilosophie* which supposedly must follow)? What, after all, have titles such as "the absolute," "mechanism," and "chemism" to do with logic proper? On the other hand, turning to the *Philosophy of Right*, a clear-cut classification of the disciplinary field covered by this work also continues to elude the interpreter. Herein Hegel develops a theory of "objective spirit"—this is the clear suggestion of the *Encyclopedia*. But then, if we look at what this theory entails we have to acknowledge that its content is hardly reducible to a straightforward practical philosophy, ethics, or moral theory at least in the canonical sense that these disciplines have received in Aristotle's or Kant's aftermath, although it may be rightly seen as encompassing them all with the addition of a theory of right and justice, a social and political philosophy, and even an action theory, an applied ethics, and a philosophy of history. In short, there seem to be way too much material and way too many fields that Hegel's *Philosophy of Right* attempts to cover—too much in order for it to be reduced to either an ethics or a moral philosophy or a political theory in the proper sense. And why, to top it off, a philosophy of history? What is the relation that supposedly connects all these fields to constitute a "philosophy of right"?

From this interpretive predicament I wish to draw two very general conclusions, which constitute the framework and starting point of my present considerations. First, it is clear in my view that in both cases—both for the *Logic* and the *Philosophy of Right*—the fault leading to these problems lies not in Hegel but in the interpreter's lack of a systematic perspective in which to inscribe the demonstrative program and the overall argument of both works, i.e. ultimately, in the lack of a principle by which to understand how and why certain contents are dealt with by Hegel in the way and systematic place they are. In short, by ignoring the overall systematic structure in which Hegel's *Logic* and *Philosophy of Right* are inscribed interpreters remain alternatively puzzled or clueless with regard to the peculiarity and novelty of Hegel's dialectic-speculative logic on the one hand, and of his theory of objective spirit on the other—and this in relation to the tradition as well as to contemporary developments of the respective disciplines. But the second conclusion is also important for my present purposes. It is significant that while both works share this common interpretive predicament, they are very rarely considered together or in connection with each other. The tendency seems rather the opposite when the *Philosophy of Right* is at stake, while it generally goes without saying that there is nothing to be gained by bringing Hegel's practical philosophy to bear on the reading of the *Logic*. Indeed, following Hegel's own apparent exhortation, the view is that his *Logic* should be approached leaving all the content of the real world—the natural as well as the human and spiritual world—out or behind. After all, the logic is described as the presentation of the "realm of shadows, [as] the world of simple essences free of all sensible concretions," i.e. as shadows taken in abstraction from the real, worldly objects to which those shadows belong (TW 5, 55).[1] In the case of the *Philosophy of Right*, by contrast, the relation to the *Logic* is harder to ignore as Hegel very often explicitly refers to it. Such reference, however, is not easy to interpret—and in the end the interpretive choice seems generally to be that it's better to ignore it entirely than to remain entangled in it trying to understand its significance.

What I set out to do in this chapter is begin to correct the shortcomings of this interpretive situation. Accordingly, I bring to the center the heretofore either ignored or

---

[1] Hegel's works are cited according to *Werke in zwanzig Bände*, ed. E. Moldenhauer and H. M. Michel, Frankfurt a.M., Surhkamp, 1986 (=TW) followed by volume and page or section number.

inadequately framed deep systematic connection between Hegel's *Logic* and the *Philosophy of Right* in order to shed light, at the same time, on the peculiar nature of both his logic and his theory of objective spirit.[2] My aim is to set up this relation from both sides, namely, as a relation that concerns the logic as much as the political philosophy—or as a relation that ultimately leads to discover the "practical" (and indeed political) significance of the logic as much as the "logical" significance of Hegel's practical philosophy. Clearly, I must limit myself here to a discussion of the general programmatic aim of both works. I am interested, in particular, in the way in which the relation between the two is established (i) on the basis of Hegel's idea of philosophy as "system," and (ii) on the basis of his conception of the philosophical "method." I shall address these topics in the first two sections of my argument. In the last section, I turn to the problem of clarifying the status of Hegel's logic and on this basis its relation to the theory of objective spirit. What is Hegel's dialectic-speculative logic properly *about*? And what is its relation to the practical—ethical, social, political— philosophy that Hegel develops in the *Philosophy of Right* but which is prepared by important episodes of the *Phenomenology of Spirit*? What is the systematic and methodological *necessity* of this relation? I will argue for two claims. First, I maintain that the fruitfulness and vitality of Hegel's practical philosophy—understood as including an ethics, a social and political philosophy, and a philosophy of history as necessary moments of the process of freedom's actualization—depend both on its being conceived as a part of the system of philosophy and on its being based on and articulated according to the dialectical-speculative method developed in the *Logic* as the first and foundational part of the system. Second, I argue that the "absolute method" that concludes the *Logic* presents the structure of a "logic of action."[3] Now, since the *Logic* is immanently developed according to the same method that, in its very conclusion, is brought to thematic focus—or, since the method is already operative *before* it can be thematized (and in order for it to be thematized)—the logical develop- ment itself must be seen as the development of a "logic of action" and thereby as the foundational moment of Hegel's *practical* philosophy. Since the logic is fundamentally (yet also formally) concerned with the basic structures of *action*[4] it constitutes the sys- tematic and methodological basis on which the *Philosophy of Right* articulates the *same* structures in their specific ethical, political, social, and historical significance. I argue that while in the *Logic* action is presented in its pure forms, independently of the nature, position, and historical constitution of the agent that carries it out, in the philosophy of objective spirit—in the spheres of right, morality, ethical life, politics,

---

[2] I have dedicated a book to the problem of the relation between Hegel's *Logic* and the *Philosophy of Right*, see my *Rappresentazione e concetto nella "logica" della Filosofia del diritto di Hegel*, Napoli, Guida, 1990. In the present considerations, however, my perspective is different, and one of the crucial differences consists in the need to read such a relation back into the *Logic* itself.

[3] I have developed an argument in favor of this claim in my "Hegel's Logic of Action," in: *Hegel on Logic and Politics*, ed. E. Ficara, forthcoming.

[4] The meaning of this purely logical "action" will be defined later, but see also my "Hegel's Logic of Action."

and history—action is qualified in relation to the specific forms assumed by spirit as the agent of that action.[5]

5.1. The "Philosophical Science of Right" and the System of Philosophy

In the introduction to the successive editions of the *Encyclopedia*, Hegel consistently brings to the center the systematic character of philosophy. Unlike previous and contemporary encyclopedias, however, Hegel's work does not assume systematicity as an extrinsic organizing principle for already given contents and material (empirically given or provided by the tradition). Rather, systematicity is for Hegel the immanent principle that first institutes philosophy as "science";[6] it is the internal, constitutive, and truly generative principle of the content itself. That philosophy as science is "essentially system" means that philosophy constitutes a "totality" (Enz. §14) or a "whole" of homogeneous parts, i.e. of parts that are themselves systematic wholes. Indeed, already in the *Phenomenology of Spirit* (1807) Hegel had advanced the famous claim that "truth" itself which is the sole object of philosophy is the "whole," and as the whole it is "actual" only in the form of a "system" (TW 3, 24, 28). This claim is based on Hegel's conviction (against Schelling and contemporary advocates of "intellectual intuition," for example) that at stake in philosophy as science is *discursive* thinking, i.e. thinking insofar as it is engaged in an ongoing process of self-production and self-actualization through finite, limited, hence contradictory forms in which different modes of finitude, limitation, and contradiction are successively and progressively corrected and overcome. Importantly, this is also, at the same time, the model of Hegel's conception of freedom. Freedom just as truth is a discrete, dynamic, ongoing process of self-production and self-actualization. Now the "system" (or systematic "whole") is the form that such process takes as it acquires objective reality—in knowledge, in action, in history. It is neither a static result that can be considered apart from the process that has led to it, nor is it a merely abstract form in which independently given contents may be taken up in order to be rendered intelligible.

Hegel famously describes the systematic structure of philosophy as "a circle of circles" (Enz. §15). Each part of the whole stages the movement of a circle the end of which, bending back to its beginning, is also the beginning of a new sphere or part of philosophy. Thereby the interconnection of the homogeneous parts of the whole is provided. Just as the overarching totality of the system, "[e]ach part of philosophy is a philosophical whole, a circle that closes up on itself." What distinguishes each part—or

---

[5] As I shall argue, this thesis is set as an alternative to the usual views according to which the *Logic* is either successively "applied" to the real world in the *Realphilosophie* or is the presentation of mere abstract forms to be then filled with the concrete content of the world. In sum, I reject both the idea of application and the abstract-concrete relation as adequate descriptions of the relation between Hegel's *Logic* and his practical philosophy.

[6] See for example Enz. §14 Remark: "To philosophy *without system* can never be a scientific activity."

philosophical disciple—in its topical specificity within the system is the fact that "the philosophical idea is present in it *in a particular determination or element*" (Enz. §15—my emphasis). While the "idea" is omnipresent throughout the whole (it is, as Hegel claims in the *Logic*, the "soul" or animating principle of the whole: TW 5, 17; 6, 551), its specific determination within a particular mode of reality is the topic of the different, successive disciplines or "circles" of the whole. Moreover, given that the systematic structure is not the structure of a static entity but the dynamic unfolding of a movement, Hegel underscores the importance of the point of connection—or rather of "transition"—between the successive circles constituting the systematic whole. "The single circle, being in itself a totality, breaks the limits of its element and grounds a further sphere" (Enz. §15). Now, the "idea" is first thematized in its "pure" structure or form—in its "in and for itself"—in the movement of the logic, which thereby constitutes the first, foundational discipline of the system. According to its circular structure, in its end the logic "breaks" the limits of its specific "element" (which is "*das Logische*": Enz. §79) and produces the beginning of a new systematic sphere. This sphere, which finds the idea in the element of its "otherness," is the realm of nature; its scientific thematization belongs to the philosophy of nature. The latter leads to the transition to the last circle, which stages the process of the idea's return to itself from its otherness (Enz. §18). This is the realm of spirit to which "objective spirit" belongs as its intermediary moment. Thereby Hegel offers the basic and broadest division of his encyclopedic system of philosophy. But in this way he also brings to light the fundamental relation that connects the logic—as the science of the idea in its purely formal structure or "in and for itself"—to the philosophy of spirit in which the logical idea is present and articulated in a specific determination or "element."

If we now turn to the opening of the *Philosophy of Right* we find these general encyclopedic considerations regarding the systematic structure of philosophy reflected in and confirmed by Hegel's more specific account of the place that the philosophy of *objective* spirit or, more precisely, "the philosophical science of right" ("*die philosophische Rechtswissenschaft*": R §1) occupies within the systematic whole. Moreover those encyclopedic remarks are also reflected in the account of the dialectic-speculative methodological principles by which, on Hegel's view, the development of the science of right should be guided in order to fulfill the function ascribed to it within the whole. Hegel's distance from traditional and contemporary accounts of natural right as well as contemporary empiricist and positivist views on the topic is measured precisely by this methodological position.[7] Significantly, following the encyclopedic claim examined earlier, Hegel's initial presentation of the scope and range of the "philosophical science of right" is also an account of the way in which the *logical* idea is now specifically determined as the "*idea of right*," i.e. as the idea in the peculiar "element" defining the sphere of objective spirit. In other words, at stake is the account of the way in which the juridical, ethical, and political realms emerge as a

---

[7] See for a general account, the preface and R §3 Remark.

"particular determination" (Enz. §15) of the logical reality of the idea. It is thereby clear that both the *systematic* position that the philosophical science of right occupies within the whole of philosophy and the *methodological* relation to the logic are of chief concern for Hegel at the outset of his presentation of the sphere of objective spirit. At stake is the problem of how this relation is carried out within the development of this science—within its own inner systematic articulation. But at stake is also the question of what this connection says of the nature of the logical idea itself in its intra-logical development. What is it in the structure and development of the logical idea that lends itself to its further determination within the element of spirit's objective—ethical, juridical, political, historical—manifestations? This latter is the side of the problem that is never addressed in the literature.

Hegel's most general assessment of the scope of the philosophical science of right is rife with systematic and logical references. Its topic is summed up in a deceivingly simple statement: such science, Hegel maintains, "has the concept of right and its realization (*Verwirklichung*) as its object" (R §1). This claim cannot be understood without the reference to the *Logic*—which, in point of fact, immediately follows. Since what we have here is a *philosophical* science of right (and not a haphazard empirical or positivistic description of what counts right), at stake are not mere ineffectual "concepts" (i.e. "abstract determinations of the understanding," or unilateral, static, non-dialectical representations—of "right, freedom, property, the state," for example: handwritten remark to R §1). At stake is rather the "concept" (*Begriff*) taken in the dialectic-speculative meaning of the term. And the concept in this sense is that which (and that which "alone") has "actuality" (*Wirklichkeit*) in the proper sense of being efficacious and effective, of having objective reality as the crystallized form of an efficacious activity. This is precisely what the logic teaches: the concept is that which is actual on the ground that "it gives itself actuality." What the philosophical science of right sets out to do then is to articulate this *same* claim once the reality at issue (or the reality that the concept gives itself) is the specific reality displayed by the *concept of right*. And here Hegel emphasizes that since at issue is the "concept" of right, it is its "actuality" and not its merely contingent existence in arbitrary opinions and representations, and in ineffectual, impermanent institutions, that should come to the fore. How does the concept of right "give itself actuality"—how does this "actualization" or "realization" take place and in which forms? This is the guiding question on which the systematic articulation of the *Philosophy of Right* is based. And this question concerns the specific "figuration" (*Gestaltung*) that the *logical* concept attains as the concept *of right*. Thereby Hegel offers not only the central methodological thread underlying the development of the science of right but also an important clue as to how we should go back to the *Logic*. With regard to the "knowledge of the concept," he claims, "the *figuration* that the concept gives itself in its realization" within the sphere of right "is the other essential moment of the idea, distinct from the *form* of being only as *concept*" (R §1). Two points on this. First, by taking the logical paradigm as his basis Hegel claims that the topic or specific "object" of the philosophical science of right is the "concept of right" in its "realization"—and the *Logic* teaches that the concept realized is the idea, or that the idea is the concept that in and by its action gives itself reality. Second, he insists that once we are dealing with the specific concept *of right*—and not only with the logical "form" of "being only as concept"—we are set to explore the other essential side or moment of the idea of which the logical form constitutes the necessary complement. While the first claim sets the *Logic* as the basis of the philosophical science of right, the latter suggests that the two are complementary investigations on the actuality of the idea—the logic offering the display of its *formal* side, the science of right developing its more specific, concrete *figuration* in the various manifestations of right. In this latter perspective, given the equal standing of the two disciplines, the science of right may indeed represent a way of going back to the logical idea that allows one to gain a new insight into the meaning of the logical development itself.

Confirming yet again the systematic conception of philosophy as "circle of circles"[8] outlined in the introduction to the *Encyclopedia*, after having identified the "philosophical science of right" through its object, Hegel proceeds to define it as a "part" of the philosophical whole. Since "[t]he science of right is a *part of philosophy*," it has its own "determinate *starting point* (*Anfangspunkt*), which is the *result* and the truth of that which precedes it and which constitutes its very proof" (R §2). As part of the systematic whole, the science of right is itself systematic. This offers a twofold methodological insight: on the one hand this science must develop its object immanently or follow the "immanent development of its topic (*Sache selbst*)," while on the other hand such development is enclosed between a starting point which is deduced from the preceding systematic sphere and an end result that constitutes in turn both the actual proof of its beginning and the transition to a new systematic sphere. This means, importantly, that the argument of the science of right is not a proof of the claim presented at the outset. For, this has already been demonstrated or indeed "deduced" in its truth in the previous systematic sphere (i.e. in the philosophy of subjective spirit) and now it is (and can be) assumed as "given" (R §2). Its argument is, instead, the "deduction" of its end result which, in turn, constitutes the beginning of the following systematic sphere (i.e. of the realm of absolute spirit). Such an end result is the concept of "world history." This systematic point is evidently crucial for the correct understanding of the demonstrative task of the *Philosophy of Right*. And this means that its entire argument is misunderstood if the connection to the system is left out.

Let's look briefly at the beginning and the end of the systematic circle the presentation of which is the task of the "philosophical science of right." These are also the systematic points (or the "transitions") in which the philosophy of objective spirit intersects with the preceding sphere of subjective spirit and the following realm of absolute spirit. The "element" (Enz. §15) and the "ground" (*Boden*) (R §4) on which the

---

[8] Enz. §15 is confirmed by R §2 Zusatz: "Philosophy constitutes a circle."

science of right develops is "*das Geistige.*" Its "point of inception" (*Ausgangspunkt*) is the "will that is free." This latter is the result that having been demonstrated—or indeed "deduced"—by the development of the sphere of subjective spirit now translates in the claim "that freedom constitutes the substance and determination [of the will] and the system of right is the realm of realized freedom (*verwirklichten Freiheit*), the world of spirit produced out of spirit itself as a second nature" (R §4). Thereby Hegel indicates the fundamental meaning of spirit's *objectivity*. Freedom is not just the (still abstract and unrealized) freedom of the subjective (individual) will; it is realized and actualized freedom, i.e. freedom that gains objectivity as the "system of right" and as "world"— the objective, collective, institutional world underlying its specification in ethical, juridical political structures. Here again Hegel's position in detailing the specific realm of the science of right matches the general view of philosophy presented in the *Encyclopedia*. In the introduction to the latter, Hegel claims that philosophy's "topic (*Inhalt*) is none other than the basic content (*Gehalt*) that has originally been produced and that produces itself in the realms of the living spirit, a content (*Gehalt*) made into a *world*, namely, the outer and inner world of consciousness." In sum, Hegel concludes, "the topic (*Inhalt*) of philosophy is *actuality* (*Wirklichkeit*)" (Enz. §6). Traditional ontology—or the idea of philosophy as the science of being *qua* being—is thereby transformed into an immanent conception of reality, where reality is the constructed and self-produced actuality of the "living spirit," realized and wholly manifested in the objectivity of a "world." Such a world, however, far from being a transcendent (cosmo-logical) object or an antinomic idea set beyond the limits of experience (as it is instead for Kant) is constitutively permeated by consciousness—it is consciousness' own, self-produced internal and external reality. We can see in this way that Hegel's conception of "objective thinking" (Enz. §25, Remark) that is the basis of his dialectic-speculative logic (which replaces traditional metaphysics and Kant's critique thereof), is also the generative point of his conception of "objective spirit" as the realm of freedom's ethical, social, political, and historical actualization. In a significant reversal, justified by the homogeneity between the part and the whole in a system, here Hegel defines the whole through the part and not vice versa. Accordingly, the topic of philosophy is the same objective actuality of spirit that occupies the philosophical science of right.

In its conclusion, the *Philosophy of Right* discloses the conflicted realm of international right and world-history. This is the broadest extension reached by freedom's realiza-tion in spirit's objective world. It is not, however, Hegel's last word on the topic. Beyond—and higher than—world-history as history of the political state, freedom continues its realization-process in the sphere of absolute spirit, in the productions of art, in the representations of religion, in the work of philosophy. The task of the *Philosophy of Right* is precisely to generate this end-result, namely, to show the intrinsic limitation of the universality achieved by freedom's historical actualization.[9]

---

[9] A detailed argument on this is to be found in my *Memory, History, Justice in Hegel*, New York and London, Palgrave Macmillan, 2012, chapter 4.

5.2. Method and Hegel's Logic as a 'Logic of Action'

We need to turn now to Hegel's conception of the *logical* method. I argued earlier that some general traits of the methodological structure of Hegel's "science of right" can be inferred from its belonging to the overall system of philosophy. The fact that this particular science is a part of the overarching system, and that it stages, in turn, a systematic development gives a first hint regarding the method that the philosophical presentation of freedom's actualization in spirit's objective world should follow. Within the system, however, the thematic place where Hegel discusses the "method" is the last chapter of the *Logic*. Herein Hegel discloses the method that has been at work throughout the movement of logical determination reaching its conclusion. The "absolute method" has immanently shaped the logical process from the unutterable immediacy of "pure being" identical with "nothing" to the complex determinations of thinking and acting developed in the forms of the "concept" up to its realization to the "idea."[10] The retrospective question left to explore at the end of the work can be summed up as follows. How has the method carried on the function of pushing the process on up to the point in which thinking self-reflectively comes to think of the method itself as that which has enabled this very reflection? In a general approximation, "method" is indeed for Hegel what Marcel Granet's imaginary etymology suggests: *metà odòs*, "after the road"—the method shows the road traveled after one has traveled it. This view finds an important confirmation in the famous claim of the preface to the *Philosophy of Right* regarding the retrospective character of philosophical knowledge with regard to the historical reality that it attempts to comprehend. Hegel famously maintains that "thought *of the world*" philosophy is necessarily bound to its historical present. This is even truer for a reflection on the world *of spirit*, on a world that is the product of spirit's activity and owes its actuality to the activity that has produced it. And yet Hegel warns that in relation to the historical reality its conceptual comprehension emerges always "too late." In such delay consists the specificity of the *philosophical* comprehension of spirit's world in contrast, for instance, to political activity. Hegel insists that as the rational comprehension of the world of spirit, philosophy "appears only at a time when actuality has gone through its formative process and has attained its completed state" (TW 7, 27f.). In an important sense, the delay or discrepancy whereby the logical method can be thematized only after it has produced its results, the discrepancy whereby the road traveled can be reconstructed in its entire length only after one has traveled it, and *Wirklichkeit* can be philosophically grasped only once the action or *Wirken* taking place in it has taken a full and concluded shape—this delay is intrinsically connected to the process-like nature of all action as such, and of *discursive* thinking's action in the first place. Now the latter is precisely the topic of Hegel's logic.

---

[10] For a detailed account of this movement and the last chapter of the *Logic* see my "The End of Hegel's Logic: Absolute Idea as Absolute Method," in: *Hegel's Theory of the Subject*, ed. David G. Carlson, London, Palgrave Macmillan, 2005, 187–205.

I have suggested elsewhere viewing Hegel's logic as a "logic of transformative processes." If contrasted against the aims and accomplishments of both Kant's transcendental logic and traditional formal logic, Hegel's dialectic-speculative logic is the only one that accounts for the dynamic of real *processes as processes*: natural, psychological, but also social, political, and historical processes. It is a logic that attempts to think of change and transformation in their dynamic flux not by fixating movement in abstract static descriptions but by *performing movement itself*. This performance is the "action" that first institutes thinking in its developmental, properly discursive nature. By bringing change to bear directly on pure thinking, by making thinking one with the movement it accounts for, Hegel's logic *does* the very thing that it purports to understand and describe (or it describes it precisely by doing it). The only way to understand change without turning it into its opposite is to take change upon oneself, that is, to perform it. Thereby the question of the intelligibility of actuality taken in its purely logical forms becomes an issue of praxis as much as one of theory. The descriptive function that the logic claims toward actuality goes hand in hand with a fundamentally normative and pragmatic function that concerns the action whereby transformations are actually (and rationally) produced. Thereby, the doctrine that Hegel finally consigns to the *Science of Logic* and the first part of the *Encyclopaedia* differs methodologically from the development staged in the *Phenomenology of Spirit*, which still distinguished the static, external standpoint of the philosophical "we" from the ever-changing, experiential position of consciousness. Unlike the *Phenomenology*, Hegel's logic is the logic of movement itself immanently enacted in its pure or purely formal structures. On the other hand, however, within Hegel's system, this is also what distinguishes the logic from the philosophy of nature and spirit. The logic offers an account (and a performance) of the structures of action independently of the question of what it is that acts, i.e. it takes transformative action in the constellation of its pure forms, independently of the subject that brings it about, independently of the concrete object in which change occurs, and independently of the particular contingent and empirical conditions under which it occurs. In this framework I suggest viewing the pure, immanent development of the logic as the "action" taking place in it. This is the action performed by pure thinking but is also the action by which pure thinking is first constituted in what it properly is. In other words, there is no *res cogitans*, no "I think"—no substantial, transcendental, phenomenological subject—that pre-exists the articulation of the action in which thinking itself, being identical with the discursive process or activity of thinking, is first developed. There is only the immanent unfolding of the action as a pure process without a pre-existing agent. At the end of the logic, such action in its accomplished developmental structure proves to be thinking retrospectively reflecting on the process—or indeed the pathway—of its own constitution. And this is the logical method.

The method, explains Hegel at the beginning of the Absolute Idea chapter, "may initially appear" in its common, more restricted sense, to be "the mere modality of cognition." And this it certainly is. However, the method comes to the fore once the "absolute idea" has been proved to be the identity of the still "one-sided" positions of the theoretical and the practical idea—the "idea of the true" and the "idea of the good" (TW 6, 548). Unlike the "logic of the understanding" (i.e. Kant's transcendental logic and traditional formal logic), dialectic-speculative logic presents the method from a position that has finally overcome the separation of theory and praxis (as well as the separation of concept and reality). Accordingly, method is not a provisional "instrument" for achieving the truth (TW 6, 552) dispensable once truth has allegedly been gained. Method is instead a position *inside* truth and constitutive of it; it is the form of truth's dynamic and systematic articulation. Thus the "absolute method" is that which the "absolute idea" properly turns out to be. It is a new *form* in which the determinations heretofore produced are thought again and are thought anew—are thought now "after the road," as it were, that is, as the pathway leading up to their reflective thematization. Hegel's insistence, then, is on the meaning of the "modality" (the *Art und Weise* and *Modalität*) that the method is—modality of cognition, to be sure, but also way or mode of being and acting (TW 6, 550f.). The modality proper of the method is the formal way in which the content—which is, at this point, the overall activity of pure thinking displayed in the entire course of the logic as a sequence of discrete and necessarily interconnected determinations—is structured so that, first, the dynamism of the whole is preserved and accounted for; second, the stages of its inner development come to light; and finally the unity of sense proper to its different actions emerges as the unity of the process that Hegel designates as the "system" of the logic (TW 6, 567). Method, Hegel shows, is itself a type of activity—it is the "universal absolute activity" (*Tätigkeit*) of pure thinking; it is the true moving principle of the process—it is its "soul and substance," the animating principle which gives life to the whole (TW 6, 551).

As the pure, immanent development of the logic stages the "action" taking place in it, all performance and all action display, in good Aristotelian fashion, three structural moments, namely, beginning, advancement, and end. These are the moments of the "absolute method," which can be detected as what they are only once the overall action has been performed, not while the action is being performed. Indeed, the account of the method can come only at the end. What I propose to do now is to concentrate on the first moment, the action of beginning or the action that begins. My first aim is to show how the methodological moment that describes the action of making the beginning as such or absolutely—i.e. (i) independently of what it is that begins, and (ii) independently of the agent that produces such beginning—is logically specified in the three spheres of the logic, i.e. within Being, Essence, and the Concept respectively. On this basis I then argue that Hegel's logic of action is directly connected (descriptively as well as normatively) to different typologies of action taking place, more specifically and concretely, at the level of spirit's social, political, and historical organization. The latter develop on the basis of the logical method by specifying (i) the *content* in which and (ii) the *agent* by which the action is performed. This, I maintain, is the relation that connects the *Logic* as the first, foundational part of the philosophical system to the "philosophical science of right." It is neither a relation of application (as it is often assumed) nor the linear relation between an abstract form and a concrete content. It is instead the connection that binds the "logic of action" in which forms of action are developed independently of any agent, to their manifold actualization and enactment by distinctively different spiritual agents—alternatively, individual, collective, institutional, economic, political agents—under the specific conditions dictated by a changing historical actuality.

5.3. Logical Method and Forms of Action: Freedom, Violence, and the Action that Begins

Hegel's presentation of the logical method begins with the beginning (TW 6, 553). What does it mean to raise the question of the beginning as a *methodological* question regarding action? Unlike the beginning of the logic, where at stake is the very first logical action (and the first logical content); and unlike the introductory considerations on the topic "with what must the science begin?" which occupies the logic before the beginning (and is still a question of content), we are now dealing with the problem of the beginning once the logic as a whole *has already begun*. What does it mean here for action as such—for pure thinking's most proper action—to begin? What is the beginning "in and for itself," as "modality" of movement? Now *to begin* (as intransitive or absolute action) is the action characterized by being an indeterminate and "immediate" that has the form of "abstract universality" (TW 6, 553). Hegel argues that as moment of the method "the beginning has no other determinateness than this: being simple and abstract," immediate and universal. In the last chapter of the *Logic*, however, immediacy and abstractness are the very *modality* with which logical thinking *begins to act as logical thinking* and *begins to know* what logical thinking is, i.e. what it *does*. In other words, at the level of the method Hegel is not concerned with "being" as the first beginning (or with the issue of *what* it is that constitutes the first beginning) but with the way in which the beginning is made (whatever the beginning in its content-determination is) in order for the logical movement, and eventually for the end of the entire movement, immanently to issue. Dynamically viewed, the act of beginning necessarily entails "the instance of the realization of the concept" (TW 6, 554), the "drive" for a further advancement (TW 6, 555). The act of beginning formally or methodologically considered (the content may be indifferently one of Being, Essence, or the Concept—but may also be a concrete "real" one) is as such immediate, indeterminate, expresses an unilateral position, is inherently deficient whereby it necessarily leads on to something else meant to complete it, and as a discursive beginning is endowed with the immanent "drive" to carry on (the dialectic beginning as such is no dead end—if it were, it would not be a beginning).

All action in its inception has consequences for which it is accountable but also leads on to unforeseen independent developments. There are, to be sure, many different ways or modalities in which thinking can begin its activity; there are many contrasting ways in which concrete actions do begin, and many contents with which beginnings can be made. What Hegel thematizes in the absolute method is that which all the actions that begin have in common insofar as they imply the formal activity of beginning. These are also the methodological characters necessarily displayed by the will that makes the beginning of the overall development of spirit's freedom in the *Philosophy of Right*. Herein, Hegel announces, the will entails "the element of *pure indeterminateness*" whereby it is able to make abstraction of all limitations and all contents—be it those imposed by nature or those that tie it to needs, drives, and desires. This is precisely what freedom in the beginning is; and this is how it acts: enacted by this utterly indeterminate will freedom is "the limitless infinity of absolute abstraction." And this is also its "universality"—in fact, an empty and indeterminate universality (R §5). The important point, however, is to stress that this is precisely—hence also *only*—the *beginning* of the process of freedom's realization. It is from the act of detecting the necessity for the will to gain determination and content that the process moves away from its abstract beginning (R §6) on to the full-fledged figure of the "substantial will" which displays its actuality in the political state (R §258). The beginning of the *Philosophy of Right* as a whole, the sphere of Abstract Right, follows precisely this methodological structure both in defining the agent of abstract property right, namely, the "person," and in defining the objective realm over which the person's freedom extends (R §35). However, all three successive spheres of the *Philosophy of Right* are characterized by different configurations of the beginning—the difference consisting, first and foremost, in the different agent enacting it.

I shall now work my way backwards from the methodological account of the beginning action at the end of the *Logic*, and look first at the opening of Being, and then at the beginnings of Essence and the Concept. My aim is to show how the logic of action sketched out in the "absolute method" is successively and differently implemented throughout the main divisions of the logic as the *formal* methodological moment of the beginning is enacted in different *content*-determined actions. On this basis I shall then turn again to Hegel's practical conception of freedom.

5.3.1. Beginning Actions: Being, Essence, Concept

The first thing that Hegel says of "being" as the "indeterminate immediate" that opens the logic is that it is "free from the determinateness against essence" (TW 5, 82). In fact, this is its difference from the beginning of essence, which does not enjoy that "freedom"—essence has always to position itself in relation to being. In the action of beginning "absolutely," i.e. in being, by contrast, there is no essence—indeed there is "nothing." For, in the position of radical indeterminateness and immediacy in which thinking begins to think, its action simply and immediately is (there is no question yet of *what* it is, which would give determinateness to such a beginning). Hence it is here, with this lack of difference and determinateness, with this utter immediacy, that thinking begins. Being is the absolute inception of thinking's pure activity and nothing more than this action (anything more than this is not a beginning action but something that is already under way). However, due to the utter immediacy and indeterminateness of this action, being merges here with nothing (and vice versa). The action of beginning is a back and forth between being and nothing, an indistinct merging and disappearing of one into the other. Being transitions into nothing and vice versa (TW 5, 83). It is action that simply and immediately happens: it is and is not at the same time. In the movement of becoming the vanishing of being into nothing is reinforced by the vanishing of their difference. This is how difference first appears: just to be dissolved in the moment in which it arises. Such is the absolute freedom of thinking, its beginning out of itself—out of nothing, as it were, because thinking itself is nothing but the very action of beginning. In this sense, the freedom of thinking is the beginning that immediately is, the action that is thanks to nothing but to itself. But it is also nothing until it develops, until it performs a determinate action and makes itself into something determinate, until it takes a distinct position. The freedom of the absolute beginning is vanishing—it is a vanishing freedom, as it were. The freedom of the beginning is the absolute lack of all presuppositions; the freedom that arises when there is no essence (and no determinate being) against which thinking can define itself. Not much value should be placed in such freedom—only the value of the absolutely necessary action of beginning, the unconditioned first condition of all development. Kant's praise of thinking's "spontaneity" as the capacity to "begin a state of affairs out of itself" (KrV B561/A533) is entirely justified. But it is only the praise of a mere beginning. It is certainly no accomplishment and has no value in itself, only in relation to the process that such action begins. In this respect, the beginning action is indeed an "intention," the very first intention and a "mere" intention. Pure being-nothing is the form that the action that begins—and begins absolutely—displays in the Logic of Being.

The beginning of essence is the action of "beginning-again"—of beginning anew after the conclusion of the sphere of being. To this extent, the beginning of essence does not enjoy the "freedom" that made of the first inception of thinking an unconditioned, presuppositionless action. In order to begin-again thinking must take a position with regard to what has happened and has been performed—what is *ge-wesen*—in being. And in particular, it must differentiate itself from it. For, the beginning-again of essence is a more advanced beginning or better, is the beginning of a different advancement, is a *new* beginning. Essence "begins from something other, namely, being" in order to find itself, hence to be able to properly begin acting as essence (TW 6, 13). This is the initial mediation embedded in essence. Yet, we know that the action of beginning is, methodologically, immediate action. Now immediacy is no longer, directly, the action that beginning is or was in being: entirely indeterminate, free with an absolute irresponsible freedom, totally daring in its coming from nothing and vanishing into nothing. Now immediacy is essence's own position *in relation to being*. For all its initial immediacy, to begin in essence is a more circumspect kind of action; unmistakably confrontational, it implies taking a position, distinguishing the "essential" from the "inessential." Indeed, although the two sides—being and essence—face each other "indifferently," apparently displaying the "same value" (TW 6, 18), essence raises a higher claim assigning to itself the side of the essential while the "overcome being" is reduced to the inessential. To begin-again is to draw this preliminary distinction, in fact an arbitrary one in its immediacy, thereby cutting out the space of an alleged "essential" action in which such beginning is seen as necessarily inscribed. The beginning of essence is a beginning in itself double, is an action in itself split: in it being and essence dialectically relate to each other. While the first absolute beginning has no true direction but in its utter indeterminacy fluctuates between being and nothing, the beginning of essence is two-faced, looking backward and forward at the same time, yet with an asymmetrical (and arbitrary) privilege for the essential, for the direction away from being. Such doubleness, which eventually culminates in the production of *Schein* or illusion, reflects the middle position of essence between being and the concept.

Immediacy and indeterminateness in their uncompromised absoluteness and abstractness characterize the beginning in being. They qualify the freedom of the incipient action of this sphere as a lack of anything with which being ought to confront itself or measure up to—be it a presupposition, a rule or law, a criterion, or a precedent. The freedom of being is the thoughtlessness that belongs to the action that initiates something radically new. This, however, is also its limitation, which forces the beginning to advance and to prove itself something more consistent and permanent than a vanishing thoughtlessness. The freedom disclosed by the beginning of essence is more laboriously obtained, and derives from uncovering the illusory character of being's freedom. Freedom is always constrained. Mediation, in the unavoidable confrontation with being and in the duality that this implies, is the character of essence's beginning-again. This is always the freedom of one at the expense of the other, the freedom that knows in the other its limit, and is still arbitrary freedom, in search of its own rule.

"Freedom" qualifies the action of the concept from the outset (TW 6, 246). This is, first, the modality according to which thinking organizes the relationship between being and essence that is the concept: what merely happens and has happened is now imputed to the concept as it finds in it its accountable center, its basis and truth. This is, second, the freedom and self-assurance of a fully justified beginning, of a beginning that recognizes its root in a "logical history" of which the concept that therein begins is, in turn, the legitimate and responsible "subject." The truly free beginning is the beginning that looks back, yet again, to its own "genesis" (TW 6, 274)—not in a distancing recollection that disavows its provenance in the moment in which it evokes it (as essence does) but in a responsible act of self-ascription. The result is truly the foundation from which the result itself issues. The concept is the action of making oneself into what one is. This is the same action of "giving itself actuality" which Hegel presents in the *Philosophy of Right* as characterizing the "concept of right" (R §1 Remark). The beginning is now the circular beginning that grants the concept's true independence and realized freedom. Neither the abruptness of being's beginning nor the one-sided arbitrary self-positioning of essence with regard to being are truly independent and free actions. Only the freedom that characterizes the beginning of the concept is the independence that comes from a grounded, justified, self-ascribed beginning, from the consciousness that the action has its ground in itself, and in its realization remains with itself (Enz. §158).

The "pure concept" begins in its immediacy as the "universal concept"; its action is in the determination of universality, which, however, does not exclude but implies particularity. While the beginning action of being is lawless in its presuppositionless, and that of essence is biased in its proclaimed "essentiality" against the inessential being, the initial action of the concept in its universality is "the determining and differentiating" that has in itself its own "criterion," and this is what confers to the concept the formal, yet "absolute identity with itself."[11] But as the concept, in its totality, embraces the differences that are its moments, its determination is "*only* to be the *universal* set against the differentiation of the moments" (TW 6, 274). In fact, the egalitarian universalism of the concept's initial action is also its limit, the insufficiency that pushes the beginning on to its further realization. For, as determinate as the beginning action claims to be it is also immediate so that, if it is to preserve its egalitarian universalism, its determination must remain a very poor one—it cannot be more than formal universality in front of the difference that divides its moments. Although the concept, owing to its "genesis," is entitled to and perfectly justified in its action, although it acts freely following the criterion that it bears within itself, it cannot take a determinate position with regard to its moments without betraying itself (i.e. its universality). It must maintain a delicate balance "in front of the distinctness" that divides its moments and can be "*only* the *universal*" (TW 6, 274) in front of them (no hierarchy or ranking or preference is allowed). This is the uneasy predicament of the concept's action "in the beginning," the precariousness of its initial—immediate and abstract—universality. Herein we find the peculiar indeterminateness that characterizes the beginning of the concept. It is the neutrality of universalism, its impartiality with regard to all particular causes that requires its not being committed to any cause (not even to the cause of universalism). This is the all-embracing and all-pervasive impartiality (but also the emptiness) of absolute toleration.

5.3.2. Beginning Actions: Violence and Freedom in the World of Spirit

Now I claim that the differential logic of the beginning action outlined earlier is, at the same time, the inner differential logic embodied in practical—moral, ethical, and political—forms of action once the agent is specified as an individual, a social, an institutional agent. I shall use the case of violence as an example. I suggest, first, that violence is logically implied by the immediacy characterizing all action in the beginning; and I maintain, second, that there is a logical spectrum along which violent action can be differentially characterized, and this is the constellation displayed by the successive action of Being, Essence, and the Concept. Accordingly, with our initial problem in view, we can claim that in his practical and political philosophy Hegel

---

[11] Respectively, TW 6, 273f. for the "*Maßstab*," and 6, 274 for the "absolute *Identität mit sich*."

does not "apply" allegedly "abstract" logical categories to "concrete" social and political phenomena, but rather specifies the way in which the formal "logic of action" is actually implemented—or gains its *Gestaltung* (R §1 Remark)—when the agent occupies determinate and varying systematic and historical positions within the development of objective spirit.

There is one important aspect in which the Terror of the later phase of the French Revolution follows the logic of being's abrupt and violent beginning—it is, as it were, its proper historical enactment. To ascertain this we need only compare Hegel's own rendition of the events of the 1790s in the *Phenomenology* with the beginning of the Logic of Being. The action whereby being begins, indistinguishable from nothing in its immediacy, leads to the movement of becoming. This is the action in which being and nothing "are inseparable, and each immediately disappears in its opposite" (TW 5, 83). Becoming is the "movement of immediate disappearing" of being and nothing into each other, and this is the "truth" of the beginning action of the logic. The movement of *Verschwinden*—of disappearing and vanishing—characterizes the dynamic of this entire logical sphere. *Verschwinden* is immediate and utterly indeterminate destruction, i.e. destruction not mediated and not motivated, blind destruction that indiscriminately invests everything that is. Logically, however, such destruction-vanishing is neither the intentional activity of a subject nor something that extrinsically "happens" to things or substrates. It is the action that characterizes being and nothing as such: vanishing, immediate destruction, and impermanence is that which being-nothing immediately is. Within the dynamic of such movement being is nothing and nothing is being. There is a fundamental fragility built into the violence and destructiveness of this movement. *Verschwinden* does not discriminate; it is not directed by motives, presuppositions, or goals, and is ultimately lawless. This is the logical figure that describes the radical action of all revolutionary violence.

This is, on Hegel's account, the logical structure that describes the extreme implication of what he calls "absolute freedom," namely, the peculiar destruction brought forth by the Terror of the French Revolution. In the *Phenomenology* chapter "Absolute Freedom and Terror," in his account of the transition from the National Assembly of 1789 to the Jacobin dictatorship of 1793 Hegel brings to light the extreme contradiction of Rousseau's general will, namely, the contradiction of a will that cannot bear any determination but must remain entirely indeterminate, hence ultimately ineffectual. Its reality and substance—the reality of its action—is just being; simple, indeterminate being that truly is nothing. As such this will accomplishes no "positive work," neither the work of language nor laws or determinate institutions (TW 3, 434). Ultimately, the ineffectual indeterminateness of being is the price that "absolute freedom" has to pay for its absoluteness. Under this condition, however, all that absolute freedom can accomplish is the "negative action" and the indiscriminate destruction proper to the violence of *Verschwinden*—an action in which every individual volition and particular aim is erased. Being immediately disappears into nothing. Such freedom is indeed the only action possible to immediate indeterminate being: it is "the fury of vanishing and destruction (*Die Furie des Verschwindens*)" (TW 3, 435–6). Absolute freedom is both vanishing freedom and the freedom of absolute destruction. Thus, Hegel concludes, "the sole work and deed of universal freedom is *death*" (TW 3, 436). Thereby he captures not only the negativity of revolutionary violence but also its suddenness and impermanence: nothing prepares it, nothing is saved from it, and nothing remains. While the beginning of the Logic of Being displays the violence of absolute immediacy—unintentional, aimless, meaningless violence—the revolutionary Terror is the theater of the violence of absolute freedom. In both cases, violence displays a dynamic that is logically accounted for by the idea of being's immediate and indeterminate action, namely, by structures that do not appeal to intentions, means–ends relations, or higher purposes (political, religious, and the like).

My general point here is twofold. On the one hand, my claim is that the *Logic* as a logic of action already presents the fundamental structures of a *practical* philosophy. On the other hand, I want to insist on the need to *logically* qualify the type of violence at play in historical events and in human agency. At stake is not the issue of justification but of qualified comprehension. The case of the French Revolution during the Terror confirms that violence is all but alien to the ideal of Rousseauian direct democracy. The gesture of construing the violence of "absolute freedom" specifically in terms of the destructiveness of pure being-nothing implies, among other things, the recognition that its action involves a new historical beginning, which creates a radical historical discontinuity, and suggests that the way out of it rests on the task of "determining" the space of that indeterminate freedom. If it wants to achieve results more permanent and positive than mere indiscriminate destruction freedom cannot remain indeterminate and cannot raise its claims through immediate purposeless and lawless action. This, I contend, is ultimately the meaning of Hegel's historical-philosophical narrative in 1807—a meaning that can be brought to focus even more precisely through the beginning of the Logic of Being.

As we have seen, the Logic of Essence begins with essence reducing being first to the "inessential," then to pure "*Schein*" in order to claim for itself the value of the "essential" action. This is essence's immediate negation of being. The violence of this action, however, does not reside in pure negativity as such but in the reflected, indirect, circumventing way in which the negation of being is carried out and made instrumental to what essence itself claims to be. For it is the violent action toward being that first institutes what essence properly is. *Schein* is reflected immediacy—reflected violence. Unlike the violence of pure being, which is aimless violence, unqualified and pre-human, the reflected violence of revenge is *human* violence. Reflected violence is, more generally, the beginning of *human* action: is the violence present in every act of beginning-again or in every *mediation* which in order to find its own way to be and to act must reject the givenness of being while still remaining inescapably bound to it. Although the beginning of human self-production still depends on (natural) being, it must fundamentally transform it—indeed do violence to it—in order to be what it (essentially) is, namely, *human* action.

In the *Philosophy of Right*, in dealing with the category of the "juridical wrong" or *Unrecht*, Hegel offers a concrete case that fulfills the logical structure of *Schein* as the initial action of essence. The juridical wrong assumes three forms: "non-malicious wrong or civil offence," "fraud," and "crime" (R §83). Right is "posited," first, in the contract. This "manifestation of right," in which the principle of right and "the particular will *immediately*, i.e., contingently correspond" turns into the "*Schein*" of *Unrecht*— the injustice of wrong (R §82, my emphasis). Herein we have the "opposition" between what is right in itself and the particular will that upholds a "particular right." While right is first "posited" with the contract, it becomes really valid, validated, and effectual only when it meets its *Schein*, clashes with its opposite, and is mediated in the process of such opposition. It is with *Unrecht* that *Recht* properly *begins* to be a valid and effectual right. "The truth of this *Schein*" Hegel contends "is that this *Schein* is nothing, and that right reasserts itself by negating this negation of itself—through which process of mediation, returning to itself from its negation, right is determined as effectual and valid *while it initially was only in itself and something immediate*" (R §82, my emphasis). This is the movement of essence: right *begins* as immediate, and it is precisely this immediacy that plunges the principle of right into the juridical wrong. But it is only on the basis of this immediate beginning that right proves its objective validity. The reflected violence of essence is needed in order to accomplish exactly the opposite of what it sets out to achieve. The beginning of right—not of its immediate being or in-itself concept but the beginning of the *action* through which right asserts itself in its real validity ("*das Sich-gelten-Machen* des Rechts": R §82 handwritten remark)—is its *Schein*, the juridical wrong action. Just as the first action of essence institutes a relation to the sphere of being whereby it declares being "inessential," so the principle of right receives its "essential" determination in relation to the "inessential," which is the particular will.[12] Unsurprisingly, the movement that characterizes the *Schein* of wrong is *Verschwinden*. In asserting itself, the wrong action shows itself as wrong, whereby the wrong disappears and the principle of right is posited as the "power" over the negativity of wrong. Right affirms itself in the act of canceling the wrong (R §82 Addition).

The beginning of the Logic of the Concept constitutes the concept as the identity that immanently differentiates itself in particularity and individuality. As the formal universal, the concept draws differences (the action of *Unterscheiden*) that are equal because they are all internal determinations or particularizations of the same abstract universal. Each "moment" of the concept is itself the entire concept as well as a determination of the concept (TW 6, 273). There is no exteriority in this relation. It is the same relation that takes place at the beginning of sphere of *Sittlichkeit*, in the "transition" from *Moralität* for which Hegel expressly refers to the "transition of the concept" presented in the *Logic*. The "determinations" of the ethical whole in its initial universality are "differences" produced by the universal in an act of self-differentiation (R §144), and are differences that in their equality are reduced "to moments, to

---

[12] This is the *Erscheinung* of right: R §82Z.

moments of the concept, which is revealed as their unity" (R §141 Remark). To be the concept in the beginning, however, is a precarious and difficult position. The universal must remain universal, fair, and neutral toward the particulars—it must be the universal and act as the universal "*only*" (TW 6, 274). It cannot judge. Judgment is the advancement from this beginning; it is that which follows it (because of its intrinsic deficiency, and by exposing such deficiency).

The universal that the concept is in the beginning "is the simple that is at the same time the richest in itself" (TW 6, 275). How does this richness inform the initial action of the concept? What kind of "power" does it lend to it; and does such power need violence to assert the concept's universality over and above particularity and individuality? In its inception, the universal is "the abstract", which implies that in it the determinations of the concrete must be "left aside." Such "leaving-aside" is the action of a double negation (it is a negation of the negation that all determination necessarily is). Although this action initially appears to be "external" to the universal and to arbitrarily discriminate among the determinations assumed as conceptual content and those left aside, even in its abstractness the speculative universal is *internal* self-differentiation: the negation of negation is the action of "mediation" (TW 6, 275) whereby the universal "maintains itself" in its determinations (TW 6, 276). While the universality of the concept of general logic excludes richness of content, the universality of the speculative concept includes it and yet still makes abstraction from it. The universal *remains* universal even though it posits itself in a particular determination. Such determination does not destroy the universal, does not negate it, does not particularize it in a way that is incompatible with universality. This is indeed the "neutrality" of the concept's position: it is not a "blind" neutrality consisting in leaving difference aside or ignoring it; it is the considered neutrality that derives from attending to the differences, from making them internal to one's own position but maintaining one's universal stance throughout this process. This is the balanced universality of ethical law (which is quite different than the undifferentiated abstractness of property rights and the intransigent universality of the moral law).[13] In sum, as the action of the concept universality is not the act of making abstraction from all contents; it is rather the attitude of not being swayed by determinations and biases but remaining impartial in attending to them. Such an attitude is the beginning or the condition of free judgment.

The non-violent power of the concept manifests itself in the relation that it entertains with its "other." The fundamental relationality (*Verhalten*) proper to essence appears in its beginning in the action of investing the other with the negativity of *Schein*. This now yields to the action whereby the universal makes itself into the very "essence" or "positive nature" of its determinations. The task is not to suppress them (reducing them to the illusion of *Schein* and subjugating them with violence) but to maintain them, revealing their truth, i.e. their conceptual, universal validity. In its other the concept finds itself. And this is the first act of freedom. It is the manifestation

---

[13] Hegel's handwritten remark to R §144 reads: "*Gesetzliche Inhaltsbestimmungen*."

of the concept's "free power" (*freie Macht*: TW 6, 277). Hegel suggests that the action that fulfills this logic of the beginning concept is the action of "formation and creation."[14] Determination is no longer a limit for the concept, a stubborn other to be reduced to *Schein* or to do violence to but is a necessary, internal moment of one's own identity (TW 6, 277). In the sphere of ethical life "the ethical" (*das Sittliche*) is introduced by Hegel according to this same model of conceptual immanent self-differentiation whereby the whole, as "the system of [the] determinations of the idea," recognizes such determinations as "the ethical powers" in which individual freedom is objectively and collectively realized (R §145). The "ethical powers" rule over the lives of individuals in a non-violent way as the citizens identify with them, trust them, and see in them the source of their self-conscious activity within the ethical whole (R §147).

To sum up my argument, I have maintained that there is a necessary *methodological* relation that connects Hegel's *Logic* and his theory of objective spirit—his political philosophy or his "philosophical science of right"; and I have maintained that such a relation is based on the idea that both disciplines are parts of the *system* of philosophy. My goal has been to begin to show how such methodological relation should be understood. On the basis of my conception of Hegel's *Logic* as a "logic of action," I have drawn to the center one moment of the "absolute method" thematized in the last chapter of the *Logic*—the moment of the beginning action. My claim has been that the relation that connects Hegel's practical philosophy to the *Logic* is not a correspondence of discrete categorical moments but the correspondence, on different systematic levels, of structures of action—the beginning action has been my focus here. I have suggested that the structure of the beginning action can be illustrated by a typology that both in the *Logic* and the practical philosophy brings into focus the connection between freedom and violence.

---

[14] See R §197 for the role of *Bildung*, and my "*Bildung* and the Realization of Freedom in Hegel," in: *Die Bildung der Moderne*, ed. M. Dreyer, M. Forster, K.-U. Hoffmann, and K. Vieweg, Tübingen, Francke Verlag, 2013, 153–66.

6

The State as a System of Three Syllogisms

Hegel's Notion of the State and Its Logical Foundations

Klaus Vieweg

The Italian architectural term *chiave de volta* is perfectly applicable to Hegel's theory that the political state is an objective form of justice. It is such an apex of the 'gothic cathedral' that his practical philosophy represents in its role as a philosophy of freedom.[1] Just like in the architecture of the arch, this apex finalizes the edifice by crowning it, and it enables the structure to carry itself—without it, the whole architecture of Hegel's temple of freedom could not persist and would collapse. It is the foundation of and reason for everything, the headstone of a 'world of freedom'. In the elevated form of 'the state' we have the beginning and the end of the entire architecture of Hegel's philosophy of objective spirit that consists in his theory of free will and action. The whole theoretical construction is akin to the breathtaking *Palazzo della Ragione* in Padua that unites free beings' various modes of living around and within itself: right, market, art, religion, and intellectual culture.

In the *Outlines*, Hegel speaks of 'the architectonic of its rationality—which [is characterized], through determinate distinctions between the circles of public life and their rights and through the strict proportion in which every pillar, arch, and buttress is held together' (Hegel 2008: 9).[2] And according to Eduard Gans, the merit of the treatise is to be found 'in the wonderful architectonic, with which each page and room is treated, in the assiduity that is bestowed upon each corner of the edifice, and all in this regular and yet varying style that can be observed from the top to its foundation'.[3]

---

[1] For more detail on this, see: Klaus Vieweg, Das Denken der Freiheit: Hegels Grundlinien der Philosophie des Rechts, München, Fink, 2013.

[2] G. W. F. Hegel, *Outlines of the Philosophy of Right*, trans. T. M. Knox, rev. ed. and intro. Stephen Houlgate, Oxford, Oxford University Press, 2008, p. 9.

[3] Eduard Gans, Vorrede zu den Grundlinien der Philosophie des Rechts, Berlin 1981, p. 3.

Hegel's Philosophy of Right can thus be condensed into the one expression that appears in the subtitle of the *Outlines*—Philosophy of freedom and of right as a *science of the state*: the highest determination of the thinking of practical freedom in the realm of politics is to be found at the standpoint of the 'highest concrete universality' (Hegel 2008: §303 remark, 292). Hegel thus took on the Herculean task of finding a new *legitimization of the political*, to justify the state as the supreme form of free willing by means of *comprehending thought*. This means that his conception is supposed to describe the state as idea, and as idea in the form of the *highest level of ethical actuality* at that, which in turn is the highest form of objective spirit. Hegel's state is thus determined as the 'actuality of the ethical Idea' (Hegel 2008: §257, 228) that has fully realised its immanent form.

This notion must be explicated as precisely as possible and the system of this idea's main determinations must be developed along the lines that the 'construction of the state' is the 'realisation of the edifice of freedom', [4] i.e. the *objective manifestation of justice*. The aim of Hegel's *science of the state*—the *ethical world*, is 'to comprehend and depict the state as something inherently rational' and this means we have to pay close attention to a demand that Hegel articulates in the *Philosophy of Right*'s preface. He there claims that although the logical development might not be explicated in all detail, 'the whole, like the formation of its parts, rests on the logical spirit [*dem logischen Geiste*]. It is [...] from this point of view above all that I should like my book to be taken and judged' (Hegel 2008: 4).

This remark refers to the logic of the constitution, i.e. to the state's logical foundation. The kind of *philosophical justification* that Hegel calls the 'speculative mode of cognition' is developed in detail in the *Science of Logic* and according to H. F. Fulda, so far, there has not been an interpretation of the *Outlines* that pays close attention to logical foundations and that Hegel explicitly requests has 'hardly been realised' and succeeded only partially.[5] The thoughts that I present in the following thus aim to continue the project that began with two seminal articles by Dieter Henrich and Michael Wolff.

'It lends gravity to Hegel's theory that he attempted to construct his philosophy of freedom with recourse to a logical theory.'[6] Akin to this evaluation by Henrich, Robert Pippin insists on the necessity of taking the *Logic* into account: 'No adequate treatment of Hegel's practical philosophy can ignore [these] claims.'[7] Also Jean-François Kervégan emphasizes that Hegel's *Philosophy of Right* is not to be read as a mere collection of theoretical notions in the context of political philosophy but rather as one element within his larger system, the *Encyclopedia of Philosophical Sciences*, which in

---

[4] G. W. F. Hegel, Vorlesungen über Rechtsphilosophie 1818–1831, ed. and comm. by Karl-Heinz Ilting. 4 Bde, Bd. 3: *Philosophie des Rechts: Nach der Vorlesungsnachschrift von H. G. Hotho 1822/23*, Stuttgart, Bad Cannstatt, 1973, p. 716.

[5] Hans Friedrich Fulda, *Georg Wilhelm Friedrich Hegel*, München, Beck C. H., 2003, p. 197.

[6] Dieter Henrich, *Hegels Grundoperation: Eine Einleitung in die Wissenschaft der Logik*, in Der Idealismus und seine Gegenwart. Hg. v. Ute Guzzoni, Hamburg, Bernhard Rang and Ludwig Siep, 1976, p. 230.

[7] Robert P. Pippin, *Hegel's Practical Philosophy*, Cambridge, Cambridge University Press, 2008, p. 8.

turn has the *Logic* at its heart and centre.[8] Unless one unearths the fundamental structures of the coordinate system of thought that is the *Science of Logic*, substantial contents of the *Philosophy of Right* will be missed out on.

And yet, most contemporary commentators of the *Outlines* argue that one ought to ignore its logical foundation. Repeatedly, the legend of the post-metaphysical age is heard aloud and wide. Insufficient, pick-and-choose-style approaches as well as sociological and so-called political theory-style engagement with the *Outlines* are the latest fads. While some admit that a number of Hegel's thoughts are worth engaging with even today, this is never said about his notion of logical justification that to many appears outdated and burdensome. In contrast to this *zeitgeist*, I will pursue a strategy that aims to uncover the work's systematic intentions, its logical foundations and thus the innermost formation of Hegel's thought with regards to the *Philosophy of Right*.

6.1. The State as a Whole Consisting of Three Syllogisms

It is not just the state in the sense of a state's inner civil or common law and the political state (the constitution) that are wholes consisting of three syllogisms. This also applies (first and foremost) to the overall structure of the idea of the state as defined in §259 of the *Outlines*. The application of the syllogistic triad thus takes place *within* the interpretation of a single totality, of a whole and its internal logical mediation out of the logico-speculative reason according to which 'only the idea that has become an actual totality by the power of the concept forms a self-referential, closed whole of syn-logisms'.[9]

The syllogistic triad

1. U – P – I
2. P – I – U
3. I – U – P

These three configurations require some detailed explanation: first, the sequence of the middle (P–I–U) remains identical; second, the last figure ends with P; and third, Hegel shows that the positioning ('*Stellung*') of the terms in figure 1 is logically identical to that in figure 2. The first syllogism implies that the individual (initially as qualitative determination) is posited by the universal. This individual, i.e. spirit as the active individual, moves towards the middle, into the mediating position. Finally, the truth of the first syllogism is posited by the second (Hegel 2010: 590ff.).[10]

---

[8]   Jean-François Kervégan, *L'effectif et le rationnel: Hegel et l'esprit objectif*, Paris, Vrin, 2009, p. 7.

[9]   Dieter Henrich, Logische Form und reale Totalität: Über die Begriffsform von Hegels eigentlichem Staatsbegriff, in *Hegels Philosophie des Rechts: Die Theorie der Rechtsformen und ihre Logik*, ed. Dieter Henrich and Rolf-Peter Horstmann, Stuttgart, Klett-Cotta, 1982, pp. 428–50, here: p. 445.

[10]   G. W. F. Hegel, *The Science of Logic*, trans. and ed. George di Giovanni, Cambridge, Cambridge University Press, 2010.

Also the second sequence is defined by the idea:

Since the particular and universal are also the extremes, and are immediate determinacies indifferent to each other, their relation itself is indifferent; each can be the major or the minor term, indifferently the one or the other, and consequently either premise can also be taken as major or minor.   (Hegel 2010: 599, 600)

The conclusion is universality, which must therefore move to the centre of the third syllogism. The sequence I–U–P represents the truth of the formal syllogism so that according to Hegel, the syllogism becomes legitimate but the conclusion becomes necessarily negative:

Consequently, it is also indifferent which of the two determinations of this proposition is taken as predicate or subject, and whether the determination is taken in the syllogism as the extreme of singularity or the extreme of particularity.   (Hegel 2010: 601)

Despite this formalism 'the conjunction [...] must likewise have its ground in a mediation that lies outside this syllogism' (Hegel 2010: 602), Hegel's syllogistic reasoning has a 'very fundamental meaning' which 'rests on the necessity that, as a determination of the Concept, *each moment* becomes itself the *whole* and the *mediating ground*' (Hegel 1991: §187 remark, 262).[11] Everything rational is such a threefold syllogism, in which the terms ultimately become interchangeable.

One can observe the path through the levels of the idea that leads to the overcoming of the syllogism's formalism in the description of the 'syllogism of the *idea*' in the *Encyclopedia*'s last section—including the argumentation's culmination in the 'absolute syllogism'. The transition from subjectivity—especially from syllogising as its last step— into objectivity has its roots in the nature of the syllogism itself, which 'gives itself external reality through particularity'. From then on, the logical form of the syllogism continues its path on a higher level and cannot be called a 'empty framework' (Hegel 1991: §192 addition, 268). We are dealing with a *rational* syllogism insofar as 'by means of the mediation the subject con-cludes [i.e. syllogises] *itself with itself*. Only then is it [truly] subject; or the subject is all by itself the syllogism of reason' (Hegel 1991: §182, 258).

6.2. The State as a Triad of Syllogisms

Qualitative syllogism:	I	–	P		–	U
	state as individual		relation of particular states			world history
	inner law of the state		outer law of the state			law of the world

Syllogism of reflexion: U – I – P
Syllogism of necessity: P – U – I

---

[11] G. W. F. Hegel, The Encyclopedia Logic (with the Zusätze): Part 1 of the *Encyclopedia of Philosophical Sciences* with the Zusätze, trans., intro., and notes T. F. Geraets, W. A. Suchting, and H. S. Harris, Cambridge, Hackett, 1991.

It is the state's duty to reconnect what has been divided and torn apart into its extremes in the context of civil society. This constitutes the state's meaning as a form of integration and connection in the sense of a 'constitution of freedom'. The last syllogism effects the sublation of the structure of the syllogism and the constitution of a system of syllogisms that is a whole and in which the determined, fixed positions of the extremes and of the middle are dissolved so that each determined moment itself represents the whole.

1. The individual state as individual is connected with the universal via its particularity (as a national state). The individual states are attached to the universal through their external particularity and their particular interests and needs.
2. The activity of the individual state (I) serves as the mediating factor that gives actuality to the relationship of the states (P) and the world-context (U) by means of 'translating' their ethical essence into the extreme of actuality. The individual states constitute inter-nationality through their relations: the external sovereignty of the state and international law.
3. The universal is the substantial middle, in which the individual states and their particular welfare have and find their mediation and subsistence. World history is the 'absolute centre' (Hegel 2010: 642) within which the extreme of the individual states (I—constitution) are connected with their external circumstances (P—international law).

This first explication of the three syllogisms is informed by Hegel's claims about the individual state as a system of three syllogistic mediations (Hegel 1991: §198 remark, 277; Hegel 2010: 622ff.): 'It is only through the nature of this con-cluding [i.e. syllogising], or through this triad of syllogisms with the same terms, that a whole is truly understood in its organisation.'

6.3. The Inner Law of the State or Domestic Right: The Second System of Three Syllogisms

The triad of three syllogisms also informs the explication of the inner law of the state, i.e. the constitution. We here encounter a *second* system of three syllogisms that Hegel—see quote in Section 6.1—alluded to in his *Logic* and in the *Encyclopedia*. In the practical sphere, 'the state is a system of three syllogisms just like the solar system'. (1) The *singular* (the person) con-cludes (i.e. 'syllogises') himself through his *particularity* (the physical and spiritual needs, which when further developed on their own account give rise to civil society) with the *universal* (society, right, law, government). (2) The will or the activity of the individuals is the mediating (term) that gives satisfaction to their needs in the context of society, right, etc., and provides fulfilment and actualization to society, right, etc. (3) But it is the universal (state, government, right) that is the substantial middle term within which the individuals and their satisfaction have and preserve their full reality, mediation, and subsistence. 'Precisely because the mediation con-cludes each of these determinations with the other extreme, each of them con-cludes itself with itself in this way or produces itself; and this production is its self-preservation' (Hegel 1991: §198 remark, 276ff.).

The triad that follows can be identified as the basic code of the state's internal right. Hegel does not develop this argument in the *Outlines* but it still represents the foundation of Hegel's idea of the state's inner rational structure, i.e. the constitution.

6.3.1. The Qualitative Syllogism I–P–U

A subject as individual 'is con-cluded with a *universal determinacy* through a quality' (Hegel 1991: §183, 259). The concrete person connects by means of its qualities, its particularity, i.e. its physical and spiritual requirements and interests (which civil society defines in more concrete form), with the universal (U)—right, law, government— so that the individuals are connected to the universal of the constitution via their needs and their external existence. In other words, the subject connects by means of its properties and interests—the abstract particularity—with the universal determinacy. However, P is subsumed under U (civil society is subsumed under the constitution) and I is subsumed under P (the concrete persons are subsumed under civil society). This only creates a two-sided relationship and prevents real mediation—the logical deficiency of this syllogism lies in the 'imperfect middle' as the *medius terminus* remains a concept-free quality. Consequently, U, P, and I are facing each other as abstract entities while in truth, all three moments of the concept are more concretely determined than that. At the same time, U and P are being connected and U becomes the mediating term of the extremes (P–U–I). However, this U only represents the 'abstract universal', resulting in the total indifference of the moments. The moments' identity remains an *external* identity of the understanding.

There are two important lessons to be learned from this development. First, individuality cannot be thought of as an isolated being, as a monad. Instead, it is a universality, the individual is an *individual citizen (Bürgerindividuum)*. Second, the logical order of the syllogism's elements takes the shape of a circle of mutually presupposing mediations (Hegel 1991: §189, 259). Its inherent deficiency motivates the further determinations of the qualitative syllogism. And since the individual is determined as an abstract universal, it assumes the middle position and becomes the mediating term. This constitutes the transition to the syllogism of reflexion where the middle is defined as all the concrete, individual subjects.

6.3.2. The Syllogism of Reflexion U–I–P

Now, all individual citizens *as* individuals (I) represent the middle, they *enact* the universal. When they bring the universal into *external existence*, they translate their ethical essence (U) into the extreme of reality and thereby constitute the actual constitution of state order. So the will and the activity of the individuals function as the mediating term, which brings satisfaction and reality to the citizens' needs and interests and bestows actuality upon the constitution and universal right. This entails that the individuals reconcile within themselves the 'extreme of the independently know-ing and willing individuality' and the 'extreme of the substantially knowing and will-ing universality'. They are actual as 'private and as substantial persons' and achieve their particularity and universality in both spheres (P and U).

The citizens' essential selfhood is partly found in the universal institutions of the state, which is 'the being in itself of their particular interests', and partly these institu-tions allow them to engage in 'an activity that aims at a universal purpose'. Still, this reflexive syllogism is deficient because the syllogism of all-ness (*Allheit*) ('all individual citizens') is first revealed to be a syllogism of induction and then a syllogism of analogy. In the meaning of the determined genus (i.e. universality) that is now disclosed, par-ticularity becomes the mediating determination and universality becomes the middle term in accordance with the syllogism's third form.

6.3.3. P–U–I: The Syllogism of Necessity

In the syllogism of necessity, the universal (the 'universal part of the constitution') constitutes the middle term in which the individuals (I) find their satisfaction and interests (P) have their reality and continued existence. The laws of the state and its institutions are the absolute centre in which the extreme that consists of the individuals (I) *is united* ('con-cluded') with their external, particular existence (P). The laws articu-late 'the determinations of the content of objective freedom' (Hegel 2007: §538, 236).[12] Concrete freedom consists in the fact that personal individuality (I) and its particular interests (P) find their complete development and the recognition of their specific right within the state (the universal of the constitution) (Hegel 2008: §260, 235).

Insofar as the acting subject has the status of '*citizen*', the agent achieves the *highest form of recognition* within an individual community, namely in the form of the unity of the dimensions of subjectivity. These are: personality, moral subjectivity, membership in a family, and in civil society. These determinations find their acknowledgement and guarantee in the status of citizenship: my rights as a person, as a moral subject, etc., are inherent in my rights as a citizen. The right of the citizen as a whole unites all the rights (and duties) that were determined so far and it is more than the sum of its parts. As a citizen, I have grasped my individuality also as a universality (for example by respect-ing reasonable laws as something universal) and thereby prove my true freedom. §263 of the *Outlines* explicitly refers to the syllogism of necessity: the Geist appears as objective universality (U) to the moments of the state (individuality and particularity) that have their immediate and reflected reality in the spheres of the family and civil society. To them, the Geist is 'the might of the rational within necessity' in the form of the laws and the institutions.

At first, the syllogism of necessity takes the form of the categorical syllogism: the state as universal, the genus of the citoyens, makes a case for a just system of education

---

[12] G. W. F. Hegel, *Philosophy of Mind*, trans. W. Wallace and A. V. Miller, rev., intro., and comm. by Michael Inwood, Oxford, Oxford University Press, 2007.

and against environmental destruction. The particular appears in the meaning of a determined kind or genus. The genus 'citizen', i.e. 'citizenship', is a 'positive unity', it is the oneness (*das Eine*) of the state, which finds its expression in the *one* constitution. As a positive singularity, it requires mediation by the individual citizens, i.e. by the individual representatives of the genus 'state', so that the logical form of the hypothetical syllogism is defined by the schema U–I–P. This constitutes the necessary relationship but there is still no steadfast necessity in the sense of an inevitable destiny as there is no compulsive demand of the genus' unity. Its demand is merely hypothetical because it is grounded in the contingency that comes with the structure of individual citizens' arbitrariness. At the same time, however, it includes the demand for a completion or affirmation of the hypothesis.

According to the hypothetical syllogism's form, the mediation lies in the activity of the individual citizens: they ought to constitute the free community—but can also fail to do so. The necessary, i.e. the universal, thus steps into the *middle position*: schema I–U–P. This mediating universal must be thought of as the totality of its particulariza-tions and as an excluding oneness (*Eines*). Here, it is one and the same universal that is differentiated into all these forms, it is the disjunctive syllogism: 'The citizens (Citoyen) as universal, individual and particular.' This logical structure exposes the moments of the concept in their *speculative unity*, each of these three moments represents the whole and contains the respective others within itself. Only a citizen (Citoyen) that is logically-speculatively thought of in this way can serve as the foundation of a political state that is truly free. So at the end of the system of the syllogistic trinity we now have the *universal and reasonable will*. The achievement of the disjunctive syllogism pro-vides us with a criterion for the evaluation of individual states and their constitutions. It follows logically that *every* moment of the concept's determination (I, P, U) *is itself the whole* and the *mediating ground*—the citizens, civil society, and the political state as community of the citizens (Citoyens). Every syllogistic moment has the function of the middle and is 'itself as the totality of the moments and thus proven to be the entire syllogism' (Hegel 1991: §187; Hegel 2008: §192). Everything reasonable must be grasped as threefold syllogism, as a system of a threefold act of syllogising. And this also means that the formalism of syllogising itself is overcome.

§260 of the *Outlines* articulates exactly this 'Being con-cluded [i.e. syllogised] together' (*Zusammengeschlossenheit*) as a core feature of the formation of modernity: 'The principle of modern states has prodigious strength and depth because it allows the principle of subjectivity to progress to its culmination in the self-sufficient extreme of personal particularity, and yet at the same time brings it back to the substantial unity and so maintains this unity in the principle of subjectivity itself.' The rights of the uni-versal, particular, and individual must be thought of as a unity of mediation. 'Precisely because the mediation con-cludes each of these determinations with the other extreme, each of them con-cludes itself with itself in this way or produces itself; and this production is its self-preservation' (Hegel 1991: §198 remark, 277). The freedom of the person and the freedom of the concrete person, i.e. the formal participant in civil society, are united in the freedom of the Citoyen, i.e. the individual citizen, the state member. Personhood must be acknowledged and the formal right must be actualized; the particular well-being of the individuals must be nurtured, the public good secured, the family protected, and civil society must be rationally regulated and designed.

6.4. A New Conception of the Separation and Interdependence of the State Powers

The basic structure of the separation or differentiation, the organization of the state into its substantial bodies—*Hegel's conception of the division of powers*[13]—can only be hinted at here. After Hegel had been championing the traditional model for a long time, the *Outlines* offered a new conception of the 'trinity' of the powers, a theory of power-interdependence that represented a paradigm shift in the history of political philosophy:

(a) the power to determine and establish the universal—the legislative power;

(b) the subsumption of individual cases and the spheres of particularity under the universal—the executive power;

(c) subjectivity, as the will with the power of ultimate decision.

(Hegel 2008: §273)

PR §275, §287, §298

I the power of the crown

P the power of government

U the legislative power

The first scheme contains the moments of the concept of the constitution and pays special attention to how force is being used. The final decision marks the endpoint and is the beginning of the actual realization of the common will. The inversion of this sequence (I–P–U) that begins in §275 is grounded in the notion that already in §273 the monarchical power of the final decider has the function of being the 'spearhead' and is named 'the beginning of the whole'. A further reason for the inversion can be found in the fact that Hegel does not focus on the functioning, activity, and application of the legislative process from §275 onwards but hones in on a possible *fundamental order of the powers* that includes the dominating role of the monarch—this is supposed to be absolute 'self-determination' that contains the three moments within: the *universality* of the constitution and the laws (U), the counsel as relationship of the *particular* to the universal (P), and the moment of the final decision (I) (§275).

However, it must be noted that the schemata—and Hegel's *Logic* proves this—fail sufficiently to develop the *entirely developed concept and the transition into the idea*.

---

[13] These thought are based on the very lucid piece: Hegels Theorie der Gewaltenteilung by Ludwig Siep, in *Praktische Philosophie im Deutschen Idealismus*, Frankfurt am Main, Suhrkamp, 1992, pp. 240–69.

Hegel's perplexing offer only consists in two forms, U–P–I and I–P–U, and in both, the particular takes the middle position. The form of the syllogism of the trinity, i.e. the *whole of three syllogisms*, does not apply here. But it is only this logical form that enables a sufficient determination of the concept of the state as something entirely reasonable, i.e. as a complete universal. The following passage underlines the crucial importance of the logical structure for the philosophical understanding of what the state is: the origin of the different spheres or powers of the state's organization as something intrinsically reasonable lies in the *self-determination of the concept*. 'How the concept and then, more concretely, how the Idea, determine themselves inwardly and so posit their moments—universality, particularity, and individuality—in abstraction from one another, is discoverable from logic, though not of course from the logic commonly in vogue' (Hegel 2008 remark: §272, 257). The final subclause—'though not of course from the logic commonly in vogue'—retains its cardinal importance today: unless one unearths the *Outlines'* specifically Hegelian logical foundations, i.e. their status as *new* logic, the architecture of political rationality remains a merely pragmatically or sociologically oriented description without legitimacy, an edifice in need of completion. Hegel comments succinctly on this issue: 'What disorganizes the unity of the logical-rational, equally disorganizes actuality' (Hegel 2007: §541 remark, 241). Political reality as a whole of different functions, i.e. as a system of powers, must be grasped as a system of three syllogisms '*of the same terms*'. According to Michael Wolff, Hegel wanted to 'place the three syllogistic forms of mediation also at the heart of the political constitution'.[14] And for Ludwig Siep, there is no doubt that Hegel 'thought of his doctrine of the division of powers as such a system of three syllogisms'.[15]

6.5. The Constitution as a System of Three Syllogisms: A Reformulation of the *Outlines*

Surprisingly, it is exactly this central thought—the trinity of syllogisms—that is neither explicated with great detail nor strictly in line with the requirements of the *Logic* in the chapter on the state! The already mentioned schemata can be found in §273 and §275ff. of the *Outlines*, where Hegel determines the state's essential moments. It is here that the careful reader will also find several important hints towards the structure of the syllogisms and the specific relevance of reciprocal implication and mediation. However, the interpreter is somewhat taken aback when he learns that the brilliant logician Hegel does not properly demonstrate the connectedness ('con-clusion') of the three syllogisms and fails to explicate the moment of the systematic whole, i.e. of the three syllogisms' unity, in sufficient detail.

---

[14] Michael Wolff, Hegels staatstheoretischer Organizismus: Zum Begriff und zur Methode der Hegelschen Staatswissenschaft, in *Hegel-Studien* 19 (1985), pp. 166–7.

[15] Siep, *Praktische Philosophie im Deutschen Idealismus*, p. 263f. Hegel was able to 'use the means of the speculative doctrine of the syllogism to describe the three constitutional powers as the three kinds of "ways in which the state's will acts"—each as a syllogism'.

Michael Wolff has already demonstrated that the monarchical power of the final decider can be associated with the deficient syllogism of reflexion (U–I–P) and that the legislative power must be associated with the highest function of finalization. However, this would contradict the very primacy of the monarchical power that the text insists on. The cardinal problem inheres in the fact that Hegel only relies on the logic of the *not yet developed, not realized* concept instead of relying on the *triad of syllogisms* that would be necessary here! Although the determinations of the concept ought to appear as 'moments of the idea', one cannot find a convincing explication of the logical theorem of the syllogistic triad. This amounts to a profound gap in the logical sequence of the *Outlines*. It is difficult to find grounds for this and my attempts at an explanation force me to venture into the highly precarious realm of conjecture: one reason can be found in Hegel's debt to his time—to the available historical-constitutional constellations as well as to the debates surrounding constitutional theory. These inspire him to find a guarantee of stability and order in constitutional monarchy and motivate him clearly to delineate this notion of monarchy from other versions and varieties of state constitutions.

Hegel's monarch appears as the 'tip in the notion of the will'. This principle of the first and final decider—the head of the state—must surely be respected by all modern states, although it also means that natural factors and arbitrariness will play a certain role in this context. Hegel is not to be argued with on this point—he profoundly altered the doctrine of the division of powers and provided a justification for the *final decider*, i.e. the head of the state, as one of the three state powers.

However, the *Outlines* also suggests that constitutional monarchy is the political form adequate for the modern world. Hegel's insistence on logical foundations especially in *this* context could be read as an indication that he has identified the logical problem but that he cannot live up to the standards of his own logic with his description of political rationality due to practical-political reasons.[16] Maybe political caution dominated his thinking in this context, an undue amount of carefulness that consciously avoids a comprehensive discussion of the true issue. According to Dieter Henrich, 'Hegel's reconstruction of the state as a system of syllogisms develops the logic of the ethical state in a form that articulates its intrinsic systematicity; but there are reasons why this form does not become explicit to the same degree in the *Philosophy of Right*.'[17] Is it a well-known fact that there were several attempts to denunciate Hegel to the Prussian king because of Hegel's notion of the monarch. Most likely, this is not an accident or a categorial mistake but Hegel cultivating the art of the '*jestful disguise*', as Goethe called this procedure. The philosopher saw the dangers that might ensue the publication of a logically grounded alternative.

---

[16] Klaus Hartmann identifies this 'mistake' in the willingness of the political state in the *Outlines*—Hegel is said to have forgotten his 'categorial insight', Klaus Hartmann, Linearität und Koordination in Hegels Rechtsphilosohie, in Henrich and Horstmann, *Hegels Rechtsphilosophie*, p. 311.

[17] Henrich, Logische Form, p. 443f.

The absence of the explicit syn-logistics appears to be the only obvious logical faux pas of the *Outlines*. Hegel has—so my rather audacious interpretation—fooled the Prussian censors with considerable finesse and chutzpa and placed his faith in his subsequent interpreters to realize a *reconstruction and correction in accordance with the requirements of Hegel's Logic* especially. The crucial elements for the understanding of the three spheres of the political structure were conceptualized by Hegel and merely the complete logical systematicity—especially the syllogism-triad—would still have to be developed.

This seems to be the only way to explain the insufficient realization of the principle of the whole as syllogisms. This interpretation follows the intentions of Henrich and Wolff, who maintain that the 'form of the concept of Hegel's theory of ethical life and of the ethical state is not easily deduced from the development of the printed *Philosophy of Right*. Hegel himself has explained with some clarity in *which logic* this conceptual form has to be constructed in passages that were more suitable for the task of conceptually determining formal relationships.'[18]

The following description connects the two already-mentioned principles of interpretation: (a) adoption of the discussed syllogistic forms, including the relations of the three powers; and (b) construction of the systematicity of the three spheres of the political in accordance with the requirements of the triad of syllogisms. Especially the latter *deviates from Hegel's own explicit claims*, but is faithful to the *logical spirit* and seems entirely appropriate given the intentions of the author of the *Philosophy of Right*—in short, this passage of the *Outlines* will be reformulated with the help of Hegel's *Logic*.

As already stated, what matters is the 'spirit' of Hegel's conception, the issue at hand is a *theory of the organic state that relies on the insights of the triad of the syllogism of Hegel's Logic*. The most crucial change concerns the explanatory sequence of the state powers: according to syllogistic logic, the qualitative syllogism (I–U–P) has to stand at the beginning. The executive power constitutes the middle of the scheme, the syllogism of reflexion. The third form is the syllogism of necessity—the legislative power, which is the only one capable of truly tying the three conceptual moments together and bringing them into the unity of the *universal reasonable will*. According to the *logical* reading, this reveals the foundation of the state's structure: the constitution and the constitutional laws, the constitution itself, and the legislative power. The ground (and reason) for the state's legitimacy can only lie here. Insofar as the legislative power in its function as terminus major (U) takes the middle position in the figure of the third syllogism (P–U–I), it renders it 'the true syllogism of state-life, in which all powers originate in the people as such'.[19] As Hegel's student Michelet put it: by the standards of the *Logic*, the schema should take this form.

<hr>

[18] Henrich, Logische Form, p. 450.
[19] Michelet, *Naturrecht oder Rechtsphilosophie*, Bd. 2, Leipzig, 1870, p. 185. Michelet adds to this fitting phrase: 'The true heart of the reasonable constitution consists in the fact that the demands of ethical life also find expression in form of a written document.'

6.6. The State as a System of Three Syllogisms: Against the Letter of the *Outlines*

1. *Syllogism of Dasein (qualitative syllogism)*

I	P	U
power of the final decision	power of government	legislative power
head of state	executive	legislature
monarchy (autocracy)	aristocracy	democracy
'one'	'some'	'all'[20]

2. *syllogism of reflexion*
U   I   P
3. *syllogism of necessity*
P   U   I

The middle terms of the syllogistic triads—*ascending* from the third syllogism and thus from the U—contain the structure of willing and of purposeful action: U—the universal will, the *cognition and determination* of the purpose of the state (*staatlicher Verband*); I—the *examination* of the purpose regarding its conformity to constitutional and legal standards and of the *final decision* regarding the realization of the purpose; and P—the relation to the particular, the *application and execution* of the purpose. The question for the nature of the purpose can be precisely answered: the people as *populous* is the 'sole purpose of the state'. Furthermore, the structure that is determined by the schema within the three syllogisms can be deciphered: *every single syllogism represents the whole of syllogisms*. In the first syllogism, this means that figure 1 I–P–U dominates, in the second, figure 2 U–I–P, the syllogism of induction, and in the third syllogism figure 3 P–U–I, the disjunctive syllogism. According to Georg Sans, the three figures of the syllogism originate in 'the complete permutation of the terms individual, particular and universal'. All of these, one after another, pass through the positions of the two extremes and of the middle. This is exactly what Hegel describes as syllogism of three syllogisms: a systematic whole of three concepts, each of which is capable of mediating the two others with each other. And because each term is able to justify the relationship of the other two, there arises a 'circle of mutually presupposing mediations' (§189).[21]

Syllogism of *Dasein*	Syllogism of reflexion	Syllogism of necessity
I–P–U	I–P–U	I–P–U
U–I–P	U–I–P	U–I–P
P–U–I	P–U–I	P–U–I

[20] Kant speaks of the different kinds of government of the body politic (*forma imperii*): (a) one—autocracy; (b) some united amongst themselves—aristocracy; or (c) all together—democracy (*Zum ewigen Frieden*, AA VIII, 352).

[21] Georg Sans, Hegels Begriff der Offenbarung als Schluss von drei Schlüssen, in *L'assoluto e il divino: La teologia cristiana di Hegel*, ed. Tommaso Pierini, Georg Sans, Klaus Vieweg, and Pierluigi Valenza, Pisa, Fabrizio Serra Editore, 2011, pp. 167–81.

On the one hand, this schema registers a change of the syllogism's moments (*terminorum*), but on the other hand, it also captures the foundation of the entire syn-logistics: the universality that stands in the middle of the disjunctive syllogism (U). This is the *universality of being a citizen* and its representation in the legislative, i.e. the law-making assembly.

6.7. The Universal, Law-Making Power: The Syllogism of Necessity (P–U–I)

From the perspective of Hegel's logic of the syllogism, the legislative power supplies the cornerstone of the entire state's structure. This power has the special function of *cognizing* and *determining* the specific purposes of the state. It is part of the constitution, which is prior to it. In its function as particular power, this power is also revealed to be a *universal* power that serves as the foundation of the division of powers. The citizens ('the people') reveal their function as a justifying instance of state power by electing their parliamentary representatives. The system of political powers finds its ground and origin precisely, in the *universal reasonable will*, which manifests itself as constitution and as legislative assembly. Both represent the *civic will* (*bürgerschaftlichen Willen*), i.e. the *universal will of the citoyen*, which mediates individuality with particularity, i.e. with the other constitutional bodies. The assembly of the polities (Politen) has the task of developing the constitution, which is also further specified in the process of defining the specific laws and the constantly changing governmental affairs (Hegel 2008: §298).

The crucial problem that Hegel has to face is how to clarify the relationship between the will of all and the universal will, i.e. the issue of the grounds for the *legitimacy of the modern state*. This is connected to the question of who wields this power, i.e. the specific participation of the Citoyen in the process of determining of the ends of the state: how do *citizens participate* in the affairs of the state? This is connected with the highly contemporary question of *how the very kind of participatory politics are formed* that enable the justification of state power. 'The principle of any sovereignty resides essentially in the [people].'[22] The parliament must be—as the French constitution of 1793 determines—at the centre of the state's structure, the people embody the sovereign in this 'republican' sense.

Every citoyen must be enabled to participate equally in the creation of the universal—be it through membership of political parties and societies, by way of direct (plebiscitary) democracy, or by indirect, representative institutions. Apart from the classical forms of political action, new, non-classical forms (e.g. popular, people's, and grassroots movements, citizens' initiatives, roundtables, participatory

---

[22] *Déclaration des Droits de l'Homme et du Citoyen*, Art. 3. According to Hegel, the main site of governmental power in the democratic constitution of 1793 France is the parliament, the legislating power has been victorious (G. W. F. Hegel, *Lectures on the Philosophy of Religion*, Frankfurt, Suhrkamp, pp. 323–404).

budgets) presently become ever-more important. However, these do not represent an alternative to parliamentary action but are a complementary element with regards to the concrete participation of the citizens in political life. In this context, Hegel's thought presents itself as a challenge and an inspiration, asking us to continue thinking—we must not simply assume that today's form of democracy is the best of all these forms *by definition*. The criteria by which we evaluate these different ways of political activity must be the successful participation in the *res publica*, the most adequate form of representation, and in general the realization of freedom in the sense of the achievement of the disjunctive syllogism—the guarantee of the freedom of every individual's particulars in one modern political community.

According to Hegel's syn-logistics, the syllogisms of necessity—the categorical, the hypothetical, and the decisive final syllogism, i.e. the disjunctive syllogism, which at the same time represents the sublation of the syllogistic form—supply the desired logical connection. In the middle position of the necessary syllogism, we find universality: it is the political will as universal, reasonable will, i.e. actuality in the form of universal, political representation of the citizens' will. This is the actual presence of the will that is free in and for itself as universal will. The universal (U) connects the universal, reasonable will in its immediate individual political representation—the individual subject of the head of state (I)—with the universal reasonable will in form of its particular political actualization: the governing power (P). Unlike the previous syllogisms suggest, universality does not have 'some immediate content', its content is not arbitrary. Instead, it has the reflexion of the extremes (P and I) within itself, while the latter have their inner identity in the middle, which in turn is determined in its content by the formal determinations of the extremes (Hegel 2010: 617)—all moments are expression of the universal and reasonable will of the citizens.

Schema:
　　　universality (U) as middle term

a) categorical syllogism	U as P	executive power
I – P – U		
b) hypothetical syllogism	U as I	power of final decision
U – I – P		
c) disjunctive syllogism	U as U	legislating power
P – U – I		

The categorical syllogism:

In the categorical syllogism that is defined by the schema of the first figure of the formal syllogism (I–P–U), we have universality as particularity, in the meaning of the determined kind 'Art' or genus. The government as particular expression of the universal will of the citizens—i.e. as mediating determination, as universal, reasonable, political will in its necessary particularity, i.e. in its particular representation as executive power—is responsible for *particularizing the universal and its realization*. The creation, realization, and application of the laws must *incorporate the universal in the laws' determinacy.* However, the other independent powers are also part of government, the final decider and the legislator because their independence is exactly that substantial universality, the species (Hegel 2010: 575f.). Governing can thus be understood as a determination of the whole.[23]

6.8. The Hypothetical Syllogism

In the hypothetical syllogism, universality moves to the centre in the form of individuality. The regent in the meaning of 'individual' is 'equally mediating as well as mediated'. In contrast to the syllogism of reflexion, no premises are simply presupposed.

The universal political will in the form of a final decision mediates the universal law (legislative power) with the particularization of law (power of government/executive power). The initial and final decision connects the cognition of the state's purpose and definition of that purpose (U) with the realization and application of the purpose (P). The adequacy of P in relation to U is tested and there is an ultimate decision about the law. This power remains *mediated* through the necessary information, counsel, and expertise of P and by the determination of the actors in U, i.e. the determination of the decider is realized by the citizens and their representatives, i.e. via the constitutionally legitimated inclusion of the traditional forms of the monarchical principle.

6.9. The Disjunctive Syllogism

The decisive concretization of 'realization' of the middle is realized in the disjunctive syllogism, the centrepiece of the syllogism of necessity. This is about the universality of universality, about the 'universality that is filled with the form', i.e. the *developed objective universality*' (Hegel 2010: 574 ff.). The middle of the syllogism includes the universal as genus (categorical syllogism) and universality as completely determined (hypothetical syllogism) and thus incorporates the objective universality in the totality of its formal determinations. This universality cannot be logically regarded as the allness of reflexion but is the totality of its particularizations—it is individual particularity, an excluding individuality.

The universal presents itself here as the 'universal sphere of its particularizations' and as determined individuality, the *medius terminus is U, P as well as I.* This has fundamental consequences for the syllogistic triad of the political organism. The middle of the disjunctive syllogism as totality of the concept itself contains both extremes in their complete determinateness, the *political trinity* in the *universal reasonable will* and in *the sovereign law-giver* as universal. In all three powers, one and the same universal is posited, the identity of these powers is the universal in the shape of the *reasonable political will.* This universal manifests itself here in this *doubled* form, as double

---

[23] Regarding government in this sense: Claudio Cesa, Entscheidung und Schicksal, in Henrich and Horstmann, *Hegels Philosophie des Rechts*, p. 205.

identity: as *constitution in general* and as *legislative power*. The legislative power's privileged position is grounded in this briefly sketched syllogistic logic, especially in the logic of the disjunctive syllogism. It is the positioning of universality in the middle of the last figure that creates a successful syllogism. *One of the powers necessarily becomes the ground of the whole, i.e. the foundation of the political organization of the state.* Recognizing Hegel's syn-logistics leads to a very surprising result compared to the claims of the *Outlines*: applying the logic correctly entails the *theoretical legitimization of a republican, democratic constitution* and of the fundamental meaning of the legislative assembly as expression of a representational-democratic structure. The universal, reasonable will manifests itself in the form of the constitution and in the form of the legislative power. Of course, this insight cannot be found in the text of the *Outlines* itself and should be developed in a continuation of Hegel's project.

So the *political trinity* has its ground in the 'holy spirit' of the universal reasonable will of the citizen, the educated Citoyenneté as lawmaker and sovereign. The notion of citizen's self-determination, i.e. of the citizenship's self-government, that is offered here, is also logically grounded in the disjunctive syllogism, which is a syllogism *and* the sublation of the logical form of the syllogism *at the same time* because the difference between the middle and the extremes is dissolved. In this way, the constitution and the legislative assembly can be thought of as a living unity filled with positive tension. Finally, one can speak of con-cluding ('*zusammenschliessen*'/syllogising) the subject not just with others but with *sublated others*. This is the subject's *syllogizing with itself,* which, strictly speaking, is no syllogizing anymore. It enables the citizen and citizenship in general to be autonomous, i.e. free, *within* the reasonably structured, legislative power in which universality, particularity, and individuality are united.

Immanent in the legislative power, universality is now present as the universal will of the citizens (the democratic principle), individuality is manifest as head of state (in the form of the *monarchical* principle of the final decider), and finally, particularity is present as government (the *aristocratic* principle). At the same time, all three moments represent the unity of the three dimensions and appear as sublated moments. The 'best constitution' must live up to what the concept of the state expresses and so it must articulate the three components' unity. However, even the best constitution is not perfect because it 'is on empirical grounds, in Dasein'—it is the state as ethical idea that is manifest in the world. Now, the political element finds its highest determination in the inner constitution, we have assumed the 'point of view of the *highest concrete universal*'. In all moments we find the '*the actual presence of the spirit that is in and for itself as the universal spirit*' (Hegel 2007: §570, 265). It is the actuality of the ethical idea, the idea of freedom as the concept of freedom that has become the political reality of the state as well as political consciousness. The state is the structure that satisfies the needs of the citizens as much as it is the product of the free activity and unification of the legal subjects. At the same time, it is its very own form of right and freedom.

In agreement with Dieter Henrich, one could thus imagine the successful achievement of Hegel's goal 'to justify the notion of the state with reference to the notion of "free spirit" in such a way that the freedom of this spirit is contained and active in the developed concept of the state. The description of the state in the form of three syllogisms is conceptually committed to this goal.'[24] This is how only the explication and application of the syllogism's triad enables an adequate comprehension of Hegel's 'science of the state' as a thinking of freedom.

[24] Henrich, Logische Form, p. 450.

7

Hegel's Shepherd's Way Out of the Thicket

Terry Pinkard

It has long been an issue not merely in the academic writing on Hegel but in the overall assessment of his philosophical achievement just how Hegel is supposed to combine his appeal to sociality and history with his otherwise timeless conceptions at work in his *Logic*. Call this the "history and/or system" problem. Hegel himself is certainly aware of it.[1] It also seems rather clear that in various places he pursues both goals rather strenuously. Nor has this gone unnoticed by Hegel scholars, and they have filled the gaps with a number of different proposals.

In this thicket of different interpretations, my purpose here is to suggest a way of looking at the relation between Hegel's method and his results that will suggest at least one way to navigate through the thicket. It is true that as we move about in the thicket, the thicket's density never lessens until we get to the end of it which brings the clearing that follows. My discussion will move between two considerations: (1) What do Hegel's claims amount to within his own terms? (2) How much do Hegel's claims depend on accepting his views on dialectic and method?

Another way of formulating those questions might be (1) What? (2) So what?

I

Here is a proposal. To grasp Hegel's work in the *Philosophy of Right*, we have to take very seriously his general claim that in the Idea, "the universal *particularizes* itself and is herein identity with itself."[2] Both empiricists and Kantians seem to think otherwise.

---

[1] "Now, right here the contradiction immediately appears, i.e., that thought should have a history. What is presented in history is mutable, has taken place, was once, and is now past, has sunk into the night of the past, is no longer…The question, then, is: how can what is outside history, since it is not subject to change, still have a history?", cited in Lauer, Q. and G. W. F. Hegel (1983). *Hegel's Idea of Philosophy with a New Translation of Hegel's Introduction to the History of Philosophy*. New York, Fordham University Press, pp. 68–9.

[2] Hegel, G. W. F. (1969). *Enzyklopädie der philosophischen Wissenschaften III*. Frankfurt a. M., Suhrkamp., §383. "Als für sich seiend ist das Allgemeine sich *besondernd* und hierin Identität mit sich."

For them (and this seems to be now by and large the accepted view) the relation of the general concept (the "universal") to the things falling under it is taken to consist in something like a rule being applied to external instances. The concept of "horse" is thus a rule (perhaps for using the English word, "horse"), and it is an entirely different matter whether there really are horses that fall under the concept. In the case of the "Idea," Hegel seems to think that there is something different going on. So if we get Hegel's idea of his "Idea" right, perhaps we get a lot of what he is trying to do in his ethical and political thought. Or we can at least tease out what the implications might be for taking the "Idea" in one way rather than the other.

That what Hegel calls the "Idea" is crucial for him is not exactly a hard case to make. He begins the *Philosophy of Right* with the claim that "the subject-matter of the philosophical science of right is the Idea of right—the concept of right and its actualization."[3] Right at the outset, we have the distinction between the concept of right and its actualization, and the Idea as the concept of the concept and its actualization. This harks back to something Hegel also says in his discussion of his *Logic* in his *Encyclopedia* to the effect that the "logical Idea" of what is comprehended in the *Logic* is itself *only* a concept, a "possibility" and not actual spirit.[4] That invites the view that the rest of the system is not simply an addition to the *Logic* but something necessary if we are to comprehend the actuality of the possibilities discussed in the *Logic* itself. (It also has to be acknowledged that this mild interpretation is complicated by the many passages in the *Logic* which speak unequivocally about the actuality of some of the items.)

One way of clarifying this at the outset is to import some Kantian language into Hegel's theory. Kant rested his critical philosophy on the distinction between appearance (the phenomenal realm) and things in themselves, the latter being unknowable. When things in themselves become objects of thought, they are called noumena. This distinction between phenomena and noumena and their unity is that expressed by Hegel's use of "*Idee*" as the unity of concept and objectivity.[5] The Idea is

---

[3] Hegel, G. W. F. (1969). *Grundlinien der Philosophie des Rechts*. Frankfurt a. M., Suhrkamp., §1.

[4] "Denn das schon in der einfachen *logischen* Idee enthaltene *Erkennen* ist nur der von uns gedachte Begriff des Erkennens, nicht das für sich selbst vorhandene Erkennen, nicht der wirkliche Geist, sondern bloß dessen Möglichkeit." Hegel, G. W. F. (1969). *Enzyklopädie der philosophischen Wissenschaften III*. Frankfurt a. M., Suhrkamp., §381, p. 18.

[5] Hegel, G. W. F. (1969). *Enzyklopädie der philosophischen Wissenschaften I*. Frankfurt a. M., Suhrkamp., §213: "The idea is *what is true in and for itself*—the *absolute unity of the concept and objectivity*. Its ideal content is nothing but the concept in its determinations: its real content is only its exhibition that the concept gives itself in the form of external existence, while yet, by enclosing this shape in its ideality, in its power, sustains itself in it…Because it has no *existence* for starting-point and point of support, the idea is frequently taken to be a mere logical form. Such a view must be left to those theories which ascribe so-called *reality* and genuine *actuality* to the existent thing and all the other categories yet permeated with the Idea.—No less false is the notion that the Idea is merely that which is abstract. It is certainly abstract insofar as *everything untrue* is exhausted in it; but within itself it is essentially *concrete*, because it is the free concept giving itself reality. It would be the formally-abstract only if the concept, which is its principle, were taken as the abstract unity, and not as the *negative return* of itself into itself and therefore as *subjectivity*." [Die Idee ist das *Wahre an und für sich, die absolute Einheit des Begriffs und der Objektivität*. Ihr ideeller Inhalt ist kein anderer als der Begriff in seinen Bestimmungen; ihr reeller Inhalt ist nur seine Darstellung, die er sich in der Form äußerlichen Daseins gibt und [der,] diese Gestalt in seine Idealität eingeschlossen, in

the phenomenal world as comprehended in thought, and in practical contexts, Hegel expresses this by saying that the Idea is the warp and the passions are the weft of world history.[6] In the Idea, there is a unity of the phenomenal world and the noumenal world. The unity of the phenomenal world is that of an infinitely extending background, not all of which can be grasped through perception or intuition. The phenomenal world as conceptually comprehended is the world of the Idea, and its "infinity" can be grasped not, as it were, as one thing after another but in the boundlessness of the conceptual.

The initial section begins with the concept of "abstract right," and (except for the discussion of punishment), there are few substantive rights talked about that would generate much controversy nowadays about their being "rights." The triad that emerged from the English Civil War play the leading roles: Life, liberty, and property. Yet the very choice of these already involves a substantive claim by Hegel. Hegel speaks of them as the abstract "rights" of a subject and also of a "person." He distinguishes the two concepts: "The person is essentially different from the subject, for the subject is only the possibility of personality, since any living thing whatever is a subject. A person is therefore a subject which is aware of this subjectivity, for as a person, I am completely for myself: the person is the individuality of freedom in pure being-for-itself."[7]

To take up a distinction recently made by Michael Thompson between agents and persons: Agents act on reasons, and agents can be singular humans or collectivities. (You are an agent, but so is the World Bank.) A person, on the other hand, is a creature that can be morally wronged. (It may be possible to construct an agent—a collective— that can act but cannot be wronged. The "Weekly Neighborhood Hegel Workshop" might be an example of such a collective.) Likewise, "persons" can also be collectives (as one sees in the definition of a limited liability corporation as a legal person in certain contexts).[8] Hegel makes a different distinction, but his is related to Thompson's. To have moral standing, it is not enough to be a "subject." One must also be a "person." A subject, on Hegel's view, is any kind of living thing to which certain predicates of "what it does in light of the kind of life it is" can be ascribed. The subjects that interest him are,

---

seiner Macht, so sich in ihr erhält...Die Idee wird häufig, insofern sie nicht eine *Existenz* zu ihrem Ausgangs- und Stützpunkt habe, für ein bloß formelles Logisches genommen. Man muß solche Ansicht den Standpunkten überlassen, auf welchen das existierende Ding und alle weiteren noch nicht zur Idee durchgedrungenen Bestimmungen noch für sogenannte *Realitäten* und wahrhafte *Wirklichkeiten* gelten.—Ebenso falsch ist die Vorstellung, als ob die Idee nur das *Abstrakte* sei. Sie ist es allerdings insofern, als alles *Unwahre* sich in ihr aufzehrt; aber an ihr selbst ist sie wesentlich *konkret*, weil sie der freie, sich selbst und hiermit zur Realität bestimmende Begriff ist. Nur dann wäre sie das Formell-Abstrakte, wenn der Begriff, der ihr Prinzip ist, als die abstrakte Einheit, nicht, wie er ist, als die *negative Rückkehr seiner in sich* und als die *Subjektivität* genommen würde.]

   [6] "These two are the warp and weft in the fabric of world history." Hegel, G. W. F. (1975). *Lectures on the Philosophy of World History: Introduction, Reason in History.* Cambridge and New York, Cambridge University Press., p. 71.

   [7] Hegel, G. W. F. (1969). *Grundlinien der Philosophie des Rechts.* Frankfurt a. M., Suhrkamp., §35.

   [8] Thompson, M. (2004). "What Is It to Wrong Someone? A Puzzle about Justice". *Reason and Value: Themes from the Moral Philosophy of Joseph Raz*, R. J. Wallace, et al., Oxford and New York, Oxford University Press, pp. 333–84.

of course, those subjects that are living things ("subjects" in his wide sense) and who are agents who act for reasons of which they can be conscious. I shall use "subject" in this sense as combining person and agent (as, for the most part but not always, does Hegel).

Such "persons" have the moral standing of possessing abstract rights. Why? At least part of the answer lies in the philosophy of history that comes at the end of the book and is supposed therefore to be the "ground" for all that has come before it. History has led us to the conclusion that we are required to think of all subjects that they are free. That view has two components: first, to put it negatively, no person by nature has the authority to rule any other person, and second, each person has the capacity for self-directed action. The idea that "all are free" is minimally the idea that there is no over-arching natural authority among persons with the conclusions, first of all, that all such authority is exclusively socially and politically constituted, and, second of all, under the conditions of "all are free," it must conform in some general sense to the concept of each individual possessing the capacity for such freedom. But why? Hegel's answer seems to be that both philosophy and history have come to the same conclusion, and that has to do with the modern conception of "rights." If it is to be rational necessity, then the necessity in history has to fall in line with some non-question-begging philosophy.

Whatever the evaluation of the conclusion, one might worry that it is circular. The idea of a "subject" is that of a creaturely agent who can be morally wronged. It would seem that therefore the very idea of a "right" already involves some kind of moral standpoint, and that has two problems. First, just by consulting the table of contents of the *Philosophy of Right*, we see that "Morality" is supposed to follow from "Abstract Right," and thus we have to determine how that is supposed to go and whether it too is unhelpfully circular in its argument (and out of that grows one of the many thickets of interpretation). Second, it seems to be presupposing a certain conception of the "moral" that makes assumptions about something like a Kantian, universalistic con-ception of morality which, whatever its attractions might otherwise be, is not exactly self-evident.

Here is another proposal: We take one step back to Hegel's theory of "the concept" and of self-consciousness. In the *Logic*, he says that the Kantian theory of the synthetic unity of apperception—the "I think" that Kant says must be able to "accompany" all my representations—is the "most true" insight of the whole *Critique of Pure Reason*. But how could the "I think" be the starting point of a piece of allegedly practical philoso-phy? As a proposal, it may also look like a non-starter in a second sense, that it would fall victim to Kant's dismissal of Fichte's philosophy as the doomed attempt to derive content from the merely formal rules of logic.

Here it is worth noting the historically obvious: In his theoretical philosophy, Kant took his objection to Fichte to rest on a knockdown argument for the necessity of both concepts and intuitions as two different sources of knowledge, but in morality, Kant claimed that pure reason on its own could produce practical knowledge with substan-tive content. Now, this is itself just yet another conceptual and historical thicket, since

the various interpretations of whether the formal statement of the categorical imperative actually leads to substantive content also cover by now most of the places opened
up in that part of philosophical space. To cover that ground adequately, one would
have to rehearse all the ins and outs of distinguishing willing (*Wille*) from freely choosing (*Willkür*) and Kant's own claim that the moral good trumps all other forms of good.
However, sometimes wandering around in the thicket is not the best way to see how to
get to the clearing, so I shall put those aside.

Hegel finds Kant's picture to be troubling for many of the usual reasons that have
been advanced over the last couple of hundred years. It has a view of subjects and the
world lying on two sides of a strict dividing line: There is the subject on the one side
with a will that legislates a formal law and there is the content of various desires, passions, and needs on the other side (and lying on the same side as the desires and needs
is a world that may or may not have some other kind of goods within it). That picture is
attractive in many ways, but there are grounds for worry about it. Besides the emptiness objection, one might doubt whether Kant has really shown that the moral good
really does trump other goods.[9] One might argue that there really are other substantive
goods that the formal moral law has to take up even if those other goods cannot trump
the moral good.[10] Still, none of those worries can be decisive, since the Kantian can
either bite the bullet or reshape some of the aspects of the theory to make room for
those worries.

Kant does have a reply that has not escaped commentators. The formality of willing
according to universal law is supposed to imply or generate in some sense a commitment to a substantive end, that of respecting all rational nature and therefore that of
respecting all humanity in oneself and in the person of another.[11] Hegel does not take
up that idea immediately in the "Introduction" to the *Philosophy of Right*, although it is
clearly an idea that he takes up later. The idea does have its problems. Contrary to
Kant's emphatic claims, so Hegel thought, no substantive content comes from the
claim that one is to respect another's capacity to set ends by promoting that capacity or
those ends. Reason is an unbounded capacity, bound only by laws of its own. Even if we
must, in some sense of "must," take that capacity to be of infinite value, it is hard to see
how this translates into the unconditional respect for humanity that Kant claims it
does, at least in any concrete way.[12]

---

[9] The best known and the *locus classicus* of the modern form of this objection is in Williams, B. A. O.
(1985). *Ethics and the Limits of Philosophy*. Cambridge, MA, Harvard University Press.

[10] This is one way of taking Barbara Herman's neo-Kantian ideas of deliberative presumption and
background salience as a presupposition of the categorical imperative.

[11] On this teleological reading of Kant's ethics, the obvious contemporary exponents are Korsgaard,
C. M. (1996). *Creating the Kingdom of Ends*. Cambridge and New York, Cambridge University Press, and
Wood, A. W. (1999). *Kant's Ethical Thought*. Cambridge and New York, Cambridge University Press.

[12] Robert Pippin makes this argument on the idea that for the finite, limited agents Kant takes us to be,
it is difficult to accept the stronger claim—that pure practical reason can set objective ends. Too many
claims about life—Pippin's example is that of the person choosing to be a rodeo cowboy—hang on matters
that do not look like the kinds of matters that can plausibly be candidates for being determined solely by
pure practical reason. Moreover, it is a stretch to think that I am under any kind of obligation to assist in

But maybe that difficulty lies in our part, in our somehow not seeing the subtleties of Kant's wider argument. Another but still related problem with Kant's view is whether, despite its clear formulation on this point, it amounts to respecting humanity at all in the way Kant surely intends for it to be. This is an argument that has also been raised by Michael Thompson.[13] When we judge that somebody has wronged another person, it seems that we are making what Thompson calls a "bi-polar" judgment of the form: X wronged Y. This is different from a monadic judgment, such as "X did wrong." Sometimes Kant speaks of his moral views as if they did consist of such monadic judgments. "Wronging someone" on that model has the structure more or less of that of committing a foul in a sport. Wronging a particular person is like having the (moral) referee blow the whistle and call a foul on you or call you offside. In the case of the foul, the other person is merely the instance which provokes the referee to blow the whistle. In such games, what counts is not even whether another person is actually wronged but what the "game" has set to count as a foul. On that conception of the relation between the subject and the moral order, any violation of a basic rule can count as a moral wrong, even if it morally wrongs no other person. For example, Kant holds that a variety of self-regarding behaviors, such as gluttony, violate a rule of the game, and the moral referee should blow the whistle on those too. There the person committing the moral wrong is the person who has been wronged, and the rules say that too is out of bounds.

Yet even though he sometimes speaks like that—especially in his stern invocations against violating the (moral) law—Kant does not seem in many other passages to want to restrict his views to such monadic judgments, and it might even seem tendentiously unfair to Kant to saddle him with the view that his moral system is so monadic. Kant after all seems to have built it into his system of pure practical reason that it include rules requiring such creatures to treat other creatures who also have pure practical reason at work in their lives with respect (just as those designing a game can simply build it into the game that "roughing the quarterback" is a bad thing and should draw a foul). Thompson has another argument that responds to that. On the Kantian view, we respect other agents because they manifest or embody the moral law, and for us to respect that, it must be the same moral law in both of us. (It cannot by accident turn out to be something like a law coming from a different legal system but with the same

---

the person's pursuit of that rodeo-oriented end. If pure practical reason really is the source of all good (or is what makes goods objective, fully rational goods), then such problems seem insurmountable. Pippin, R. B. (1993). "Review of Allen Wood, 'Hegel's Ethical Thought'." *Inquiry: An Interdisciplinary Journal of Philosophy* 43: 239–66. Pippin also undercuts the idea that we can save that thought by appealing to the infinite value of giving oneself the law in "On giving oneself the law". One of the examples is that of the stock character in B-Westerns who refuses to let the doctors amputate his leg. What does his "autonomous" choice in that context mean? (His choice now, or the one he would make in the very near future? In what sense is he choosing "autonomously" at all?) The end remains too indeterminate to be of any practical guidance.

[13] Thompson, M. (2004). "What Is It to Wrong Someone? A Puzzle about Justice". *Reason and Value: Themes from the Moral Philosophy of Joseph Raz*, R. J. Wallace, et al., Oxford and New York, Oxford University Press, pp. 333–84.

content, in the same way that a law from one legal system—say, that of Japan—is not binding on someone else in a different legal system—say, Germany—even if the two laws have the same content.) How is it possible that the same law manifests itself in different agents (and that it need not be restricted to human agents but extends to any and all those entities that can manifest such laws)? Kant has an elaborate metaphysics to answer that question, and if his metaphysics were true, it would perhaps save the view.[14] Kant's metaphysics is, to be sure, a rather weird metaphysics, but, on the other hand, the world is a pretty weird place, and so the weirdness of the metaphysics should not per se count against it.

It looks as if Hegel might be landing himself in a similar pickle, since he holds that there is something in people which does historically come to demand respect for itself. This occurs in passages such as "The religiosity and ethicality of a restricted sphere of life (for example, that of a shepherd or peasant) in their concentrated inwardness and limitation to a few simple situations of life, have infinite worth…This inner focal point…remains untouched [and protected from] the noisy clamor of world history."[15] Moreover, although for him to hold the view he does of nature, Hegel cannot hold that nature is devoid of value (as some take Kant to have done). He also states that if not Kant's "good will," it is nonetheless "freedom" that the basis of calling things "right" (as when for example he says apparently unequivocally that "*Right* is any existence in general which is the *existence* of the *free will*. Right is thus in general existent there as freedom, as Idea," and "Right is something *utterly sacred*, for the simple reason that it is the existence of the absolute concept, of self-conscious freedom"[16]). This might seem as if it makes all valuing, or all the valuing that really counts, oddly and probably indefensible, relative to our wills.[17] If so, many of the worries we might have about the Kantian

---

[14] However, as Thompson points out, the elaborate Kantian metaphysics is exactly what the contemporary Kantians wish to deny. His argument on that point is that they cannot have it both ways. The Kantian position is logically possible, but for it to be real, there must be "present in me a practical law, the operation of which is alas often impeded, which has all the cosmic scope of the laws of interaction of fundamental particles; its operation, we may suppose, is busily being impeded even in distant galaxies" (p. 383). On Kantian grounds themselves, the existence of such a law must be unintelligible to us.

[15] See Hegel, G. W. F. and J. Hoffmeister (1994). *Vorlesungen über die Philosophie der Weltgeschichte.* Hamburg, F. Meiner, p. 109; Hegel, G. W. F. (1975). *Lectures on the Philosophy of World History: Introduction, Reason in History.* Cambridge and New York, Cambridge University Press, p. 92. ["Die Religiosität, die Sittlichkeit eines beschränkten Lebens—eines Hirten, eines Bauern,—in ihrer konzentrierten Innigkeit und ihrer Beschränktheit auf wenige und ganz einfache Verhältnisse des Lebens hat unendlichen Wert und desselben Wert als die Religiosität und Sittlichkeit einer ausgebildeten Erkenntnis und eines an Umfang der Beziehungen und Handlungen reichen Daseins. Dieser innere Mittelpunkt, diese einfache Region des Rechts der subjektiven Freiheit, der Herd des Wollens, Entschließens und Tuns, der abstrakte Inhalt des Gewissens, das, worin Schuld und Wert des Individuums, sein ewiges Gericht, eingeschlossen ist, bleibt unangetastet und ist dem lauten Lärm der Weltgeschichte und nicht nur den äußerlichen und zeitlichen Veränderungen, sondern auch denjenigen, welche die absolute Notwendigkeit des Freiheitsbegriffs selbst mit sich bringt, [entnommen]."]

[16] PR, ¶29: "Dies, daß ein Dasein überhaupt *Dasein des freien Willens* ist, ist das Recht.—Es ist somit überhaupt die Freiheit, als Idee" and "Das Recht ist etwas *Heiliges überhaupt*, allein weil es das Dasein des absoluten Begriffes, der selbstbewußten Freiheit ist" (¶30).

[17] This is a criticism made most forcefully by Thompson, M. (2004). "What Is It to Wrong Someone? A Puzzle about Justice". *Reason and Value: Themes from the Moral Philosophy of Joseph Raz,* R. J. Wallace, et al.,

setup might equally well apply to Hegel, even though the terms at stake ("free will" versus "*Geist*," and so forth) are on the surface different.

Hegel's way out of the pickle has to do with one of his criticisms that he makes of Kant in terms of Kant's own principle. In his later work, Kant adopts what Henry Allison has called the "incorporation thesis." In place of the view of sensibility giving the subject one set of motivations and reason giving him another, Kant substituted the view that "an incentive can determine the will to an action only so far as the individual has incorporated it into his maxim (has made it the general rule in accordance with which he will conduct himself); only thus can an incentive, whatever it may be, co-exist with the absolute spontaneity of the will (i.e., freedom)."[18] No natural incentive can actually be a motive for action unless the subject makes it a motive for action. Hegel's argument was that if the incorporation thesis were truly Kant's view, then the struggle between passion and duty, which seemed central to Kant, could really only be the struggle of reason with itself. What looks at first like two great forces meeting each other in one individual—passion battling it out with reason to see who will win—in fact becomes the battle within the subject of which reason has the greater weight: Do my passions give me a greater reason to do such and such than do the formal demands of the moral law? What is supposed to be the battle between two forces turns out really to be a form of "shadowboxing" of reason with itself.[19]

To see how this view works in terms of Hegel's criticism and absorption of the Kantian view, we need to continue to look at his arguments in a wider perspective.

Oxford and New York, Oxford University Press, pp. 333–84; Thompson, M. (2015). "Forms of Nature: 'First', 'Second', 'Living', 'Rational' and 'Phronetic'." <https://www.academia.edu/9666637/Forms_of_nature_first_second_living_rational_and_phronetic_>. The same type of criticism has been made by Frey, J. (2014). "Against Autonomy: Why Practical Reason Cannot Be Pure". On the interpretation proposed here, Thompson's view stands in substantial agreement with Hegel's, but differs on the issue of life-form versus historicism.

[18] Kant, I. (1960). *Religion within the Limits of Reason Alone*. New York, Harper, p. 19.

[19] In the *Phenomenology*, Hegel had argued that point when he contrasted the knight of virtue to the way of the world. The knight of virtue thinks he is struggling to realize "the good" as opposed to the subject who embodies the wicked way of the world (the world of passions and egoism). The knight of virtue takes himself to have made reason his motive, whereas he takes the subject of "the way of the world" to be moved by only natural self-interested desire. This amounts only to shadowboxing (*Spiegelfechterei*—"fencing with a mirror") since what is at stake is what counts as a good or overriding reason for each of them. In Hegel's telling of the story, the way of the world wins out not because animal passion triumphs over virtue, but because the constellation of reasons at work in the emerging early modern world win out over the antiquated conceptions of virtue. After authors such as Mandeville in his *Fable of the Bees* had already made the claim that in the newly emerging modern world, private vice could actually be public virtue, Hegel broadened considerations like that into the view that the structure of reasons that we have can itself only be comprehended in terms of its sociality and historical embeddedness, and in the modern world that comes with market-oriented practices that provide a basis for thinking that self-interested reasons can be actually be legitimate, ethically based reasons. I discussed this in Pinkard, T. P. (1994). *Hegel's Phenomenology: The Sociality of Reason*. Cambridge, Cambridge University Press. See the discussion of how this plays out in terms of self-individuation in Hegel's thought in Yeomans, C. (2015). *The Expansion of Autonomy: Hegel's Pluralistic Philosophy of Action*. New York, Oxford University Press.

II

Hegel's absorption of the incorporation thesis is not the view that somehow the passions lose their force in moving people to action, nor that they are dissolved into the more bloodless ideas of weighing reasons against each other. It does claim that they stand in a different relation to the subject than they do to a non-self-conscious animal. The incorporation thesis brings, as he puts it, the "form of self-consciousness" to the passions, and this makes all the difference, since, as Hegel puts it, "the great difference that matters in world history is what has to do with this difference."[20]

Following Matthew Boyle, we can characterize this in terms of the difference between the "additive" and the "transformative" conception of rationality.[21] The additive conception of rationality views it as a property simply added or grafted on to an existing stock of animal powers such that it can monitor them and maybe even exercise some causal power over them, but is essentially a different set of powers from the stock of animal powers. A "transformative" conception of subjectivity understands the capacity for rationality not simply as adding powers to an existing stock of animal powers but as producing a new genus of animal—the rational animal—which transforms those animal powers. A rational animal is not just an animal with rational powers grafted on to itself. It is an animal that stands in a very different relation to itself than do non-rational animals. For an animal to become a rational animal, the "I think" must be able to accompany all its representations, so that the capacity for self-consciousness is constitutive of such a rational animal. In such a transformative conception, "the kinds of perceptual episodes which we rational creatures undergo must themselves be characterized in terms that imply the power to reason about the import of such episodes" (an idea made well known by John McDowell).[22]

Likewise, as Boyle explains, even in cases of "passive" self-knowledge (paradigmatically, knowledge of our sensations), such rational animals are still ascribing such states to a subject.[23] The difference between the parrot who has been taught to say "I am in pain" when it is in pain and the rational animal who does the same thing has to do with the cognitive relation to the state—more generally with the relation of the rational animal to its states. We do not merely "have" these mental states (for example, of sensation or brute desire), we also represent them as ours. Without that capacity for self-ascription, of representing them as ours, we could not make cognitive statements about those states. The trained parrot can make no such cognitive statement.

---

[20] Hegel, G. W. F. (1969). *Vorlesungen über die Geschichte der Philosophie I*. Frankfurt a. M., Suhrkamp., p. 40. "Der Mensch, der an sich vernünftig ist, ist nicht weitergekommen, wenn er für sich vernünftig ist. Das Ansich erhält sich, und doch ist der Unterschied ganz ungeheuer. Es kommt kein neuer Inhalt heraus; doch ist diese Form ein ungeheurer Unterschied. Auf diesen Unterschied kommt der ganze Unterschied in der Weltgeschichte an."

[21] Boyle, M. (forthcoming). "Additive Theories of Rationality: A Critique." *European Journal of Philosophy*.

[22] Ibid.

[23] Boyle, M. (2009). "Two Kinds of Self-Knowledge." *Philosophy and Phenomenological Research* 78(1): 133–64.

As Boyle suggests, the "additive" picture is fundamentally Cartesian in its overall structure, since it suggests that there are two very different sets of powers that are simply joined to each other. The true-blue Cartesian explains this difference in terms of two different types of substance which are at work in those cases, whereas the more contemporary Cartesians, usually while vehemently denying Descartes' original dualism of thinking and extended substances, nonetheless keep the additive structure intact, often nodding to evolutionary theory as showing that the rational component had to get added later to the animal component in the course of evolution.

Hegel is certainly not the only "transformative" theorist of rationality, but that view adequately captures his overall approach. He subscribes to the view of action that understands the subject's knowledge of what he is doing as essential to the action.[24] Or, as he puts it, the subject gives the "form of self-consciousness" to his life.[25] In giving this form, he does not automatically give it a reflective form of self-consciousness, although his self-consciousness requires the capacity for such reflection. (In reading this sentence, you know you are reading the sentence and not, for example, gardening, jogging, taking a bath, etc., and you do this without any reflective knowledge being necessary in that case.) In Elizabeth Anscombe's gnomic formulation, the subject knows what he is doing, and this knowledge is both non-inferential and non-observational. Without this knowledge, there would not be an action at all.

In defending this kind of account of action against, for example, causal accounts (on the model of those suggested by Donald Davidson), Michael Thompson has given an account of action in general as a kind of teleologically structured event—an event or series of events whose explanation requires us to specify the end that gives it its sense. The dog going after the squirrel, the mantis honing in on its prey, and the human going to the market are all engaged in actions that require such explanations. Only in the human case does the explanation also require a reason in the form of self-consciousness. This is not knowledge of an inner, psychic event (of a mental state) but knowledge of a material process.[26] Unlike the standard causal account, which specifies an action by the mental state (the intention) which causes it, Thompson's view understands the action as composed of smaller intentional actions in which there are no actions that can count

---

[24] The relation to Hegel's own conception of action is made by Pippin, R. B. (2008). *Hegel's Practical Philosophy: Rational Agency as Ethical Life*. Cambridge, Cambridge University Press. The more general developments of the Ancombeian view appear in Thompson, M. (2004). "What Is It to Wrong Someone? A Puzzle about Justice". *Reason and Value: Themes from the Moral Philosophy of Joseph Raz*, R. J. Wallace, et al., Oxford and New York, Oxford University Press, pp. 333–84; Rödl, S. (2007). *Self-consciousness*. Cambridge, MA and London, Harvard University Press; Pippin, R. B. (2008). *Hegel's Practical Philosophy: Rational Agency as Ethical Life*. Cambridge, Cambridge University Press; Thompson, M. (2008). *Life and Action: Elementary Structures of Practice and Practical Thought*. Cambridge, MA, Harvard University Press.

[25] Hegel, G. W. F. (1969). *Grundlinien der Philosophie des Rechts*. Frankfurt a. M., Suhrkamp., §26.

[26] Thompson, M. (2015). "Forms of Nature: 'First', 'Second', 'Living', 'Rational' and 'Phronetic.'" <https://www.academia.edu/9666637/Forms_of_nature_first_second_living_rational_and_phronetic_>. See also the discussion in Frey, "Analytic Philosophy of Action: A Very Brief History," and "How to be an Ethical Naturalist" <https://jennfrey.wordpress.com/research/>.

as basic, as actions that are not means to any other action.[27] Thus, when asked why I am studying Kant so assiduously, I might respond with something like, "I am studying for my BA at the college here." That same reply might also follow from being asked why I am studying organic chemistry so assiduously, etc. If asked why I am participating in the environmental consciousness study group, I might reply that it too is part of studying for the BA, or of going to college, although the participation in the environmental consciousness group is not for credit. Those smaller component actions themselves may also be explained in different ways. (The Kant question—"Why are you studying the *Critique*"—may prompt a reply such as, "If I understand what in the world a pure intuition is, I may be able to write the mid-term paper satisfactorily and get a better grade.") The point is that an action may be explainable by its reason, but its components need not be just one intention plus an action but a set of other actions, done for their own reasons but also done for the overarching reason of the whole action. Throughout all these different explanations, I know what I am doing—going to college, getting my BA—even if I do not often think to myself any thought such as "I am going to college."

Examples like this have been taken to suggest an overall account of action in terms of instrumental reasoning, typified elegantly by Hume's statement: "Ask a man *why he uses exercise; he will answer, because he desires to keep his health.* If you then enquire, why he desires health, he will readily reply, *because sickness is painful.* If you push your enquiries farther, and desire a reason *why he hates pain,* it is impossible he can ever give any. This is an ultimate end, and is never referred to any other object."[28] Hume's view pushes us to something like a doctrine of ultimate ends that effectively stop the chain of reasoning. One can easily understand how Kant takes his own view of treating humanity as an end in itself as another way of ending the chain that is more in keeping with the conception of pure practical reason. (And one can understand how to generate the metaphysical see-saw that gets set up once one assumes that picture.)

Thompson's argument is that this Humean picture of action flies in the face of the form that reasons for action assume.[29] "Studying Kant" is an action, an event unfolding over time characterized by its end, and its explanation, its "reason" can be a more general action, "studying for the BA" for which "studying Kant" is one component. The form of the explanation need not be Hume's purely instrumental "exercise to promote health to avoid pain" but a series of actions, each of which is explicable in terms of the overall reason of "studying for the BA" but which themselves may not be linked instrumentally to each other. It may have the shape: "I am reading the 'Introduction to the second edition' of the *Critique* not for the purpose of reading the 'Transcendental

---

[27] See Lavin, D. (2013). "Must There Be Basic Actions?" *Nous* 47(2): 273–301.

[28] Hume, D. and J. B. Schneewind (1983). *An Enquiry Concerning the Principles of Morals*. Indianapolis, Hackett Pub. Co., p. 87. Hume's statement is all the more ironic, since it seems Hume did relatively little to no exercise at all.

[29] "Naïve Action Theory" in Thompson, M. (2008). *Life and Action: Elementary Structures of Practice and Practical Thought*. Cambridge, MA, Harvard University Press.

Aesthetic', nor am I reading the 'Transcendental Aesthetic' for the purpose of reading the 'Metaphysical Deduction', etc.," and each of these may have as its reason, "working to get the BA" or "getting to know Kant." (Of course, there may turn out to be a crude instrumentalism at work in that sequence, as in the stereotype of the student who does all the work and learns nothing, but it is not a priori fact that it must be so explained, and in many cases of seeking a specific form of goodness, that kind of instrumentalism will even in fact be unproductive or counterproductive of the end.[30])

If such a distinction is intelligible, then "leading a human life" may well function as such a general reason, with many actions falling underneath it as subordinate to it and explicable in terms of it. Thompson uses this to conclude that if such explanation is possible, then it cannot be in terms as formal as Kant's use of "rational nature." A "life form" (Thompson's term) explains in a general sense why a creature acts as it does. (For example: "That's what bears do.") Thompson takes this to be required in explaining any type of life (as does Hegel, so I would argue).[31] The amoeba and the bear do what they do because of their "life form." But, as Hegel puts it, in the case of self-conscious creatures, the life form is aware of itself as a life form.[32] The "life form" figures as a reason in the subject's actions, and it is formal because it does not specify what exactly the individual of the genus will do, but it is substantive in that it will explain why it does these things and not those. (Rabbits will eat lettuce, but foxes will eat rabbits. Moreover, the foxes are not eating the rabbits in order to be foxes but because they are foxes.) The distinguishing feature of human action is its self-consciousness: Knowing what I am doing will include doing this because (in the sense of its being a "reason") of the human life form under which I fall. On Thompson's account, therefore, we must know the life form in which we participate in a non-empirical manner.[33]

To shift from Thompson to Hegel: To be an apperceptive life is to know that one is this shape of life exactly by being the life that falls under the concept, and an apperceptive

---

[30] Jennifer Frey makes this point in Frey, J. (2014). *How to be an Ethical Naturalist.*

[31] Thompson, M. (2015). "Forms of Nature: 'First', 'Second', 'Living', 'Rational' and 'Phronetic'." <https://www.academia.edu/9666637/Forms_of_nature_first_second_living_rational_and_phronetic_> "At the level of thought: the *representation* of given phenomena here and now as amounting to a process of reproduction, or as a phase of it, depends on a conception of how things stand with the individual's so-called species or life form or 'first nature'. This form-dependence or first-nature-dependence or species-dependence, or whatever you want to call it, extends, I think, to every ordinary tensed description of an individual organism precisely as alive."

[32] Actually, he says roughly the same thing in different terms: The genus is aware of itself as a genus. Hegel, G. W. F. (2010). *Phenomenology of Spirit* translated by Terry Pinkard., ¶172: "Rather, in this *result*, life points towards something other than itself, namely, towards consciousness, for which life exists as this unity, that is, as genus."

[33] "The human form, my form, what I am, the unity to which I bring my thoughts, etc. is evidently also exhibited in the specific unity, outlined by Anscombe, of concept-of-itself governed process, i.e. of intentional action; coming into possession of this form is coming into possession of a will, if all goes well. I know that it is possible by sharing in it, that is, as a sort of *factum* of reason; I have no similar way of knowing that the opposed idea is *impossible*." Thompson, M. (2015). "Forms of Nature: 'First', 'Second', 'Living', 'Rational' and 'Phronetic'." <https://www.academia.edu/9666637/Forms_of_nature_first_second_living_rational_and_phronetic_>, p. 731.

life falls under that concept just by bringing itself under that concept.[34] We are self-conscious animals by being the animals that bring ourselves under the concept, "self-conscious animal." We know this in a non-empirical way because it is a feature of our subjectivity that we are the subjects we are by bringing ourselves under the concept of "subject."[35] We are participating, as Hegel says, in the life of spirit, and that is the reason for many of the progressively unfolding actions we take.

III

To keep Hegel within the more familiar but less expressive terms of contemporary philosophy, we can say that we are concept-mongering creatures because we make ourselves into concept-mongering creatures. That much is part of Hegel's "soft" naturalism which he shares with Thompson and others. However, as Thompson has also argued, nothing ethical follows from this. It does not follow from the form of being a concept-mongering creature that it include moral or ethical concepts about, for example, wronging others within itself.[36] It may be that some concept-mongering creatures do have that written into the rules of their game, but there does not seem to be any necessity at least at first for that rule to be there. For Hegel to get to a "science of right" out of these considerations will take an extra step.

However, in taking his next step, what Hegel does not do is argue that the next step has to rest on some kind of fact about human nature. That is, he does not distinguish between concept-mongering creatures who, were they to appear in some other area of the cosmos, might be bereft of moral feeling, and us, who are not so bereft, and claim

---

[34] In what I now think to be a very confused way, I discussed this many years ago as the self-subsuming and self-explaining aspect of conceptual thought in Pinkard, T. P. (1988). *Hegel's Dialectic: The Explanation of Possibility*. Philadelphia, Temple University Press. Nonetheless, however clumsy and ultimately unsatisfactory my original treatment of the idea was, the basic idea behind it had more or less something approaching the right target in view (even if, while in flight, the arrow fell far away from the goal): A subject is a subject by being the kind of substance that does not sense itself as a substance and then apply a category to itself, but is rather a thinking substance that knows it is a thinking substance by being the substance that brings itself under that concept. Subsequent reading of several authors helped me to see the inadequacy of my earlier way of putting things, in particular, in representative works of theirs: Pippin, R. B. (2010). *Hegel on Self-Consciousness: Desire and Death in Hegel's Phenomenology of Spirit*. Princeton, NJ, Princeton University Press.; Henrich, D. (2007). *Denken und Selbstsein: Vorlesungen über Subjektivität*. Frankfurt am Main, Suhrkamp; and also Henrich, D. (1999). *Bewusstes Leben: Untersuchungen zum Verhältnis von Subjektivität und Metaphysik*. Stuttgart, Reclam; Farrell, F. B. (1994). *Subjectivity, Realism, and Postmodernism: The Recovery of the World*. Cambridge and New York, Cambridge University Press. One of the other major failings of *Hegel's Dialectic* is its Adorno-ian infused rejection of the absolute. This led me—in what I now think was a rather twisted way—to think that the question Hegel was posing in the philosophy of history was a kind of Kantian, "what are the conditions of the possibility of history at all." This is not Hegel's primary question (or, if to the extent that it is a question at all for him, it is only one of the minor ones he raises along the way for the purpose of explicating his real concerns).

[35] See Rödl, S. (2007). *Self-consciousness*. Cambridge, MA and London, Harvard University Press.

[36] Thompson, M. (2004). "What Is It to Wrong Someone? A Puzzle about Justice". *Reason and Value: Themes from the Moral Philosophy of Joseph Raz*, R. J. Wallace, et al., Oxford and New York, Oxford University Press, pp. 333–84.

this difference is just a fact, however deep and central a fact it might be, about us.[37] How does he get away with that?

In his *Logic*, Hegel at least claims to argue for a view that is Aristotelian in origin and spirit: To understand a concept fully, we must understand how it may be actualized in use, and in the case of a practical concept, how, in Hegel's way of putting it, it must be able to "actualize itself" if it is to count as a practical concept at all. A purportedly practical concept that could not be made real (be "actualized") would in fact not be a practical concept at all. It might be a wish or a daydream, but it is not practical, not anything that the subject could entertain as a real possibility, as something it could in principle do (in some appropriately metaphysical sense of "could").[38] When Hegel speaks of a "concept's actualizing itself," he qualifies it by saying that the only way a concept can "actualize itself" is by subjects taking up the concept and putting it into practice. By putting it into practice, the subject resolves a certain indeterminacy in any concept considered merely as a possibility of actualization. In acting, the agent specifies what she takes the concept to mean.

Although at this level of abstraction, we are indeed still speaking in Kantian terms of a generalized rational agent who brings together the "form" of self-consciousness (as universal law) and whatever are the inclinations and passions with which she is confronted. So it seems, the most that the agent can do is choose a general end (such as, for example, happiness or something similar) and subordinate all those passions into serving that end (or at least represent to herself the way they ought to be ordered if they were to serve that end), such as "avoid pain." Or the subject can choose the formal end—I shall act only on those maxims I can always and at the same time will as universal law—and conceive of all of her maxims as means to serving that end. Yet, in acting on the basis of that, the subject cannot act as a generalized rational agent who also happens to be a human being (as we would be if rationality were something like a Platonic form which at least some of us happened to manifest).[39] To the extent that the

[37] See Thompson, on the idea of logical and local Footianism in Thompson, M. (2008). *Life and Action: Elementary Structures of Practice and Practical Thought*. Cambridge, MA, Harvard University Press. He sees the problem with his own position as finding the right epistemology for the Aristotelianism he defends. See Thompson, M. (2004). "What Is It to Wrong Someone? A Puzzle about Justice". *Reason and Value: Themes from the Moral Philosophy of Joseph Raz*, R. J. Wallace, et al., Oxford and New York, Oxford University Press, pp. 333–84. In Thompson, M. (2015). "Forms of Nature: 'First', 'Second', 'Living', 'Rational' and 'Phronetic'." <https://www.academia.edu/9666637/Forms_of_nature_first_second_living_rational_and_phronetic_>, he provisionally understands this problem to be solved by understanding that the knowledge of one's life form to be a *Faktum* of reason.

[38] Hegel, G. W. F. (1969). *Enzyklopädie der philosophischen Wissenschaften III*. Frankfurt a. M., Suhrkamp., §383. "Als für sich seiend ist das Allgemeine sich *besondernd* und hierin Identität mit sich. Die Bestimmtheit des Geistes ist daher die *Manifestation*. Er ist nicht irgendeine Bestimmtheit oder Inhalt, dessen Äußerung oder Äußerlichkeit nur davon unterschiedene Form wäre; so daß er nicht *etwas* offenbart, sondern seine Bestimmtheit und Inhalt ist dieses Offenbaren selbst. Seine Möglichkeit ist daher unmittelbar unendliche, absolute *Wirklichkeit*." He also notes: "der absolute Geist aber ist die absolute Einheit der Wirklichkeit und des Begriffs oder der Möglichkeit des Geistes." Ibid., §383, p. 29.

[39] See Thompson, M. (2015). "Forms of Nature: 'First', 'Second', 'Living', 'Rational' and 'Phronetic'." <https://www.academia.edu/9666637/Forms_of_nature_first_second_living_rational_and_phronetic_>.

subject has to choose in terms of a good (such as happiness), she has to choose in terms of a human good. This good functions like a norm, and hence like all norms, it can be transgressed. The very "form of self-consciousness" implies the possibility of such transgression.

Now, if we take the Kantian idea seriously that the subject is independent, or can make herself independent, of all sensuous desire and passion, then the subject exercises a kind of negative freedom as "independence of determination from outside of itself."[40] It is not necessarily free with regard to the passions to which it gives form, but it is free in giving those passions form. To actualize its freedom, it must seek an end with regards to which it itself is free, and, so Kant thought, this has to be its own autonomy, the moral law itself. Here I shall follow Hegel's assumption, which would take too long to fully explicate at this point, that the Kantian end of respecting rational nature as an end in itself cannot be formally cashed out in any adequate way that rescues the pure Kantian program. (This is a big assumption, but I take others to have made a case for it.[41]) If we give up on the claim that the end of treating humanity as an end in itself follows from the form of rational willing, then the Kantian position turns into just a version of the Humean position with the formula of universal law added to it. Moreover, any way to bail out Kant with appeal to something like a "practical identity" really would amount only to fusing the formula of universal law with what Hume would call a "convention."[42] (This leaves aside the causalist-psychological leanings of Hume's views on volition, but that is not important here.)

What one is left with is a self-conscious subject as a subject of "life," who because of her self-consciousness is always possibly not completely absorbed in such "life." There are natural goods that come with such a life, and there is the distinction of the subject as the choosing agent from all those goods.[43] If the Kantian position when pushed thus collapses into a kind of modified Humean view, the modified Humean view also has to become something else. The agent is not the "additive" agent whose internal psychological states are causing the action. Understanding the agent's actions as her action is to comprehend "a process as a phenomenon of agency, in this sense, when I see the concept through which I describe or represent the process as itself at work in the genesis of the process I describe or represent."[44]

[40] See Hegel, G. W. F. (1969). *Grundlinien der Philosophie des Rechts*. Frankfurt a. M., Suhrkamp., ¶14: "As such, the subject stand above its content, i.e., its various dives, and also above the further individual way in which these are actualized and satisfied."

[41] I take the arguments to be decisive in "Giving Oneself the Law" in Pippin, R. B. (2008). *Hegel's Practical Philosophy: Rational Agency as Ethical Life*. Cambridge, Cambridge University Press. And Pippin, R. B. (1993). "Review of Allen Wood, 'Hegel's Ethical Thought'." *Inquiry: An Interdisciplinary Journal of Philosophy* 43: 239–66.

[42] In essence, this seems to be the position to which Christine Korsgaard found herself driven in Korsgaard, C. M. (1996). *The Sources of Normativity*. New York, Cambridge University Press. Her more recent "constitutivism" position would not necessarily be prone to that objection.

[43] See the very helpful article: Longuenesse, B. (2012). "Kant and Hegel on the Moral Self." *Self, World, and Art: Metaphysical Topics in Kant and Hegel*, D. Emundts, Berlin, Walter de Gruyter, pp. 89–113.

[44] Thompson, M. (2004). "What Is It to Wrong Someone? A Puzzle about Justice". *Reason and Value: Themes from the Moral Philosophy of Joseph Raz*, R. J. Wallace, et al., Oxford and New York, Oxford University Press, pp. 333–84, p. 352.

Instead of the Humean or the Kantian subject, we now have the hybrid, the Kantian-Humean subject, who chooses among all the alternatives before her by acting in such a way to realize a concept of what she is doing (although that need not be, but might be, a reflective activity) but who does so in light of instrumental principles. If there is nothing to block the regress of such instrumental reasoning except avoidance of pain or conforming to the law, then we have a monadically conceived subject.

Hegel next imagines two such monadically conceived agents coming into relations with each other, and at some point, one of them, for her own reasons (perhaps out of egoism, madness, or just randomness) demands that the other recognize her as possessing the true system of concepts. To the extent that they see each other as occupying, metaphorically speaking, two different legal systems, there is no way of conceptually adjudicating the dispute. One of them might of course kill the other, or they might do each other in, or they might manage to strike a reasonable and pragmatic truce. However, if one of them does not see the reasonableness of a truce and is still willing to kill for the sake of such recognition, then there has to be a struggle. If out of fear for her life, one of them submits, she becomes the slave, and the other becomes the master. However, at that point, no matter how monadically they may have conceived of themselves before the outcome of the struggle, they have now entwined their fates. One now has life and death authority over the other, and the other must bend her will to the former. Such a structure exists because of such mutual recognition of the authority. Without that dyadic authority, there is no such relationship.

The move from the modified Kantian-Humean position to the social practice conception of subjectivity takes place in working out what has happened in the imagined encounter. As concept-mongering living creatures, the subjects find themselves not merely confronting desires and passions but as occupying a social space structured by a kind of authority. Each, like Hegel's shepherd, possesses an "inner focal point" that "remains untouched [and protected from] the noisy clamor of world history." That does not make them recognize each other as ends in themselves, recognizing that the other ought never be used merely as means. For them to reach that point, they have to work out a longer struggle for recognition in history. What they have is a social space in which what they do is done for a reason that is part of a larger context, that of being human, but this "being human" is always socially and historically indexed, even for those subjects who do not think of themselves as acting in light of socially and historically indexed concepts. That takes us very abstractly from the Kantian-Humean subject to the more historically embedded Hegelian subject. However, it does not get us all the way there. A few more signposts have to be erected before the guide gets us out of the thickets.

IV

Hegel has several theses about subjectivity and life whose explication and defense can only be pointed out here rather than fully fleshed out. Each is, however, plausible on its own as a starting point for discussion. Taken together, they are pointers on how to exit the thicket.

Here is the first of Hegel's theses: Individual actions take place under the "Idea" of the human—the "Idea" in the sense of the unity of concept and objectivity, the warp and weft of world history. People seek to lead a human life, and that concept of the human life is always tailored around the objectivity, the reality, of what is and is not possible for them. Hegel's shepherd fits this picture. He is self-conscious and thus possesses what we can call his "concept" of himself. The goods of his life will include freedom—the ability to act on his own and efficaciously will certain things into being—even though freedom may not be especially high on his list of goods.

This shepherd acts for reasons, and that places two kinds of constraints on his actions: For him to have a will, he must be able to reason from a standpoint from which he can conclude that there are things he can do and things he cannot do. He must, that is, have at least a vague sense of his specifically human powers. (He cannot fly like a bird, there are some weights too heavy for him to lift, he cannot defy death indefinitely, he can run only so fast, etc.) He must also have a conception of what can be actualized and what cannot. Hegel's shepherd knows that he can make changes in the world by willing certain things. At a certain point in history, he probably also thinks he knows that husbands have natural authority over their wives, just as aristocrats have natural authority over him. In all of these cases, his actions will be components of a larger activity, that of living an appropriate human life.[45] That is, he brings the "form of self-consciousness" to bear on the goods of the historically situated life in which he finds himself. At most points in history, the shepherd will also think he also knows that it is a universal truth that only some are free, in that there are only some who have the authority to command others but are not themselves under the command of anyone else, and that he (perhaps regrettably) is not among those "some" who are free in that sense. Because of that, he will think he knows that there are things he cannot change. Some will be masters, some will be servants. Even though by a stroke of fortune he might become a master, that will just mean that somebody else will have to remain or become a servant. Dreaming of a masterless world is just that: Dreaming. It is a possible thought, but it cannot become real. It is thus not a practical concept.

The second of Hegel's key theses is this: What is distinctive about subjectivity in its practical outlook is that it takes its own concept, its concept of itself, to be the truth to which the world should measure up, not the other way around. It is also one of his key theses that the development of this view is nowhere near as neat and tidy as the former sentence might suggest.

Here is the third of Hegel's theses: Each shape of life has its own absolute contours, typically expressed in its art, religion, and philosophy, about what ultimately a human life signifies. When within its absolute contours, a shape of life begins to exhibit conceptual tensions, even contradictions, within itself, it makes things difficult for people living in terms of it. When a shape of life cannot comprehend what it is doing, it begins

[45] In the beginning of the NE, Aristotle says: "if any action is well performed when it is performed in accordance with the appropriate excellence...But we must add 'in a complete life.' For one swallow does not make a summer, nor does one day; and so too one day, or a short time, does not make a man blessed and happy."

to lose its normative allegiance among people living in terms of it. People may not—in fact usually do not—stop behaving in terms of it, but they do not comprehend the point of what they are doing, and they become thereby alienated from it. Those periods mark breakdowns of a shape of life, times when things fall apart for the participants. Typically, in living among the ruins of such a meaning breakdown, they have to pick up the remaining pieces that still seem to work, discard those that do not, and put what still functions to work in a different order of things. (Hegel uses the German term, *Aufhebung*, cancelling and preserving, to signify that process.) As we might put it, when a shape of life is functioning well, its inhabitants see its terms as constitutive of practical reason, such that failure to adhere to them is itself a practical failure. When it begins to unravel, its terms become norms, and norms can always be transgressed without there being a clear practical failure at work.

Hegel has a view of history such that people have under many different conditions lived through such breakdowns of meanings in a way that has compelled them to a conclusion about human life such that nobody by nature has authority over anybody else, and therefore "all are free." The "form of self-consciousness," the metaphysical and normative core of subjectivity, is the basis from which any such ideal of progress in history is based.

Hegel's fourth thesis: Such subjects, who seek to bring the world into conformity with their "concept," arrive at two interests. For the first part, they want to insure that their judgments about what a human life is has subjective validity.[46] The subject takes up some good or some inclination and forms a rational practical judgment about it. The subject recognizes that its maxims are those that would also be taken up from the viewpoint of any other practically judging subject in their position.[47] She says to herself, "This is what those of us would do in this case."

For the second part, and this is a big supposition on Hegel's part, because of its form the subject is also driven to concern herself not merely with subjective validity but also with the objective validity of her maxims.[48] Not merely the idea of the "good" but also the idea of the "true" plays a role in its being the kind of being it is, namely, a human subject with the form of self-consciousness. In acting, the subject intends something or other, which is also, seen from another angle, the actualization of a concept, and in these cases, actualizing the concept of what it is to be a human being within that specific shape of life. The subject's reasoning about these actions is not simply instrumental to

---

[46] Hegel, G. W. F. (1969). *Grundlinien der Philosophie des Rechts*. Frankfurt a. M., Suhrkamp. ¶25.

[47] This would be consistent with Hume's own position and with Kant's when he says, "Instead, we must [here] take *sensus communis* to mean the idea of a sense *shared* [by all of us], i.e., a power to judge that in reflecting takes account (a priori), in our thought, of everyone else's way of presenting [something], in order *as it were* to compare our own judgment with human reason in general and thus escape the illusion that arises from the ease of mistaking subjective and private conditions for objective ones, an illusion that would have a prejudicial influence on the judgment. Now we do this as follows: we compare our judgment not so much with the actual as rather with the merely possible judgments of others, and [thus] put ourselves in the position of everyone else, merely by abstracting from the limitations that [may] happen to attach to our own judging." *Critique of Judgment*, §40.

[48] Hegel, G. W. F. (1969). *Grundlinien der Philosophie des Rechts*. Frankfurt a. M., Suhrkamp. ¶26.

achieving humanity.[49] Rather, she is acting in light of what it means at this place and at this time to act as a human conforming to her concept. From the standpoint of subjective validity, the subject reasons, "This is what we do." From the standpoint of objective validity, the subject reasons (or should wonder if) whether "What we do" is true, that is, is what a true human being would do. (This much depends on a central claim in Hegel's *Logic* to the effect that assertions about "substance" have to do with the way things appear or what causes them, whereas assertions about the "concept" have to do at least minimally with what follows from what—as when one says that your conclusions do not follow from your premises or that what you say is at odds with current understandings of evolutionary theory. A subject is minimally a creature who moves in the normative space of reasons, and thus, just as there are good and bad cases of reasoning, there are good and bad subjects. It makes sense to speak of better and worse versions of subjectivity but not better and worse causal processes.)

With those two claims about subjective and objective validity, the "science" of right is almost ready to begin. It requires two more theses, which will here just be stated. First, there is a deeply historical claim that history has pushed us to the position that it would be irrational to hold anything other than the view that "all are free." We have arrived at a point of "subjective validity" where "what we do" has something like the respect for human dignity as its norm. At that point, the old world has gone, and the "inner focal point" of the shepherd may appropriately demand that he too participate in political rule and lead his own life, such that if he demands such recognition from recalcitrant authorities, he will be in the right even if "what we do" in his particular world still runs completely contrary to that. The shepherd will also find that his wife, who in earlier periods owed him a kind of natural authority, also begins to demand her own right of participation. Second, there is therefore the idea that now, in our modern social space, we begin our inquiry into right with something like a modified Kantian view on dignity. Given the building blocks with which history has left us, that will have three parts: a section on the rights that all such agents can rationally claim; an understanding that these rights demand a moral point of view, a reasoning from the standpoint of what any rational human would do; and a conception of those social goods that make it good for any individual subject to think of his concept as good—that means that it is good to be a rights-bearing, moral agent, in the sense that one is doing what ultimately matters in a human life—so that even when the world fails to conform to this concept, it has the means to right itself.

With that, we are out of the thicket and into a clearing, where what shows up for us is the Hegelian and very modern triad of rights, morality, and ethical life. The *Wissenschaft* of right takes these as its building blocks and moves from there—most likely into new and not yet adequately charted thickets.[50]

---

[49] Thompson, "Forms of Nature."

[50] Hegel's notes in his own copy of the Hegel, G. W. F. (1969). *Grundlinien der Philosophie des Rechts*. Frankfurt a. M., Suhrkamp, ¶29, p. 81: "Die große Stellung des *Rechts*—Geist sich wirklich machen;—Natur ist, was sie ist; wird begriffen—daß der Geist—als eine *Natur*—als das System einer *Welt sei*,—Sitte, Ordnung [eine]r *Vorstellung*, Idee notwendig—für sich. Ob das, was in Idee notwendige Bestimmung, das sei, was die Menschen *Recht* heißen."

8

To Know and Not Know Right
Hegel on Empirical Cognition and Philosophical Knowledge of Right

Sebastian Stein

Introduction

What does the relationship between empirical cognition and philosophical knowledge mean for our engagement with the *Philosophy of Right*?[1] While much attention has recently been paid to the difference between empirical and philosophical knowledge in Hegel's work in general and in the *Philosophy of Right* in particular,[2] there is no agreement on whether Hegel's philosophical claims are at least partially informed by empirical experience and history (e.g. Pippin 2008, Honneth 1995), whether they relate to empirical experience in way similar to Kant's 'a priori'-claims,[3] or whether the knowledge they represent undercuts the difference between thought and reality that the notion 'a priori' can be argued to imply. It also remains disputed whether Hegel thinks that having philosophical knowledge amounts to taking 'god's point of view',[4] whether it describes the conceptually and empirically unconditioned truth of Kant's '(thing) in itself' (Sparby 2014: 34) or if it is limited to the perspective of particular, finite thinkers, i.e. 'us'.[5]

The difficulty in describing Hegel's position on this issue is not diminished by his seemingly contradictory statements about the nature of philosophical knowledge in the *Philosophy of Right* and the *Encyclopedia*'s equivalent, 'objective Geist' (Hegel 2007: §482ff., 214ff.). On the one hand, he claims that all his 'philosophical'[6] (Hegel 2008: 3)

---

[1] For comments on earlier versions of this chapter, I would like to thank (in alphabetical order) Thom Brooks, Michael Inwood, Robert Pippin, Felix Stein, Kenneth Westphal, and Allen Wood.

[2] See, e.g., Vieweg 2012, Ostritsch 2014, Sparby 2014, Longuenesse 2000, Beiser 2005, Kreines 2007.

[3] See e.g. Pippin 1989.   [4] Longuenesse 2000.

[5] Others wonder whether philosophy's claims are of a natural or a 'supersensible' kind (Sparby 2014: 34).

[6] Some recent commentators prefer what Thom Brooks (2012) calls 'non-systematic' approaches. These detach the claims of the *Philosophy of Right* from Hegel's other writings, e.g. the *Logic* and its justification of the concept.

statements represent the unconditioned truth that is 'eternal',[7] universally and objectively valid, brings forth time and space itself,[8] has been, is and always will be valid everywhere[9] (Hegel 1986: 24), ought to be accepted by all rational individuals, describes thought and reality at its most 'supreme' (Hegel 2007: §573 remark, 270) and, in short, defines the unconditioned (onto)logical principle that articulates itself in pure thought, in nature,[10] and in all Geist-informed phenomena (Hegel 1991a: §18, 42).[11]

Such claims seem to suggest that empirical cognition and experience neither define the content of the kind of knowledge that philosophical knowledge (from here on 'PK') represents nor that they affect it conceptually. For if they did, so Hegel's worry seems to be, PK's validity could be relative to the validity of the empirical experience, historical circumstance, etc. that informs it: if PK's content were conditioned, it would be just as good as—and thus limited in its validity to—its condition. To evaluate the condition, one would need a criterion in the form of a further condition and so on, resulting in an infinite regress. Alternatively, one might simply stop asking for justification of a given condition and thereby open oneself to the charge of assuming the condition's validity unquestioningly.[12]

The same holds for the conceptual relevance of empirical experience for PK: if PK is *conceptually* conditioned by experience—i.e. experience is ontologically first and philosophical knowledge is confined to exploring the conditions of the possibility of experience—experience would be in need of justification. This could be either done by appeal to experience or to some conceptual criterion. While doing the former would lead into infinite regress, doing the latter undermines the conceptual priority experience was argued to have in the first place.

So *if* PK were conditioned by empirical experience—empirically or conceptually—it would fail to live up to Hegel's explicit requirements[13] of (a) being informationally and conceptually unconditioned (Hegel 2007: §574, 275–6), (b) having absolute ontological priority (Hegel 1991a: §17, 41),[14] and (c) being an independent standard for all empirically existing thought and reality (Hegel 1986: 24).

---

[7] Hegel 1986: 24.   [8] Hegel, 1986a: §254ff., 41ff.

[9] 'For philosophy's aim is to cognize that, which never passes, is eternal and in and for itself; philosophy's aim is the truth' (Hegel 1986: 24 translation by author). The concept is time and space itself (Hegel 1991: §§254–9).

[10] 'Nature has proven to be the idea in the form of otherness' (Hegel, 1986a: §247, 24).

[11] '[P]hilosophy as thinking of the time's substantial [Geist] turns this [Geist] into its object' (Hegel 1986: 74).

[12] Hegel thinks Spinoza opens his notion of substance as ultimate condition of all conditioning to this charge due to his inability to deduce 'substance' itself — i.e. there is no 'method' by which substance is known (Cf. Stein 2016).

[13] These requirements have to be met by philosophical knowledge in order to avoid (a) infinite regress, (b) an arbitrary suspension of justification, (c) empty circularity.

[14] 'But what we have here is the free act of thinking putting itself at the standpoint where it is for its own self, producing its own object for itself thereby, and giving it to itself' (Hegel 1991a: §17, 41).

At the same time, however, Hegel seems to suggest that all PK—including the claims he makes in the *Philosophy of Right*—depend on particular empirical factors such as the thinker's historical context:

> To comprehend *what is*, this is the task of philosophy, because *what is*, is reason. Whatever happens, every individual is a *child of his time*; so philosophy too is *its own time apprehended in thoughts* [...]. The teaching of the concept, which is also history's inescapable lesson, is that it is only when actuality is mature that the ideal [*das Ideale*] first appears over against the real and that the ideal grasps this same real world in its substance and builds it up for itself into the shape of an intellectual realm.   (Hegel 2008: 15, 16)[15]

Such passages suggest that the finite, empirically informed thinker who strives for PK must first have the historical 'luck' of living during a time when philosophical truth has manifested itself so that PK depends at least on the condition 'historical circumstance'. While some consider this seeming dependence a strength that enables Hegel to avoid Kantian formalism,[16] others worry that it brings Hegel dangerously close to relativism: if the content of PK depends on thinker and thought-internal and -external conditions, it is at least *possible* that Hegel's own philosophical claims are just as good as his personal, conditioned thinking and the conditions he formed them in. What has been true for the historical thinker Hegel about political rationality in 1820s Prussia does not need to hold for twenty-first-century Western democracies.

In the following, I will argue that the apparent contradiction between Hegel's claims about the unconditioned *and* conditioned nature of PK disappears once one differentiates between proper philosophical knowledge ('PK'), empirical knowledge ('EK'), and potentially conditioned philosophical knowledge ('PCPK'[17]). While PK represents knowledge that is unconditioned, empirical knowledge is conditioned by definition and PCPK's knowledge is *potentially* conditioned. Since PK is ontologically prior to both empirical knowledge and PCPK, these two do not contradict PK on the same conceptual level:[18] unlike EK, PK is always already true[19] and known, and the possibilities of doubt and error are confined to 'our', empirically informed and thus potentially conditioned, PCPK-style perspective.

These observations about Hegel's notion of philosophy enable an explanation of how best to engage with Hegel's claims in the *Philosophy of Right*: from 'our', PCPK-style

---

[15] 'It follows from this that philosophy is completely identical with its time. Philosophy does not stand above its time, it is knowledge of what is substantial about its time.' (Hegel 1986: 74).

[16] E.g. Pippin 2008: 196ff., Sedgwick 1988: 98.

[17] 'PCPK' might be misleading insofar as PK is unconditioned by definition. However, 'PCPK' is to mean that PK is always already there and that PK's *potential* conditioning is ontologically second (PCPK is (1) philosophical knowledge that (2) is potentially conditioned due to the potentially conditioned perspective from which it is thought).

[18] One might say that PK is *the* (i.e. truth's own) perspective onto truth, PCPK is *our* perspective onto truth.

[19] For Hegel, this does not mean that PK is dogmatically or rationalistically (cf. Hegel 1990: 153–4) presupposed but that it has the ontological structure of a self-positing 'negative unity' (Hegel 2010: 212).

perspective, Hegel's PK-claims might have failed to express unconditioned knowledge. For 'us' they are open for potential revision by the always already present standard of PK. Insofar as Hegel failed to express PK and we succeed, true thought is manifest and recognizes itself in 'our' thinking. When this happens, PCPK is replaced by PK and the contradiction between PK and PCPK is avoided.

The argument proceeds in four steps: in the next two sections, Hegel's notion of philosophical knowledge (PK) is contrasted with his notion of empirical knowledge (EK) and with the notion of possibly conditioned philosophical knowledge (PCPK). The third section ties the preceding discussions to the specific claims of the *Philosophy of Right*, describing how a philosophically constructive engagement with Hegel's claims about socio-political rationality would have to look like according to Hegel's own notion of philosophy. The results of this enquiry are then contrasted with a selection of other interpretations from this volume.

Argument

From empirical cognition to philosophical knowledge

What does Hegel mean when he claims that philosophical knowledge is unconditioned? In the early paragraphs of the *Encyclopedia*, Hegel gives his first account of how best to conceptualize the unconditioned nature of PK and how this differs from other ways[20] of relating to truth. He distinguishes between two ways of thinking PK: first, there is representational thinking, which he associates mostly with understanding ('Verstand' Hegel 1986c: 16) and sometimes reflexion (e.g. Hegel 2007: 389 addition, 32) or abstraction (Hegel 1991a: 7, §9 remark: 31, §79, §1). Second, he mentions *conceptual* thinking and argues that doing philosophy, i.e. having and articulating PK, amounts to putting 'thoughts and categories, but more precisely concepts, in the place of representations' (Hegel 1991a: §3 remark, 26).

According to Hegel, 'representations' are formed in the finite thinker's mind and are based on seemingly knower-externally received, mediated, and reflected sensual content that originates in a presupposed reality (Hegel 2007: §§45–6, 184–202). When the individual thinker correctly conceives of and actively applies such representations to his experience and intuiting, he *understands*[21] or reflects what he encounters and thinks, i.e. he identifies and differentiates empirical phenomena and representations. One might thus be able to define and think the representations of 'family', 'civil society', and 'state', to recognize their empirical correspondents when one encounters them in reality, in one's or others' thoughts and actions. One might also exchange with others about their name, definition, and what thought-content ought to be subsumed under them (e.g. Hegel 2007: §445 remark).[22]

---

[20] For example intuition, feeling, etc. (Hegel 1991a: §3, 26).
[21] See, e.g., Hegel 2008: 3, 4.   [22] Cf. Thompson 2016: 8ff. and Winfield 1988.

However, the finite thinker need not stop at the level of understanding and representational thought.[23] Instead, he can decide[24] to go one step 'further' and engage in philosophical thinking. Doing so amounts to comprehending[25] the 'supreme' (Hegel 2007: §573 remark: 270) unconditioned principle that engenders thought, nature, and geistige reality. (Hegel 2010: 670) When the thinker grasps this principle, he comprehends what there unconditionally and necessarily *must* be so that there *can* be anything[26] (Hegel 1991a: §18, 42).

Hegel calls this principle 'the concept'[27] and describes it as the eternal 'soul' (Hegel 2010: 10) that resides within all thought and reality.[28] However, even if the concept is unconditioned by definition, why should individually held knowledge of it be unconditioned, also? It would seem that at least the finite, philosophical knower must be conditioned in his philosophical knowing as long as PK is something he achieves via insight into representations whose content is conditioned.

Two notions of empirical cognition

However, the act of philosophically grasping the unconditioned concept includes the thinker's realization that the *finitude* of his own reality and thinking is part and product of the very infinite principle that gives rise to the finite, seemingly conditioned content of empirical knowledge (EK).[29] So when the finite, empirically cognizing thinker replaces conditioned representations with the unconditioned concept and its determinations, the separation of finite thinker and finite thought content is overcome *within* the unconditioned concept: both finite thinker and finite content of philosophical thought are grasped as articulations of the unconditioned concept.[30]

---

[23] While I agree with Thompson when he argues that representational thought cannot be the last word when it comes to philosophy (e.g. Thompson 2016: 5) from PCPK's perspective, it is an inevitable means for achieving philosophical insight.

[24] '[T]hat the beginning [of science] only has a relation to the subject who takes the decision to philosophise' (Hegel 1991a: §17, 41).

[25] German: 'Begreifen'. E.g.: 'In point of fact, the *conceptual comprehension* of a subject matter consists in nothing else than in the "I" making it *its own*, in pervading it and bringing it into *its own* form, that is, into a *universality* which is immediately *determinateness*, or into a determinateness which is immediately universality' (Hegel 2010: 516, 517).

[26] 'But philosophy ought not to be a narrative of what happens, but a cognition of what is *true* in what happens, in order further to comprehend on the basis of this truth what in the narrative appears as a mere happening' (Hegel 2010: 519) Cf. also Knappik 2016: 6ff.

[27] In its self-adequate form, it is 'idea', i.e. 'the rational concept that in its reality only rejoins itself' (Hegel 2010: 735). For a contextual analysis and explanation of his notion, see Koch 2003 and Koch 2011. Cf. also deBoer 2012: 91: 'The *Philosophy of Right* is confined to an analysis of the *idea* of the state, that is to say, of the totality of determinations that are contained in its very concept.' Each concept can be described as a circle, encompassing other concepts—a 'circle of circles' (Hegel 1991a: §15, 39).

[28] Due to the unity of thought and being (cf. Houlgate 2006: 117ff.).

[29] Hegel calls this act 'the liberation of the free intelligence': 'The concept of [Geist] has its reality in the [Geist]. That this reality be knowledge of the absolute Idea and thus in identity with the concept, involves the necessary aspect that the implicitly free intelligence be in its actuality liberated to its concept, in order to be the shape worthy of the concept' (Hegel 2007: §533, 257). Cf. Stern 2006.

[30] Cf. 'The absolute [Geist] is identity, both an identity that is eternally within itself and an identity that returns and has returned into itself: the one and universal substance as spiritual, the judgement discerning

Since this reveals that the knower and the known of EK are unconditioned determinations of the unconditioned concept, Hegel's notion of EK differs from the orthodox empiricist notion of EK—at least on Hegel's reading of empiricism.[31] For according to Hegel, orthodox empiricism's notion of EK implies that it is itself a finite, conditioned fact that cognition consists in finite, conditioned thinkers' experiences and the forming of representations[32] about a conditioned world.[33] And Hegel disqualifies this conception on the grounds that it cannot explain its own implicit and unavoidable claim to unconditioned validity.[34]

As an alternative to the orthodox empiricist notion of EK, he offers what he calls 'theoretical Geist' (Hegel 2007: §445, 173ff.). This notion of empirical cognition defines empirical cognition as a relation of the unconditioned concept with itself: the unconditioned concept in form of knowing Geist (Hegel 2007: §441, 167) knows about itself in the form of a presupposed, conditioned reality.[35] It is this conceptual structure of empirical cognition that renders EK conditioned: since the concept in the form of known reality is defined as ontologically *prior* to the concept as knowing Geist, knowing Geist's knowledge is *by definition* conditioned, namely by the presupposed reality.[36]

In contrast, the thinker and the thought content of philosophy are unconditioned: both are the unconditioned concept in the form of Geist *as it is*, i.e. unconditioned and free. Neither is presupposed and thus prior to the other and so neither is conditioned by the other.[37] So when an empirically knowing subject assumes the philosophical point of view by thinking through correct but conditioned representations, the subject grasps that its own Geist is as unconditioned as is the content of its thought: the thinker assumes what Hegel calls the eternal[38] standpoint of the concept as self-thinking, absolute

---

itself into itself and an awareness, an awareness for which the substance is as such' (Hegel 2007: §554, 257). From the 'presuppositionless' (Thompson 2016: 13ff, Houlgate 2006: 29ff.) perspective of philosophy, no specific determination of thought is presupposed: Neither a knowable world nor a difference between subject and object.

[31] See Stein 2016.   [32] I.e. 'ideas' (Hume 2009: 17).

[33] Although Hume is careful enough to not commit to the world's nor to the ego's existence.

[34] For Hegel, empiricism self-contradictorily implies that it is necessary knowledge that there can be no necessary knowledge. Cf. Stein 2016.

[35] Cf. Hegel 2007: §445ff., 173ff. Cf. '[Geist], therefore, sets out only from its own being and is in relationship only with its own determinations' (Hegel 2007: §440, 165). Cf. also Hegel 2007: §441, 167.

[36] Ibid. See also: Stein 2016a.

[37] Cf. 'Even finite or subjective mind, not only absolute mind, must be grasped as an actualization of the Idea' (Hegel 2007: §377 addition, 3).

[38] 'Eternal' here in the sense of 'unconditioned' and 'self-referential': The philosophical knower is the concept, the philosophically known is the concept. In PK, the concept refers to itself, independently from any external conditioning. This is *ontological* eternity, not temporal eternity. It does not imply that the finite thinker or his/her representation as a mental event is beyond or above or outside of time but that the concept as origin of truth and finite thinkers is temporally unconditioned. The unconditioned concept gives rise to time (and space) and manifests itself in the form of finite, truth-thinking thinkers: Time (and space) are determinations of the very concept (similar to how space and time are because Spinoza's substance is or are abstractions of Humean experience (cf. Hume 2009: 66ff.) that informs all finite thought and reality. Since time is (a determination of) the concept, the concept cannot be conditioned by it (Hegel 1986a: §254ff.). I owe this notion to a conversation with Sebastian Ostritsch.

Geist, i.e. of true, unconditioned thought that thinks itself *as it truly is*.[39] So as empirically cognizing, knowing subjects, 'we' have to think through 'our' conditioned representations to comprehend the unconditioned concept that always already animates 'us', our thinking, and 'cognized' reality.

Empirical and conceptual priority

Hegel's philosophical notion of the relationship between EK and PK thus implies an inversion of the logical sequence that defines their relationship form the empirical point of view. From EK's perspective, experience and representation are first and grasping the concept is second. From PK's perspective onto empirical reality, the concept is first and its manifestations are all there is. For example, from the empirical point of view, the insight that 'the state' is a determination of the concept and thus part of PK comes after experience, intuition, and representation of objectively existing, political states. 'We', as finite thinkers must *first* have experience and *then* form the representation 'state' to *then* achieve the philosophical knowledge that 'the state' is part of PK, i.e. that it is a determination of the unconditioned concept.[40]

However, from the philosophical perspective, the conceptual determination 'state' is first.[41] The unconditioned concept determines itself as 'state' (Hegel 2008: §257, 228), which in a second, PK-irrelevant step gives rise to the empirical reality that is cognized by the subject, providing it with the content for the subject's representation 'state'. While the empirically cognizing subject requires subject-external content for forming representations, the philosophically *knowing* subject comprehends that it is the unconditioned concept that determines itself as thinker, reality, and 'state' (Hegel 2008: §257, 228).

Attaining PK thus reveals that to the finite thinker the conditioned, empirically cognizing subject and the conditioned, empirical thought and reality only exist because there is the unconditioned concept that manifests itself in conditioned, finite form (see e.g. Hegel 2008: §3, 19, 20).[42] Without it, there could neither be ideal nor

---

[39] This is akin to Kant's 'god's point of view' (Longuenesse 2000), only that Hegel's god is the unconditioned thinking via the finite thinker that thinks unconditionally.

[40] Cf. '[F]or learning is always acquired in this way, by advancing through what is less intelligible by nature to what is more so....] so it is our task to start from what is more intelligible to oneself and make what is by nature intelligible intelligible to oneself' (Aristotle 1933: 1029b1).

[41] Cf. Hegel's philosophy of nature: 'Philosophy must not only coincide with the experience of nature but the *genesis* and *development* of the philosophical science has empirical physics as a presupposition and condition. However, the path of the creation and the preliminary preparations of a [philosophical] science are something entirely different from the [philosophical] science itself. Within [philosophical science] these [preparations] cannot function as a foundation since this is supposed to be the necessity of the concept [Begriff] itself' (Hegel 1986a: §246 remark, author's translation). Cf. '[The] "determinations of thinking" have the "value and significance of being in and for themselves the ground of everything" (Enz. [1817] § 17)' (Thompson, 2016: 15).

[42] E.g. any empirical, existing, conditioned state is only state insofar as it is manifestation of the concept in the determinations of statehood (Hegel 2008: §1 remark, 17). Cf. Siep 2015 and Koch 2007.

non-ideal reality,[43] history, or experiencing subjects so that empirical cognition (EK) itself would be as impossible (see Hegel 2007: §440 addition, 165, 166)[44] as PK itself.

According to Hegel, it is this conditionality-accommodating character of the philosophically accessible concept that undermines any notion of its own conditioning.[45] Since the concept's 'true', i.e. conditionality-incorporating, unconditionality consists in the ontological *simultaneity* of unconditionality[46] and conditionality, there is nothing 'outside' the concept at the same ontological level that could condition it.[47] Crucially, this undermines the notion that the truly unconditioned concept *as such* is conditioned by its self-posited conditionality, for example by its own historical manifestation. Since the concept *contains* conditionality within itself, it cannot itself be conditioned by conditionality as this would mean that the concept would be conditioned by its own internal ontological moment.[48] This would contradict the very notion of conditioning as something that is effected on the same ontological level.

So from the perspective of PK, the truly unconditioned concept does not have to 'wait' for historical conditions to be 'right' or for the empirical experience of individuals to enable its reality and thinking because the finite conditioned thinkers, their experience and history result always already from the truly unconditioned concept's own activity.[49] More precisely, these *are* the unconditioned concept, only in the form of

[43] 'Instead, the Concept is what truly comes first, and things are what they are through the activity of the Concept that dwells in them and reveals itself in them' (Hegel 1991a: §163 addition 2: 241).

[44] Insofar as the manifestation of the concept (its objectivity) lives up to the concept-inherent standard and forms an unconditioned 'negative unity' (Hegel 2010: 717) with it, it is *idea* and thus the concern of philosophy (e.g. Hegel 1991a: §18, 42).

[45] Cf. 'Philosophy must wield an autonomous reason, free in both the negative sense of overcoming dependence upon presuppositions and the positive sense of determining what its own method and subject matter should be. As such, philosophy cannot begin with any determinate claims about what is or about knowing. It must start from utter indeterminacy and generate from that presuppositionless commencement determinacy that is not grounded on any given or given procedure of specification. This indeterminate commencement allows philosophy to be a theory of determinacy, accounting for determinacy without begging the question by beginning with some given determinacy' (Winfield 2016: 1).

[46] I.e. 'abstract' (Hegel 2010: 519) universality or unconditionality. This is the understanding's or reflection's 'horizontal' negation of conditionality. While the concept's 'true' and thus speculative unconditionality *contains* abstract conditionality and abstract unconditionality, abstract conditionality is merely the opposite of conditionality. Cf. Trisokkas 2009.

[47] The incorporation of conditionality, i.e. particularity, into the concept's 'true universality' (Hegel 2010: 615) enables Hegel's claim that the concept is real, worldly, objective, finite, historically manifest, etc., and that it can be felt, experienced, intuited, etc. (Hegel 2007: §446ff., 176ff.) Cf. 'Of political justice part is natural, part legal,—natural, that which everywhere has the same force and does not exist by people's thinking this or that; legal, that which is originally indifferent, but when it has been laid down is not indifferent [...]. [W]ith us there is something that is just even by nature, yet all of it is changeable; but still some is by nature, some not by nature' (Aristotle 2009: 92).

[48] Cf. 'Whatever is, is in God and nothing can be or be conceived without God' (Spinoza 2002: 224). However, unlike the way in which Spinoza's unconditioned, universal substance ontologically eclipses the conditioned, particular modi, so Hegel would argue, the concept's conditionality (i.e. particularity) is not eclipsed by the concept's unconditionality (i.e. universality) but both are contained within its 'true' unconditionality. Cf. Stein 2016.

[49] Some readings suggest that history, experience, society, practices of recognition, etc. are something concept-external as if they condition the concept, the concept depends on these, etc. (e.g. O'Connor 2015, Deligiorgi 2012, 2014, Pippin 2008, against this view: Nuzzo 2012) However, this appears untrue to the

mere conditionality and particularity[50] insofar as they do not live up to its standard and in the form of unconditionality-informed, i.e. 'true' or *conceptual* conditionality insofar as they do live up to it.

According to Hegel, this renders the concept an inherently 'speculative' (Hegel1991a: §9, 33, Hegel 1991a: §82, 131) notion, i.e. something that in its true, free form cannot be merely intuited, represented, understood, or reflected since understanding and reflection either posit conditionality's particularity absolute[51] or privilege it over abstract, i.e. conditionality-negating rather than –incorporating, unconditionality. In contrast, 'speculative' thinking allows for conceiving of the concept as both unconditioned *and* 'unconditioned in the form of conditionality' *at the same logical time*. Speculation comprehends both elements as aspects of an overarching, accommodating unity without losing the distinct meaning of either.[52]

The perspective of PCPK

However, conditioned empirical knowledge (EK) and unconditioned, philosophical knowledge (PK) are not the only notions of knowledge that Hegel mentions. Sometimes, he seems to suggest that PK itself depends on the activity of empirical, particular thinkers that are historically situated and rely on empirical experience and thus thought-conditioning factors for achieving philosophical insight.[53] In the following, I will refer to this perspective as the perspective of *potentially conditioned philosophical knowledge* (PCPK) because it implies that the particular, finite, empirically informed thinker is potentially conditioned by truth-external elements in the attempt to think philosophical truth. As opposed to the conditioned empirical knower and the uncon-ditioned philosophical knower, PCPK's knower is *potentially* conditioned.

So while PK disqualifies the notion of any conditioning factors onto knowledge and empirical knowledge as conditioned by definition,[54] PCPK *presupposes* the existence of conditions and their *potential* effect on knowledge. According to PCPK, philosophy is the attempt by finite, potentially conditioned thinkers to articulate the unconditioned truth of PK. PCPK thus allows for conditioning and PK-irrelevant factors, both thinker-internal[55] as well as thinker-external,[56] to potentially condition PK. So while PK disqualifies

---

logical relationship between the true, conditionality-incorporating unconditionality of the concept and its objective manifestation: Nothing is concept-external because everything is because of the concept's activity of self-manifestation. Against such readings: 'The concept of spirit [in the context of the philosophy of history] rather refers [...] to the attempts of thought to comprehend itself' (deBoer 2010: 182). For a pragmatist reading, see, e.g., Westphal 2015.

[50] Since all reality is the concept, neither the concept nor its thinking can be conditioned by anything other than itself so that in one sense, there is no conditioned reality or thought. However, the concept can be thought in its self-inadequate (i.e. non-ideal) form and in logical differentiation from the thinking subject (as is the case with empirical knowledge) *as if* it were conditioned.

[51] 'Understanding' (Hegel 2010: 10).   [52] E.g. Hegel 2010: 12. Cf. Stein 2014.

[53] See Hegel 2008: 15ff.   [54] See, e.g., Houlgate 2006: 29ff.

[55] E.g. bias, assumptions, prejudices, confusion, etc.

[56] E.g. history, language, geography, anthropology, etc.

error by definition, PCPK renders its possible: the aspiring philosopher might claim to have PK but could actually be just opining, confused, biased, etc.

The priority of PK over PCPK

Given this difference between PK and PCPK, one might ask which of the two Hegel thinks is more fundamental, i.e. ontologically first. Is there PCPK because there is PK or is there PK because there is PCPK? While PK represents unconditioned thought and reality at its most fundamental by definition, its lack of consideration for non-conceptual, conditioned, empirical reality can make it seem dogmatic and unconscious of empirically caused fallibility: PK seems to naïvely assume that the finite thinker does indeed think unconditioned truth. At the same time, it might seem that PCPK presupposes the very unconditioned thought and reality that PK describes: without what PK describes, i.e. the concept and its determinations there could be neither empirical reality nor thought.[57]

Both notions seem to articulate essential features of knowledge. From PCPK's perspective onto PK, there have to be fallible, potentially conditioned thinkers and conceptually inadequate reality so that the unconditioned thinking that PK describes can take place. In contrast, from PK's point of view onto PCPK, it is impossible to conceive of empirical thinkers who possibly get PK wrong without implying the unconditioned concept that PK describes: there only are empirical, potentially conditioned thinkers who can get PK wrong and empirical conditions because there is the unconditioned concept that enables their existence and which potentially fails to connect to itself via the thoughts of these thinkers. From PK's perspective, there is only a potential lack of true thought and reality because true thought and reality always already exist (e.g. Hegel 2011: 79ff.).

PCPK's self-contradiction

Hegel undermines the perspectives' rivalry for ontological priority by arguing that PCPK disqualifies itself if granted fundamental status. Conceptually, PCPK must pre-suppose that PK is always already the case.[58] If it did not, there could be no notion of PK, and consequently, no notion of PCPK. This is because PCPK is unable to justify, i.e. to conceptually guarantee its own inevitably required necessity.

---

[57]   E.g. Hegel 2011: 79ff., Hegel 1991a: §18, 42.

[58]   Since Hegel does not differentiate between being and thought from PK's point of view, logical priority amounts to existential/ontological priority: PCPK logically presupposes PK since PCPK is a modification of PK: PK + mere particularities, historical, linguistic, etc. conditions = PCPK. PCPK is '◊PK' and thus PK1 + possibility. This also applies to Hegel himself: PCPK allows for the possibility that what the particular thinking individual, e.g. the historical Hegel, is thinking is just Hegel's *own* thought and not true thought *in general*.

If PCPK were first:

(1) All PK is only potential (There is only PCPK).[59]

(2) (1) is PK.

Conclusion: (1) claims to be true but according to itself is only potentially true, i.e. is potentially false → (1) is false insofar as it implies a claim to (non-potential) truth.[60]

To Hegel, putting PCPK first thus amounts to implying that all PK is PCPK, i.e. that PCPK is PK. However, since PCPK only allows for *potential* PK, doing so undermines PCPK's—and thus PK's—inherent, inevitable claim to being actually and thus necessarily true. This fatally undermines the very notion of what PCPK and PK are because PCPK must imply its own necessity in order to deserve its status as PK:

(1) (It is necessary/It is PK that) All PK is PCPK.

(2) (1) is PCPK.

Conclusion: (1) is not necessary/PK but must imply that it is → contradiction.

So if all PK were PCPK, the claim that 'all PK is PCPK' would itself be PCPK and therefore not necessary. However, since this claim must imply its own necessity, putting PCPK first results in a contradiction.

So bestowing logical priority upon PCPK would not only undermine PCPK's—and by extension, PK's—own necessity. It would also fail to explain how an empirical individual can know *that* he or she philosophically knows. If all knowledge is *potentially* philosophical knowledge (PCPK first), there is no way to know whether one's thought is or is not philosophically true. The very notion that 'all PK is potential' implies that there is no criterion available to differentiate PK from non-PK since the criterion of differentiation between true and false PK would itself have to be undistorted, true thought. It would be the very PK—i.e. universal and necessary thought—that one is seeking in the first place. However, such a criterion must be available if the notion of PK is to have any sense at all. In order for PCPK to be PC-*PK*, it must imply the existence and availability of PK. At the same time, it denies it by implying that all PK is PCPK.

According to Hegel, this contradiction can only be avoided by giving (onto-)logical priority to PK: if the criterion for true thinking is always already present within the philosophical thinker, he or she recognizes his or her own or others' truthful thinking in virtue of this criterion. This also applies to the recognition of truth in the thought of one thinker by others. If there is to be truthful individual thinking and recognition

---

[59] The same holds for the claim 'it seems to me that all PK is PCPK' as this amounts to 'I do not *know* that PK'.

[60] This and all other reductio arguments in this chapter are supposed to communicate a sense of the unconditioned perspective of PK itself.

thereof by other thinkers, all thinkers involved must be in possession of the criterion of truthful thought. The thinker who makes *philosophical* claims and the thinkers who evaluate these claims only recognize the truthfulness of thinking insofar as it is the truth they always already know. If they did not, they could not recognize it when they encounter it, anyone's opinion would be as good as any other's, or rather, the notions of opinion and knowledge[61] would cease to exist in lack of a conceptual contrast between them.

Error as deprivation of truth

So while every potentially conditioned thinker is capable of being deceived about himself having PK, this deception can only be made sense of as a distortion of PK: the notion of a thinker erring about philosophical truth implies that PK is something that one always already possesses so it can be erred about. The mistaken thinker aims at full awareness of the PK he always already has in virtue of him or herself being part of the concept-engendered reality and thought but instead, he or she has his or her own thought distorted. Like the notion of error presupposes knowledge—it is knowledge, which is not—so the notion of *potential* knowledge (PCPK) presupposes knowledge (PK): PCPK is PK (first) that only potentially is (second). For Hegel, this entails that the only conceptually tenable notion of PCPK is from a PK-informed perspective, i.e. that PCPK implies PK: PCPK means that, there always already is PK that can be gotten wrong or that is not fully realized.

Reasons for PK's failure to fully manifest originate in the concept's own activity of regularly less than perfect self-manifestation and -thinking and include historical contingencies such as the accident of birth. Some empirical thinkers cannot but fail to articulate PK fully because *from the perspective of PCPK*, the concept has not yet manifested itself in the form of an empirical state during or before the empirical thinker's lifetime and its determination can thus not be discovered as its ontological origin of reality. For example, pre-historical thinkers may not be able to form the required representations they need to achieve the philosophical insight that 'state' is one of the unconditioned concept's determinations.

So from a PCPK-perspective onto PK, one might ask: How can the finite thinker achieve PK? And the answer would be: by preventing *mere* particularities and thus external conditions from affecting his or her thinking and by engaging in the very speculative thinking that incorporates and overcomes representational thinking to achieve PK—insofar as the sometimes arbitrary circumstances and abilities of the thinker allow. From PCPK's perspective, undistorted PK is something to be achieved, something that is rarely explicated clearly and that relies on the demanding process of excluding mere particularities from one's thinking by letting go of prejudice,

[61] Cf. 'And how will you search for something, Socrates, when you don't know what it is at all? I mean, which of the things you don't know will you take in advance and search for, when you don't know what it is? Or even if you come right up against it, how will you know that it's the unknown thing you're looking for?' (Plato 2005: 80d–e, 113).

unwarranted assumptions, etc., i.e. of all that is *just* the thinker's.[62] From PK's perspective onto PCPK, PK is always already present in all finite thinkers at all times and places, albeit in varying degrees of clarity and at different levels of development.[63]

The truth and 'us'

If PK ontologically grounds PCPK—there must be unconditioned truth so that 'we' as finite, PCPK-style thinkers *can* get it right or wrong—then for 'us', as finite thinkers doing philosophy means to attempt to describe the unconditioned truth of PK from a potentially conditioned perspective. The same applies to Hegel: since his claims are made by a historically situated, finite individual, they are possibly conditioned, deserve others' critical scrutiny, and are in potential need of revision.

The very possibility of philosophical error is thus due to 'our' and Hegel's' finitude and possible distortion of true PK. Insofar as there is philosophical error, it is 'us' as potentially truth-missing, finite thinkers who err and not PK's self-thinking, unconditioned concept—in the form of what Hegel calls self-thinking, absolute Geist[64]—that enables 'us' and our thinking in the first place. From PK's own, conceptually self-transparent perspective onto PCPK, it is not 'we' as potentially erring thinkers who are first and successful thinking of truth is second. Instead, truth in the form of self-thinking, absolute Geist is first and every finite, truth-thinking thinker articulates it. When 'we' think and express the truth conceptually, 'our' thinking is an expression of absolute Geist's self-thinking. The same applies to doubt. Like error, so the very structure of 'doubt' implies a potential difference between absolute Geist and finite thinker that is untrue to the self-referential, conceptual structure of PK as self-thinking absolute Geist. Insofar as there is doubt whether it is truly absolute Geist that knows itself in 'our' thinking, this doubt is *just* 'our's' when Geist *is* thinking itself in 'us'. And 'our' doubt is motivated by Geist's self-thinking in 'us' insofar as the doubt is directed at what is *just* our's' in 'our' thinking.

Truth's criterion

It also follows from PK's absolute Geist's priority over 'us' as PCPK-style thinkers that the *criterion* by which to evaluate any finite thinker's cannot be *just* 'our', PCPK-style thinking, a zeitgeist different from Hegel's own, contingent empirical facts or an irrational detour taken by history. Instead, it must be unconditioned PK's self-thinking Geist that 'our' thought expresses if 'we' are to speak with the authority of PK itself. So any critical reformulation of present and past philosophers' work that lays claim to being a philosophical 'improvement' cannot be done *just*[65] in 'our' name but must be

---

[62] From PCPK's perspective, exchange with other thinkers is necessary for achieving PK. From PK's perspective, PK is always already achieved. Since every geistige being always already participates in PK, the most 'complete bias' possible is when a thinker is utterly mistaken about PK: independently of how false a notion of PK is, it is still a notion of PK.

[63] Cf. Hegel 2007: §393 and remark and addition, 39–44.   [64] Hegel 2007: §572, 267.

[65] For a helpful discussion of this problem, see Brooks 2014.

done by the authority of 'self-knowing reason' (Hegel 2007: §577, 276) that knows itself in 'us' rather than it did in whoever 'we' criticize.[66]

So who is to judge whether it is indeed 'absolute Geist' that explicates itself via 'our' thought? How do 'we' know that 'we' know? It follows from PK's ontological priority over PCPK that the criterion and only eligible true 'subject' of philosophical thinking that is able to judge the truthfulness of 'our', PCPK-style thinking is the presence of the unconditioned concept in the form of absolute Geist itself.[67] When absolute Geist thinks itself in 'our' thinking, it knows that it is doing so. So the question 'How do "we" know that it is absolute Geist that thinks itself in "us" and not just "us" falsely thinking that it does?' implies PCPK's perspective and not the perspective of PK's absolute Geist with regards to the subject of true knowing. If absolute Geist knows itself in 'us' and there is PK, it is not the PCPK-style 'us' who know or need to know. As truthfully knowing subject, 'our' thinking *is* articulation of PK's self-thinking Geist.[68] Along with PCPK, 'our' worries, doubts, or ignorance[69] also disappear when PK's absolute Geist's fully knows itself in 'us'. And since absolute Geist always already knows itself in 'us', the question is not *if* it does but to which degree it does so where, in whom, and in what form.[70]

However, the demand for 'our' certainty regarding the truthfulness of our thinking can also be understood as a demand for another criterion apart from true thinking that allows 'us' to judge whether 'our' thinking and true thinking as such coincide: 'How do we know that we think what is necessary rather than contingent—i.e. that 'we' think the concept rather than mere particularity?' However, with the replacement of PCPK's finite, conditioned thinkers by PK's infinite, unconditioned Geist, the call for such a criterion becomes superfluous. Since all true PK *is* Geist's self-knowing, there is no finite, PCPK-style subject that requires a further criterion to judge the truthfulness of

---

[66] This recognition can only take place because absolute Geist is always already thinking itself in 'us'. *In principle*, 'we' always already know the truth—everything is always already transparent. The PCPK-style question is just to what degree this realization is manifest and in what conceptual detail in 'our' thinking.

[67] Cf. 'Cunning of reason' (Hegel 1991a: §209). From 'our', PCPK-style point of view, we must decide to think philosophically so that truth recognizes itself. From the truth's own, i.e. PK's, perspective, truth has always already recognized itself. From 'our' perspective, this 'always already happened' self-recognition of the truth by the truth takes place in the decisions, acts and thoughts of finite, geistige thinkers. However, since PK is ontologically prior to 'us', our decisions and levels of truth-awareness do not affect *whether* PK is real but only the way in which it is present in 'our', PCPK-style reality.

[68] Cf. Hegel 2007: §576, §577.

[69] What Hegel demands in terms of presupposing conceptual 'nothing' (cf. Hegel 2010: 48). If there is a 'we' in thinking, 'we' have failed to 'lose our mere particularities' and 'we' must try harder to rid 'our' minds of distortion and overcome what is *just particular* about thinking.

[70] Cf. Hegel 2008: §3, 19ff. Reason can be present or at work without the finite subject's reflexive awareness of it: 'In the course of this activity [*Geschäft*] of the world spirit, states, peoples, and individuals arise animated by their particular determinate principle which has its exposition and actuality in their constitutions and in the whole range of their life and condition. While they are conscious of this actuality and are absorbed in its interests, they are all the time the unconscious tools and organs of this inner activity' (Hegel 2008: §344, 317).

its own thought.[71] It is within and by absolute Geist's self-recognition in thinking alone that our or Hegel's or anyone else's philosophical claims are legitimately refuted or affirmed.[72]

(Dis-)agreeing with Hegel

These observations enable a reconstruction of what Hegel thought it conceptually means for other finite thinkers to engage with his own philosophical claims. According to Hegel's notion of philosophy, 'his' philosophical claims aspire to represent Geist's self-thinking (PK). When other PCPK-style thinkers such as 'we' disagree with them, 'we' see them as a challenge to test to what degree Hegel was unable to overcome conditioning and make room for unconditioned Geist's self-thinking. In so doing, we assume that 'we' might articulate PK and thus that 'we' express Geist's truthful self-thinking whereas 'Hegel' might not have. And insofar as 'we' overcome 'our merely particular selves' and manage to comprehend and prove that 'Hegel' failed PK's standard,[73] there is less distortion in 'our' account of PK—because it is *not* 'ours' but Geist's own.

'Our' engagement with Hegel's claims about unconditioned socio-political truth might thus reveal that Hegel's thoughts on the monarchy,[74] the family,[75] the unelected second chamber of the legislature, the inappropriateness of having a constitutional court, the corporations,[76] the vices of democracy,[77] the inevitability of poverty and decadence,[78] etc., fall short of allowing absolute Geist's self-expression.[79] 'We' might thus have to improve on Hegel's account of PK by overcoming what makes 'us' merely 'us' with regards to thought to a greater degree than what made Hegel 'merely Hegel' in his thinking.[80]

---

[71] For example, the demand for a principled criterion by which to distinguish what forms part of necessary PK and what is merely contingent, conditioned, empirical fact: 'How does Hegel know that the empirical fact that there are "x" different kinds of parrots in the world or that Britain has a first past the post electoral system do not form part of PK?' Hegel would answer that from the perspective of PCPK, only truthful thinking itself can establish to what level of *conceptual* detail necessary, philosophical knowledge extends. I owe this idea to an exchange with Michael Inwood. Cf. (Hegel 2010: 518).

[72] Cf. '[P]hilosophical investigation cannot begin by examining anything distinct from its own thinking' (Winfield 2016: 1).

[73] For one way of doing just that, see Winfield 2016: 26ff.

[74] Cf. Vieweg 2012.   [75] Cf. Stone forthcoming.

[76] Cf. Vieweg 2012.   [77] Cf. Vieweg 2012.   [78] Cf. Ruda 2011.

[79] So insofar as Hegel is a 'historical' (see e.g. O'Connor 2015) thinker in the sense of reporting on merely empirical, particular reality as it happened to be in his time rather than on the idea's historical manifestation, he has failed the standard of PK. Insofar as his being a 'historical' thinker means that he reports on unconditionally valid determinations of conceptual truth that are historically manifest, he has met that standard.

[80] This allows for an explanation in which sense Hegel's system is open *and* closed (an 'open closure') (Sparby 2014a). From PK's own perspective, the truth *as it truly is*, is always already achieved and thus non-statically 'closed'. From 'our', PCPK-style perspective, every finite thinker might be mistaken about truth unless he is not and so there might be plenty of room for improvement of Hegel's system—it is 'open' for revision by 'us' in the name of truth.

Hegel's notion of philosophy does therefore not mean that one sceptically questions *that* there is unconditioned, PK-style truth.[81] This must be the case for if it were not, no being nor thought, i.e. neither reality nor 'we' nor thought could and would exist. 'We' as PCPK-style, philosophically inclined thinkers know that we always already know (PK) the unconditioned truth that must exist so that anything is and can be.

At the same time, 'we' as finite, PCPK-style thinkers must remain critical about 'our' descriptions of the truth, for they might be just 'ours' and not Geist's true self-thinking. So 'we' must inquire whether 'our' doubts about 'our' thinking are directed at just 'our' thinking or at absolute Geist's self-thinking in 'us'. And we must reject the doubts with the authority of absolute Geist's self-thinking insofar as they fall short of it. So while 'we' must avoid the naïve dogmatism of *assuming* that 'we' automatically articulate the Geist's self-thinking *as it truly is,* 'we' must equally avoid the unjustified doubt that 'our' thinking can not be Geist's own because 'we' are always *just* finite thinkers and not infinite Geist itself. From 'our' finite, PCPK-style perspective, 'we' must be equally open for the possibility of being right as 'we' are about the possibility of being wrong about the truth: when 'we' *do* think the truth, absolute Geist thinks itself in 'us' and the difference between 'us' and the truth is dissolved *within the truth.* So when 'we' are right about truth, the truth in which we always already participate is right about itself. It is in this sense that 'we' (always already) know *and* (potentially) do not know right.[82]

Alternative Readings

How does this reading of Hegel's notion of philosophy compare to others of current popularity? From the PK- and PCPK-differentiating perspective that his chapter has argued for, several commentators confine their descriptions of Hegel's notion of PK to a finite, historically, socially, or pragmatically conditioned perspective that implies that all knowledge is of the kind that Hegel describes as empirical, conditioned knowledge, rather than philosophical (PK) or potentially philosophical knowledge (PCPK). For them, the philosophical truth about socio-political rationality is neither informationally nor conceptually unconditioned in the sense that Hegel insists on because, for example, historical conditions, or the pragmatic, practice-externally determined 'success' of practices functions as a condition for their 'truthfulness'.

---

[81] Any such questioning inevitably implies a claim about truth. Cf. the beginning of the *Science of Logic* where truth is defined as 'pure being' or 'nothing' (Hegel 2010: 59): 'The truth just is/the truth is nothing/ nothing is the truth'.

[82] Unlike Socrates' suggestion, so Hegel might argue, it is not that 'we know that we don't know' but that 'we know that we always already know' (we always already participate in PK) *and* that "we" might not think and express that knowledge properly' ('we' might err—PCPK): 'We' know (PK) that 'we' might not know (PCPK). Strictly speaking, Hegel would thus claim that it is wrong to say that for example, 'Heraklitos' knew the truth about becoming. Instead, it was true thought that knew its own form of becoming and the historical Heraklitos participated in this self-knowing of reason, losing his mere particularity—and thus what made him 'this Heraklitos'—to the degree that he was able to participate.

In contrast, the socio-political practices that Hegel identifies as part of PK—for example abstract right, morality, and ethical life—are not known to be part of PK because 'history' or truth-external 'success' qualify them as such. On the contrary, there only are 'history'[83]—in the sense of 'rational progress'—and 'success' [84] because there is the truth (PK) that 'successfully' manifests itself historically.[85] If it were the other way around, the truth would be contingent upon truth-external conditions and would fail to avoid infinite regress that it evades by grounding itself.

If truth ('PK') were conditioned:

(1) (It is unconditionally true that) the truth is whatever a condition 'X' (e.g. 'historical circumstance', 'success-deciding conditions', 'finite practices of recognition') enables

(2) (1) is true.

Conclusion: Contradiction: (1) implies to be unconditionally true but argues that all truth is conditioned.

In contrast to the self-contained, unconditioned notion of PK that Hegel commits to, readings that imply that philosophical knowledge is conditioned thus open themselves to the criticism of undermining their own, unavoidable claim to unconditioned truth.

One might respond that one has to differentiate between (a) unconditionally true truth-defining practices (e.g. 'practices of recognition', practices of public justification, or practices of 'sense-making' on the one hand, and (b) conditioned content of truth—i.e. the concrete determinations and shapes of the institutions, norms, and practices that the practices under (a) produce. On this reading, Hegel's PK is formally necessary *and* contingent with regards to its content.

However, from the point of view assigned to Hegel by this chapter, this would amount to invoking a self-contradictory, truth-internal split:

(1) The truth is necessary (form) and contingent (content)

(2) (1) is necessary truth.

Conclusion: Contradiction: (1) implies that truth is necessary *and* that truth is 'necessary *and* contingent'.[86]

---

[83] Cf. earlier section on 'PCPK's self-contradiction'. It is only from 'our', PCPK-style perspective that history (Pinkard 2016: 28) enables grasping the idea of right in its forms of abstract right, morality, and ethical life. Cf. Pinkard 2016: 28.

[84] Or discriminate 'more from less effective self-critical assessment' (Westphal 2016: 3).

[85] The same applies to the notion of the 'fallibility' (Westphal 2016) of philosophical knowledge. For Hegel, there is only failure because there is the 'success' that is the truth (PK). This is why Hegel's notion of PCPK implies PK *and then* allows for the possibility of its incomplete or conditioned articulation.

[86] Cf. Stein 2016.

Differentiating between 'form' and 'content' of truth would introduce an element of conceptual contingency into the notion of truth that contradicts truth's inevitably implied, all-pervading necessity.[87] Hegel would wholeheartedly agree that from the perspective of PCPK, we are 'very finite [...] creatures' who 'make sense' or 'give accounts' of themselves, nature, and of thinking in the historical, cultural, ideological, linguistic, etc., contexts of the empirical world 'we' inhabit. However, as long as this is thought to be *all* there is to PK there is no proper PK at all. Reading Hegel in this way means to not describe PK *as PK* but to think of PK as PK-presupposing PCPK, or worse, EK.[88] And this perspective is absorbed into PK as soon as PK's inevitability if recognized. When 'we' succeed[89] in grasping and articulating PK,[90] it is the unconditioned truth's most concrete determination—absolute Geist— in the form of which PK comprehends itself, thereby replacing PCPK.[91]

Furthermore, Hegel thinks of his own account as an account of unconditionally true PK that is valid irrespective of what kind of logic happens to be popular at a given time and place. Insofar as he is right, his claims cannot be 'outdated' since the very concept of 'being outdated' can only apply to knowledge that can be evaluated by a criterion that differs from itself. In the case of PK, this is impossible since conceptually, there is nothing 'outside of', i.e. conditioning of PK—only the truth itself is qualified to function as its own standard. This unconditioned truth is the only thing of 'interest and value' to any philosopher irrespective of when and where, in which culture, ideological context, etc., she or he happens to live and think.

For Hegel, philosophy is thus not about reconstructing how a thinker of the past thought about truth—be this done systematically or unsystematically—from a supposedly privileged, inescapably presentist or zeitgeist-indebted perspective. Instead,

---

[87] Technically, Hegel's notion of the concept is 'free' (Hegel 2010: 505) and thus articulates necessity's identity and contingency's difference *at the same logical time*. Cf. Hegel 2010: 529ff.).

[88] So while it is true that from the perspective of PCPK, 'rational justification is in principle fallibilist' (Westphal 2016: 6), this does not hold for the perspective of PK, where true thought correctly 'justifies' itself by definition. The 'public' nature of the solution to the social coordination problem does not exist 'in principle' (Westphal 2016: 7) for the publicity-enabling, true principle that finds articulation in PK. So insofar as 'we' do philosophy—rather than reconstruct how Hegel as historical, PCPK-style potentially erring thinker thought—'we' must articulate PK, i.e. reason's self-thinking. Allen Wood seems to reject this notion of philosophy when he argues that 'We cannot simply look at Hegel's own writings and doctrines for the right answers to our questions' (Wood 2016: 24). Insofar as 'our' questions are philosophical, i.e. about the truth (PK), we should look to Hegel's answers and *rationally evaluate* whether they articulate the unconditioned truth. Cf. 'The finite, philosophising subject "reasons" (or should wonder if) whether "What we do" is true, that is, is what a true human being would do' (Pinkard 2016: 27).

[89] So while Hegel's own account is thus not beyond revision insofar as it is *just* his account and is 'deeply functional' (Westphal 2016: 7) in the sense that what 'functions' is true thought (PK), the criterion and content for what 'functioning' means is not thought- and thinker-external or -internal: the truly thinking thinker and the true content of thinking are immanent aspects of 'functioning' truth that sublates the 'internal-external' difference by being all there is and relating to itself within itself.

[90] As opposed to falsity or inadequacy, which merely appears or merely exists (cf. Pippin 2016: 13).

[91] From the perspective of PCPK, this is done when 'we engage cogently and critically with others' critical assessments of our own reasons, reasoning and judgments' (Westphal 2016: 3), but it can only yield philosophically *valid* results, because existence and knowledge of PK is always already present in the reasoners.

doing philosophy means overcoming whatever is 'just' zeitgeist, historical circumstance, logical fashion, or 'just present paradigm' and to enable the unconditioned truth to think itself *as it is*. While this might reveal that Hegel's method and the claims of his system were totally or partly erroneous, such an evaluation would have to be reasoned for philosophically—i.e. by means of the actually true description of PK or any account based on a different notion of truth insofar as this notion itself is reasonably shown to be superior to Hegel's. No alternative's supposed superiority should be simply assumed if it is to give a non-dogmatic answer to the question about the relationship between empirical and philosophical knowledge that Hegel's notion of philosophy is designed to address.[92]

Conclusion

This contribution's initial question about the relationship between empirical cognition and philosophical knowledge motivated the argument that Hegel differentiates between three kinds of knowledge: unconditioned philosophical knowledge (PK), conditioned empirical knowledge (EK), and potentially conditioned philosophical knowledge (PCPK). Of these three, EK and PCPK both presuppose PK and as soon as real PK is obtained, PK replaces PCPK.

From 'our' finite, potentially conditioned, PCPK-style perspective, this means that 'our' claims about PK can be mistaken *and* that they can be true. What 'we' take to be the truth in conceptual form might just be 'our' historically, geographically, or otherwise conditioned representations and not the unconditioned concept as absolute Geist. The same applies to Hegel. Instead of describing the 'idea of right', his *Philosophy of Right* and the *Encyclopedia's* 'objective Geist' might just have articulated what his times, intellect, and experience allowed 'him' to represent. However, while 'his' and 'our' errors and doubts are only possible because PK's unconditioned truth is always already enabling us and them, 'we' as subjects of thinking and 'our' PCPK are replaced by true thinking's self-thinking when true PK is achieved. Whenever philosophical claims are true, they are nobody's but unconditioned Geist's—and thus the truth's—own:

The unfolding of the mediation pulls itself together out of its dispersal and out of its temporal and external succession also in the form of *thinking* [...] to achieve its result: [Geist's] joining together with itself. When the unfolding expands in thinking's immanent simplicity, it is known as the indissoluble unity of the universal, simple and eternal Geist within itself. It is in this form of the truth that the truth is the object of *philosophy*.[93]

---

[92] If it is Hegel's notion of philosophy that is thought to be mistaken, then this would also have to be argued for (e.g. by engaging with the arguments Hegel makes against other available notions of philosophy in the *Encyclopedia's* 'attitudes', the *Phenomenology*, the *Logic*, or his *Lectures on the History of Philosophy*).

[93] Hegel 1986b: §571, 377 original italics, translation by author based on Michael Inwood's (2007) in: Hegel 2007.

References

Aristotle (1933) *Metaphysics* in Aristotle in 23 volumes, vols 17, 18, translated by Hugh Tredennick. Cambridge, MA, Harvard University Press; London, William Heinemann Ltd.

Aristotle (2009) *The Nicomachean Ethics*, trans. Ross, David, rev. intro. and notes Lesley Brown, Oxford: Oxford University Press.

Beiser, F. C. (2005) *Hegel*, New York: Routledge.

Brooks, Thom (2012) *Hegel's Political Philosophy*, 2nd ed., Edinburgh: Edinburgh University Press.

Brooks, Thom (2014) 'Natural Law Internalism' in *Hegel's Philosophy of Right*, Thom Brooks ed., Oxford: Wiley Blackwell.

deBoer, Karin (2010) *On Hegel: The Sway of the negative*, London: Palgrave Macmillan.

deBoer, Karin (2012) 'Hegel's Conception of Immanent Critique:Its Sources, Extent and Limit' in *Conceptions of Critique in Modern and Contemporary Philosophy* Karin de Boer and Ruth Sonderegger eds., London: Palgrave Macmillan, 2012.

Deligiorgi, K. (2012) *The Scope of Autonomy*, Oxford: Oxford University Press.

Deligiorgi, K. (2014) 'Actions as Events and Vice Versa: Kant, Hegel and the Concept of History' in *Internationales Jahrbuch des deutschen Idealismus Bd X*, Stolzenberg, Jürgen and Rush, Fred eds, Berlin: de Gruyter Verlag.

Hegel, G. W. F. (1986) *Vorlesungen über die Geschichte der Philosophie I*, Frankfurt: Suhrkamp.

Hegel, G. W. F. (1986a) *Enzyklopädie der philosophischen Wissenschaften im Grundrisse 1830: Zweiter Teil -Die Naturphilosophie—Mit den mündlichen Zusätzen -Werke 9*, Frankfurt: Suhrkamp.

Hegel, G. W. F. (1986b) *Enzyklopädie der philosophischen Wissenschaften im Grundrisse 1830: Dritter Teil—Die Philosophie des Geistes—Mit den mündlichen Zusätzen—Werke 10*, Frankfurt: Suhrkamp.

Hegel, G. W. F. (1990) *Lectures on the History of Philosophy: The Lectures of 1825–1826 Volume III Medieval and Modern Philosophy*, Brown, R. F. (ed.), Brown, R. F., Stewart J. M., and Harris, H. S. (trans.), Berkeley: University of California Press.

Hegel, G. W. F. (1991) *Enzyklopädie der philosophischen Wissenschaften (1830)*, Hamburg: Felix Meiner.

Hegel, G. W. F. (1991a) *The Encyclopaedia Logic (with the Zusätze): Part I of the Encyclopaedia of Philosophical Sciences with the Zusätze*, trans., intro. and notes by T. F. Geraets, W. A. Suchting, and H. S. Harris, Cambridge, MA: Hackett Publishing Company, Inc.

Hegel, G. W. F. (2007) *Hegel's Philosophy of Mind*, trans. W. Wallace and A. V. Miller, rev. and intro. M. J. Inwood, Oxford: Oxford University Press.

Hegel, G. W. F. (2008) *Outlines of the Philosophy of Right*, trans. T. M. Knox, rev. ed. and intro. Stephen Houlgate, Oxford: Oxford University Press.

Hegel, G. W. F. (2010) *The Science of Logic*, trans. & intro. Di Giovanni, George, Cambridge: Cambridge University Press.

Hegel, G. W. F. (2011) *Lectures on the Philosophy of World History: Volume I, Manuscripts of the Introduction and the lectures of 1822-3*, ed. and trans. Robert F. Brown and Peter C. Hodgson, assis. William G. Geuss, Oxford: Clarendon Press.

Honneth, A. (1995) *The Struggle for Recognition: The Moral Grammar of Social Conflicts*, trans. J. Anderson. Cambridge MA: MIT Press.

Houlgate, Stephen (2006) *The Opening of Hegel's Logic: From Being to Infinity*, La Fayette: Purdue University Press.

Hume, David (2009) *A Treatise of Human Nature: Being an Attempt to introduce the experimental Method of Reasoning into Moral Subjects*, The Floating Press.

Inwood, Michael J. (2007) *A Commentary on Hegel's Philosophy of Mind*, Oxford: Oxford University Press.

Knappik, F. (2016) 'Hegel's Essentialism. Natural Kinds and the Metaphysics of Explanation in Hegel's Theory of "the Concept"'. *European Journal of Philosophy*, DOI: 10.1111/ejop.12129.

Koch, Anton (2003) 'Sein—Wesen—Begriff' in *Der Begriff als Wahrheit. Zum Anspruch der Hegelschen 'Subjektiven Logik'*, A.F. Koch, A. Oberauer, and K. Utz eds, Paderborn, 17–30.

Koch, Anton (2007) 'Metaphysik und spekulative Logik' in *Metaphysik heute—Probleme und Perspektiven der Ontologie*, Matthias Lutz-Bachmann and Thomas M. Schmidt eds, Freiburg/München, 40–56.

Koch, Anton (2011) 'Hegel: Die Einheit des Begriffs' in *Einheit und Vielheit als metaphysisches Problem*, Johannes Brachtendorf und Stephan Herzberg eds, Tübingen: Mohr Siebeck.

Kreines, James (2007) 'Between the Bounds of Experience', *Inquiry* 50: 3.

Longuenesse, Beatrice (2000) 'Point of View of Man or Knowledge of God' in *The Reception of Kant's Critical Philosophy*, Sally Sedgwick ed., Oxford: Oxford University Press.

Nuzzo, Angelica (2012) *Memory, History, Justice in Hegel*, New York: Palgrave Macmillan.

O'Connor, Brian (2015) 'The Neo-Hegelian Theory of Freedom and the Limits of Emancipation', *European Journal of Philosophy* 23:2: 171–94.

Ostritsch, Sebastian (2014) *Hegels Rechtsphilosophie als Metaethik*, Münster: Mentis.

Pinkard, Terry (2016) 'Hegel's Shepherd's Way Out of the Thicket', chapter 7, this volume.

Pippin, Robert (1989) *Hegel's Idealism: The Satisfactions of Self-consciousness*, Cambridge: Cambridge University Press.

Pippin, Robert (2008) *Hegel's Practical Philosophy: Rational Agency as Ethical Life*, Cambridge: Cambridge University Press.

Pippin, Robert (2016) 'In What Sense is Hegel's *Philosophy of Right* "Based" on His *Science of Logic*?', chapter 3, this volume.

Plato (2005) *Meno and Other Dialogues: Charmides, Laches, Lysis, Meno*, Trans., intro., and notes R. Waterfield, Oxford: Oxford University Press.

Ruda, Frank (2011) *Hegel's Rabble: An Investigation into Hegel's Philosophy of Right*, New York: Continuum.

Sedgwick, Sally S. (1988) 'Hegel's Critique of the Subjective Idealism of Kant's Ethics' in *Journal of the History of Philosophy* 26:1: 89–105.

Siep, Ludwig (2015) *Der Staat als irdischer Gott: Genese und Relevanz einer Hegelschen Idee*, Tübingen: Mohr Siebeck.

Sparby, Terje (2014) 'The Problem of Higher Knowledge in Hegel's Philosophy' in *Hegel Bulletin* 35:1: 33–55.

Sparby, Terje (2014a) 'The "Open Closure" of Hegel's Method and System: A Critique of Terry Pinkard's *Naturalized Hegel*' in *Clio*, 44:1: 115–45.

Spinoza, Baruch de (2002) *Complete Works*, trans. Samuel Shirley, ed. and notes Michael L. Morgan, Indianapolis: Hackett.

Stein, Sebastian (2014) 'Hegel and Kant on Rational Willing: The Relevance of Method', *Hegel Bulletin*, 35: 273–91.

Stein, Sebastian (2016) 'Hegel's Twofold Critique of Empiricism: Cognition, Ontology and the Question of Universality', *Revista Eletrônica Estudos Hegelianos/Online Journal of Hegelian Studies* 13:22.

Stein, Sebastian (2016a) 'Freedom for Free: Hegel on Cognition, Willing, Free Mind and the Methodological Cost of Finite Freedom' in *Hegel's Philosophical Psychology*, L. Ziglioli and S. Herrmann-Sinai eds, New York: Routledge.

Stern, Robert (2006) 'Hegel's Doppelsatz: A Neutral Reading', *Journal of the History of Philosophy* 44:2, 235–66.

Stone, Alison (forthcoming) 'Hegel on Law, Women, and Contract' in *Feminist Encounters with Legal Philosophy*, Maria Drakopoulou ed.

Thompson, Kevin (2016) 'Systematicity and Normative Justification: The Method of Hegel's Philosophical Science of Right', chapter 2, this volume.

Trisokkas, Ioannis (2009) 'The Speculative Logical Theory of Universality', *The Owl of Minerva* 40:2: 141–74.

Vieweg, Klaus (2012) *Das Denken der Freiheit: Hegels Grundlinien der Philosophie des Rechts*, München: Wilhelm Fink.

Westphal, Kenneth (2015) 'Hegel's Pragmatic Critique and Reconstruction of Kant's System of Principles in the Logic and Encyclopaedia', *Dialogue: Canadian Journal of Philosophy/Revue canadienne de philosophie*, 54:2: 333–69.

Westphal, Kenneth (2016) 'Hegel's Natural Law Constructivism: Progress in Principle and in Practice', chapter 13, this volume.

Winfield, Richard D. (2016) 'The Logic of Right', chapter 11, this volume.

Wood, Allen W. (2016) 'Method and System in Hegel's *Philosophy of Right*', chapter 4, this volume.

9

Individuals

The Revisionary Logic of Hegel's Politics

Katerina Deligiorgi

A common place in the interpretation of Hegel's political philosophy is that it contains powerful criticisms of liberal individualism and advances strongly institutionalist proposals.[1,2] My aim in this chapter is to contribute indirectly to this discussion, by examining Hegel's analysis of the category of 'individual' in the *Science of Logic*. Getting to grips with the logic of 'individual' is important in helping us make sense both of his criticism of the politics of individualism, discussed extensively in the literature, and his recognition of the positive, liberating function of modern individualism.

---

[1] References to Hegel's texts are given parenthetically as in-text citations. After an abbreviation a reference is given to the page number of the translations, after a comma a volume and page number is given to the Suhrkamp edition of Hegel's works, *Werke* in 20 Bd., E. Moldenauer and K. M. Michel eds, Frankfurt am Main: Suhrkamp, 1986. For the *Philosophy of Right* and the *Encyclopedia* only the paragraph numbers are given. The English translations and abbreviations used are:

A: *Hegel's Aesthetics*, trans., T. M. Knox, volume 1, Oxford: Clarendon, 1998.

EM: *Hegel's Philosophy of Mind: Part Three of the Encyclopedia of Philosophical Sciences (1830)*, trans. W. Wallace, with Zusätze trans. A. V. Miller, Oxford: Oxford University Press, 1988.

L: *Hegel's Science of Logic*, ed. H. D. Lewis, trans., A. V. Miller, Atlantic Highlands, NJ: Humanities Press, 1991 [1969].

LPH: *Lectures on the Philosophy of World History: Introduction*, trans. H. B. Nisbet, Cambridge University Press, 1980.

NL: *Natural Law: The Scientific Ways of Treating Natural Law, Its Place in Moral Philosophy, and Its Relation to the Positive Sciences of Law*, trans. T. M. Knox, Philadelphia: University of Pennsylvania Press, 1975.

PhS: *Phenomenology of Spirit*, trans. A. V. Miller Oxford: Oxford University Press, 1977.

PR: *Hegel's Philosophy of Right*, trans. T. M. Knox, Oxford: Oxford University Press, 1967.

[2] See Wood 1990, 1991, Franco 1999, Neuhouser 2000, Honneth 2010, McCumber 2014. Criticism of liberal individualism does not mean also outright rejection of liberalism, see Brooks 2012 and also Sayers 2007 and Moyar 2011. Exemplifying recent trends in rehabilitating individualism in Hegel is Ross 2008. Interestingly there is also a reverse trend, inspired by the recent rehabilitation of notions of collective intentionality; see Chitty 2014. Traditionally the debate has centred on whether it is possible or indeed desirable for Hegelian objective 'Spirit' to accommodate individuals politically, socially, or metaphysically. An early contribution to this discussion, Hartmann 1929, contains an extensive argument that seeks to demystify 'Spirit', arguing that the term does not mean 'group-mind', but rather, it captures just the social sphere of familiar everyday interactions; see too Williams 1992, 1997, Pinkard 2008, and Deligiorgi 2010.

What the discussion in the *Logic* shows is that there are two ways of understanding the category of 'individual'; Hegel's argument aims to undermine the first and preserve the second. On the first way, 'individual' is understood as something that counts as one by virtue of not being reducible to something else. This sense of individual comes very close to what modern metaphysicians call a 'simple', which is whatever is taken as basic in our discussions about the world.[3] If we look at contemporary moral and political philosophy, we will have no difficulty in finding examples of this understanding of 'individual'. References to the cognitive and volitional powers of individuals, their practical skills, level of epistemic competence, rights, self-expression, want-satisfaction, preferences, and so on, presuppose that we use 'individual' to mean something that counts as one by virtue of not being reducible to something else. The substantive moral and political claims advanced on behalf of individuals, so understood, can, of course, be criticized without recourse to logical arguments, Hegel's or anyone else's.[4] Our task here, however, is not to argue for or against substantive positions in politics or ethics. Rather it is the more modest one of understanding Hegel's own views. The advantage of going about it through the *Logic* is that his criticisms of the political manifestations of these simples are shown to be not mere correctives of individualism. They are an invitation to rethink systematically what we mean by 'individual', and, by extension, to reflect on what we care about politically and who is the 'we' who undertakes such critical reflection on our words and on our aspirations.

I just said that there is a second way of understanding 'individual' that Hegel's argument preserves. If we look in the literature on Hegel's social and political philosophy, however, we do not find such a notion. We find attention focused on his positive arguments about interpersonal relations, such as recognition, and the institutions of ethical life, such as the family or the state. The notion of individual presupposed in these discussions is that notion of a simple, as outlined above. This presupposition gives rise to the familiar interpretative conundrum about how Hegel can strike a balance between 'the individual' and 'the social'.[5] A rare exception is Kenneth Westphal, who comes up with an explicit definition of individuality summarized in three theses that make up what he calls 'moderate collectivism':

> MC1. Individuals are social practitioners. Everything a person does, says, or thinks is formed in the context of social practices that provide material and conceptual resources, objects of desire, skills, procedures, techniques, and occasions and permissions for action et cetera.

---

[3] For this use of 'simple' see Russell 1992, who introduces the term in part to distance his views from Hegelianism.

[4] See Wolf 1990, esp. chapters 2 and 3 on moral individualism, and Skorupski 2015 for an overview of criticisms of political individualism.

[5] Writing about recognition, for example, Robert Williams says that Hegel 'struggles to formulate a theory of individuality, to do justice to the individual and individual freedoms...Individuality and difference must be given their due without, however, reducing the social to something inherently oppressive' (Williams 1992: 83).

MC2. What individuals do depends on their own response to their social and natural environment.

MC3. There are no individuals, no social practitioners, without social practices and vice versa no social practices without social practitioners, individuals who learn, participate in, perpetuate, and *who modify* those social practices as needed to meet their changing needs, aims, and circumstances (including procedures and information). (Westphal 2003: 107, emphasis in original)

These three theses do not appear to be making excessive philosophical demands of the sort that would warrant a reconception of the category of individual.[6] Moderate collectivism is a readily graspable view about the ways we form—and are formed by— our environment. It is moreover a view that is routinely assumed in disciplines such as social anthropology or political economy. What I want to show is that, for Hegel, to think *consistently* in this fashion requires that we give up on the unitary conception of individual and replace it with one that is quite a bit more demanding than the moderate theses Westphal attributes to Hegel. Hegel's alternative to the unitary conception is one in which 'individual' is an incomplete term: in order to fully characterize what makes someone an individual, further information must be adduced. Hegel's logical revision of the category of 'individual' partly confirms the theses that make up moderate collectivism and partly confronts us with an open question about the complete specification of any given individual.

Section 9.1 examines the material from the *Logic* and substantiates the claims made in this introductory section about Hegel's criticism of the unitary conception of individual. Questions about his positive conception are answered in Section 9.2, using the resources of an argument by Peter Geach. Section 9.3 shows how Hegel's logical arguments map on to practical arguments. Section 9.4 identifies a recurrent interpretative puzzle and draws some tentative conclusions about the relation between logic and politics.

9.1. 'Posited Abstraction': The Category of 'Individual' in the *Logic*

Hegel treats the logical category of 'individual' (*das Einzelne*) in the second and final volume of the *Science of Logic* entitled 'Subjective Logic or the Doctrine of the Notion'. The volume has three sections, 'Subjectivity', which is where the discussion of 'The Individual' is located, 'Objectivity', and 'The Idea', which concludes the whole book.

Under 'Subjective Logic' Hegel treats mainly, though not exclusively, certain aspects of Kant's transcendental philosophy. The introduction to this volume, entitled 'The

---

[6] The sort of philosophical demands traditionally have been thought of as excessive in the Hegelian context concern the existence of a supra-individual spirit that manifests itself through individual thoughts and actions. The *locus classicus* of this view, in the Anglophone reception of Hegel's thought, is Taylor 1975.

Notion in General', contains a detailed discussion of Kant's transcendental deduction from the first *Critique*. Given the prominence of this discussion, it is plausible to think that the whole volume on 'Subjective Logic' is concerned with the subjectivity of the synthetic unity of apperception or 'I', which Hegel also calls a 'unity of consciousness' (L 584, 6:254) and the conceptual nature of its synthesis, which allows Hegel to refer to the thinking activity of this 'I' as the 'Notion' (*Begriff*). Hegel credits Kant with the categorial expression of the unifying function of the 'I':

> It is one of the profoundest and truest insights to be found in the *Critique of Pure Reason* that the *unity* which constitutes the nature [*Wesen*] of the *Notion* is recognized as the *original synthetic unity of apperception*, as unity of the *I think*, or of self-consciousness.   (L 584, 6:254)

The purpose of this introductory discussion is to set out the problem the second volume aims to resolve, namely to uncover the nature of the Notion, 'what the Notion is' (L 585, 6:255). The question arises for Hegel because Kant does not fully explain how the thinking activity of the I can truly be thought of as ground of all objectivity. Having acknowledged Kant's contribution then, Hegel aims to show that this Kantian inheritance needs revision and extension.[7] He argues that in order to grasp the I's unifying function, precisely so as to account for the 'unity of the Notion and reality' (L 587, 6:258), neither the (Kantian) categories of the understanding nor the mere thought of the 'I' can help. This is where he introduces what he calls 'the Idea' (L 587, 6:258), which is a concept that represents or expresses 'the unity of Notion and reality'.[8] These general introductory remarks on 'The Notion in General' give us not just the context of the whole volume, but also of the chapter that immediately follows, on 'The Notion', which ends with a discussion of 'The Individual'. Prior to this discussion, however, Hegel makes some puzzling remarks in which he attributes individuality *to* the 'Notion'. I will therefore first examine this material and then turn to the explicit treatment of the category of the individual.

Hegel attributes individuality to the Notion in the course of his critical engagement with Kant. He starts the section by identifying the limitations of Spinoza's conception of substance as lacking a unity that is manifest. I take this to mean that the unity of Spinozan substance is just given.[9] The requirement for such unity to be investigated

[7] In both the *Science of Logic* (e.g. in L 581, 6:251) and in the *Encyclopedia*, Hegel defines the Notion as 'the principle of freedom, the power of substance self-realised' (§ 160). This suggests that his aim is to move beyond a formal conception of the principle of unity of cognition as such.

[8] The discussion of Kant in this section can help us understand the 'Idea' Hegel presents here in relation to something Kant says in the first *Critique*, when Kant identifies the 'common principle' from which the categories arise as 'the faculty of judgement' (Kant 1999: A81, B107). Kant claims that a full account in the sense of definition of that principle is not possible (see Kant 1999: A727, B755). The function the 'Idea' at this stage of the *Logic* then can be seen as a promissory note that such a full account is possible. At the same time, Hegel is using familiar Kantian terminology in making these claims: '[t]he pure concept [*Begriff*] in so far as it has its origin in the understanding alone (not in the pure image of sensibility), is called a notion [*Notio*]. A concept formed from notions and transcending the possibility of experience is an idea [*Idee*] or concept of reason' (Kant 1999: A 320/B377).

[9] It is not my aim to adjudicate whether this is a justified criticism or not, for extensive treatment see Macherey 1990.

and explained brings the 'Notion' qua transcendental unity of apperception into the discussion. The thought is that Kant presents us with a notion of unity for which he gives an argument and attempts to show why it is right that we think about unity in this way. It is in this context that Hegel makes the claim that 'the Notion is the *individual*' (L 582, 6:252). He then explains the claim as follows: the identity of the Notion has 'the determination of negativity', which in turn, gives us the 'Notion of the Notion' (L 582, 6:252). These claims appear very opaque; one way of understanding what Hegel is saying here is by taking them as a Hegelian summary of an argument that can be found in Kant and which states that the notion (*Notio*) (Kant 1999: A320) of transcendental subjectivity 'is known only through the thoughts that are its predicates' (Kant 1999: A346/B404), i.e. it is not known in itself. So in Hegel's terms it is a 'negatively' determined individual.

At the same time, Hegel says, the Notion is also a universal (L 582, 6:252). This is again a difficult claim to understand, not least because Hegel has not yet explained what theory of universals he espouses. Still, from the negative determination alone, just discussed, it is possible and plausible to reach two negative conclusions about the Notion: that it is not a substance and also not a universally distributed particular. At this stage then, 'universal' can at most mean a class to which all particular acts of unification of the manifold belong. This is a Hegelian rendering of a Kantian claim, that is, a way of saying that the Notion is a necessary principle of *all* cognition for *every* subject of cognition. So Hegel's understanding of the transcendental 'I' is as a Notion that possesses universality and an individual identity that is to be conceived of negatively.

Given the specificity of the context of the discussion of the individuality of the Notion, it would seem unlikely that we can draw any conclusions besides those relating to Hegel's interpretation of Kant. However, there is something interesting going on here that has broader relevance to his conception of 'individual' as such. In attempting to convey more precisely the identity of the 'I', Hegel describes it as 'self-related negativity' that has individuality in the sense of 'opposing itself to all that is other and excluding it' and which is individuated 'through its unity with the positedness' that constitutes the '*nature* of the I as well as of the Notion' (L 583 emphasis added, 6:252). The basic description of the individuality of the 'I' is given precisely in terms of what we called previously the standard modern view, as 'opposing itself to all that is other and excluding it', its individuation, however, is presented as something that is not a straightforward matter. Rather, what makes something the individual it is has to do with its 'positedness', so individuation is a sort of relation that reveals the nature of the thing as individual such and such. It is in this manner, Hegel concludes, that the concept of 'individual' gains 'concreteness' (L 603, 6:277).

With this in the background, let us now turn to the section on 'The Individual'.[10] The argument repeats the basic moves we found in the discussion of the individuality of the

---

[10] A word of caution is perhaps apt here concerning with the well-documented and ongoing controversy about what the precise philosophical task Hegel set himself when embarking on his *Science of Logic*, very

Notion, adding detail and clarifying the structure of the presentation: we start basically with what seems to be an easy and unproblematic way of picking out individuals, and then Hegel points out that the 'individual' is not thereby determined and that determination requires at least two relata. The first move is to describe individuality partially as what is involved when we identify something specific, a particular, a 'this …' (L 618, 6:296). This identification is 'illusory', Hegel claims. This basic understanding of individuality makes it 'an illusory being within the universal' (L 619, 6:297). The idea seems to be that in seeking to determine that which is individual, we resort to features that are general, we seek to determine it 'through abstraction which lets drop the particular and rises to the higher and the highest genus' (L 619, 6:297). This abstraction, Hegel notes, 'is a sundering of the concrete and an isolating of its determinations; through it only single properties and moments are seized' (L 619, 6:297). So what is individual then? Hegel wants to hold on to the idea of its connection to the original 'this' of particularity and also to the abstraction or formality of universality. His designation of individuality is 'posited abstraction' (L 621 and 622, 6:299 and 300).[11] I want to suggest that we understand this designation as an invitation to consider fully determined individuality as a unity of form (the universality) and a substantive or 'concrete' element (the particular).

How is individuality to be fully determined though? The clue to answering this question is in the structure of the section on Subjectivity. On the one hand, we have an analysis of subjectivity as a concept that has a very distinctive nature, it is a unifying concept (the Notion) and as such it is an individual, in the sense of an 'I'. On the other hand, 'individual' is one element, together with 'universal' and 'particular', in the forms of thought about reality. At the end of the discussion of individuality we do not have a full determination of it either as a form of thought nor as an 'I', and the reason for this is that Hegel has not yet discussed judgement, which on Kantian grounds is the basic unit of cognition. To determine something fully is a matter of a special kind of judgement that gives us just what the thing is; Hegel calls this 'essential determination [*Wesentlichkeit*]' (L 643, 6:326). Judgement for Hegel is both an 'original partition' (L 622, 6:301 and 628, 6:304) and a unity, bringing together subjects, 'this' or what something '*simply is* [das *Seiende*] or *is for itself*' with predicates that signify something

---

roughly whether he is developing his own metaphysics or whether he is attempting to give a systematic inventory—or perhaps deduction—of fundamental concepts of thought; see Burbidge 2006 and Houlgate 2006, chapter 1. It is apt to raise this now, because unlike the introduction to 'Subjective Logic' with its extensive discussion of Kant's arguments, which can be read as a philosophical commentary, the section on 'The Individual' cannot. So the question of what kind of philosophical genre the *Logic* is arises here perhaps more urgently. My view, the defence of which exceeds the scope of the present chapter, is that the *Logic* is a kind of content logic, aiming to offer a systematic exposition of thought *qua* thought *of* things. Nonetheless, the sort of 'systematic' reading I propose (using Brooks's 2012 terminology) requires only that Hegel is engaging in an analysis of concepts, on which all sides of this debate agree—whatever else they claim he is also doing while doing this. And it is this conceptual analysis of 'individual' that concerns me here.

[11] As Paul Redding pointed out in discussion, there is an Aristotelian dimension to this passage and also Hegel's reception of Leibnizian logic transmitted through Gottfried Ploucquet, whose textbook Hegel was using in Tübingen.

universal (L 627, 6:306). Using traditional subject-predicate logic, Hegel seeks to show that the basic form of thought in which a genus or universal is predicated of something aims at something that is not quite captured in the judgement form. To say truly of x that it is y, requires a certain agility in thinking that the universality of the x is concrete and the particularity of the y is an 'invidualised universal' (L 662, 6:349). Hence, Hegel says, 'we have before us the determinate and fullfilled [*erfüllte*] copula, which formerly consisted in the abstract "is"' (L 662, 6:350). The emphasis on the unity achieved through this new perspective on the copula or the judgement function, 'S is p', Hegel says, amounts to a step forward from judgement to syllogism (L 663, 6:351). While I am not going to follow Hegel's argument here, except to note that the move to syllogism is pivotal for the transition from the section on Subjectivity to that on Objectivity, it is clear from the material we have covered so far that the direction of argument about the categories that Hegel puts in the section on Subjectivity is towards forms of thought that permit gathering together single elements of thought into systematic wholes in which these elements signify by virtue of the role they play in the bigger whole.[12]

So given this context how is individuality determined? In other words, what is Hegel's positive theory? And following from this: can a positive theory of individuality be extracted without committing to every claim contained in the *Logic*? Taking each question in turn: first in some sense individuality cannot be fully determined without losing its individual character, that is to say, we have to acknowledge what, especially in the *Encyclopedia Logic*, Hegel designates as the 'negative' character of individuality (see §163 and §165). At the same time, a positive theory can be extracted given that individuals are determinable in judgements. In what follows, I will make a sideways step that can help extract such a positive theory from the material Hegel has given us in the *Logic*. The step is sideways because it does not treat Hegel's arguments but Geach's reconstruction of the Aquinian conception of 'form'. While this interpretative path may look unpromising, rendering the obscure yet more obscure, I believe that Geach's 'thin'—i.e. guided by logico-linguistic concerns—reconstruction of Aquinas' argument, can help us advance our understanding on Hegel's positive theory of individuality.

9.2. A Hunch About Form: Geach on Aquinas

Hegel's *Science of Logic* is both about basic categories of thought, that is, how we—or philosophers—think about what there is, and about what there is. The ambition of embracing thought and being in a single project can seem very remote from the logico-linguistic concerns of the tradition we are about to discuss. However, as we shall see, one of Geach's motivations for getting predication right, in part by drawing on medieval sources, is that logic can save us from being metaphysically misled.

---

[12] In Hegel's terms the advance is 'from simple determinateness' to 'succeeding ones becoming ever richer and more concrete'; he also describes this process as 'expansion' and also as forming 'a system of totality' (L 840, 6:569).

Of particular interest and relevance to our current concerns is Geach's discussion of form in Aquinas. I want to suggest that Hegel's positive theory of the category of individual can be illuminated if we think of 'individual' as a 'form' in the manner Geach explains. The key advantage of understanding 'individual' as form is that we do not need to replace the concept with some other, all that is needed is to reflect more deeply about the conceptual commitments we make when using the term. Admittedly, drawing on medieval arguments recast in response to post-Fregean logico-linguistic concerns is a rather roundabout way of making sense of the category of Hegel's individual, especially of its positive content. However, neither the thirteenth- nor the early twentieth-century aspects need intrude. My aim is not to engage in scholarly debate about Aquinas, nor to champion a specific position in the philosophy of language, rather it is to show how Geach's interpretation of 'form' is very fruitful when applied to Hegel's conception of the individual.[13]

Geach's work aims to show that the formal analysis of language undertaken by logicians has an important role in clarifying our everyday use of language, and this purpose can be served by drawing on both medieval and Fregean theories of logic and language.[14] The particular argument that concerns us here on Aquinas's notion of form is a perfect example of this approach. Geach's interpretation of form takes its cue from Frege's notion of a concept (*Begriff*). Frege delimits sharply between concepts and objects, assigning to them different logical roles. One way of putting this by means of an example, is to say our thought 'Socrates is a man' can be divided into two constituents, the object-expression 'Socrates' and the concept-expression 'is a man'. On Geach's interpretation, Aquinas' notion of 'form' falls on the concept side of the distinction; what falls on the other side is what Aquinas calls the *supposit*, which he uses to designate a complete entity.[15]

This does not take us very far because it is not really clear what forms are. Geach illustrates the meaning of 'form' with Aquinas's example 'quo albedus Socrates est', 'that by which Socrates is white'; what interests us is the phrase introduced by *quo*, because this is what designates the form function. It is useful here to consider how one might say otherwise 'that by which Socrates is white' given how odd it sounds to contemporary ears. A synonymous expression, Geach claims, is 'albedo Socratis', or 'the whiteness of Socrates' (Geach 1955: 5).

Although Geach's clarification enables us to recognize form expressions without the use of the cumbersome *quo*, it leaves us in the dark about their role. One may ask, for

---

[13] While the influence of Geach's Fregean interpretation can be seen in Kenny 2002, it is not uniformly accepted; see Weidemann 1986 and Wippel 2000.

[14] Geach sets himself equally against logicians who see logic as a branch of mathematics and against ordinary language philosophers; see Geach 1980: 8–10.

[15] 'For Aquinas, the real distinction between a form and the self-subsistent individual (*suppositum*) whose form it is comes out in the logical distinction between subject and predicate' (Geach 1955: 2–3). Geach refers to self-subsistent individuals and to individualized forms, to avoid confusion with the notion of individual I want to illuminate through Geach's analysis of form, I shall only refer to supposits and to fully specified or determined forms.

example, why should a contemporary audience, which is not especially interested in the history of philosophy, spend time considering 'that by which...' expressions. The contemporary philosopher may argue that she has to hand an accepted theory about subjects and predicates, according to which, as Geach himself reminds his audience, the logical subject and predicate have different ways of signifying. Another way of putting this concern is why can't we absorb 'that by which X is y' expressions into 'X is y' expressions? The reason Geach gives, and the motivation for focusing on Aquinas, is that he wants to add something controversial to the accepted theory, namely that the 'realities signified' (Geach 1955: 5) are *not* different in type. This is what thinking about forms contributes to the debate; it allows us to think of 'realities signified' without committing ourselves to the search of a thing, such as 'whiteness'—a form in the Platonic sense—which would then lead us to a confused search of how Socrates partakes of whiteness or how whiteness belongs to Socrates.

Although Geach is making his argument in the context of Anglophone post-Fregean philosophy of language, the point he makes about predication and how we think about the ontological basis of what we say is clearly of much broader application. Another way of talking about Aquinian forms is to say that the attributes of the particulars we are talking about, the 'whiteness' of Socrates, for example, are themselves particulars—not Platonic forms.[16] This view, popularized in contemporary metaphysics in the discussion of 'tropes', speaks to the intuition that the whiteness of Socrates is a different whiteness to the whiteness of his chiton or the whiteness of his eye. To return to the Aquinian terminology, Geach uses to make his point, the idea that a *supposit* relates to form by being an instance of something, e.g. 'here is Socrates' and 'here is something white', and something recognizable as such, e.g. 'this here Socrates is such and such'. By contrast, form signifies by enabling us to focus on the kind of thing something is, the kind of designation that is applicable to the thing. The important point is that forms direct us to look at what in the world they signify. 'Forms', Geach says, 'are what answer *in rebus* to logical predicates' (Geach 1955: 6). So he recommends that we should allow that 'logical predicates stand for something, as well as being true or false *of* things' (Geach 1955: 6). It is this idea of 'standing for something' that makes the Aquinian notion of form especially interesting in the Hegelian context.

How does Aquinas' concept of form allow us to think of the realities the logical predicates stand for? Let us go back to 'the whiteness of Socrates'. The claim is that this phrase stands for something and at the same time that 'whiteness' does not stands for a substance—or what amounts to the same thing that 'whiteness' is not a subject. Geach's answer is to point out first of all that 'whiteness' is of no use to anyone. What we in fact say is 'the (whiteness) of...'. If we take this as the Aquinian form, rather than the abstract term 'whiteness', we see that 'the X of...' is not complete, 'it needs to be completed with a name of something that has the form'. So we treat 'the whiteness of...' in

---

[16] As Anthony Kenny remarks, for Aquinas 'there is not, in the world, any dogginess which is not the dogginess of some particular dog' (Kenny 2002: 180).

exactly the same fashion as the predicate '...is white', which also needs to be completed by a subject (Geach 1955: 5). Aquinian form, whether in the phrase using the abstract term 'the Xness of...' or the predicate phrase '...is x', is in Fregean terms 'unsaturated'. The 'of' in the first phrase is a 'logically inseparable part' of the phrase indicating 'the need to put a name after this sign' (Geach 1955: 5). Here, as Geach notes, we have to tread carefully or we shall lose the distinction between form and logical individual. Form *simpliciter* is the reference of the predicate '...is white', form characterized or made specific is the reference of a phrase such as 'the whiteness of Socrates'. So we understand the original '*quo*' as a way of connecting a logical individual with some form, in the familiar manner of subject/predicate, but also as distinguishing the individual from its individualized forms, so we speak of Socrates and also his whiteness, wisdom, humanity. etc., and similarly we can say *of* the whiteness of Socrates that it is off-putting, and *of* the whiteness of Alcibiades that it is attractive, etc.

Let us see now how this discussion can help us with a positive theory of the Hegelian 'individual' as a concept that we may use in ordinary discussions. Hegel as we saw repeatedly refers to the individual as a 'this' (L 621, 622, 6:300), which naturally fits the position of *supposit* in our previous analysis: 'here is x' 'here is something y'. But it is precisely such a use that Hegel calls illusory. If we don't think of the individual as a this, or at least if we entertain the thought that such a conception of the individual is in some way problematic, we will not be tempted to give metaphysical sustenance to the 'this' by considering the individual as a simple. The alternative that Hegel gives us in the *Logic* is to think of 'individual' as a 'posited abstraction', which in light of the arguments from Geach just discussed, we can understand to mean that the term is asserted but it is not complete.

To put the same thing more simply: to assert that someone is an individual, as in '...is an individual' and 'the individuality of...' is to say something that is in need of completion. Replacing the unitary conception of 'individual' with this revised conception in which individual is a form has the advantage of leaving open the term to admit the further information of the kind we seek. To say '...is an individual' sounds a lot less informative than '...is white'. But they are different forms and different realities signified when we speak of the whiteness of Socrates or the whiteness of his chiton. Similarly, when we are thinking of the form '...is an individual' we ought to concern ourselves with the realities signified and ask about what fills *that* in, what characterizes that form. So if we say 'Mary is an individual' we may mean that her manners somehow mark her out in a specific context, the how and the what of the context serving further to characterize the form. But we may also mean that she is a being capable of choice and that she can make up her own mind about something. In each case we mean something and something is understood depending on the filling we put to the form. Also in each case, if there is doubt then more questions can be asked, such as: what instances of dress count as distinctive, what behaviour do we identify as distinctive, what transactions show capacity of choice? Discussion concerns concrete instances either of particular things ('this email here') or of further forms ('...is thoughtful').

The advantage of thinking of Hegel's positive theory of the category of the individual in terms of a form that needs specification is that we can think of individuals and objective spirit as being on the same side, so to speak. In other words, the individualized form of 'individual' stands for some portion of reality, or in more Hegelian terms, some portion of spirit. By 'spirit' I understand here both 'subjective spirit', the whole range of states of mind we display in interacting with our environment, including our social environment, and 'objective spirit', the roles we occupy in institutional settings within organized social and political wholes. When we seek to characterize the portion of spirit we pick out with the term 'individual', we commit ourselves to referring to worldly specifics. As Hegel puts it in the *Logic*, seeking to clarify the idea of posited abstraction, 'the *this is*; it is immediate; but it is only *this* in so far as it is *pointed out*' (L 622, 6:300).[17] In each case, we are effortlessly referred to the world and specific encounters in the world to substantiate, explain, and clarify what we say. Neither individuals nor individuality disappear in this way, rather we are directed to consider what they stand for.

9.3. Individuals in Practice

The position defended in the previous two sections comes to this: to say that someone is an individual is to say something, though not very much, unless further information is at hand to help us specify, *individualize*, the individual in question. At issue is not the pragmatics of conversations, filling in missing information by knowing something about the context. For Hegel, this filling in is a matter of the logic of individuality. The category 'individual' signifies through being completed, fully determined. The purpose of the present section is to find out what such full determination amounts to.

In part, to complete or specify an 'individual', we need an extended description of the social, political, and also cultural properties, which mark out this or that individual as this or that region of spirit. But an interesting and distinctively Hegelian twist complicates this story. Hegel's critical discussion of individuality in both his logic and in his practical philosophy is historically alert and specific. 'Individual' is not a found term, it comes with specific philosophical contents. While Hegel's positive account emerges out of his critical engagement with philosophical positions that advance forms of practical individualism, he does not assume that they thereby disappear or lose their hold on our thinking. So 'individual' is not completed or specified *just* through positive identification of roles, choices, or interests, but also through reference to aspirations that attach to modern conceptions of individuality, either empiricist-inflected aspirations to self-determination and non-interference by others, or universalist aspirations that come with a moral self-conception of individuals. Although it would seem that logically

---

[17] Given this analysis, it makes sense that for Hegel the category of the individual cannot ultimately be treated in isolation from that of judgement with its relata, which in turn explains why the section on 'The Individual' immediately precedes and serves to introduce precisely the chapter on 'The Judgement'.

we are asked to do away with the understanding of individual as a simple, this understanding is current in a historically specific slice of spirit. So the revisionary logic of individual allows and indeed requires that we keep in view precisely what we are in effect asked to move on from. I will illustrate what I mean by looking at a couple of examples.

In his practical philosophy, Hegel targets versions of moral and political individualism in the name of freedom. Already in his early work, the so-called 'Theological Writings' dating the mid-1790s and including the Jena-period writings of the early 1800s, Hegel was centrally concerned with articulating a positive conception of freedom, a conception that is 'positive' in the sense that it contains substantive commitments that express or constitute human freedom.[18] Integral to this project is Hegel's criticism of individualistic conceptions of freedom, on the grounds that they are merely negative and thus cannot find genuine expression in specific practical commitments (cf. NL 66, 2:448-9), or, alternatively, because they are concerned with the availability of alternatives, to do or to refrain from doing, which Hegel considers vacuous (cf. NL 89f., 2:477f.). The clearest example of such arguments can be found in the 'Natural Law' essay, Hegel takes issue explicitly with empiricist and idealist conceptions of freedom—these last represented by Kant and Fichte. The empiricist ones are paradigmatically negative on Hegel's presentation, because they advocate non-interference with individual choices. At the same time, empiricist accounts offer no resources for a normative conception of the individual they seek to defend from external interference. She has a valid claim for her choices are to be respected, but it is not clear why. The idea of a contract as providing a normative foundation does not fill this gap since the individual brings her authority with her to the contractual relation and enters the contract for instrumental reasons. Hegel's concern is not with a specific theory, but rather with what Frederick Neuhouser calls the individual in 'substance', who is the political equivalent of the individual as a simple (see Neuhouser 2000: 182). Kant and Fichte, on Hegel's account, fill the normative gap with the idea of the individual as moral agent who realizes her freedom through her choices. However, the idea of spontaneity underpinning this normative conception remains mysterious.

Although a question may well arise about whether Hegel's criticisms hit real targets or straw men, the point of looking at this intellectual trajectory is to identify recurrent elements of his engagement with the modern empiricist and idealist ways of thinking about freedom and individuals. Although it is tempting to think of this criticism in terms of a confrontation between different conceptions of freedom, there is a deeper point that emerges clearly in the *Phenomenology*. As Robert Pippin argues, Hegel's criticism of the 'ultimacy of individuality' (Pippin 2006: 135) in the *Phenomenology* targets the very model of mind presupposed by individualist conceptions of agency.

---

[18] This use of 'positive', current in the contemporary debate, is owed to Berlin 1969. For detailed discussion of Hegel's distinctive use of the term 'positive', especially in his early works from the Berne period (1793–1796), see Deligiorgi 2012.

On Pippin's reconstruction, there is such a basic model and it consists of prioritizing something that counts as 'inner' over whatever is thought to be 'outer'. What Hegel seeks to show for each version of the model is that we are agents only insofar as we are also members of a social world that allows us to have and make sense of intentions, interests, and aims.[19]

There is no one lesson from Hegel's engagement with various forms of individualism. There is a negative claim that individuals are not basic practically, which is consistent with the criticism of individuals as simples in the *Logic*. There is a conditional claim that if they are conceived as basic or simples, then individuals cannot play the normative role ascribed to them by different theories. There is a positive claim that there is a modern demand or aspiration to freedom. Finally there is a positive, possibly action-guiding, in any case modally complicated, claim that individuals are-and-can be free qua members of a social world. What I called earlier the Hegelian twist is that the philosophical inheritance of individualism in its connection with freedom is criticized and also *presupposed* in Hegel's last claim, which is what most identify as a Hegelian position. The upshot of this distinctive feature of Hegel's treatment of individuality in his practical philosophy gives us a dynamic practical notion that helps answer the familiar questions about how Hegel negotiates between collectives and individuals.

Let us start with a text that appears to support an extreme form of collectivism. In the *Lectures on the Philosophy of World History*, Hegel describes the relation of members of the state to the whole in which they belong as follows:

The living reality of the state within its individual members is what we have called its ethical life. The state and its laws and institutions belong to these individuals; they enjoy their rights within it, and they have their external possessions within its nature, its soil, its mountains, its air, and its waters, for it is their land, their fatherland. The history of their state, its deeds and the deeds of their forefathers, are theirs too...for it is their substance and being (*Wesen*).

(LPH 102–3, 12: 123)

Hegel describes here what he later summarizes as the 'spiritual being'—or 'essence'—of the individual (LPH 103, 12: 124). This is a statement of fact of how things stand with individuals considered as members of ethical life. At its most comprehensive, ethical life extends to encompass the 'spirit of the nation' (LPH 103, 12: 124) and so not just the laws and practices of the present, but also the history of the state and the natural environment it encloses within its boundaries. This discussion easily fits an organic view of ethical life where all that matters is the collectivity and the shared 'spiritual being' that makes the 'living reality' of the state. There is little evidence here of the moderation that Westphal claims we should bring to our understanding of Hegel's collectivist claims.

---

[19] Pippin's argument about what he calls 'the reciprocal dependence of the "inner" on the "outer"' (Pippin 2006: 136) concerns in particular the role of intentions: he argues that Hegel's critique of the ultimacy of individuality extends into an area in which 'the privileged and prior status of the individual or first-person point of view seems intuitively strongest: the dependence of outer manifestations of the subject's will on the inner intentions of that subject' (Pippin 2006: 135).

Note, however, that the context of the quotation is a discussion of world history. Arguably, from the vantage point of world history, the inner articulation of ethical life would be undetectable. The mid-range perspective we seek can be found in the relevant passages in the *Philosophy of Right*. This material shows that not every item in the quoted list above makes equally *authoritative* claims in the lives of the members of ethical life. Hegel argues that it is the 'ethical substance', the laws and powers that regulate the lives of individuals not their natural environment (PR §§145–6). This ethical substance, in turn, is a highly organized whole in which different spheres of activity are sustained by a range of institutions and are defined by distinct roles that make up the worldly specifics of individuals and thereby give us their being (or 'essence' see PR §147). So members of ethical life are very finely characterized as family members, members of particular estates, classes, and so on. These contents have normative weight: to be a son, a citizen, and a farmer is to be under certain obligations, there are certain things you have to do, they are marked out as the 'rules of his own situation' (PR §150 A). The conformity of the individual 'with the duties of the station to which he belongs' (PR §150) appears as a 'second nature' (PR §151). That Hegel describes second nature as an attainment indicates that whatever the facts of membership in *Sittlichkeit*, induction into ethical substance is not spontaneous. As Hegel explains, there is a process whereby the 'self-will of the individual' vanishes 'together with his private conscience which had claimed independence and opposed itself to ethical substance' (PR §152). Ultimately it is the 'individuality of the state' that takes precedence over particular individualities and it is duty to this political whole that ties members of the state together (PR §325).[20]

Let us take stock. The emphasis Hegel places on belonging, on being a member of a larger organized whole, fits with a classical view of what we may call 'embedded' values, one understands values and value-based demands by virtue of belonging to particular organized communities and having certain roles in these communities. This view is consistent with the logic of individuals we discussed in the previous Sections 9.1 and 9.2. This is because 'individuals' can be spoken about as segments of spirit. In the *Encyclopedia*, the consecutive layers of 'mind' (*Geist*) from physical soul to ethical substance provide a very rich resource for such a task of specification. The content of the specified individual is given by propositions that are potentially extremely fine-grained, giving us the physical as well as moral, social, political, and religious properties of the being in question; they are individual *because* not despite of the multi-layered spiritual being that defines them. In line with this finding, the term individual has use by directing us to the specifics. Without spirit, 'individual' is an abstraction 'devoid of life, colour and filling' (L 619, 6:297).

The question now is whether there is any further content to 'individual' that allows us to square the classical view of embedded value with claims such as 'the individual's destiny is the living of a universal life' (PR §258A). What we have found so far is that

---

[20] See too Neuhouser 2000: 244f. on how the state permeates non-political institutions.

the world-historical perspective locates individuals in a broad-brush way—or to put it differently the individuals in question are states, peoples, or groupings. Focusing within the state or the *Sittlichkeit* allows us to pin down regions of spirit that identify individuals that are people. We can then speak of the things that count for them as authoritative and make them the individuals they are. We are now at a level in which the new logic of individual helps us refer to what the undermined logic took as basic. We can have contentful discussion about individuals and their lives, because we can identify them properly. This identification of individuals for the purposes of referring to them is cold comfort to those who fear that it also requires that individuals fully identify *with* the region of spirit they are. As many commentators have argued, Hegel is not advocating blind adherence to whatever ethical substance one is born into.[21] He argues that the individual has a rational relation to her environment guided by her aspirations of freedom, which only the rational state can fulfil. Here again we have to confront the historical and conceptual inheritance of 'individual', including empiricist and idealist conceptions of individuality. While Hegel is critical of them, he does not deny that they have taken root in our thinking and express aspects of who we, at a certain historical juncture, are and aspire to be.[22] Hegel is a historical thinker, which, in this context, means that he appropriates and seeks to integrate the modern normative and psychological content of 'individual', despite the atomistic presuppositions of such content.[23]

We are now in a position to revisit Westphal's moderate collectivism. If we just stick to the moderate collectivist theses, we have a reasonable but rather weak position that directs us to attend to the context in which individuals form what they say and do, learn, become who they are, and which, in turn, they transform. What is missing is the normative dimension of Hegel's argument. Driving what members of societies do is

---

[21] For detailed analysis see Neuhouser 2000: 244–8.

[22] Brooks 2012: 55–61 offers a more negative picture of what I call here integration, arguing that Hegel treats Kant's moral theory as an example of a theory that treats individuals in abstraction from their communities and that Hegel's aim is to reject that perspective and therefore overcome the standpoint of morality as such. I think that this reading underestimates what I see as the Kantian elements that Hegel wants to preserve and the positive claims he makes in the 'Morality' sections. More importantly, for our present purposes, the abstraction from content is itself a *content* for modern individuals, the moral standpoint is plainly available to them as a set of theoretical commitments well apart from anything else.

[23] It is only in this historical sense that I think the self-actualization interpretation of freedom, popularized by Wood 1990 is plausible. See for example the discussion of property rights, in which Hegel hails the recognition of 'the freedom of personality' as a 'universal principle' (PR §62 A), even while he is keen to show that abstract right is not the only form of right shaping human relations in the state. Further on he says: 'in considering freedom, the starting point must be not individuality, the single self-consciousness but only the essence of self-consciousness; for whether man knows it or not, this essence is externally realised as a self-subsistent power in which single individuals are only moments' (PR § 258 A). In his *Lectures on Aesthetics*, he writes about the liberating function of modern individualism which offers new opportunities for the artist who 'acquires his subject-matter in himself and is the human spirit actually self-determining' (A 607, 15: 237–8). See too: 'the individual subject may of course act of himself in this or that matter, but still every individual, wherever he may twist or turn…does not appear himself as the independent, total, and at the same time individual living embodiment of this society, but only as a restricted member of it' (A 194, 14: 254–5).

their desire to attain reflective awareness of their choices, 'since man alone, as distinct from the animals, is a thinking being' (LPH 144, 12: 175). One way of adding this missing element is by supplementing moderate collectivism with what Neuhouser calls methodological atomism. Methodological atomism permits references to interests at the atomic level, but does not stand in the way of formation of shared interests, most importantly, for our purposes it allows for the non-instrumental participation in a social whole (Neuhouser 2000: 13, 182). Although it is a methodological proposal, it has a normative dimension, the idea of an end that ought to be pursued for non-instrumental reasons. Methodologically then the following is endorsed:

> Laws and principles have no immediate life or validity in themselves. The activity which puts them into operation and endows them with real existence has its source in the needs, impulses, inclinations, and passions of man.…Thus nothing can happen, nothing can be accomplished unless the individuals concerned can also gain satisfaction for themselves as particular individuals. For they have their own special needs, impulses, and interests which are peculiar to themselves.   (LPH 70, 12:113)

Accepting individual self-satisfaction is a step towards a more demanding normative end that is consciousness of freedom:[24]

> Consciousness of freedom consists in the fact that the individual comprehends himself as person, i.e. that he apprehends himself in his individuality as inherently universal, as capable of abstraction from and renunciation of everything particular, and therefore as inherently infinite.   (LPH 144, 12:175)

This consciousness of freedom gives us a normative aim that, on Hegel's account, pulls individual strivings forward and gives them their overall shape. Whether we take this as a basic Hegelian metaphysical commitment, a thesis about what thinking beings do, or as an acknowledgement of the history of individuals, a thesis about how individuals have been thought of, or as a complex claim that encompasses both, it does not matter to our present concerns. What matters is that Hegel sees his account of membership to societies, including the receptive and active features of such membership captured in Westphal's theses, as contributing or fitting in an overall account of the realization of the modern promise of freedom.

9.4. Incomplete Individuals

Section 9.3 described some of the practical implications of Hegel's revision of the category of individual. The conception of individual Hegel preserves integrates classical and modern normative contents of individuality. The embedded value perspective directs us

---

[24] In EM §408 and Z Hegel associates such separation of the self and individualization of aims and interests with insanity. He contrasts this view with the conception of the 'I' as 'something away and beyond' (EM §415), which he attributes to Kantian and Fichtean idealism. And although he seeks to correct this transcendent conception of the I, he also wants to keep a positive conception of universality that involves the 'negation of immediacy' (EM § 429), and so also of individuality understood as mere given segment of spirit.

to a conception of individuals as segments of spirit. The same logic invites us to confront the historical content of our conception of individuals, as desirous atoms seeking satisfaction unless impeded in their course, and as moral agents guided by universal values and aspirations. The plurality of content leaves a lot of room for negotiation between the inherited normative content of individuals and Hegel's positive claims regarding individuals as sections of spirit. This can be seen as a virtue of Hegel's political philosophy because it allows us to conceptualize different meanings of individuality. The resulting dynamic conception of individuals, however, is not Hegel's final word on the matter.

In the *Logic*, Hegel claims that the fully specified individual is 'the determinate determinate' (L 618, 6:296). If in reality determination is in accordance with the dynamic conception sketched above, then any content of 'individual', outside the *Logic*, will be partial. Logical determinations attain their deteminateness because of the whole to which they belong. Stephen Houlgate explains this holistic commitment in terms of 'moments': 'a moment gains its character from the whole that it helps to constitute' (Houlgate 2006: 428). Logical holism has epistemic implications, since we cannot get to grips with a determination or concept without having the whole in view, but we cannot have the whole in view from some external vantage point. So given some version at least of logical holism, we are confronted with a practical question: the determinate individual is made determinate as part of a stage or 'moment' that is then taken up in further moments, till we reach the absolute Idea. Holism supports the dynamic conception of individuality, merely adding that no individual is ever completely individualized. This, however, raises anew the question of perspective we encountered in the context of Hegel's discussion of world history. The dynamic, practical conception fits with and is sustained by a pluralistic theory of the contents of 'individual'. On the pluralistic model there is no finality of contents and that allows for ongoing redefinition of political, social, or cultural identities and also friction among competing models. We may, however, take a more strongly integrationist line, and entertain the possibility of someone who reflectively accepts her world and finds in it simply what is her own and nothing else. Such acceptance pushes beyond the demand of specification, leaving the category of individuality behind.

What shall we make of this? On the one hand, the pluralist versus integrationist model of understanding specification is a replay of issues we encountered before, one level up, so to speak. One the other hand, the very re-emergence of this by now familiar problematic suggests that the resources for understanding the category of individuality are not to be found within this category, perhaps not even in subsequent sections of the *Logic*. Although in some respects unsettling, this negative conclusion may be instructive about how logic and politics relate.

9.5. Conclusion

In conclusion then, and bringing the different strands of the discussion together, we can identify at least four ways in which Hegel's revisionary logic informs his politics.

First, logic provides a detailed conceptual analysis of the term, which adds support to the criticisms of individualism while also providing a genuinely novel positive notion; this positive notion fits Hegel's substantive positive claims, his corrective of modern individualism.

Second, the positive logical notion sustains a practically dynamic conception of individuals; this dynamic conception goes some way to explain how familiar conundrums about the role of individual in Hegel's politics arise. It also shows how Hegel seeks to integrate classical and modern views of social and political life.

Third, the logical demands of determination of individuality are never met fully in reality. Whether we take the view that the pluralistic model is the right one, or whether we find ourselves having to sort out which is the right way to proceed, logic does not dictate practice, it underdetermines it.

Fourth, the underdetermination of the practical notion of individual by its logical form leaves open the possibility that the category of individuality is itself superable in thought if not in practice.[25]

References

Berlin, I., 1969, 'Two Concepts of Liberty', *Four Essays on Liberty*, London: Oxford University Press.

Brooks, T., 2012, *Hegel's Political Philosophy: A Systematic Reading of the Philosophy of Right*, 2nd edition, Edinburgh: Edinburgh University Press.

Burbidge, John, 2006, *The Logic of Hegel's Logic*, Ontario: Broadview Press.

Chitty, Andrew, 2014, 'Hegel's *Philosophy of Right*: A Collective Intentionality Interpretation', unpublished manuscript, presented at the Sussex Idealism Conference.

Deligiorgi, K., 2010, 'Doing Without Agency: Hegel's Social Theory of Action', A. Laitinen and C. Sandis eds, *Hegel on Action*, London: Palgrave Macmillan, 97–118.

Deligiorgi, K., 2012, 'Religion, Love, and Law: Hegel's Early Metaphysics of Morals', M. Baur and S. Houlgate eds, *The Blackwell Companion to Hegel*, Oxford: Blackwell, 23–44.

Franco, P., 1999, *Hegel's Philosophy of Freeedom*, New Haven, CT: Yale.

Geach, P.T., 1955, 'Form and Existence', *Proceedings of the Aristotelian Society*, New Series, 55: 251–72.

Geach, P.T., 1980, *Reference and Generality: An Examination of Some Medieval and Modern Theories* [1962], Ithaca, NY: Cornell University Press.

Hartmann, N., 1929, *Die Philosophie des deutschen Idealismus*. BD II. Hegel. Berlin: De Gruyter.

Honneth, A., 2010, *The Pathologies of Individual Freedom: Hegel's Social Theory*, Princeton NJ: Princeton University Press.

Houlgate, S., 2006, *The Opening of Hegel's Logic: From Being to Infinity*, West Lafayette, IN: Purdue University Press.

Kant, I., 1999, *Critique of Pure Reason*, trans. and ed. Paul Guyer and Allen Wood, Cambridge: Cambridge University Press [A and B edition pagination provided].

[25] Acknowledgements: I owe thanks to many for helping me think through some of the issues discussed here, in particular, Stephen Houlgate, Paul Redding, Thom Brooks, and Sebastian Stein.

Kenny, A., 2002, *Aquinas on Being*, Oxford: Oxford University Press.

Macherey, P., 1990, *Hegel ou Spinoza* [1979], Paris: La Découverte.

McCumber, J., 2014, *Understanding Hegel's Mature Critique of Kant*, Stanford, CA: Stanford University Press.

Moyar, D., 2011, *Hegel's Conscience* Oxford: Oxford University Press.

Neuhouser, F., 2000, *Foundations of Hegel's Social Theory: Actualizing Freedom*, Cambridge, MA:Harvard University Press.

Pinkard, Terry, 2008, 'What Is a Shape of Spirit?', Dean Moyar and Michael Quante eds, *Hegel's Phenomenology at 200*. Cambridge: Cambridge University Press.

Pippin, R.B., 2006, 'Recognition and Reconciliation: Actualized Agency in Hegel's Jena *Phenomenology*', K. Deligiorgi ed., *Hegel: New Directions*, Montreal: McGill-Queen's University Press, 125–42.

Ross, N., 2008, *On Mechanism in Hegel's Social and Political Philosophy*, London: Routledge.

Russell, B., 1992, 'Analytical Realism' [1911], J.G. Slater and B. Frohmann eds, *Logical and Philosophical Papers 1909–13*, London: Routledge, 132–46.

Sayers, S., 2007, 'Individual and Society in Marx and Hegel: Beyond the Communitarian Critique of Liberalism', *Science & Society*, 71:1: 84–102.

Skorupski, J., 2015, 'The Conservative Critique of Liberalism', S. Wall ed., *Cambridge Companion to Liberalism*, Cambridge: Cambridge University Press, 401–21.

Taylor, C., 1975, *Hegel*, Cambridge: Cambridge University Press.

Weidemann, H., 1986, 'The Logic of Being in Thomas Aquinas', S. Knuutila and J. Hintikka eds, *The Logic of Being*, Dordrecht: Reidel Publishing, 181–93.

Westphal, K.R., 2003, *Hegel's Epistemology: A Philosophical Introduction to the Phenomenology of Spirit*, Indianapolis: Hackett.

Williams, R.R., 1992, *Recognition: Fichte and Hegel*, Stonybrook: State University of New York Press.

Williams, R.R., 1997, *Hegel's Ethics of Recognition*, Berkeley: University of California Press.

Wippel, John F., 2000, *The Metaphysical Thought of Thomas Aquinas: From Finite Being to Uncreated Being*, Washington, DC: Catholic University of America Press.

Wolf, S., 1990, *Freedom within Reason*, Oxford: Oxford University Press.

Wood, A., 1990, *Hegel's Ethical Thought*, Cambridge: Cambridge University Press.

Wood, A., 1991, 'Editor's Introduction', *G. W.F. Hegel Elements of the Philosophy of Right*, trans. H.B. Nisbet, Cambridge: Cambridge University Press.

10

Hegel on Crime and Punishment

Thom Brooks

Introduction

Perhaps the least controversial issue for most commentators on Hegel's political and legal philosophy concerns his theory of punishment. The orthodox consensus is that Hegel was a retributivist who justified punishing deserving criminals in order to 'annul' their crimes.[1] Broadly speaking, the classic 'positive' view of retribution is that punishment can only be justified where deserved and to the degree it is deserved.[2] In that light, some commentators have claimed Hegel is 'one of the most famous and important retributivists'.[3]

While they are often deeply divided on so many other issues in his philosophy, the orthodox consensus among Hegel scholars is no accident. Hegel offers us comments about punishment that support this interpretation. Hegel is clear that punishment is only justified where it is deserved by an offender for committing a crime.[4] Punishment aspires to be a 'cancellation' of a crime and its ill-effects in a 'restoration of right'— restoring rights violated by a crime (*PR*, §99). Hegel says: 'the cancellation [*Aufheben*] of crime is *retribution*' (*PR*, §101). For most scholars, these well-known and widely

---

[1] See Jami L. Anderson, 'Annulment Retributivism: A Hegelian Theory of Punishment', *Legal Theory* 5 (1999): 363–88; Stephen Paul Brown, 'Punishment and the Restoration of Rights', *Punishment and Society* 3 (2001): 485–500; David E. Cooper, 'Hegel's Theory of Punishment' in Z. Pelczynski (ed.), *Hegel's Political Philosophy: Problems and Perspectives* (Cambridge: Cambridge University Press, 1971): 151–67; J. Angelo Corlett, 'Making Sense of Retributivism', *Philosophy* 76 (2001): 80, n11; John Cottingham, 'Varieties of Retribution', *Philosophical Quarterly* 29 (1979): 244–45; Markus Dirk Dubber, 'Rediscovering Hegel's Theory of Crime and Punishment', *Michigan Law Review* 92 (1994): 1577–621; J. N. Findlay, *Hegel: A Re-examination* (London: George Allen & Unwin, 1958): 312–13; Lewis P. Hinchman, 'Hegel's Theory of Crime and Punishment', *Review of Politics* 44 (1982): 524; Michael Inwood, *A Hegel Dictionary* (Oxford: Blackwell, 1992): 232–35; Igor Primoratz, *Justifying Legal Punishment* (Atlantic Highlands, NJ: Humanities Press, 1989): 69–81; Peter G. Stillman, 'Hegel's Idea of Punishment', *Journal of the History of Philosophy* 14 (1976): 169–82; and Allen Wood, *Hegel's Ethical Thought* (Cambridge: Cambridge University Press, 1990): 108–24.

[2] See Thom Brooks, *Punishment* (London: Routledge, 2012): chapter 1.

[3] Mark Tunick, *Punishment: Theory and Practice* (Berkeley: University of California Press, 1992).

[4] For example, see PR, §95R ('Right, whose infringement is crime').

cited passages make clear that Hegel understood his own theory of punishment as retributivist and it is such a theory. Allen Wood calls Hegel 'a genuine retributivist'.[5]

The orthodox consensus rests on a mistake. It fails to take sufficient account of Hegel's distinctive form of argumentation that runs deep throughout his philosophical system, including his comments about punishment. Hegel did not present his system and its unique argumentative structure in the standard form we find with most modern philosophers—and it is easy to downplay or overlook this fact, not least since Hegel's dialectical form of argument is deeply controversial and seen as more of a problem for understanding Hegel's views than enlightening us as to what his views are.

In the following sections, I offer a *systematic reading* of Hegel's comments about punishment in his philosophical system with careful attention to his *Philosophy of Right*.[6] I argue that the conventional reading which claims his theory of punishment is mostly confined to the section Abstract Right raises interpretive difficulties. One problem is the inadequacy of punishment as described in Abstract Right to be a complete theory of punishment so often overlooked. A second problem is accounting for apparent inconsistencies between what Hegel says in Abstract Right versus comments stated elsewhere in the *Philosophy of Right* and larger system. I argue that later sections like Ethical Life matter for our understanding Hegel's penal theory and a systematic reading of his texts—where we consider his arguments in light of their systematic structure—can help make best sense of this. I conclude by reflecting on the implications this reading has for our understanding Hegel's philosophy and its contemporary appeal.

The Orthodox Consensus of Hegel the Retributivist

The orthodox consensus on Abstract Right started with a landmark essay by David Cooper, published in 1971. He begins: 'In this essay I discuss Hegel's theory of punishment for its own sake. I am not concerned with its relation to the rest of the *Philosophy of Right*, and even less with its place in the dialectic as a whole.'[7] Cooper's sole focus is on Hegel's comments about punishment in Abstract Right. Cooper argues that 'reform and deterrence cannot be the reasons' for justifying punishment—only a guilty person's desert can serve as such a reason.[8] He does not find these arguments novel and notes that Kant's retributivist theory of punishment accepts the same view.[9]

---

[5] Wood, *Hegel's Ethical Thought*, 109.

[6] On the systematic reading, see Thom Brooks, *Hegel's Political Philosophy: A Systematic Reading of the Philosophy of Right*, 2nd edition (Edinburgh: Edinburgh University Press, 2013). See Thom Brooks, 'Is Hegel a Retributivist?' *Bulletin of the Hegel Society of Great Britain* 49/50 (2004): 113–26; Thom Brooks, 'Hegel's Ambiguous Contribution to Legal Theory', *Res Publica* 11(1) (2005): 85–94; and Thom Brooks, 'Hegel and the Unified Theory of Punishment' in Thom Brooks (ed.), *Hegel's Philosophy of Right* (Oxford: Blackwell, 2012): 103–23.

[7] Cooper, 'Hegel's Theory of Punishment', 151.

[8] Cooper, 'Hegel's Theory of Punishment', 152.

[9] See Cooper, 'Hegel's Theory of Punishment', 152, 156.

Cooper's interpretation of Hegel's theory of punishment views it as a retributivist theory that can be understood within Abstract Right alone. This position has become the orthodox consensus over the near half century later. While there remain other important differences in the interpretations offered by Hegel scholars, they nonetheless are committed to the position first identified by Cooper.[10] For example, Dudley Knowles remarked that Hegel's discussion of punishment beyond Abstract Right 'merely recapitulates the philosophical points made in the discussion of crime and punishment of Abstract Right'.[11] Allen Wood argues that Hegel's 'theory of punishment is well grounded in Hegel's theory of abstract right, and it succeeds, without appealing in any way to consequentialist considerations'.[12] In his groundbreaking *Hegel's Ethical Thought*, Wood discusses punishment in his section on abstract right—providing a section-by-section interpretation of key ideas in Hegel's political philosophy.[13] Cooper's central claims about Hegel's theory of punishment have become the consensus view.

The current orthodoxy can find evidential support for its position. In Abstract Right, Hegel provides a number of comments that could appear to justify a retributivist theory of punishment. He defines crime as an infringement of a right as a right, denying its relevance or importance (*PR*, §95). Where a right is violated, it is crucial that its existence is acknowledged and reasserted. Hegel claims we should try to cancel the crime—so it cannot be 'regarded as valid'—and produce 'the restoration of right' through punishing the criminal (*PR*, §99). This need for restoring rights arises not from a desire to cancel evil but recognize our rights (*PR*, §99R). Moreover, Hegel says the restoration of rights by punishing crimes 'is *retribution*' (*PR*, §101). The case for viewing Hegel's theory of punishment as retributivist might appear compelling.

However, such a conclusion is premature. Hegel understands a crime like theft as a denial of an individual's right to private property. The punishment of theft aims to recognize and support the right violated by crime. Punishing offenders is a way to protect and maintain the rights of individuals. This includes offenders, too. Hegel goes so far as to say that punishment is 'a right for the criminal himself' (*PR*, §100). Punishment provides for the acknowledgement and reassertion of rights for all. Punishing a thief for his theft recognizes the importance of the right to property that was infringed by the crime by restoring its status as a right that should not be violated. Through punishment, the rights of all—including the offender's rights—are reasserted. Punishment is not about damaging an offender's rights, but maintaining them.

---

[10] For example, see Knowles, *Hegel and the Philosophy of Right*, 147 ('I am content to endorse the drift of Cooper's original reading').

[11] Knowles, *Hegel and the Philosophy of Right*, 153.

[12] Allen Wood, 'Hegel's Ethics' in Frederick Beiser (ed.), *The Cambridge Companion to Hegel* (Cambridge: Cambridge University Press, 1993): 221.

[13] See Wood, *Hegel's Ethical Thought*, 108–24. While he does make reference to later sections in the *Philosophy of Right* and other works by Hegel, Wood's discussion is focussed firmly on Abstract Right.

This appears to lead Hegel to reject non-retributivist theories of punishment like deterrence. Punishment aims at achieving justice, restoring rights because they should be so maintained. The problem with deterrence justifying punishment is that it might fail to honour the offender by punishing her not to protect and maintain the rights of all but for some other purpose (*PR*, §100R). Hegel says that such a view justifies punishment 'like raising a stick at a dog; it means treating a human being like a dog instead of respecting his honour and freedom' (*PR*, §99A). The rights that every individual should respect are worthy of our respect and capable of being recognized as such. To justify punishment as a deterrent or form of rehabilitation is to regard offenders like 'a harmful animal which must be rendered harmless' (*PR*, §100R). Such statements support the orthodox retributivist reading of Hegel's penal theory.

Retribution also appears to inform how Hegel justifies the distribution of punishment. This seems unequivocal. He says: 'the cancellation [*Aufheben*] of crime is *retribution*' (*PR*, §101). Hegel explains that crime and retribution share an 'identity' based not on strict equality, but on equal value (*PR*, §101). Rejecting the eye for an eye doctrine of the *lex talionis*, Hegel argues:

> It is very easy to portray the retributive aspect of punishment as an absurdity (theft as retribution for theft, robbery for robbery, an eye for an eye, and a tooth for a tooth, so that one can even imagine the miscreant as one-eyed or toothless)...equality remains merely the basis measure of the criminal's essential deserts, but not of the specific external shape that theft and robbery [on the one hand] and fines and imprisonment etc. [on the other] are completely unequal, whereas in terms of their value, i.e. their universal character as injuries [*Verletzungen*], they are *comparable*. (*PR*, §101R)

Hegel's point is that giving offenders what they deserve is not the same as doing a similar act to them that they did to others. A reason for this view is strict equality does not seem to apply to most, if any, crimes. Some crimes are self-regarding like consuming an illegal substance or parking violations. But it is far from obvious how a like for like punishment could work for someone parked illegally or smoking crack cocaine. Even visiting physical harm on those that did violence to others does not work in any clear sense. Part of what makes a violent assault wrongful is the innocence of the victim. If the state were to do to violent offenders what they did to others, they do not impose a harm on someone innocent and the circumstances are very different—even here it is no like for like treatment.

Hegel argues instead for the view that we do not consider crimes separately—in terms of how to punish equally a theft or a murder as different entities—but in relation to each other that is comparable in value. Crimes share a common nature as wrongful violations of rights that justify imposing punishment on a deserving offender. Crimes differ with respect to the relative value of their wrongfulness and corresponding punishment—some crimes require greater punishment than others. But it is the value of wrongfulness that does this work. Offenders are punished because they deserve it and to the degree it is deserved. An offender's punishment 'is merely a manifestation of the crime' (*PR*, §101A).

In sum, my purpose in this section was to indicate the key textual evidence that supports the orthodox consensus view that Hegel held a retributivist theory of punishment and that this account can be understood from Abstract Right without substantive recourse to other parts of the *Philosophy of Right*. There is a case to argue and few consensus views commanding such widespread agreement—not least among commentators on Hegel's controversial philosophy—lack some form of support.[14]

The Poverty of Abstract Right

The orthodox consensus is able to provide textual support for a retributivist theory of punishment drawn entirely from the section Abstract Right that starts Hegel's substantive discussion of his political philosophy. However, this interpretation suffers from two flaws. The first is that Abstract Right does not provide the unambiguously retributivist picture that orthodoxy claims. The second flaw is that the orthodox consensus fails to interpret Hegel's comments in Abstract Right within the *systematic* philosophical structure by which they are meant to be understood. I will now consider these flaws in turn, and show how the orthodox consensus overlooks key features of Hegel's comments about punishment in Abstract Right, and that they are mistaken about how these comments should be considered in light of his remarks beyond Abstract Right.

Abstract Right plays a central role in setting out a retributivist vision, but this section develops a more complex analysis than that—the closer we look, the less retributivist his views become. Hegel defines 'crime' in Abstract Right in a particular way. His understands it as a wrong where an individual fails recognize what is right: 'the recognition of right' is 'the universal and deciding factor' (*PR*, §85). This failure to recognize what is right is neither unintentional nor meant to deceive, but acting without regard to what another's point of view could plausibly consider what is right.[15] Crime is different because of what it is 'in itself': an appeal to my particular point of view alone (*PR*, §83).

This is a problem because what is right is not determined by reference to my own view without regard to others. Right is held universally in common (*PR*, §87A). Crimes fail to recognize the special status possessed by right. Hegel's example of a crime in Abstract Right is 'the violation of a contract through failure to perform what it stipulates' (*PR*, §93R). He is discussing the contractual stipulations arising from the unreal hypothetical scenario where two persons agree about the property possessions of the other. Hegel is not considering who they are or their other particularities. Nor does he discuss what the property is or how it became possessed. This contractual agreement is not subject to any law or courtroom, but merely a hypothetical mutual recognition of

---

[14] My discussion has not been comprehensive, but indicative. My aim is to make clear there is some support in Hegel's Abstract Right for the orthodox consensus view. In following sections, I show that Abstract Right is ill-suited as the sole repository of a retributivist theory of punishment and that these comments may be incoherent with Hegel's comments elsewhere.

[15] Hegel speaks of 'the point of view of right in itself' (*PR*, §83A).

right between two nondescript persons—where the 'crime' is one's failure to respect and validate the other's claim to some thing.

It is striking that Hegel's description of crime in this case is of breaking a contractual stipulation. Contracts are commonly understood to be the province of private law—and so not a part of the criminal law. Nor is this scenario clearly theft. Typically, theft is defined as dishonestly intending to permanently deprive another of some possession belonging to another.[16] But this criminal view of theft is not clearly the picture that Hegel has in mind. For Hegel, crime 'in itself' is a failure of recognition akin to general illegality.

My point is that not all illegality is criminal—it can be civil, such as with contract law. This is important because it begins to highlight that Hegel's understanding of a 'crime' is not ours. Instead, it should be thought of in terms of general illegality, including what might constitute criminality. So not only is Hegel's use of 'crime' not about crimes *per se*, they are not about laws from a parliament or king either.[17]

But it is clear that while Abstract Right may be the key to understanding an important part of Hegel's views at the beginning, it cannot be the conclusion at its end. This problem of interpretation concerns not only *what* is claimed for Hegel's views but *how* we should understand them. Hegel is clear that his discussion of crime and punishment in Abstract Right matters for later consideration of these issues. He says: 'But the substantial element within these forms is the universal, which remains the same in its further development and in the further shapes it assumes' (*PR*, §95R). This means that the key understanding of crime as general illegality characterized by a failure of recognition is the 'substantial element' that is 'universal' to all forms of illegality remaining 'the same in its further development'.[18]

Punishment 'is merely the negation of the negation' (*PR*, §97A). Its purpose is to nullify crime by reaffirming the right that illegality contravened and restoring right to its proper recognition. This is called 'the restoration of right' whereby punishment cancels the existence of some criminal wrong 'which would otherwise be regarded as valid' (*PR*, §99). Hegel's point is that illegality is wrongful as a failure to recognize what is right and universal. The offender asserts a private view above what is right and without regard for what is right. Hegel's thief is a thief because he seeks to possess

---

[16] For example, see the five-part definition of the offence of theft in England and Wales: section 1(1) of the Theft Act 1968.

[17] A crucial implication follows from this insight. If by 'crime' Hegel means any form of illegality (including, but not only, crimes), then punishment—as a response to crime—is a response to 'crime' and so connected to (criminal and civil) illegality (including criminality). My point is that Hegel's discussion of crime and punishment at this stage is so generalized as to be about illegality and its response, but not the criminal law and sentencing in particular. The following discussion will focus on crime and punishment, but broadly speaking—in Abstract Right—neither Hegel's use of 'crime' or 'punishment' is what we might initially expect from his using such terms. It should now be clear he has a different meaning for them which is routinely overlooked. But it should also be clear that this non-standard way of understanding everyday terms may go some way to helping explain why interpreters have been mistaken about his theory of crime and punishment.

[18] See also *PR*, §99R ('the essential factor is the concept').

something now; the thief is not making any claims about the property rights for all in general—because these are not his concern.

The 'cancellation of crime', for Hegel, 'is retribution' (*PR*, §101). If this were left unpunished, then it sends out a signal that such behaviour is permissible and not contrary to right. You or I could be led to the false belief that we might act similarly. For right to exist 'externally', it must be reasserted and restored through some form of reaffirmation. False claims of ownership must be exposed for what they are, possessions returned to their rightful owners and thieves punished in relation to the gravity of their wrong. Justice should be done and punishing deserving offenders is an important part of doing justice for Hegel. This helps explain Hegel's comment that punishment is 'a right for the criminal himself' (*PR*, §100). By punishing the offender, we reassert and restore the right violated for all. Additionally, we also reassert and restore this right for the offender, too. The restoration of rights is more than a benefit for the law-abiding community, but it honours the rights of offenders as well.[19]

The comment that receives a great many approving citations as proof that Hegel is a retributivist is this claim that all relevant modalities of punishment 'take it for granted that punishment in and for itself is just' (*PR*, §99R). Such a view is thought to be a clear case of Hegel's retributivism. It is supported further by Hegel's comment in the section's Addition that deterrence should be rejected because 'it means treating a human being like a dog instead of respecting his honour and freedom' (*PR*, §99A).

However, this is also incorrect. Hegel's claim about punishment being just 'in and for itself' is consistent with his view that 'crime' as general illegality is following one's own subjective view without regard to what is right and held in common. So Hegel's apparent retributivism is hardly retributivist: it is only the claim that punishment can only be justified for illegality, and that punishment is a response to this illegality with a view to reaffirming and restoring violated rights. Hegel says nothing about moral responsibility for wrongdoing here, nor how much punishment is deserved. This is very different from classic views of retributivism which hold that criminals are to be punished because they are morally responsible for some immoral wrongdoing—and punished to the degree they are responsible for this wrongdoing irrespective of the wider context. Hegel says no such thing.

His comment about deterrence is very specific. Hegel's criticism is of those who 'justify punishment…like raising one's stick at a dog' (*PR*, §99A).[20] If we confirm that someone meets the test of illegality through a failure of recognition, then punishment is not justified in that way and so its different justificatory foundation may be open to the use of deterrence where punishment is deserved. This might avoid the objection that an offender's 'honour and freedom' were not respected. So long as deterrence is not

---

[19]   See *PR*, §100R ('In so far as the punishment which this entails is seen as embodying the criminal's own right, the criminal is honoured as a rational being').

[20]   Some penal theorists take Hegel's comment here about deterrence to be a complete rejection of the place of deterrence in penal theory. This reading misunderstands the narrowness of Hegel's rejection. See R. A. Duff, *Punishment, Communication, and Community* (Oxford: Oxford University Press, 2001): 14, 16, 85.

the primary ground for punishment, it might still serve a justificatory purpose.[21] This important point must be kept in mind when we consider later passages where Hegel says more about how retribution, deterrence, and rehabilitation might fit together. All that should be noted here is that his criticism of deterrence is only as the ground for distinguishing someone as a criminal. The use of deterrence in other ways is not ruled out provided the ground is justified by what he means by retribution.

Likewise, Hegel's remark that 'the cancellation of crime is retribution' is also very specific (*PR*, §101). Hegel notes that crime and punishment share an equivalency of value, but not 'the specific character of the infringement' (*PR*, §101). We are not to punish offenders in the same form they have harmed others, such as punching someone convicted of battery. The crime will have a value of wrongdoing that should be equivalent to the value of punishment.

For Hegel, this kind of retribution gets right the fact that there is a 'universal feeling of peoples', that a crime 'deserves to be punished', and 'that what the criminal has done should also happen to him' (*PR*, §101R). This will appear a strong statement of retribution whereby punishment must be deserved and in proportion to what is deserved—and this is where Hegel's discussion is more nuanced.

Hegel recognizes that 'the determination of equality has brought a major difficulty into the idea of retribution' (*PR*, §101R). Foreshadowing his later comments on punishment, he notes that 'even if, for this later determination of punishments, we had to look around *for principles other than those which apply to the universal aspect of punishment*, this universal aspect remains what it is' (*PR*, §101R, emphasis added). Hegel's point is that punishment can only be justified where it is deserved—and this link between crime and punishment is a 'necessary connection' (*PR*, §101R).

Their value can only be of an 'approximate fulfilment' (*PR*, §101R). Hegel claims that:

> it is very easy to portray the retributive aspect of punishment as an absurdity (theft as retribution for theft, robbery for robbery, an eye for an eye, and a tooth for a tooth, so that one can imagine the miscreant as one-eyed or toothless); but the concept has nothing to do with this absurdity, for which the introduction of that [idea of] *specific equality* is to blame.   (*PR*, §101R)

This still reads like a fairly conventional understanding of retribution. Few retributivists argue that the state should rape rapists or torture torturers. Hegel still defends the idea that punishment should be deserved and its value an 'approximate fulfilment' of the value of its corresponding crime.

But we must attend to the distinctive meaning that Hegel has in mind here. He says that the value equality between crime and punishment 'remains merely the basic measure of the criminal's *essential* deserts, but not of the specific external shape which the retribution should take' (*PR*, §101R). This is explained further in an Addition where Hegel says 'retribution is the inner connection' between crime and punishment (*PR*, §101A). Hegelian retribution is but one essential part of punishment that requires

---

[21] See Brooks, *Hegel's Political Philosophy*, 44.

that punishment is only justified as a response to crime where the value of one is linked to the other. This connection is not explicitly moral insofar as punishment is not set in accordance to the evil performed by someone, but instead to reaffirm and restore rights. In this sense, Hegel's view of desert is more political than moral, although there is no denying the moral significance that rights can have.[22]

Immanuel Kant's retributivist theory of punishment is a useful counterexample to help sharpen the emerging differences between Hegel's understanding of 'retributivism' and how most retributivists view it.[23] In his *Metaphysics of Morals*, Kant argues that legal punishment 'can never be inflicted merely as a means to promote some other good for the criminal himself or for civil society. It must always be inflicted upon him only because he committed a crime.'[24] This is important because it means that the *amount* of punishment should never be determined by *external factors*—offenders are to be treated individually and the wider socio-political context is irrelevant for determining what is deserved.[25]

This understanding of retributivism as centred on an individual's desert and absent any external factors is attributed to Hegel.[26] However, his theory of punishment is a significant break from this view insofar as he argues—and this is found clearly in Abstract Right—that contextual external factors can shape the amount of punishment that is deserved by an offender. The importance of these factors for determining punishments is developed in greater detail in later sections like Ethical Life.[27] Yet it is clear already that such factors are relevant. This is one key feature that distinguishes what Hegel means by retribution from how most retributivists have.

Kant's retributivism is different from Hegel's penal theory for a second reason. Kant argues that there is a 'principle of equality' where:

accordingly, whatever undeserved evil you inflict upon another within the people, that you inflict upon yourself. If you insult him, you insult yourself; if you steal from him, you steal from yourself; if you strike him, you strike yourself; if you kill him, you kill yourself.[28]

---

[22] See Thom Brooks, 'Punishment: Political, Not Moral', *New Criminal Law Review* 14(3) (2011): 427–38.

[23] See Thom Brooks, 'Kant's Theory of Punishment', *Utilitas* 15(2) (2003): 206–24 and Thom Brooks, 'Kantian Punishment and Retributivism: A Reply to Clark', *Ratio* 18(2) (2005): 237–45.

[24] Immanuel Kant, *The Metaphysics of Morals*, ed. Mary Gregor (Cambridge: Cambridge University Press, 1996): 105 [6:331].

[25] I qualify my statement with 'for determining what is deserved'. This is to recognize that there can be some flexibility exercised by the monarch to grant pardons or alternative sanctions like deportation. But this does not invalidate the fact that, for Kant's retributivism, offenders deserve a different punishment that they should otherwise receive. See Kant, *The Metaphysics of Morals*, 107 [6:334].

[26] See Wood, 'Hegel's Ethics', 221.

[27] To restate this point in now older political theory terminology of liberalism versus communitarianism, standard retributivist accounts like Kant argue for a more liberal conception because it is individualistic. Our concern is only with the offender's desert and not any external factors. However, Hegel's account is a more communitarian conception where the offender's desert is important—if it is absent, no punishment can be justified—but external factors are relevant for whether we punish and how much we should punish.

[28] Kant, *The Metaphysics of Morals*, 105 [6:332].

As we have seen, Hegel rejects the view that the external shape of punishment must somehow mirror the external action of the offender. Hegel is opposed to the *lex talionis*. Instead, we should aim for an approximate fulfilment in value of what an offender deserves. Hegel might criticize Kant's retributivism on these grounds as a kind of 'empty formalism' and so not only a concern about Kant's moral theory, but his penal theory, too (*PR*, §135).

Nonetheless, to claim Kant's theory of punishment blindly supports doing to offenders what they did to their victims would be uncharitable at best. For Kant, the equality of a crime with its punishment—in what he calls 'the law of retribution (*ius talionis*)'—is about punishing 'every criminal in proportion to his *inner wickedness*'.[29] Offenders do not merely break the law, but the *moral* law, and so every criminal act or omission is immoral to some degree. Offenders deserve punishment because they have performed an immoral wrong where the greater the evil—or 'inner wickedness'—the more severe they should be punished. For Kant what matters is the inner wickedness of the offender: his deserving punishment for his immoral activity is what counts and not other factors.

However, for Hegel, an offender deserves punishment on account of violating right—which may or may not be understood as 'wickedness' or evil—and this alone is what *retribution* means for him. It is not an offender's inner wickedness alone that determines how much punishment is deserved. Retribution for Hegel is about considering *if* punishment might be deserved. Whether or not it is distributed—and its amount—must take account of additional factors.

Some interpreters, like Knowles, argue that Hegel offers an identifiable retributivism not far away from Kant's theory. If more than one form of punishment is consistent with the value of crime, then we are perfectly entitled to appeal to other non-retributivist factors 'without sacrificing the retributivist ideal' in making our sentencing choice.[30] So long as the values are approximately equal, the purposes by which we choose one form of punishment over another is unimportant or non-consequential—or so Knowles argues. He might similarly claim that not unlike how Kant determines a value for punishment linked to the moral wrongness of its corresponding crime, so too does Hegel. The form that punishment takes is unimportant as long as whatever punishment is selected has the appropriate value.

Knowles misunderstands how retribution works for Hegel. It does not offer us a timeless, 'ideal' value that is fixed irrespective of background circumstances. So it is not the case that there is some ideal value—provided to us by way of retribution—that we can use to set deterrent or rehabilitative punishments to.

Alan Brudner provides us with a useful distinction.[31] He argues that most retributivist theories of punishment should be understood as theories of *moral* retributivism. These accounts give morality central importance: an act or omission is criminal for its

[29] Kant, *The Metaphysics of Morals*, 105–6 [6:332–3].
[30] Knowles, *Hegel and the Philosophy of Right*, 158.
[31] See Alan Brudner, *Punishment and Freedom: A Liberal Theory of Penal Justice* (Oxford: Oxford University Press, 2009): 38–55.

meeting some threshold of immorality—and it is to be punished in proportion to its immorality. Some retributivist theories of punishment rest on a different justification and these views are called *legal* retributivism. This account claims that offenders deserve punishment on the more narrow and limited justification that the offender commits a crime. It is this act or omission resulting in a public wrong like illegality that is what any offender must possess to be held deserving of punishment.

Brudner rightly views Hegel as an early exponent of legal retributivism, and this perspective is illuminating as an accurate interpretation of Hegel's position in Abstract Right. Commentators accepting the orthodox consensus that Hegel is a retributivist fail to see how narrowly Hegel understands how crime and punishment are related. In Abstract Right, Hegel makes the case for their necessary connection—but he has not made a full case for determining when it should be distributed and setting the amount of punishment that can and should be deserved. Yet even here Hegel breaks clearly from standard retributivist accounts, such as Kant's retributivist theory, with a *legal* form of retributivism where external factors like the wider context matters.

In sum, this section has looked more closely at Hegel's discussion of punishment in Abstract Right. It reveals several findings. First, 'crime' is understood in a non-legal way. It is about the failure to recognize right. This is important for Hegel because it is a fundamental feature that must be present for any further determination of crimes like theft, murder, and the like. However, this view of crime is not unique to it and funda-mental to any form of justified illegality, including violations of contracts in private law. To argue that Hegel offers a fleshed-out theory of criminal law because he uses the word 'crime' misunderstands the distinctive meaning that Hegel has for it.

Second, punishment is a response to crime that seeks to cancel it by restoring and reaffirming what is right. If all illegality is fundamentally violations of right, then pun-ishment attempts a reversal. This is to send a signal that what is right has existence—through punishment we secure the rights of all, including the rights of the punished offender. As a response, punishment is deserved in a narrow, legal sense: an offender deserves punishment because he has committed an offence. It is this necessary con-nection of crime and its deserved punishment that is called retribution by Hegel.

Third, Hegel's use of retribution is not explicitly individualistic or moralistic. This is made clear by the contrast with Kant's retributivism. Kant argues that criminals are to be punished for their moral wrongdoing—in violating the moral law—and in propor-tion to its gravity. External factors are irrelevant for determining the amount of pun-ishment any offender can deserve. On the contrary, Hegel argues for an 'approximate fulfilment' between the value of crime and its linked punishment, but he does not yet say how it should be set. While retribution is an essential 'inner connection' between crime and its punishment, Hegel is open to non-retributivist factors determining the distribution and amount of punishment (*PR*, §101R). Admittedly, his discussion of what this might look like is not fleshed out in Abstract Right. This fact coupled with the unconventional use of the words 'crime' and 'retribution' may go some way to explain-ing why the orthodox consensus has failed to notice its interpretative errors before.

This leads us to consider two issues. The first is what Hegel has to say beyond Abstract Right that might help flesh out the gaps in his theory concerning the distribution and amount of punishment. The second concerns how later remarks should be understood in relation to his comments in Abstract Right. This is the second interpretive flaw noted at the beginning of this section: namely, that the failure to understand Hegel's comments within the systematic philosophical structure they are meant to be considered is a reason why the orthodox consensus is mistaken about Hegel's theory of punishment. I turn to these issues now.

Why Ethical Life Matters

The orthodox consensus view on Hegel's theory of punishment claims that only Abstract Right matters—the later discussion in Ethical Life has little significance. This is a reading that fails to take Hegel at his word, as he explicitly argues that his work should be read in a systematic way where concepts, including crime and punishment, are developed and fleshed out as we proceed through a dialectical process.

The orthodox consensus is endorsed in different ways by all leading commentators. For example, Wood says that only in Abstract Right does Hegel provide 'his treatment of punishment proper'.[32] Knowles says of Ethical Life that 'although it adds much more detail concerning its institutional articulation and practical application' Hegel's theory of punishment is not developed in any substantive way from this later discussion.[33] Peter Stillman says:

Neither morality nor society exist at the level of abstract rights, where Hegel primarily discusses punishment. Hegel does introduce further, non-abstract right aspects of punishment later—a law code, some concern with intention, pardon, crimes against the state, and a system for the administration of justice—but these produce only minor additions and no essential changes to the theory of punishment at abstract right—except, of course, to make the abstract into the concrete and existent.[34]

To summarize in the words of John Findlay, Hegel's treatment of punishment after Abstract Right is 'in no way remarkable'.[35]

But all this is incorrect. Towards the end of Abstract Right, Hegel says that 'in this sphere of the immediacy of right, the cancellation [Aufheben] of crime is primarily revenge' (PR, §102). Hegel qualifies this statement in the section's Addition: 'In a social condition in which there are neither magistrates nor laws, punishment always takes the form of revenge' (PR, §102A, emphasis added). Recall that Hegel's discussion in Abstract Right is about individuals abstracted, and so thus removed, from their concrete circumstances. There are no laws, no police, no courts, and no prisons. We should

[32] Wood, Hegel's Ethical Thought, 118.
[33] Knowles, Hegel and the Philosophy of Right, 153 and see 161.
[34] Stillman, 'Hegel's Idea of Punishment', 170 n5.
[35] Findlay, Hegel, 8.

remember that by 'crime' Hegel is not even talking about the criminal law, but general illegality—and that it shares a fundamental feature, namely, a failure to recognize rights. Abstract Right's use of 'retribution' is little more than a claim that the failure to recognize right must be corrected by reaffirming right, to breathe life once again into what should exist—and this is the purpose behind punishment and how we should respond to illegality overall. Hegel separates form from content.

Scholars should not play down the philosophical importance of Hegel's discussion of crime and punishment in Ethical Life. It is often overlooked that the idea that context matters—undermining any claims to some strong retributivist picture—can be found in Abstract Right, too. Hegel says:

Various qualitative determinations [of crime], such as *danger to public security*, have their basis in more precisely determined circumstances, but they are often apprehended only indirectly in the light of other circumstances rather than in terms of the concept of the thing [*Sache*]. Thus, the crime which is more dangerous in itself, in its immediate character, is a more serious infringement in its extent and quality.   (*PR*, §96R)

Public security as societal maintenance of right has a key role in determining the seriousness by which we see crime and consider its punishment. Context clearly matters not for informing us of *what* is criminal, but helping us determine *how* wrong it is and so what punishment is appropriate. Hegel adds: 'It is not the crimes or punishments themselves which change, but the relation between the two' (*PR*, §96A).

It is remarked by interpreters like Knowles—quoted at the beginning of this section— that Hegel's later treatment of punishment in the *Philosophy of Right* is merely detail and nothing philosophically substantive. But this claim that all the philosophical activity is to be found in Abstract Right alone does not survive scrutiny. An example regularly touted in support of the orthodox view that later comments are philosophically less substantive or important can be found here:

The various determinations which are relevant to punishment as a phenomenon [*Erscheinung*] and to its relation [*Beziehung*] to the particular consciousness, and which concern its effect on representational thought (as a deterrent, corrective, etc.), are of essential significance in their proper context, though primarily only in connection with the *modality* of punishment. But they take it for granted that punishment is and for itself is *just*.   (*PR*, §99R)

Hegel's comments are thought to make clear that the form of punishment has little general importance because they concern only 'the modality of punishment'. Hegel is making the point that whatever else punishment is that it must be just—and this is true for all the 'various determinations' relevant to punishment.

This is incorrect. The modality of punishment is not determined here. Hegel avoids saying here that punishment is *in toto* retribution, deterrence, rehabilitation, or some other view. It is striking that Hegel's claim that modality is to be determined later is somehow taken as evidence that he is accepting only one—retributivism— here. It is hardly surprising that Hegel takes seriously form and content, and not least with punishment where the form's 'essential significance' in its 'proper context' has yet to receive consideration. And so no judgement can or should be made in Abstract Right about punishment's modality across all cases.

While many commentators play down Ethical Life as a mere application of ideas found in Abstract Right, Hegel does not view the relation of these sections in that way. In his discussion of law, he claims that 'when right comes into existence primarily in the form of being posited, it also comes into existence in terms of *content* when it is *applied to the material* of civil society' (*PR*, §213). Right gains content through its application—it has substance and is not purely formalistic. Part of this content is found in the contingency of applying concepts to the world (*PR*, §214A). Hegel says: 'For example, the magnitude of a punishment cannot be made to correspond with any conceptual definition, and whatever is decided will in this respect always be arbitrary. But this contingency is itself necessary' (*PR*, §214A).

As already foreshadowed by his early remarks in Abstract Right, Hegel claims that the distribution and amount of punishment is *not* determined by an individual's state of mind alone, but external factors like a crime's potential 'danger to society' (*PR*, §218). He says: 'its danger to civil society is a determination of its magnitude…This quality or magnitude varies, however, according to the *condition* of civil society' (*PR*, §218R). The argument can be explained in the following way. Crime is a failure to recognize right. Punishment seeks to cancel this failure and reaffirm right. This transpires within a wider context—and Hegel takes this context seriously. All thefts may share specific features in general as attempts permanently to deprive another of her possessions. Hegel's point is that the damage done to this right to own property, in this example, and reaffirm it can shift in value due to external factors.

Hegel clarifies what these factors relating to the condition of civil society might look like. Of importance is 'the very stability of society' (*PR*, §218A). The more stable a society is—or when it is more 'sure of itself'—then the 'greater leniency in its punishment' (*PR*, §218). Crime might then be seen 'in a milder light, so that its punishment also becomes milder' (*PR*, §218A). A stable society that is self-confident and relatively harmonious is less threatened by crime; offences do not pose as chilling a threat to it.

The situation is very different for a civil society that is less stable. For example, a society plagued by deep internal tensions or engaged in war provides a very different context. Criminal violations are viewed as more dangerous as a result, and 'a penal code is therefore primarily a product of its time and of the current condition of civil society' (*PR*, §218R). This means that the punishment of crime must take into account contextual matters like the stability of civil society and the potential harm a crime might pose to it. Such factors might be contingent and a product of circumstances beyond the control of any government, but for Hegel this contingency is a necessary feature in helping us determine if we punish and how much punishment we distribute.[36]

---

[36] I mention that only in Ethical Life do we gain insight into *if* we should punish. Hegel is clear that monarchs can issue pardons and remarks that the wider context—and possible consequences of issuing a

Hegel's theory of punishment will justify different punishments for the same kinds of offences over time as circumstances change. He says: 'harsh punishments are not unjust in and for themselves, but are proportionate to the conditions of their time; a criminal code cannot be valid for every age, and crimes are semblances of existence which can meet with greater or lesser degrees of repudiation' (PR, §218A). This is not relativism. Hegel is not defending an overly conservative view that however we punish is justifiable. Crime and punishment share a necessary connection—and we cannot punish the innocent. This fundamental building block for how we should approach crime and punishment is crucial.

It is also of central importance that what we change over time is not the conception of what a theft, murder, or rape is, but how they are punished. All thieves commit thefts and all murderers have murdered. These offence-types like theft or murder exist over time as categories. For Hegel, a theft during peacetime is the same offence-type as a theft committed during civil war. But the thieves are not the same all the way down because the circumstances surrounding their thefts can be different. It is this difference in circumstances that is substantively important for informing how we should punish offenders. Hegel distinguishes between 'crime *in itself* is an infinite injury' and so as an offence-type is resistant to change over time (PR, §218R). Yet its measurement 'in terms of qualitative and quantitative differences' are context-dependent 'since its existence is essentially determined as a representation and consciousness of the validity of the laws' with 'its danger to civil society is a determination of its magnitude' (PR, §218R). Interpreters that claim context has no substantive part to play fail to grasp the fact that punishment is an institutional practice *in the world* and not apart from it. Only in some heavenly, unreal beyond are all crimes to be the same independently of their becoming *real*. Punishment is a practice in human community and the wider circumstances pertaining to justice are relevant to the just administration and distribution of any criminal justice system.

An example of how crimes are never fixed for any specific punishment is Hegel's views on the death penalty. A well-known defender of capital punishment, Hegel says:

although retribution cannot aim to achieve specific equality, this is not the case with murder, which necessarily incurs the death penalty. For since life is the entire compass of existence [*Dasein*], the punishment cannot consist [*bestehen*] in a *value*—since none is equivalent to life—but only in the taking of another life.   (PR, §101A)

---

pardon—can justify its use. So whereas Abstract Right merely tells us crime and punishment have a necessary link with each other, the fact of crime need not mandate punishment where there are suitably important contextual factors supporting the use of pardons. But note that no circumstances would warrant the punishment of an innocent person. Punishments are only deserved by criminals, but not every criminal may deserve the same punishment—or any punishment—even where two or more have committed the same offence. Context matters and this is another reason why Hegel's theory of punishment is not like any other retributivist theory—and why it should be understood as a different approach altogether. See Thom Brooks, 'No Rubber Stamp: Hegel's Constitutional Monarch', *History of Political Thought* 28 (2007): 91–119.

Hegel's argument is that death is an appropriate punishment for murder, but not because it is a life for a life. Instead, murderers should be executed because the most serious offence should be punished with the highest gravity. That the murderer has taken a life and the most appropriately grave punishment is his death is a coincidence.[37] What counts is the comparative value and we should not be misled into thinking Hegel's support for the death penalty is grounded on some view of the *lex talionis* or some idea that punishments should mirror their corresponding crimes.

But nor is Hegel's support for capital punishment absolute or timeless. In making some remarks about Beccaria's theory of punishment, Hegel says: 'The death penalty has consequently become less frequent, as indeed this ultimate form of punishment deserves to be' (*PR*, §100A). For Hegel, a crime may warrant execution as a punishment, but this might change over time as circumstances evolve. And his support for the death penalty is far from unequivocal in claiming it 'deserves' to become less frequent. This comment fits his later remarks about how the stability of civil society influences the amount of punishment: as society becomes more secure, the need for punishments like the death penalty start to dissipate.

In Ethical Life, Hegel explicitly refers back to his Abstract Right discussion claiming that 'the right against crime takes the form of revenge' and that 'it is merely right in itself' (*PR*, §220). It is not yet 'in a form that is lawful' and lacks 'existence' (*PR*, §220). Punishment becomes 'objective' when it 'restores' what is right 'through a cancellation of crime' (*PR*, §220). What is key here is that there is a difference between a restoration of right in theory versus what would be entailed in practice. If circumstances recommend more lenient or harsh punishments to achieve its goal of the restoration of right, then this has real significance for our thinking about punishment's justification as a practice in theory and in fact.

This still leaves a missing part in the argument. If context matters and conditions might warrant more or less punishment to deserving offenders, how should we make judgements about when and how to punish? How we distribute punishment seems opaque.

The orthodox consensus has not caught on to this problem. This is because it fails to take seriously Hegel's comments—even in Abstract Right—where he says the context matters in a non-retributivist way, and it turns a deaf ear to Hegel's later remarks in Ethical Life where he substantiates these comments further. Before making further progress, it must be noted that the standard orthodox reading is not the best interpretation of the comments Hegel offers. Abstract Right is not the only source of comments detailing the substantive content of his theory of punishment. But even if it was, Hegel still denies the standard retributivist reading widely attributed to him.

Punishment aims at the restoration of right. The context within which we punish has significance for shaping the values of crime and punishment that we seek to fulfil approximately. If non-retributivist factors can matter, how should they? This crucial

[37] I am grateful to Brian O'Connor who first raised this crucial point with me. See Thom Brooks, 'Corlett on Kant, Hegel and Retribution', *Philosophy* 76 (2001): 562–73, at 576 n71.

question may be answered if we look elsewhere in his philosophical system—after all, Hegel claims his arguments are linked in a systematic way across texts.[38]

In his *Science of Logic*, Hegel says:

Punishment, for example, has various determinations: it is retributive, a deterrent example as well, a threat used by the law as a deterrent and also it brings the criminal to his senses and reforms him. Each of these different determinations has been considered the *ground of punishment*, because each is an essential determination, and therefore the others, as distinct from it, are determined as merely contingent relatively to it. *But the one which is taken as ground is still not the whole punishment itself.*[39]

This passage is remarkable in two ways. First it defines 'retribution' in a very narrow way—which is consistent with Hegel's use of this term in Abstract Right. Hegel's understanding of 'legal' retribution is only the necessary connection between crime and punishment. This leaves open a space for determining the amount of punishment so long as it is distributed to a deserving person. So the first point we should recognize is that Hegel's later view of retribution in the *Philosophy of Right* is consistent with his view published several years earlier in the *Science of Logic*.

The second remarkable feature about this passage is that it is perhaps the first explicitly 'unified theory' of punishment defended. Hegel is claiming that punishment is more than any one penal feature. In the words of British Idealist Thomas Hill Green, 'it is commonly asked whether punishment according to its proper nature is retributive or preventative or reformatory. The true answer is that it is and should be all three'.[40] Punishment is not one or the other, but all together.

This perspective on punishment has roots that predate even the *Science of Logic*. In his earlier essay on natural law, Hegel says:

In the case of punishment, one specific aspect is singled out—the criminal's moral reform, or the damage done, or the effect of his punishment on others, or the criminal's own notion of the punishment before he has committed the crime, or the necessity of making this notion a reality by carrying out the threat, etc. And then some such single aspect is made the purpose and essence of the whole. The natural consequence is that, since such a specific aspect has no necessary connection with the other specific aspects which can be found and distinguished, there arises an endless struggle to find the necessary bearing and predominance of one over the others.[41]

---

[38] Hegel says of the *Philosophy of Right* in its opening paragraph: 'This textbook is a more extensive, and in particular a more systematic exposition of the same basic concepts which, in relation to this part of philosophy, are already contained in a previous work designed to accompany my lectures, namely my *Encyclopaedia of the Philosophical Sciences*' (PR, 9). The *Encyclopaedia* is Hegel's philosophical system in outline and the *Philosophy of Right* fleshes out one part of it, 'Objective Spirit'. See G. W. F. Hegel, *Philosophy of Mind* (Oxford: Oxford University Press, 1971): §§483–552.

[39] G. W. F. Hegel, *Science of Logic*, 465 (emphasis added).

[40] Thomas Hill Green, *Lectures on the Principles of Political Obligation* (London: Longmans, 1941): §178. Green is discussing his own theory of punishment, but he was an early Hegel scholar and familiar with Hegel's political thought—and familiar with Hegel's logic in a way that few commentators are today.

[41] G. W. F. Hegel, *Natural Law: The Scientific Ways of Treating Law, Its Place in Moral Philosophy and Its Relation to the Positive Sciences of Law*, trans. T. M. Knox (Philadelphia: University of Pennsylvania Press, 1975): 60.

Here Hegel acknowledges 'an endless struggle'—seemingly without a clear resolution—between specific aspects of punishment. His point remains that the problem is that philosophers of punishment insist on one-sided thinking claiming one aspect or view of punishment as a full theory of punishment. This is a problem because it neglects the fact that punishment is more than any one aspect. Punishments should be deserved and their uses can have deterrent or rehabilitative effects. It is unclear whether Hegel makes this point because he believes punishment's capacity to deter means deterrence is a necessary aspect of punishment's existence as a practice—even if he rejects deterrence as a reason to punish.

Hegel's unified theory of punishment might be thought of as bringing these different penal aspects together in a particular way. Punishment must be deserved, but its distribution is determined by the relevant circumstances affecting the crime's impact on the stability of a particular civil society. The restoration of right may call for more deterrence, rehabilitation, or other penal factors depending on these circumstances. In setting the value of punishment, we seek to restore the violated right, and the form that punishment might take is justified where it best approximates what is required for the restoration of right.

This can avoid the concern that such a mix will lead to clashes because Hegel's framework is guided by restoring right and not retribution, deterrence, or rehabilitation. If it was guided by one aspect, then it is easy to see that clashes can arise between trying to punish offenders as much as deserved while trying to deter others—as what is deserved may be very different from what might deter. But since no one aspect is our guiding principle, this conflict is overcome. In seeking the restoration of right, we implement different aspects alone or in combination in the service of a shared goal—and so can avoid potential conflicts between them.

Conclusions

Few areas of Hegel's philosophy are less controversial than his views on crime and punishment. The orthodox consensus claims Hegel was a retributivist. This reading is built off of the view that we need only concentrate on but one section—Abstract Right—in Hegel's *Philosophy of Right* in order to gain a complete, or near complete, grasp of his views. This orthodox consensus has become the dominant reading of Hegel's theory of punishment since Cooper's classic essay on this topic.

I have argued that the orthodox consensus runs into serious difficulties when we compare Hegel's comments about crime and punishment in Abstract Right with later parts of his *Philosophy of Right* and other writings. If the orthodox consensus is correct, then much of Hegel's claims must be wrong for reasons of inconsistency or incoherence. The consensus view that he endorses some standard view of retribution does not hold up when we consider his comments on punishment—and the case begins with remarks found in Abstract Right. Hegel is open to non-retributivist aspects so long as there is a necessary connection between crime and punishment. This connection is how he narrowly understands 'retribution'. For a philosopher who celebrated taking standard vocabulary and transforming it into something different in his philosophical lexicon, this should not come as any surprise.

I argued that Hegel's comments are coherent if we take his philosophical methodology more seriously in a systematic reading of his texts. His works are not meant to be read as a series of sections or chapters that build on each other like a story with a beginning, middle, and end. Instead, there is a structure where these different parts interpenetrate each other so that what is at the start foreshadows what comes later and retains its presence, while following sections develop earlier insights in new directions.

Punishment offers an illustration of this at work. The earlier discussion about it in Abstract Right helps establish a foundation for what is to follow. This legal retributivist core—understood in Hegel's distinct way—does not rule out non-retributivist aspects from determining the shape of punishment as a practice. But as a practice in the world, it is necessarily affected by contingency—and so the circumstances under which crimes occur and punishment is distributed matter to how this is undertaken. Punishment never loses its retributivist heart mandating that it is deserved, but its distribution and amount can have shifting values depending on the possible harm that a crime threatens the stability of civil society with. For Hegel, such external factors are not a problem, but part of how punishment is conceived and practiced. Yet this is distinctly non-retributivist, as standard views can reject their use.[42]

Hegel does not offer any clear guide for how punishment should be distributed. I have argued that his views in Abstract Right foreshadow his later comments in Ethical Life in ways that show his theory is inconsistent with retributivism. I further argued that we can find comments in other texts, such as the *Science of Logic*, that are consistent only with this non-retributivist reading of Hegel's theory. Moreover, they indicate that he held a unified theory of punishment, bringing together aspects of retributivism, deterrence, and rehabilitation. While he does not say much about how they might work together, his endorsing a unified theory—and not retributivism—appears to have been noticed by British Idealists like Green who echo similar positions.[43]

---

[42] Retributivism is a broad church—and my argument is it's not broad enough to include Hegel's theory of punishment. But at least one view of retributivism—negative retributivism—can also take stock of external factors. It does so in different ways from standard and positive retributivism. Elsewhere, I argue it is the more problematic and inconsistent of retributivist views. See Brooks, *Punishment*, 96–99.

[43] See Thom Brooks, 'T. H. Green's Theory of Punishment', *History of Political Thought* 24 (2003): 685–701; Thom Brooks, 'Rethinking Punishment', *International Journal of Jurisprudence and Philosophy of Law* 1 (2007): 24–34; Thom Brooks, 'Was Green a Utilitarian in Practice?' *Collingwood and British Idealism Studies* 14 (2008): 5–15; Thom Brooks, 'Punishment and British Idealism' in Jesper Ryberg and J. Angelo Corlett (eds), *Punishment and Ethics: New Perspectives* (Basingstoke: Palgrave Macmillan, 2010): 16–32; Thom Brooks, 'Is Bradley a Retributivist?' *History of Political Thought* 32 (2011): 83–95; Thom Brooks, 'What Did the British Idealists Ever Do for Us?' in Thom Brooks (ed.), *New Waves in Ethics* (Basingstoke: Palgrave Macmillan, 2011): 28–47; Thom Brooks, 'On F. H. Bradley's "Some Remarks on Punishment"', *Ethics* 125 (2014): 223–5; and Thom Brooks, 'Defending *Punishment*: Reply to Critics', *Philosophy and Public Issues* 5 (2015): 73–94.

Peter Steinberger makes the comment about his own interpretation of Hegel on crime and punishment that 'it may be wondered how much of this account is really Hegel, and how much is merely inspired by certain Hegelian insights'.[44] There is an orthodox consensus about Hegel's views that can find textual support for its positions. But it cannot account for all of Hegel's comments about punishment. Taken together, Hegel offers a theory that breaks from the retributivist tradition and in so doing breaks new ground. The new reading of Hegel's theory of punishment developed here is made possible by taking more seriously the argumentative structure that Hegel uses to construct his philosophy both within the *Philosophy of Right* and elsewhere in his system. A greater attention to the systematic structure—through a systematic reading—presents us with a deeper appreciation of Hegel's philosophical contributions that corrects even widely held assumptions, and so opens new possibilities previously obscured or closed off.

---

[44] Peter J. Steinberger, 'Hegel on Crime and Punishment', *American Political Science Review* 77 (1983): 870.

11

The Logic of Right

Richard Dien Winfield

Philosophy, Logic, and Ethics

Truth and right are fundamentally tied to self-determination. The quest for truth cannot free itself of opinion unless it liberates inquiry from the hold of given opinion and validates all its claims through its own independent labors. Philosophy must wield an autonomous reason, free in both the negative sense of overcoming dependence upon presuppositions and the positive sense of determining what its own method and subject matter should be. As such, philosophy cannot begin with any determinate claims about what is or about knowing. It must start from utter indeterminacy and generate from that presuppositionless commencement determinacy that is not grounded on any given, or given procedure of, specification. This indeterminate commencement allows philosophy to be a theory of determinacy, accounting for determinacy without begging the question by beginning with some given determinacy. Moreover, since philosophy develops determinacy as something generated in its own presuppositionless process, it develops self-determined determinacy. Philosophy thus begins as a development of self-determination per se.

To do so, however, philosophical investigation cannot begin by examining anything distinct from its own thinking. Any inquiry that addresses a topic different from its own knowing is doubly conditioned and relative. On the one hand, such an investigation must take its method for granted since it investigates not its own thinking but something distinct from method. On the other hand, such an investigation must presuppose the boundaries of its subject matter, since it only addresses something different from its method by confronting a topic with a given content distinguishing it from the thinking that addresses it. Hence, any investigation that begins by distinguishing its method from its subject matter, or its knowing from its object, is relative to both the given method it employs and the given determination of its topic. Philosophy can overcome this dual relativity if it overcomes the opposition of knowing and its object. This is why philosophy must begin with logic, whose thinking of thinking proceeds upon the elimination of the distinction of method and subject matter. Logic is equally autonomous in the dual sense that it proceeds without any given method or subject matter and instead generates both at once in thinking thinking. As such, logic, with which philosophy must begin, is autonomous reason. Instead of beginning with any given determination of knowing or its object, logic must establish what thinking is in the process of thinking thinking. Beginning with neither any predetermined method or subject matter, logic can only be a logic of self-determination, a logic in which determinacy is established without taking any determinacy for granted, a logic which overcomes all dependency upon foundations, a logic which thereby can validly think valid thinking.[1]

The legitimacy of conduct involves a very analogous centrality of freedom. Conduct cannot be valid unless it liberates itself from the domination of given authority and overcomes the divide between what confers legitimacy and what possesses legitimacy. So long as putatively valid conduct owes its validity to a separate foundation, that privileged factor must remain suspect. To be consistent with its own standard of validation, the privileged foundation must derive its validity from itself. Yet, insofar as the foundation must be self-grounding, its own legitimacy subverts the distinction between ground and recipient of validity, supplanting its own foundational structure of justification with self-determination as the only tenable substance of normativity. As such, ethics becomes a philosophy of the reality of self-determination, a philosophy of right, where right is understood as the actuality of freedom in all its totality.

Does the pivotal role of self-determination in both logic and ethics signify that ethics will exhibit the same logic as the logic of autonomous reason, whose development of self-determination per se is an ingredient in logic's overcoming the opposition of subject and object with its thinking of thinking? Ethics may share self-determination, but ethics concerns the reality of self-determined *action*, not self-determination as a development of the categories of self-thinking thought. Moreover, ethics consists not in logic, but in a philosophy of non-logical reality, which may follow from the presuppositionless development of logic, but in so doing supplements logical determinacy with non-logical categorization. On both counts, the relation of the pure logic of self-determination with the logic of the reality of freedom, the logic of the philosophy of right, is far from straightforward.

Hegel, who pioneers both presuppositionless logic and ethics as a philosophy of the reality of self-determination, provides us with the basic categories of logic and ethics with which to determine what the logic of the philosophy of right should be and how it relates to logic proper.

In the *Science of Logic*, Hegel presents self-determined determinacy as something that becomes thematic in the third and final section of logic, the Logic of the Concept.[2] Self-determined determinacy is shown to be nothing other than the determination

---

[1] Hegel develops these arguments for why philosophy must begin as a presuppositionless development of self-determined determinacy and as a self-thinking logic in the two introductory sections of his *Science of Logic*, entitled respectively, "General Notion of Logic" and "With What Must the Science begin?" See G. W. F. Hegel, *Science of Logic*, trans. A. V. Miller (New York: Humanities Press, 1976), pp. 43–59 and 67–78.

[2] Hegel, *Science of Logic*, pp. 575ff.

of the concept as such, that is the universal. The universal differentiates itself in particularity and in so doing determines nothing but itself, thereby attaining a completely self-originating character, comprising individuality. Although the concept exhibits self-determined determinacy in the process whereby the universal entails particularity and individuality, it still arises from two preceding logical developments, unfolding, respectively, the Logic of Being and the Logic of Essence. The Logic of Being accounts for how indeterminacy gives rise to determinacy, which, through its own development, renders its own immediate givenness something posited or mediated by an underlying essence. The Logic of Essence then develops all the two-tiered relationships whereby a determiner determines some determined determinacy. That development achieves closure when what determines and what gets determined become indistinguishable. This yields self-determined determinacy, not as something that owes its self-determined character to itself, but as something that immediately results from the elimination of the difference between determiner and determined. Hegel recognizes that self-determination cannot be immediately given. Instead logic must move from indeterminacy to determinacy, which the relation of determiner and determined incorporates and presupposes. Only with determinacy and determined determinacy at hand, can self-determination obtain the factors it needs for its own constitution. Even though self-determined determinacy is what it determines itself to be, it cannot begin its self-determining activity without these enabling conditions, determinacy on the one hand, and determiner and determined determinacy, on the other.

This dependency upon enabling conditions applies as much to the reality of self-determined conduct as it does to the logical development of the concept. As Hegel points out in the Introduction to the *Philosophy of Right*, the ethics of self-determination has its only deduction in the prior philosophical development of the real preconditions of conduct.[3] This "deduction" is supplied by the systematic philosophies of nature and of "subjective spirit" which develop the conceptually determinate reality of the biosphere in which animal life can develop to the point of providing individuals with theoretical and practical intelligence. This work of nature and psychology provides all that is required for conduct, that is, self-determined willing, to take place. Significantly, these natural and psychological enabling conditions in no way determine what conduct should be. Precisely because nature and mind are the enabling conditions for all conduct, they are completely neutral with regard to what distinguishes that conduct which is right from that which is wrong. This neutrality is necessary for the very possibility of normativity in conduct. Otherwise conduct would be juridically conditioned by antecedent factors. That would reinstate the incoherent framework of foundational justification, which ethics overcomes as a philosophy of right, of the reality of freedom. The reality of self-determination is determined in and through itself and for just this reason the philosophy of right can have no juridical foundations. This absence of prior

---

[3] G. W. F. Hegel, *Elements of the Philosophy of Right*, trans. H. B. Nisbet (Cambridge: Cambridge University Press, 1991), ¶2, p. 26.

THE LOGIC OF RIGHT 225

legitimating principles has mystified legions of thinkers trapped in foundationalist dogmatism. They wonder whether the *Philosophy of Right* can be an ethics at all, since all it does is determine the reality of freedom, without appealing to any separate standards of validity.

This independence from the heteronomy of external grounding is basic to the logic that properly informs ethics. Hegel broadly identifies ethics as consisting in the Idea of Right, that is, the Idea of the reality of self-determined willing.[4] The Idea is the proper subject matter of each and every part of philosophy, from the logic with which philosophy must begin through the philosophies of nature and of mind that follow. In each case the Idea consists of the unification of concept and objectivity in which truth resides. Objectivity, unlike appearance or existence, does not rest upon some undisclosed ground, but is determined in and through itself, as should be the proper object of true knowledge. The concept, as exhibiting self-determination, is precisely suited to lay hold of that which is independently determined. Thanks to the concept's fundamental autonomy, conceptualization can grasp a subject matter as it is determined in and through itself. The form of representation, by contrast, represents given intuitions and recollected images. Representational cognition always reflects upon given contents, modifying them in terms of the forms of its understanding. What representation apprehends is always a mere given appearance, which its general representations may correctly fit, but never know to be what is true in itself. Ethics properly develops the *Idea* of Right because this consists in presenting the conceptually determinate, self-constituted objectivity of freedom. The *Philosophy of Right* conceives its subject matter by allowing the "*Sache selbst*" to unfold in its own structural objectivity.

This requires a purely conceptual development, freely following the immanent unfolding of the concept of right. Does this signify that the logic of the *Philosophy of Right* will mimic that of logic proper?

In considering this question, it must be recognized that it is not meta-ethical in character. Meta-ethics proceeds upon the logical positivist dogma that reason is empty and cannot generate any content of its own. On this impoverished basis, thinking can only be analytic, at most confirming the consistency of given content in accord with the principle of non-contradiction, but never establishing the truth of any such content. The logic of thought can then only be formal, mapping a thinking whose form is always distinct from its content, which must be received from some other source, such as experience or linguistic usage. Meta-ethics presumes that the logic of ethics is equally formal, specifying a form of ethical reasoning that can be determined without specifying the particular content of ethical values. In other words, meta-ethics presumes that the logic of ethics can be identified without distinguishing between right and wrong, as if one could distinguish the ethical from the non-ethical without distinguishing what is ethical from what is unethical. Such formalism is precluded by the concrete logic of self-determination. Since the "form" of self-determination,

---

[4] Hegel, *Elements of the Philosophy of Right*, ¶1, p. 25.

namely the unity of the self, is the very content it determines itself to have, the logic of freedom, whether purely logical or ethical, cannot be an external form, indifferent to what it orders. As self-ordering, self-determined determinacy has a form that is pregnant with a content of its own. This means that the logic of right is uniquely tied to the one and only content of the reality of freedom. Since ethics *is* the philosophy of right, meta-ethics is as much a fraud as formal logic's pretention to have anything to do with philosophical thinking.

Nonetheless, this does not preclude asking whether the reality of free willing shares the same concrete self-ordering form as the pure logic of autonomous reason. Hegel might appear to draw a strict connection between the two from the very start of ethical investigation. In the introduction to the *Philosophy of Right*, he introduces his concept of the free will by sketching out how the will achieves self-determination by exhibiting universality, particularity, and individuality.[5] The will first of all displays the negative freedom of universality by being able to abstract itself from any given end and instead pursue some other goal. This abstract universality, Hegel notes, must be supplemented by particularity, for unless the will makes a particular choice, it fails to *determine* its self. Finally, the will must not succumb to external dictate in the particular determinacy it gives itself. Rather, to be free, the will must remain at one with its self-determining self in engaging in a particular action, and to the extent that it does so, it unites its particularity with its universality, thereby exhibiting individuality.

Does this connection signify that the *Philosophy of Right* begins with the same logical development as the Logic of the Concept, which starts by conceiving universality, particularity, and individuality? Moreover, should we expect that the unfolding of the structures of right will map on to the progression of the rest of the Logic of the Concept, with judgment and syllogism being followed by the forms of objectivity and then the logical determinations of the Idea?

Two important factors weigh against any close correspondence of ethical and logical development. The first concerns the general relation between the self-ordering of logic and the development of the non-logical part of philosophy, or what Hegel calls *Realphilosophie*, to which belongs ethics, that is, the philosophy of right. The second concerns how the self-determination of the will fundamentally differs in structure from the self-determination of the concept per se.

Logic per se versus the Logic of *Realphilosophie*

The self-development of autonomous reason achieves closure when logic completes its valid thinking of valid thinking, which culminates in the so-called Absolute Idea, where the entire logical development is methodically recapitulated as the self-constitution of logical science. Once this culmination is achieved, the totality of logical determination has come into *being*. This addition of the form of being to the

---

[5] See Hegel, *Elements of the Philosophy of Right*, ¶5–7, pp. 37–41.

Absolute Idea constitutes something that is irreducible to any logical determinacy, since it incorporates all the logical categories within its form. Insofar as the emergent being of the Absolute Idea is the least determinate qualification that could be added to logical totality, it comprises the minimal determinacy of what is extra-logical, providing the starting point for *Realphilosophie*, arriving at something beyond logic without illicitly introducing any putative "given" content. This minimal threshold of non-logical determinacy can be described by Hegel as the self-externality of the Absolute Idea[6] since it consists of nothing but the totality of logical determinacy as immediate, as beyond its own self-mediating, self-constitution. Any further development of non-logical determinacy must proceed upon this minimal self-external totality, which Hegel appropriately identifies with space,[7] the most basic factor of nature that all further natural realities incorporate. Although the Idea, that is, the conceptually determinate objectivity, of nature will constitute itself from this structural starting point, the development of nature cannot consist in a simple application of the succession of logical categories to the completed Absolute Idea. Nature cannot consist in such a "development" for that would involve an external application of the logical ordering to the antecedently given logical totality. Although being may indeed immediately be nothing, and nothing and being may comprise becoming, their transitions are not that of a logical totality to which being has been added. Space can yield time and then matter and motion insofar as each stage along the way builds upon the entirety of what has heretofore been provided, without the contribution of any further content or the application of any categories to some given content by an external *deus ex machina*. The ultimate ordering principle of the development of nature will consist in the natural totality that arises when all natural relationships have come into being in their structural unity. This totality, which consists of the natural universe that has become a biosphere, then provides the starting point for the development of the non-natural reality of the "psychozoids", the rational agents that animal life makes possible. Here, on the basis of the psychological reality of intelligent individuals, the threshold of ethical reality emerges. At each stage in the development leading up to this enabling platform for self-determined willing, what determines the succession of real factors is something more specific than an application of particular logical categories to the absolute Idea. Once space has provided nature with a minimal non-logical realization, what orders the ensuing development are two converging considerations. On the one hand, each subsequent development will build itself from nothing more than what has already emerged and, on the other hand, the unfolding that proceeds will determine itself to be the development of the totality whose self-constitution brings that realm to closure. Space will therefore be not a determination of and by the Absolute Idea but rather the most rudimentary feature of a universe that exhausts its natural possibilities

---

[6] Hegel, *Science of Logic*, pp. 843–4. See also, G. W. F. Hegel, *Philosophy of Nature*, trans. A. V. Miller (Oxford: Oxford University Press, 1970), ¶247, pp. 13–14.

[7] Hegel, *Philosophy of Nature*, ¶254, p. 28.

by being the biosphere of animal life. Similarly, that biosphere will turn out to be the incorporated threshold on which rational agency constitutes its historical world, culminating in the cultural achievement of philosophy, by which the totality of reality comes to contain that which knows it in its whole truth. Accordingly, to comprehend the "logic" of right, it will be necessary to focus on the structural interrelationships of the different spheres comprising the reality of freedom, in light of the natural and psychological materials that provide the enabling conditions of ethics. That this involves more than applying the logical ordering of categories is reflected in the second factor that bars any simple parallelism.

Self-determination in Logic versus Self-determination in Ethics

This second factor consists in the key difference in the self-determination of the concept and the self-determination of the will. Unlike the concept, free will inextricably involves the interrelationship of individuals.

The logic of the concept begins by developing universality, particularity, and individuality without reference to any plurality of individuals.[8] Hegel presents universality, followed by particularity, and then by individuality, indicative of how the particularization of the universal does not presuppose a plurality of differentiated particulars, that is individuals. Instead, universality, poised to determine itself, differentiates itself as particularity per se, which gives rise to individuality only *after* particularity affirms its unity with universality. Only once universality and particularity take on individuality in their contrast with one another does the concept divide itself into a plurality of individuals, setting the stage for judgment.

By contrast, the will achieves self-determination only by participating in an interaction of right, in which the self-determination of one individual is interdependent upon the self-determination of others.

Hegel's application of the categories of universality, particularity, and individuality to the self-determination of the will might suggest that an individual can act autonomously without interacting with any other agents. Simply by having the capacity to choose, the individual can wield the universality of negative freedom, deciding which end to pursue without being bound to any given goal. Moreover, by making a choice, irrespective of relating to others, one can exhibit the particularity of giving one's will determinacy. What, however, can enable that particular choice to exhibit universality and provide for the individuality of volition? What can allow the will to give itself a

---

[8] Admittedly, in Judgment, the factors of the concept will be determined by one another in relationships that involve a plurality of individuals, but in the preceding account of the concept, individuality as such is determined through nothing but universality and particularity. For a detailed discussion of these logical developments, see Richard Dien Winfield, *From Concept to Objectivity: Thinking Through Hegel's Subjective Logic* (Aldershot: Ashgate, 2006), pp. 67–105 and Richard Dien Winfield, *Hegel's Science of Logic: A Critical Rethinking in Thirty Lectures* (Lanham, MD: Rowman & Littlefield, 2012), pp. 207–60.

determination that is its own, rather than being a content given *to* the will by external circumstance or given inclination? How can the choosing will escape being bound to options mandated not by will, but by outer or inner conditions? How can choice escape remaining a slave to contingent externality and subjective desire?

So long as the individual wills monologically, that is, without interacting with other agents, the choice it makes fails to achieve self-determination on two fundamental counts. On the one hand, the individual does not determine the identity of its own agency. Rather than individuating the self that wills, the single agent instead wields a faculty of choice that is given antecedently to every decision it makes. Since that faculty is the enabling condition rather than the product of every choice, it is not a product of willing. Rather than being an artificial agency, it is a natural will, comprising an inherited capacity that is merely a potential whose actualization adds nothing to its defining character. The natural agency of the monologically choosing will is thus not self-determined, but given independently of willing, as a psychological endowment that comes into being through the natural maturation of the individual.

Furthermore, the faculty of choice fails to determine not only the form of its own agency but also the content of what it chooses. The individual agent may wield the negative freedom, the abstract universality, of deciding which goal to pursue, but the faculty of choice does not itself supply the options among which it can decide. The faculty of choice is formal, having no intrinsic content. What it chooses are ends that must be found outside the will itself—ends given by such independent factors as external circumstance and internal drives and representations. Instead of achieving self-determination, the natural will employs a faculty of choice that leaves it unable to determine by itself either the form or content of its volition. Who the agent is and what the agent wills are both heteronomous, determined not by willing but by other factors, be they objectively external or subjectively psychological. This double conditioning is why Socrates in Plato's *Republic* declares the very idea of self-rule, that is, self-determination, to be unintelligible. After all, Socrates observes, how can any individual be both agent and patient at once? How can the isolated agent possibly will its own character when it must employ itself to determine itself?[9]

What overcomes the otherwise insoluble enigma of self-determined willing is the intersubjective practice of rights. Individuals, who by nature are endowed with the faculty of choice, can use their natural wills to achieve self-determination provided they interact with one another in the function of determining both the form and content of their respective agencies. They are able to do this in the most basic way by embodying their wills in separate objective realizations that they mutually recognize to be the actualizations of one another as self-determined persons. Through such reciprocally coordinated willing, they establish for one another a type of agency that comes to be in and through their interaction, an interaction in which they will both

[9] Plato, *Republic*, Book IV 430e–431a in Plato, *Complete Works*, ed. John M. Cooper (Indianapolis: Hackett, 1997), p. 1062.

who they are as self-determined individuals and what they will to do so. Their inter-action establishes an agency whose identity is defined by the recognized embodiment it gives itself rather than by any features given independently of their willing. Further, what each individual thereby wills is an embodiment of that agency, which, as its self-determination, is defined not by any given features of that embodying factor, but by the recognition that it actualizes the self-determination agency that wills it as its own realization. Since each participant can determine itself only by facilitating in its counterparts the same type of willing that it itself engages in, each partakes in a universal, lawful willing. This lawful willing is an exercise of right because it is a recognized self-determination that is shared by all participants in their interaction.

These mutual features are minimally exhibited in the self-determination of individuals as persons, that is, as owners. One cannot determine oneself as an owner without having the exclusive embodiment of one's will recognized as such by others who have established their own domain of ownership in some other exclusive embodiments. To give oneself the character of being an owner, one relies upon nothing other than embodying one's will in some factor that is acknowledged by others to be one's exclusive domain, acknowledged by their refraining from infringing upon that property. Nothing about one's natural identity renders one an owner. No matter what may physiologically, psychologically, or culturally individuate one from others, unless one wills an embodiment that is recognized by others, one cannot distinguish oneself as an owner. Similarly, no given feature of the factor that becomes property makes it something owned. Only the recognized presence in it of the will of the person renders it property. This is what allows the acquisition of property to be a self-determination, for what individuates the agent as an owner is determined through the coordinated willing of the mutually recognizing individuals rather than by any antecedently given features of those individuals or of the factors they appropriate. To be an owner, one must abstract from all features by which one is individuated by nature or external circumstance and acquire an identity determined through nothing but the convention of property ownership consisting in the coordinated acts of will in which one participates. To be an object of property, by the same token, a factor must figure as a pure receptacle for the embodiment of the will. Its identity as an object of property is determined solely by that embodiment, and only insofar as that is the case can the factor be the vehicle for the self-determination of the individual as an owner.

Although both person and property realize self-determination by obtaining an individuation produced by the coordinated choices of the participants in the exercise of property right, the most elementary and primary actuality of self-determination consists in the acquisition of a very specific type of property, without whose appropriation no other property can be obtained or relinquished, nor any other exercise of right can be had. This form of property is that of the agent's own body, which every person must be recognized exclusively to own before that person can engage in any further acts of self-determination. Self-ownership of one's body is primary because unless one is recognized to be the exclusive proprietor of one's facticity, nothing one does can count juridically as one's own deed. Instead, one has the status of a mere factor, susceptible of appropriation by the will of another, who is responsible for whatever the enslaved individual causes to happen. Only once individuals mutually recognize one another as having taken exclusive ownership of their respective bodies, can they take further actions that can be attributed to themselves. For this reason, one's ownership of one's body has the unique character of being inalienable. One cannot transfer ownership of one's body to another because to do so would be to annihilate the entire actuality of one's self-determined embodiment, leaving one incapable of retaining the status of recognized person.[10]

This primacy of self-ownership renders property right equally primary in the reality of freedom. It does not, however, make property right a first principle of ethical construction, as social contract theory believes. If property right were made a determining foundation of all further ethical validity, it would confer validity upon other institutions and activities which would thereby be conditioned on property right instead of being self-determined. In order for any further conduct to be autonomous, property right must enter in not as a determining principle but as an elementary ingredient in an exercise of freedom that contains but is irreducible to property relations.

In developing the Idea of Right, Hegel properly begins with property right and unfolds property relations in the order of their self-constitution.[11] First comes the original acquisition of property, which starts with the mutual recognition of individuals as persons who have taken exclusive inalienable ownership of their respective bodies. With this primary property at hand, agents who have freely individuated themselves as self-owning persons can now make the next logical move in extending their freedom. This consists in taking ownership of other factors by recognizably laying their will in them, be it by physically seizing them, altering their form, or marking them. In each case, these actions take ownership of alienable property only by being recognized by other individuals who have correlatively determined themselves as persons. Once this has occurred, persons are able to use their property and then to alienate their alienable possessions either in full or for limited use. Since ownership is a self-determination on the part of the owner, alienation of property can only involve a transfer of title if the receiving party wills to acquire the object or limited use of it. Hence, all transfer of property consists in a relation of contract, where persons agree to accept property, either with an exchange of property or of use of property, or without exchange, as in gift contract where only one party receives ownership or use.[12] Logically enough, only once the acquisition, use, and alienation of property have been developed, can the violation of property right occur in its full totality of non-malicious and malicious wrongs. Moreover, only with the determination of wrong does the task of righting

[10] See Hegel, *Elements of the Philosophy of Right*, ¶47–8, 67, pp. 78–9, 97.
[11] Hegel, *Elements of the Philosophy of Right*, ¶40, p. 70.
[12] Hegel, *Elements of the Philosophy of Right*, ¶80, pp. 110–12.

wrong arise in the way that property relations allow. These structural implications dictate how the Idea of the first, primary sphere of right must be developed.

Where, however, should the logic of right lead after property relations have been thought and realized? The precarious situation in which the righting of wrong finds itself on the basis of property relations indicates that the reality of freedom cannot consist just in the practice of property relations. Since persons have choosing wills they can always enter into disputes in good faith concerning the boundaries of their ownerships, disputes for which the plurality of persons offers no recognized authority to adjudicate conflicts. Further, persons can always choose to violate the property of others maliciously, leaving others in the predicament of having to determine what wrong has been committed and what punishment and compensation are warranted, under conditions where none have any authority to take coercive actions without risking accusation of committing new wrongs of their own. This difficulty suggests, as it did to social contract theorists confronting the insecurity of liberty in the "state of nature", that further institutions of right must be enacted to uphold property. If, however, normativity consists in self-determination, any further institutions that secure property right must involve an irreducible freedom of their own. Further, the connection between any such institutions and property relations must be determined by an exercise of freedom, for otherwise the different spheres of right will be ordered by a power external to self-determination, leaving the totality of conduct under heteronomous control.

These considerations dictate that property right should be supplemented at least by an encompassing sphere of right in which individuals codetermine the whole reality of conduct in which they participate. In addition to property relations there ought to be self-government, where individuals will themselves as citizens who exercise self-rule and thereby determine how their political activity presides over their non-political freedoms. This presents a mandate not unlike the two-tiered framework of social contract theory, which places property relations under the governance of a civil administration of law that provides legal regulation and enforcement of property rights. The difference here is that the upholding of property relations should take the form of an institution of political freedom, not just an enforcement of civil legality, which may or may not involve self-government.

Hegel, however, does not restrict the Idea of freedom to a two-tiered structure of property relations and self-government, where individuals determine themselves as persons and citizens. Instead, he offers a threefold division of self-determination into the abstract right of property relations, the moral domain of conscientious subjects, and the institutional reality of ethical community, which itself contains the three spheres of the emancipated family, civil society, and self-government.[13]

---

[13] See Hegel, *Elements of the Philosophy of Right*, ¶33, p. 62.

Is the Threefold Division of Abstract Right, Morality, and Ethical Community Valid?

Is this division valid and comprehensive, and are the major subdivisions within each of its three domains proper and exhaustive? The broad logical terms with which Hegel distinguishes the three spheres of abstract right, morality, and ethical community do not immediately exhibit the necessity of the division. Property relations are characterized as a form of self-determination in which the will obtains its free actuality in given external facticity. By contrast, in morality, the will achieves self-determination through subjective determinations that ought to be realized by conduct that is valid insofar as it reflects them. Finally, in ethical community, agents determine themselves through membership in existing associations where their freedom has an objective existence that contains the subjective activity by which it is realized. One is tempted to observe that abstract right presents self-determination in the form of the given determinacy of the Logic of Being, that morality presents self-determination in the form of the reflected, determined determinacy of the Logic of Essence, and that ethical community presents self-determination in the form of the self-determined determinacy of the Logic of the Concept. Even if this is the case, one may question why this need be and how it uniquely identifies the exhaustive division of the Idea of right, that is, of the reality of freedom.

Support for these divisions can be sought on an alternative, if complementary, logical basis. The delineation of the spheres of right can be judged in terms of the two correlative provisos that govern the self-constitution of any independent totality: namely, both as conceived and as internally structured, a free-standing totality should involve a development in which each of its prior divisions presupposes nothing of what is found in those divisions that follow upon them, whereas those successive formations should have their sufficient enabling conditions in those preceding structures which they equally incorporate.

These dual considerations are amply satisfied by Hegel's three-fold development of abstract right, morality, and ethical community. To begin with, the self-determination of persons presupposes nothing but a biosphere and the existence therein of a plurality of rational animals that are able to interact in terms of their respective choices. On the other hand, individuals can engage in none of the self-determinations of moral subjects or members of an ethical community unless they have determined themselves as property owners. Otherwise, they lack recognized self-ownership, without which no further exercise of right can be had.

Moral self-determination, for its part, requires a plurality of property owners, whose actions are their own responsibility and not that of some master. On the other hand, individuals do not need to belong to any ethical community to exercise their moral freedom. Indeed, moral autonomy is characterized by a subjective determination where conduct must draw its bearings from the internal purposes, intentions, and conscience of the individual rather than from the institutional practices in which they may be embroiled. Whereas membership in family, civil society, or state is not an enabling condition for interacting with others as morally accountable subjects, acting on conscience requires turning inwards for guidance, which is precisely where one is left when ethical community provides no unequivocal normative direction.

Further, the three subdivisions Hegel ascribes to morality exhibit these dual provisos of systematic unity.[14] The first exercise of moral freedom, where moral subjects hold each other accountable only for that part of their actions that are prefigured in their purpose, does not depend upon the other two aspects of moral freedom, the right of intention and welfare and the right of conscience to determine the good. Rather, both of these latter aspects of morality presuppose that individuals interact in recognition of their morally circumscribed responsibility for only that part of their conduct that they do on purpose. Only once this is done can moral subjects proceed to attribute responsibility to the ramifications of what they do on purpose in function of the intentions that give the motive for their purpose. This right of intention necessarily follows upon the right of purpose since if refers explicitly to the intended consequences of what is done on purpose. The right of intention, however, does not depend upon conscience, for recognition that moral subjects be held responsible for the consequences they intend does not itself involve the additional consideration of whether their intentions and purposes are good. On the other hand, moral self-determination with respect to purpose and intention provides all that is necessary to exercise the freedom of conscience, where moral subjects hold one another accountable for acting on purposes and intentions that conform to a good they independently determine. Moral subjects can only act conscientiously if they already interact in function of their right to be held responsible for what they do on purpose and what they intended to result from their moral deeds. On this basis, conscience need only employ its choosing will to determine which purposes and intentions will realize a good that is not yet at hand, but should be objective. The whole actuality of morality thus involves the sequential self-constitution that Hegel presents.

Nonetheless, does participation in ethical community depend upon moral accountability in addition to recognition as a property owner? It is not hard to see that individuals who determine themselves as persons and moral subjects are fully able to enter into matrimony and establish an ethical household, from which they then can enter into the social interdependencies of civil society, and from there, into the activity of self-governance.

Yet does the functioning of ethical community necessarily require that its members hold one another accountable as moral subjects? Consider what it would mean to be an individual whose moral accountability is not recognized. Although one might not be treated as a slave, one would have no positive rights or duties, including any positive welfare, extending beyond ownership. One would be a mere person, restricted to a

---

[14]   Hegel, *Elements of the Philosophy of Right*, ¶114, p. 141.

minimal autonomy that cannot make any further purposes or intentions its normative concern.

Can individuals with no moral rights of purpose, intention, and conscience still exercise their ethical rights of household, social, and political community? Persons can observe the negative, prohibitive rights of property ownership without concerning themselves with purpose, intention, and conscience. Respecting ownership does not involve the inner, subjective aspects of conduct, but only the external actions that honor or infringe upon the property of others. Motive plays a role solely in determining punishments for perpetrators of malicious wrong. By contrast, in each and every sphere of ethical community, the realization of right includes the subjective activity by which it is achieved. Spouses exercise their household rights and duties not just by respecting property, but by taking a positive interest in the household autonomy and welfare they share. That conscientious ethical commitment is a constitutive ingredient in the domestic association their actions aim to sustain. The same role for moral agency applies to civil society, whose members pursue self-selected particular ends that can only be realized by enabling others to do the same. Unless market participants and legal subjects aim at upholding the particular right and welfare of one another, they cannot interact in terms of market interdependence, civil legality, and the public securing of economic well-being. Although civil society provides an institution in which particular interests can legitimately be pursued, that normatively *civil* pursuit is predicated upon it being a right that all members of society can exercise. For this reason, acting only as a property owner without moral consideration is not compatible with exhibiting civil rectitude. Nor is the exclusive restriction to property right that libertarians endorse compatible with political freedom. Self-government depends upon citizens acting with a patriotism consisting in making the good of the body politic one's individual purpose and intention.

In each case, ethical conduct incorporates moral subjectivity, but clothes it in an institutional framework that overcomes the dilemma that haunts conscience as it operates outside of ethical community. Conscientious moral subjects hold each other accountable for acting with purposes and intentions that are good, where each is responsible for determining what counts as good. The good should be objectively valid, but since morality has only the subjective resource of conscience to determine what the good should be, what one conscience determines to be good can always conflict with what another prescribes. This discrepancy confronts moral subjects with the dilemma of either respecting the conflicting conscience of another while ignoring one's own conscience, or following one's own conscience while disregarding that of others. In ethical community, by contrast, the good one pursues is neither something yet to be realized nor subjectively determined. Rather, in exercising the role to which membership entitles one, each individual acts to fulfill a good that is both already actual in the institution in which they participate and commonly pursued by all its members. Since every exercise of ethical conduct sustains the institution to which its

236 RICHARD DIEN WINFIELD

members belong, no one exercising their household, social, or political rights will pursue an end that violates the corresponding rights of their counterparts. Citizens, for example, may use their political prerogatives with different views on what will uphold the totality of freedom, but so long as they act within the constitutional limits of self-government, they will not prevent others from exercising their political rights. However, citizens disagree, and their constitutional political involvements will continue to sustain the body politic as an institution of self-rule realizing their shared political freedom.

Are Family, Civil Society, and the State the Exhaustive Differentiations of Ethical Community?

Hegel's broad division of the Idea of Right into spheres of abstract right, morality, and ethical community may therefore fit the logical demands of systematic unity, but can the same be said of his division of ethical community into the three institutional domains of the family, civil society, and the state?

Admittedly, Hegel fails consistently to develop the full content of these three ethical spheres. Unable to free his conception of holdovers of the pre-modern arrangements of his day, he leaves key features of each ethical sphere structured by factors extraneous to self-determination. In the family, Hegel restricts marriage to a monogamous heterosexual relation in which the male spouse lords over the female spouse as household manager and exclusive representative of the family in civil society and the state.[15] In civil society, he compounds the heteronomy of gender disadvantage by substituting estates for economic classes[16] and corporations for social interest groups.[17] Thereby he lets hereditary relations determine social function and opportunity, while allowing the natural subsistence of a peasantry to intrude upon the social interdependence of market freedom. These hereditary and natural dependencies carry over into Hegel's determination of political institutions, doing so on the backs of the corporations and estates he inconsistently foists upon civil society. Instead of conceiving the legislature as a representative assembly in which all citizens have equal political opportunity, Hegel adopts an estate assembly, allowing estate distinctions to ground political privileges.[18] Finally, he undercuts self-rule by endorsing the hereditary reign of a constitutional monarch.[19]

All of these violations of self-determination can be overcome without undercutting the basic division between family, civil society, and state offered by the *Philosophy of*

---

[15] Hegel, *Elements of the Philosophy of Right*, ¶165–7, pp. 206–7.
[16] Hegel, *Elements of the Philosophy of Right*, ¶202–5, pp. 234–7.
[17] Hegel, *Elements of the Philosophy of Right*, ¶250–4, pp. 270–2.
[18] Hegel, *Elements of the Philosophy of Right*, ¶300–14, pp. 339–52.
[19] Hegel, *Elements of the Philosophy of Right*, ¶279–80, pp. 316–22.

Right.[20] What allows this is that Hegel firmly differentiates the three ethical spheres in terms of the character of their ends and the scope of their association, neither of which have any necessary connection to the heteronomous holdover traditions he fails to discard. The end of family ethical community is the co-determined joint private good of the household, an end that is common to its members, but particular in scope, since the family is one domestic union among indefinitely many others. Civil society, by contrast, entitles the pursuit of ends that are particular, but its association is universal in scope since market interdependence, as well as the conventions of civil law and the public administration of welfare, extend as far as there are individuals who interact in terms of self-selected particular interests. Political association aims at the universal end of freely ordering the totality of freedom over which it presides, but unlike civil society, the state can have a particular boundary limited by other states.

Is ethical community properly divided into these three ethical spheres? Is the reality of ethical self-determination exhausted by the willing of ends that are universal but limited to an association particular in scope, ends that are particular but pursued through a global association, and ends that are universal but advanced by a particular totality of freedom? It might seem that this division covers all the possible permutations with two exceptions: an ethical community whose ends are particular and whose association is particular, and an ethical community whose ends are universal and whose association is universal.

The former option, however, is already contained within civil society in the association of social interest groups, characterized by Hegel as corporations. The members of social interest groups pursue a shared particular interest by making a common front in relating to other groups whose particular interests are different from theirs, but must be accommodated in order to satisfy the former's interests.

The latter option is also already contained in the threefold division of ethical community, in this case within political association, which may be universal both in end and in scope. Although the state can be one among others, there is nothing about political unity that requires that it be a particular state confronting others in international relations. Contrary to Carl Schmitt, for whom political association depends upon a friend–foe opposition,[21] what defines political association are its self-ruling reflexivity, autonomy, supremacy, and the universality of its ends, all of which are secured through the domestic subordination of all other spheres of freedom under

---

[20] This is substantiated in the four books in which I have remedied the shortcomings in Hegel's account of ethical community: *The Just Family* (which reconstructs the family as an institution of self-determination), *The Just Economy* and *Law in Civil Society* (which together reconstruct civil society in accord with right), and *The Just State: Rethinking Self-Government* (which reconstructs the institutions of political freedom). See Richard Dien Winfield, *The Just Family* (Albany: State University Press of New York, 1998), *The Just Economy* (New York: Routledge, 1988), *Law in Civil Society* (Lawrence, Kansas: University Press of Kansas, 1995), and *The Just State: Rethinking Self-Government* (Amherst, NY: Humanity Books, 2005).

[21] See Carl Schmitt, *The Concept of the Political*, trans. George Schwab (New Brunswick: Rutgers University Press, 1976), p. 26.

the sway of self-government.[22] Self-government can proceed without the state having any other states with which to contend. In principle, the state could be global or a solitary body politic with no relations to any other.

What validates family, civil society, and self-government as necessary and comprehensive realizations of ethical community is the systematic unity they exhibit. The emancipated family does not itself incorporate any civil or political relationships, but without household freedom, neither civil nor political self-determination can be realized. This is not because every civilian and citizen must be married or raised in a family, since individuals can certainly exercise their social and political rights even if they are single and have been brought up in public orphanages. Rather, the emancipated family serves as a structural prerequisite of civil society and self-government because if household emancipation has not been achieved, heteronomous family organization will impede the equal social and political opportunities of family members. Any deficit in household co-determination will prevent competent adult family members from being able to participate in civil society and politics on an equal footing with their household counterparts.[23] Similarly, civil society does not itself involve political relationships, which is why individuals may exercise their social, as well as household rights, in conditions where self-government is lacking. Nonetheless if equal social opportunity is unrealized, relations of social domination will prevent individuals from having equal opportunity to engage in self-rule. For this reason, the social emancipation provided by a civil society that regulates market activity through civil law, private social interest group activity, and the public administration of welfare, is a structural prerequisite for political self-determination.

Indeed, precisely because self-government cannot operate unless household and civil rights are guaranteed, the actuality of political freedom necessarily insures that the totality of pre-political freedoms are realized and sustained within the state. Only with self-government crowning the system of self-determination can the specter of political oppression be removed and all rights be adequately upheld. This truth provides the logical capstone of the development of the Idea of Right.

[22] For further analysis of these four cardinal features of political association, see Winfield, *The Just State*, pp. 129ff.

[23] Moreover, since normativity consists in self-determination, there can be no legitimate excuse for not leaving room for a type of self-determination that is compatible with the other institutions of freedom.

12

Hegel, Autonomy, and Community

Liz Disley

Hegel's account of community, particularly ethical community, rests on a picture of the human agent as incomplete, vulnerable, and constantly changing. A number of recent accounts and discussions of Hegelian community and ethical agency rest on precisely such a view of human life and individuality. The picture of *Sittlichkeit* and civil society in general in the *Philosophy of Right*, however, at least on the face of it, seems to rest much more on a concept of the individual as fully formed and with a far greater degree of autonomy, at least on the public level. Is the resolution to or *Aufhebung* of this tension to be found in Hegel's method itself, and, if so, does it inevitably shape all practical consequences of this method?

In Section 12.1, I describe the Hegelian account of intersubjectivity that demonstrates the incomplete, changing, and vulnerable nature of Hegelian personhood. In Section 12.2, I discuss the Hegelian view of autonomy as seen in the account of civil society in the *Philosophy of Right*. In Section 12.3, I examine further the tension between these accounts and how they interact with the relationship between Hegel's method and its practical corollaries. I offer here a few introductory remarks.

In asking what the relationship between a Hegelian notion of community and Hegelian *Sittlichkeit* is, we must break the enquiry down into several sub-questions. First, to what extent is Hegelian *Sittlichkeit* and the idea of civil society foundational to the account of community in his system? Second, what can we use as a working notion of Hegelian community which takes into account his importance for current political and social philosophy? And third, what lies at the core of this contemporary notion?

Richard Dien Winfield points out that Hegel's *Philosophy of Right* preserves and emphasizes the foundation-free nature of ethics:

Hegel is the first to recognize that ethics can be neither a science of a highest good nor a procedural construction because what is normative cannot derive its legitimacy from any foundation, be it a privileged given content or a privileged determiner. If what is ethical has its normativity conferred upon it by something other than itself, the ground conferring validity upon it cannot have validity of its own unless it grounds itself.[1]

---

[1] Richard Dien Winfield, *Hegel and the Future of Systematic Philosophy*. Palgrave Macmillan, 2014, p. 131.

As Winfield notes, the absence of any foundations of this kind has led many to doubt whether the *Philosophy of Right* can be called an ethics at all.[2]

Here, I examine the relationship between Hegelian community, which relies to a great extent on a notion of the individual that is in some way incomplete or, as Jane Dryden describes it, vulnerable, and the ethical life in Hegel's later philosophy, which rests on a non-foundationalist account of ethics. The notion of the ethical agent as in some way incomplete accords particularly well with a notion of ethics and the ethical life as starting from something other than an already established ground. In this way, contemporary accounts of Hegelian community that focus on intersubjectivity and interdependence mould well with an overall system with a phenomenological basis rather than a foundationalist one.

John O'Neill sketches out the problem in a 2001 paper:[3]

The practice of minoritarian politics presupposes the civic recognition of ethical identity claims. Unless this is cancelled, one's life, reasons and desires only achieve currency in a public world and a public discourse that they presuppose for their identification, evaluation and acknowledgement. The self, in other words, is a communicative self, endlessly invoking other similarly communicative selves to sustain its projects…This is a message that is lost once we put Hegel into a bottle and toss it out into the sea—or into the Seine!

Hegelian recognition, and particularly ethical recognition, depends upon a context of civil society. Recognition—as in the *Phenomenology*—is a condition of possibility for what, in Hegelian terms, we might call subjectivity, and in the terminology of current moral and social philosophy, might be called selfhood or agency. It is only within a civil context that our (ethical) actions become meaningful. This is not merely true by definition—not the case merely because the ethical sphere is what gives individual action ethical meaning. Rather, it is so because the self, by itself, is incapable of sustaining projects, as O'Neill puts it. The self is constantly reaching out to the others purely in order to continue to be, to sustain itself. Whether or not this proves to be an insurmountable challenge for an ideal of rational autonomy (or indeed whether rational autonomy itself turns out to have a crucial social component, which I also discuss) is discussed in Section 12.2. With Hegel and his system in mind, there is a further question to answer. If the problem with Hegelian social philosophy is not that a social context is needed for any meaningful action, but that it is a particular type of social context that is required, then it is clear how the objection to both system and social philosophy emerges from the practical, rather than the obscurely theoretical, aspect of criticism. It is this question, too, that I tackle in Section 12.2. First, however, I trace out the Hegelian social self in his early works with reference to twentieth-century criticism.

---

[2] Ibid., p. 132.
[3] John O'Neill, 'Oh, my others! There is no other: Civic Recognition and Hegelian Other-Wiseness'. *Theory, Culture & Society* 18:2–3 (2001): 77–90.

12.1. The Hegelian Self: Incomplete, Vulnerable, Changing

Judith Butler's early work on Hegel, *Subjects of Desire*, points out explicitly the mistake that is made by mid-twentieth-century French readers such as Sartre when considering the Hegelian self. As the foreword to the 2012 edition states:

[Sartre et al.] impute to the Hegelian subject an ontological autonomy and self-sufficiency, whereas the very fact of being a 'subject of desire'…puts into play a negativity and a dialectic of intersubjectivity that renders eminently problematic the supposed plenitude of this subject.[4]

Since it is precisely that autonomy that is thought to be politically problematic from a postmodern point of view, this is a confusion which needs urgently to be cleared up. This autonomy and self-sufficiency is, on one account at least, guilty of both an empirical neglect of human independence and a more theoretical neglect of genuine human intersubjectivity. For someone like Sartre, this level of self-sufficiency might seem like nothing more than an insistence on subjectivity and a denial of one's objecthood—a mere struggle for domination with no real chance of success for either party. One particular account of selfhood or subjecthood from a postmodern or post-structuralist point of view questions precisely this kind of self-sufficiency.

Judith Butler, in her recent *Giving an Account of Oneself*, tackles this problem directly by exploring how people can be moral agents even without being completely autonomous subjects—and indeed, as moral agents, cannot be completely autonomous. This is a continuation, in many ways, of her earlier work in *Subjects of Desire*. There, she states:

As it becomes clear that the same truths hold true of the Other's relationship to the self, the Other is also viewed as the author of the subject. Desire here loses its character as a purely consumptive activity, and becomes characterised by the ambiguity of an exchange in which two self-consciousnesses affirm their respective autonomy (independence) and alienation (otherness).[5]

Recognition, for Butler and for Hegel, has the character of an exchange between self and Other that involves each one establishing themselves as both subject and object. Put this way, it becomes clearer how it is precisely this ambiguity that means autonomy is restricted, and also why the self is not a fixed quantity (and recognition therefore always involves some kind of error). Butler's insight and main line of argument in *Giving an Account of Oneself* is that the self does not have to be truly autonomous for

---

[4] Judith Butler, *Subjects of Desire: Hegelian Reflections in Twentieth-century France.* Columbia University Press, 2012, p. viii.
[5] Ibid., p. 51.

moral responsibility to be possible.[6] The fact that we are socially constituted is not a barrier to being a genuinely free ethical agent. Butler poses the question as follows:

Does the postulation of a subject who is not self-grounding, that is, whose conditions of emergence can never fully be accounted for, undermine the possibility of responsibility and, in particular, of giving an account of oneself?[7]

Butler's strategy is to contrast the social phenomenon of recognition with the epistemological practice of judgement. Traditional moral responsibility sees the subject as accountable for its actions, but Butler wishes to extend the practice of 'accounting' to include the narrative of the subject and the sense in which the subject is socially constituted. In other words, the subject is not complete by itself, but must always include the social context in which it finds itself—the subject is always already embedded. Rather than being a barrier to the possibility of moral responsibility, recognizing the extent to which the self is socially constituted during the narrative of its life is a precondition for honest moral judgement.

Thus, Butler brings the traditional picture of moral autonomy into question. What she is fundamentally attacking is the fixed Cartesian subject. As she puts it in her earlier *Bodies that Matter*:

One might be tempted to say that identity categories are insufficient because every subject-position is the site of converging relations of power that are not univocal. But such a formulation underestimates the radical challenge to the subject that such converging relations imply. For there is no self-identical subject who houses or bears these relations, no site at which these relations converge. This converging and interarticulation is the contemporary fate of the subject. In other words, the subject as a self-identical identity is no more.[8]

As a matter of fact, Butler does not see Hegelian reciprocal recognition as providing the crucial kind of sociality that is required by an ethics as described in *Giving an Account of Oneself*.[9] Nevertheless, particularly in terms of the freedom that Butler's non-autonomous self can enjoy, much of the analysis relates well to the discussion of Hegel as defining the limits of autonomy. As she puts it:

[The forswearing of traditional autonomy is] a chance—to be addressed, claimed, bound to what is not me, but also to be moved, to be prompted to act, to address myself elsewhere, and so to vacate the self-sufficient 'I' as a kind of possession.[10]

The self-sufficient I, for someone with Hegel's systematic commitments, is merely a source of heteronomy and a barrier to mediated self-consciousness. It is precisely this freedom from a predefined self that ought to interest someone who ultimately wants

---

[6] J. Butler, *Giving an Account of Oneself.* New York: Fordham University Press, 2005.

[7] Ibid., p. 19.

[8] Judith Butler, *Bodies That Matter: On the Discursive Limits of 'Sex'*. London and New York: Routledge, 1993, pp. 229–30.

[9] Butler, *Giving an Account of Oneself*, p. 31.   [10] Ibid., p. 136.

to sublate the subject/object dichotomy and get away from the slave mentality of merely clinging to the apparent self, to life.

How can the death of the subject as announced by postmodernists be reconciled with the philosophy of the subject, the Copernican revolution of rejecting an ultimate heteronomous goal of knowledge (which I discuss in Section 12.2)? To answer this question involves taking Butler's initial idea of the non-autonomous, incomplete, and changing subject—a theme which in fact runs throughout a lot of her writings and does not just emerge in her 2005 work—in connection with the observation of Hegelian anti-foundationalism, and re-examining what is crucial about autonomy for Hegel.

12.2. The Hegelian Subject: Autonomous in the Ethical Life

True autonomy, for Hegel, is mediated autonomy, as Robert Williams points out in his defence. In particular, 'autonomous freedom is intersubjectively mediated'.[11] What might this actually mean in practice, and does it not mean that any practical application of Hegel's accounts of autonomy and freedom are doubly bogged down, in incomprehensible details of an all-encompassing system as well as with the particular need for the right sort of (ethical) community, and indeed, as Hegel's system has it, a state? The assertion central to Hegel's argument in the *Philosophy of Right* that freedom is only possible in the context of a state seems paradoxically conservative and anti-individualistic, and the effect on the autonomy of the self equally so. For Hegel, autonomy is no less important than it is for Kant. As Paul Stern points out: 'Hegel attempts to expose the limits of a strongly rationalist, formal strategy in ethical theory, but does not at the same time abandon the view that ethical principles must fulfil the demands implied by the idea of rational autonomy.'[12]

Hegel criticizes Kantian morality for neglecting the social context in which moral lives are lived, but does not wish to criticize, and much more wants to preserve, the idea of autonomy. Indeed, Hegel thought that it was Kant's picture of autonomy that failed to preserve freedom properly, given that, with its dualism of reason and sensibility, it merely replaced an outer tyrant with an inner one.[13] Paul Stern has argued that Hegel's account of ethical community and *Sittlichkeit* preserves the foundations of an idealist ethical theory in rational autonomy while overcoming the difficulties of a Kantian account of morality.[14] Nevertheless, the problem of whether Hegel advocates a 'command account' of morality, as Dean Moyar puts it, is a vital question to which an

---

[11] Robert R. Williams, *Hegel's Ethics of Recognition*. Berkley: University of California Press, 1998, p. 6.

[12] Paul Stern, 'On the Relation Between Rational Autonomy and Ethical Community: Hegel's Critique of Kantian Morality'. *Praxis International* 3 (1989): 234–48.

[13] Robert Stern, *Understanding Moral Obligation: Kant, Hegel, Kierkegaard*. Cambridge: Cambridge University Press, 2012, p. 137.

[14] Ibid., p. 235.

answer is clearly required.[15] If morality commands us, how does it do so except from without, and how can rational autonomy be preserved in the face of this? On one reading at least, either an inner or an outer tyrant is required for morality but problematic for autonomy. On a view put forward by Robert Stern in 2007, it is *Sittlichkeit* that allows both morality and autonomy to be preserved, and Moyar quotes him as saying: 'whereas in the sphere of *Moralität*, duty still has the feeling of a command imposed on the agent, in the sphere of *Sittlichkeit*, this is precisely what is lost.'[16] I argue at the end of this section that the distinction between *Moralität* and *Sittlichkeit* is a crucial indicator of the importance ascribed to autonomy, even within the highly social context of the ethical life.

12.2.1 Rationality, autonomy, and system

How crucial is the idea of rational autonomy to a Hegelian politics? To what extent does the concept of the self outlined in Section 12.1 conflict with the idea of a rational, as well as an autonomous self? What is the relationship here between rationality and autonomy? As William Maker puts it: 'Can we somehow make sense of a Hegel whose agreement with the postmoderns on antifoundationalism, holism, and historicism can be seen not as an aberration, but rather as a consequence of his conception of philosophical rationality?'[17]

This chapter asks the question the other way around—is Hegel's commitment to philosophical rationality in the public ethical sphere an aberration, given that his theoretical philosophy commits him to a much more fluid and interdependent view of the self? Nonetheless, the basic matter at hand remains the same. Hidden behind Maker's question is, of course, an affirmative answer, which leads one to answer the converse question in the same way. Maker correctly notes the question as being of ahistorical significance, and also of constituting nothing less than a reconciliation of modernity (broadly understood as a commitment to autonomy and self-sufficient reason) and postmodernity.[18] On one interpretation, what is being reconciled (what Maker's analysis, and indeed Hegel's own position as regards system) are two opposites: the insistence on system as the proper context for philosophy, and the rejection of system.

Is this an inherent contradiction? Maker has an account of Hegel's relation to philosophical system-building that involves the claim that he is not a 'metaphysical idealist', and that this is a misinterpretation that stems from Hegel's Marxian critics and followers.[19] Metaphysical idealism, Maker claims, is defined by its setting in opposition 'thought, and the materially or empirically given, in order to deny the primacy of such

[15] Dean Moyar, 'How the Good Obligates in Hegel's Conception of *Sittlichkeit*: A Response to Robert Stern's *Understanding Moral Obligation*'. *Inquiry* 55:6 (2012): 584–605.
[16] Robert Stern, *Understanding Moral Obligation: Kant, Hegel, Kierkegaard*. Cambridge: Cambridge University Press, 2012, p. 256, quoted in Moyar, 'How the Good Obligates in Hegel's Conception of *Sittlichkeit*', p. 536.
[17] William Maker, *Philosophy Without Foundations: Rethinking Hegel*. Albany: SUNY Press, 1994, p. 24.
[18] Ibid.   [19] Ibid., p. i.

a given in favour of the primacy of thought'.[20] This is not what Hegel (or, one might argue, Kant) is trying to do—for Hegel, systematic philosophy requires the *suspension* of the opposition between thought and the given. Systematic philosophy is not an attempt to reconcile the world of phenomenal experience with the world of the 'real', not an exercise in the correspondence theory of truth.

To take Maker's analysis a step further, that is, to follow it through as it relates to autonomy, we can argue that Hegel *does* reject an account of rational autonomy that sees self-sufficient reason as a lone attempt to make one's way from the world of phenomenal experience to the world of the real; to interpret one's phenomenal experience in such a way as to make it correspond for practical purposes with the world of the real. The opposite of autonomy, of course, is heteronomy, and the kind of analysis or system that merely attempts to build a bridge between the ideal and the real is itself introducing a kind of heteronomy into the supposedly self-sufficient rational process, that is, the guiding hand of the Myth of the Given, of being able to justify with relation to knowledge-claims what one says and making claims about entitlement to say what one does.[21] In such a scenario, the self does not find its way to knowledge, but is guided by a way of thinking and talking about knowledge which assumes an opposition between the ideal and the real. This all seems convincing; it is less convincing that all 'metaphysical idealism' attempts to do this, but this becomes largely a question of semantics. It also suggests that no genuine autonomy is possible if there is a gap posited between the ideal and the real, or at least if this is a gap that the process of gaining knowledge is supposed to close or negotiate (so that Kantian autonomy might be possible, but that autonomy might be impossible for someone like an empiricist). This is a bold claim, but one we can see Hegel, and indeed anyone who wants to argue for this particular kind of autonomy, would want to make. It is also the only kind of autonomy or system that might appeal or be acceptable to a postmodernist who wants to reject the idea of systematic philosophy—perhaps what they really want to reject is the sort of philosophical system that posits the given as being in opposition to thought or phenomenal experience. Certainly, we might say this of someone like Husserl, a forerunner of postmodernism and post-structuralism, whose phenomenological method does not aim at some objective reality, but the examination of the life-world of human experience. We might say that someone like Marcuse, who argues that the transcendental reduction in philosophy from Descartes, to Kant, to Husserl, represents an abandonment of the true Hegelian project (or its materialist continuation) of restoring the real dynamics of essence and appearance, is precisely wrong.[22] Such a materialist continuation of the Hegelian legacy does nothing other than set up the ideal and the real against each

---

[20] Ibid., p. 171.

[21] Cf. Wilfred Sellars, 'Empiricism and the Philosophy of Mind', in *Science, Perception and Reality*. London: Routledge and Kegan Paul, 1963; reissued Atascadero, CA: Ridgeview, 1991.

[22] Herbert Marcuse, 'The Concept of Essence', in *Negations: Essays in Critical Theory*. Boston: Beacon Press, pp. 43–87, p. 70, referenced in John O'Neill, *The Poverty of Postmodernism*. London: Routledge, 2002.

other, pursuing the real. It is Husserl and his existentialist/postmodernist successors—Jean-Paul Sartre, Jacques Lacan, and Judith Butler—who are the true heirs of Hegel's legacy, not the Marxian materialists.

The main objection to such a line of argument is that it simply begs the question against the materialist, claiming from the outset that truly systematic philosophy, and true autonomy, is bound up with the philosophy of the subject, and excluding from the outset the possibility of rational autonomy within an empiricist or realist context. Systematic philosophies are divided up into those which can allow for this particular sense of autonomy, and those which cannot. This would seem arbitrary and question-begging were there no external reasons for thinking that a certain kind of philosophy of the subject provides a way out of the seemingly unnavigable gap between thought and the given, system and atom, isolated subject and subsumed subject. It is at this point that the 'rational' in rational autonomy provides a new angle on the question of Hegel, autonomy, community, and system.

As Robert Pippin points out in his 2005 *The Persistence of Subjectivity*, Kant's real break with what came before was the insight that the autonomy of reason is crucial for freedom: Kant insists on 'the autonomy of the normative domain, the claim that the only thing that bears on the sufficiency of a reason is another reason, never a mere state of affairs or cause on its own'.[23] Nothing extra-mental can determine the mental, and knowledge is not a matter of reconstructing an extra-mental reality inside the mind. Only reason can determine what belongs inside the mind. This is another sort of Copernican revolution, placing rationality ahead of the extra-mental, the active subject over the world of objects. Pippin sees Hegel as continuing Kant's project, its natural extension being the replacement of what had hitherto been philosophy's central dichotomy, that between thinking and extended substance, with the dualism of Spirit and Nature—in other words, between behaviour controlled by social norms (that is, intersubjective others) and behaviour controlled by the inanimate world of objects. This is the completion of the revolution—social philosophy naturally becomes first philosophy, with any notion of a metaphysical or epistemological system occupying at best a distant second place.

Given this, it becomes easier to see how a system that does not try to bridge the gap between appearance and reality is a necessary precondition for genuine autonomy, in a Hegelian context or at all. It is a much further step, of course, to see how a Hegelian subject who was autonomous in this way could also be incomplete and vulnerable in the sense described in Section 12.1. Pippin's analysis, combined with the insights on system offered by O'Neill, additionally make it clear just how important freedom as a concept will be as the background to reason, autonomy, and the social world. With these considerations in mind, I go on now to discuss autonomy in practical terms, as described in the *Philosophy of Right*.

---

[23] Robert B. Pippin, *The Persistence of Subjectivity: On the Kantian Aftermath*. Cambridge: Cambridge University Press, 2005, p. 115.

12.2.2 Autonomy and Hegelian civil society

Which features of civil society and the state, according to Hegel, are crucial for the intersubjective mediation of absolute freedom? Is it necessary to make a clear distinction between civil society as viewed in political theory today, and *Hegelian* civil society? Craig Calhoun offers a succinct definition of the former:

The value of a public sphere rooted in civil society rests on three core claims: first, that there are matters of concern important to all citizens and to the organization of their lives together; second, that through dialog, debate and cultural creativity citizens might identify good approaches to these matters of public concern; and third, that states and other powerful organizations might be organized to serve the collective interests of ordinary people—the public—rather than state power as such, purely traditional values, or the personal interests of rulers and elites.[24]

The first two aspects can be clearly mapped on to a Hegelian account of civil society. It is the vital similarities between members of a community that shape interaction at the most fundamental level of the master–slave dialectic: each fears the complete oblivion of objecthood and strives for complete subjecthood, relegating the Other to the status of pure object, lacking agency. Because both fear death and oblivion, but are incapable of escaping the oblivion of objecthood without the help or recognition of the Other, they are locked into a process which either fails on both sides—failed recognition, just as in the case of the master and the slave in paragraphs 178–92 of the *Phenomenology*— or succeeds because it is mutual. Hegel offers us no model of this in the *Phenomenology*, but this characterization of an important aspect of civil society suggests how a success-ful attempt might be made. It is reasonably easy to see how mutual recognition could work on a one-to-one level in the context of certain phenomena such as love and forgiveness;[25] it is a further question as to how a general social context could be imagined, but civil society as described by Hegel, and by Calhoun in relation to the current world, would seem to be a possible contender.

The second aspect of civil society mentioned by Calhoun, that of debate and discus-sion shaping the world, is also applicable to Hegelian civil society. As an approach to studying Hegel, civil society, and *Sittlichkeit*, the question might be posed as follows: is interaction in the form of discussion within civil society intended to get at the ideal form of state or community organization, or to define this ideal form? The answer, for Hegel even more obviously than for Kant, must surely be the former, for there is nei-ther a simple assumption about the inherent rationality of human judgement (such as might arguably be claimed in the case of Kant) nor a positing of some ideal societal form standing over and above the realm of human judgement. For Hegel, looking back once more to the *Phenomenology*, it is clear that actual combative interaction is absolutely

---

[24] Craig Calhoun, 'Civil Society and the Public Sphere', in Michael Edwards (ed.) *The Oxford Handbook of Civil Society*. Oxford, Oxford University Press, 2011, pp. 311–23, p. 311.
[25] See Liz Disley, *Love and Forgiveness: Positive Recognition in German Idealism*. London: Pickering & Chatto, 2015.

critical if the foundations of human interaction and sociality are to be formed. The dialectic is not simply a critical tool; just as for Plato/Socrates, it is an indispensable creative tool as well. The public sphere has to work this way for genuine intersubjectivity to be possible. This is the case precisely *because* the human subject is not fully autonomous and self-sufficient—it is, as O'Neill points out, a communicative self.

In this way, it becomes clear why the state in Hegel's view is not some external apparatus acting heteronomously to restrict freedom, but is in fact the context in which freedom is possible. Nevertheless, Hegel does make a distinction between the state and civil society; they are not synonymous, as they might be in certain versions of liberalism.[26] Civil society, for Hegel, is a vital part or 'moment' of political community. Ethics on the micro-level of the family are cancelled (sublated, or *aufgehoben*), and reconfigured to work on the macro-level of public life.[27] Pelcynzski points out the historical context of Hegel's moving the emphasis from the state to civil society: it coincides, in the setting of the Industrial Revolution, with a division between political and economic power, with power centralized in the state (be that a republic or a principality) and the arguably more significant economic power in the hands of various groups in society. Thus, political and civil spheres become separated. To a great extent, in political theory terms, this historical power shift represents a shift towards something like a classical Greek polis, and the movement from the familial sphere to the public sphere is a move between *oikos* and *polis* which could be completed only by those deemed capable of participating in the *polis* (not, for example, women or slaves). Hegel's remarks on women in civil society are well documented, and not fully excused by a reference to the historical context, as Seyla Benhabib points out.[28]

What bearing does this have on considerations of autonomy? That autonomy might be compromised within a family situation, that is, that one may act in a domestic setting as something other than a fully rational and autonomous being, seems empirically correct and philosophically unproblematic, even if autonomy were to be a precondition for ethical action more generally. But it seems part of the point of a distinction between *oikos* and *polis* that a different attitude is assumed, and that the human subject should be able to represent their domestic unit in a rational manner and pursue projects relating to the ethical sphere in a way that does not interfere with others (as contrasted with the domestic sphere, where the same arrangement of individual freedoms coexisting would not be possible).

Hegel's emphasis during the crucial passages of the *Philosophy of Right* is often on sentiment or emotion, and he talks repeatedly about love, the characterizing feature of the family unit, as being subjective. But love itself, as the resolution of a process

---

[26] Cf. Zbigniew A. Pelczynski, *The State and Civil Society: Studies in Hegel's Political Philosophy.* Cambridge: Cambridge University Press, 1984, p. vii.

[27] Ibid., p. 1.

[28] Seyla Benhabib, *Situating the Self: Gender, Community, and Postmodernism in Contemporary Ethics.* New York: Psychology Press, 1992, p. 17.

of mutual recognition, is something which aims at sublating the subject/object dichotomy:

Love, therefore is the most tremendous contradiction; the understanding cannot resolve it since there is nothing more stubborn than this point of self-consciousness which is negated and which nevertheless I ought to possess as affirmative. Love is at once the producing and the resolving of this contradiction. As the resolving of it, love is unity of an ethical type.[29]

The two subjects Hegel refers to as producing this contradiction cannot be fully autonomous, in one sense at least, as they are not both acting as subject and object simultaneously. But Hegel says that love *resolves* this self-caused contradiction. Being in the family and then moving on to the civil society sphere is a movement towards this autonomy, away from the initial stages of love which display a dependence on another person that rules out full autonomy. It is a step much too far to assume that being influenced by an emotional state means that rational autonomy is impossible.

In terms of higher- and lower-order ethical frameworks, however, the first moment of *Sittlichkeit* in the form of the family is lacking, since individual moral consciousness can only be fully articulated in the context of social norms—Kant, according to Hegel, was quite wrong to think that *Moralität* and *Sittlichkeit* could be entirely separated from one another. In the final development of the dialectic, *Moralität* is comprehended within *Sittlichkeit*. Thus it is not the emotional aspect of interactions in a familial context that make rational autonomy impossible, but the lack of a social context that means individual moral action on this level will remain less than fully developed or articulated. Even at the other levels of the ethical life, civil society, and the state, *Sittlichkeit* remains at the level of ethical substance, not Spirit—it remains at the level of subjectivity. This is due to its nature as immediate:

Since self-consciousness knows itself to be a moment of the being-for-self of this [ethical] substance, it expresses the existence of the law within itself as follows: sound Reason knows immediately what is right and good. Just as it knows the law immediately, so too the law is valid for it immediately, and it says directly: 'this is right and good'—and, moreover, this particular law. The laws are determinate...filled with a significant content.[30]

The law has a social context, and is as it is only because of this social aspect. The collective ethical reality here goes far beyond a concept of a social contract or other loose agreement. At the same time, the law is given immediately, which seems as if it could constitute heteronomy, even if the source of the law is the community. This state of affairs must therefore ultimately be overcome, since it would impinge on autonomy to have the law as immediately given.

To some extent, then, the tension remains. So important is the commitment to autonomy in moral agenthood that even the communally formed *Sittlichkeit* cannot

---

[29] G.W.F. Hegel, *Elements of the Philosophy of Right*, trans. Allen Wood. Cambridge: Cambridge University Press, 1991.
[30] Ibid., §422.

serve as a fully adequate account of our moral lives. There is a high bar set for autonomy in that the sublation, on an individual level, of the subject/object dichotomy is required for an individual to be a fully functioning (moral) agent—but of course, at the same time, a social context is required for any meaningful articulation of the moral. The crucial division between the state and civil society does much to underline the social context of norms and laws, but in order for autonomy to be preserved the higher levels of abstraction involved in the interaction between *Sittlichkeit* and *Moralität* must be observed. Despite the key involvement of the social world, how can such a persistent commitment to autonomy be compatible with the postmodern idea of an incomplete, changing self? For this to be fully answered, we need to look more broadly than Hegel's account of the self and look at his system in general. This is the task of Section 12.3.

12.3. The *Aufhebung* and the Effect on the System

The apparent tension described in Sections 12.1 and 12.2 plug into a wider tension in Hegel scholarship in general. Returning to Judith Butler's *Subjects of Desire*, we can see how the scholar who first characterized the tension broadens the discussion out to Hegel's metaphysics in general:

Although Hegel is often characterized as the philosopher of totality, of systematic completeness and self-sufficient autonomy, it is not clear that the metaphysical totality he defends is a finite system. Indeed, the abiding paradox of Hegel's metaphysics seems to consist in the openness of this ostensibly all-inclusive system. For a metaphysics to be simultaneously complete and infinite means that infinity must be included in the subject itself, but 'inclusion' as a spatial relation is a poor way of describing the relationship of the infinite to the system itself.[31]

The tension in the system between different accounts of the self is just the most obvious and potentially problematic instantiation of this tension, which is actually between the finite and the infinite or, perhaps more accurately, between totality and infinity. The self is not posited as something over and above this 'metaphysical totality' which, since infinity cannot be enclosed within it, is always itself looking for a completion that can never come. Just like the human subject or self, the totality, that which is covered by any systematic approach, is incomplete and looking beyond itself. The looking beyond itself is towards the *Aufhebung* or sublation of the difference between subject and object. Alper Turken, in a recent article, reads a passage from the *Phenomenology* beside one from the *Logic* in order to demonstrate that the goal of true infinity is the elimination of this distinction.[32] The *Phenomenology* passage is as follows:

The goal lies at that point where knowledge no longer has the need to go beyond itself, that is, where knowledge works itself out, and where the concept corresponds to the object and the

---

[31] Butler, *Subjects of Desire*, p. 13.

[32] Alper Turken, 'Brandom vs. Hegel: The Relation of Normativity and Recognition to the True Infinite'. *Hegel Bulletin* 36 (2015): 225–47, 237–8.

object to the concept. Progress towards this goal is thus also unrelenting, and satisfaction is not to be found at any prior station on the way.[33]

The ultimate goal is to achieve a totality of knowledge, so that knowledge does not have to seek outside itself. Turken sees this as closely linked to the following passage from the *Encyclopedia Logic*:

[T]he Logical is to be sought in a system of thought-determinations in which the antithesis between subjective and objective (in its usual meaning) disappears.[34]

Christoph Halbig sees this approach to the subject/object dichotomy at this relatively early stage as a clear piece of evidence for its importance (that is, the importance of sublating this dichotomy or antithesis) in Hegel's system; it precedes the opposition between conceptual scheme and mind-external reality, and enables Hegel to give an informative answer to the question of how reality can be accessible to our thinking about it.[35]

Taken together, these remarks on Hegel and the references to passages in different works from different periods draw together the broadest possible central themes and considerations from his philosophy. They involve making claims about the *telos* of philosophy and knowledge, the sublation of at least three dichotomies—subject/object, appearance/reality, and totality/infinity, which of course are all themselves connected at the most fundamental level. But in moving to this level of theoretical philosophy, questions which encompass and precede metaphysics and epistemology, do we help answer the original question, which concerned the apparent tension between the 'modern' conception of the autonomy of the person, as ethical subject and more generally, and the 'postmodern' conception of the person as incomplete and changing? Does this level of abstraction help at all on the more practical level of how Hegel's apparently shifting view of the human subject fits into his philosophical system? How can the human capacity for self-legislation possibly be illuminated by meditations on infinity, the logical and the sublation of the antithesis between subject and object?

It is precisely because there is such a clear link, or perhaps lack of dividing line, between the theoretical and the practical in Hegel's system that observations on the phenomenal level can shed light on the level of totality and infinity. For further elucidation of this kind of argument, we can turn to Emmanuel Levinas' text of that name. There, Levinas observes:

To approach the other in conversation is to welcome his expression, in which at each instant he overflows the idea a thought would carry away from it. It is therefore to receive from the Other beyond the capacity of the I, which means exactly: to have the idea of infinity.[36]

---

[33] G.W.F. Hegel, *Phenomenology of Spirit*, trans. A.V. Miller, with analysis of the text and foreword by J.N. Findlay. Oxford: Clarendon Press, 1979 (1977), §80.

[34] G.W.F. Hegel, *The Encyclopedia Logic*, trans. T.F. Geraets, W.A. Suchting, and H.S. Harris. Indianapolis and Cambridge: Hackett Publishing Company, 1991, §24.

[35] Cf. Christoph Halbig, *Objektives Denken*. Stuttgart–Bad Cannstatt: Frommann-Holzboog, 2002, p. 370.

[36] Emmanuel Levinas, *Totality and Infinity*, trans. Alphonso Lingis. Pittsburgh: Duquesne University Press, 1969, p. 51.

It is precisely our relation to infinity, which must of course be related to the link between infinity and the limits of human knowledge, that defines and determines our interactions with the Other. 'To approach the other in conversation' is Levinasian jargon referring to a face-to-face encounter; the message is that we seek actual encounters with others because we are finite and thus by definition incomplete. The form of the encounter is not unimportant or arbitrary. It is not knowledge from others that we seek, and not some kind of verification of particular properties. It is precisely this in-person encounter that displays, and aims at transcending, our finite and incomplete natures. This does not interfere with our capacity for self-legislation or self-determination, since the encounter is not forced and is not aimed at serving some heteronomously dictated goal. We can determine our own actions, but that does not mean that we are capable of seeing every meaningful project to completion without encounters with other (autonomous, rational) agents. Crucially, as I have argued in this section, it is precisely because of Hegel's particular systematic commitments that the apparently contradictory situation can retain theoretical consistency: thus the self is not closed off to the Other, but rather needs him to operate fully in both a practical and an epistemological self, and nevertheless remains autonomous in the sense that is important to Kant, Hegel, and their successors.

13

Hegel's Natural Law Constructivism

Progress in Principle and in Practice

Kenneth R. Westphal

Pour être bon philosophe, il faut être sec, clair, sans illusion. Un banquier, qui a fait fortune, a une partie du caractère requis pour faire des découvertes en philosophie, c'est-a-dire pour voir clair dans ce qui est.

Stendhal[1]

13.1. Introduction

Legend has it that, in principle, Hegel's *Philosophical Outlines of Justice*—to render more idiomatically his main title—cannot afford any progress in morals, nor any progressive politics, for either of two reasons: Either his entire moral philosophy is derived *a priori* from his first principles, ultimately, from his *Science of Logic*, by inflexible, inexorable dialectical logical deduction; or alternatively his putative theory of 'justice' must simply endorse whatever lurch the *Weltgeist* next takes in its mythological self-development through world history, dragging us haplessly in tow. However ideologically useful such legends may have been—whether to the Prussian reaction, which called the embittered, aged Schelling and Schopenhauer to Berlin to root out the 'dragon-seed' of Hegelianism;[2] to Marx (1843) grappling with those same reactionary forces grown more virulent (cf. Beck 1992; Böhme and Heidenreich 1999); or to the vociferous individualist ideologues of the twentieth century[3]—these legends are literally *in*credible (Stewart 1996), though they do underscore one important point: Anyone who tries to pigeonhole Hegel's views within their own preconceived philosophical

---

[1] Quoted approvingly by Nietzsche, *Jenseits von Gut & Böse* (1886), §39.
[2] In these terms the newly crowned Friedrich Wilhelm IV instructed his minister of culture, Bunsen (1869, 2:133), to call Schelling to lecture in Berlin (1 August 1840).
[3] Esp. Popper and Isaiah Berlin; on Popper see Kaufmann (1951), on Berlin, see Wood (1990), 38–52.

taxonomy winds up with rubbish, which itself belongs on the ash heap of history. The ideological inflammations of the twentieth century ravaged philosophy, too, in ways mainstream Anglophone philosophers are only beginning to consider (Reisch 2005, 2007; Erickson et al. 2013; Westphal 2013d, 2016a, §§39–43).

I agree with many contributors to this volume that Hegel's methodology and his *Science of Logic* are important to understanding his moral philosophy. However, four related methodological precautions must be observed (§13.2). Following those observations, I consider some substantive fundamentals of Hegel's moral philosophy, central to his version of what I call 'Natural Law Constructivism' (§13.3). Thus prepared, I detail several specific regards in which Hegel's normative social morality is progressive both principally and practically (§13.4), and conclude by reflecting on Hegel's career of public activism on behalf of liberal republican reform (§13.5).[4]

13.2. Some Methodological Fundamentals

Against schematizing formalism. The first methodological observation is: Appeal to Hegel's *Science of Logic*, or to his *Encyclopaedia*, as if it were the master premiss from which follows Hegel's practical philosophy, would result in schematizing formalism, of exactly the kind for which Hegel justly criticized Schelling.[5] Instead, through immanent analysis of the phenomena pertaining to practical philosophy, Hegel must construct indirect, regressive proofs of his substantive conclusions. If such analysis and proof exhibit the kinds of structures and relations Hegel analyses abstractly in the *Science of Logic* or *Encyclopaedia*, then (and only then) has Hegel justified philosophically the relevance of his more abstract 'logical' principles to his practical philosophy. This can be done, but Hegel's regressive method also allows his moral philosophy to stand to a remarkable extent on its own.

Against petitio principii. Second, appeal to Hegel's *Science of Logic* or philosophical *Encyclopaedia* to justify an interpretation of his *Philosophical Outlines of Justice*, or to justify any of Hegel's views stated or defended in those *Outlines*, launches a justificatory regress: That interpretation or those views are thus only conditionally justified to the extent that the cited portions of Hegel's *Logic* or *Encyclopaedia* are themselves justified— together with their putative links to the points at issue in Hegel's moral philosophy. Hegel's expositors have on the whole been preoccupied with the challenges of expositing Hegel's difficult texts; few have paid significant—not to say sufficient—attention to whether or how Hegel justifies any of his philosophical views. Hegel devoted concerted, subtle, and insightful attention to fundamental issues regarding philosophical justification (Westphal 2013a), starting in the middle of the Introduction (*Einleitung*; not his

---

[4] My substantive interpretation of Hegel's normative social theory is presented in Westphal (1993), (2002), (2007), (2010); the first diagrams Hegel's institutional analysis.

[5] Unnamed but unmistakably in the Preface to the 1807 *Phenomenology* (*GW* 9:17, 36–7, 41/¶¶15, 16, 51, 56), expressly in his Lectures on the History of Philosophy (*MM* 20:443–5, 450, 452).

Preface) to the 1807 *Phenomenology*, where he restates the Pyrrhonian Dilemma of the Criterion (*GW* 9:58.12–22/¶81).

The Pyrrhonian Dilemma raises the issue of how (and how well) to justify any first-order claim, how (and how well) to justify one's criteria of justification for those first-order claims, *and* how (and how well) to justify one's meta-theory of justification for one's criteria of justification for those first-order claims. This Dilemma can be neither solved nor avoided by foundationalism, coherentism, or the many varieties of constructivism now popular in moral philosophy, because these latter all appeal to some sort of subjective factors, e.g. validity claims, desires or passions, intuitions, or affective responses. Any theoretical construction based upon such elements can only justify principles for and to whomever shares sufficiently in those (allegedly basic) elements; to whomever denies, disowns, or genuinely lacks those elements, that theory can justify nothing (Westphal 2013c, §2; 2016a).

In the Introduction to the 1807 *Phenomenology* Hegel shows that the Pyrrhonian Dilemma of the Criterion can be solved by a sophisticated account of the possibility of constructive self-criticism (Westphal 1998). However, because we are very finite semi-rational creatures, actually exercising constructive self-criticism, and successfully discriminating more from less effective self-critical assessment, further requires that we engage cogently and critically with others' critical assessments of our own reasons, reasoning, and judgments. Hegel's analysis of rational, justificatory judgment and our fallible rational competence shows that we can each *be* maximally rational and actually *justify* our best judgments rationally, only insofar as we recognize our mutual interdependence for the critical assessment of our own best judgments and their grounds and principles. Our *being* rational, so far as we are able, requires us to be public reasoners: reasoners who justify their most considered judgments on principles, grounds, and evidence which *can* be communicated to, understood by, and assessed and adopted in thought or in action by all concerned (i.e. all affected) parties, consistently with one's own judgment and action on that, and on all relevant such occasions; this is the ultimate, fundamental thesis demonstrated by Hegel's analysis of mutual recognition (Westphal 2013b). This finding raises challenging questions about how and how accurately to distinguish between critical assessment and anyone's dogmatism, defective judgment, insufficient competence, or outright deviousness. No *theory* or *method* of justification can circumvent such problems; they belong to the human condition. Identifying whether or when defective reasoning occurs, and properly assessing it and its redress, itself requires exercising critical self-assessment, which includes considering seriously the critical assessments of others—of the circumstances in question, and of one's assessment of them. This crucial thesis Hegel justifies in his analysis of 'Evil and Forgiveness', which culminates his analysis of mutual recognition and its roles in rational judgment and justification.[6]

---

[6] *PhdG, GW* 9:359.9–23, 360.31–361.4, 361.22–5, 362.21–9/¶¶666, 669, 670, 671; see Westphal (2009c).

In these regards, Hegel's analysis of rational justification further develops Kant's Critical account of the social dimensions of rational judgment, which Onora O'Neill (1992, 2004, 2015) has rightly emphasized in connection with public reason, including the modality involved in Kant's universalization tests, which is fundamental not only to Kant's moral philosophy, but throughout his Critical methodology. At the end of 'What does it Mean to Orient oneself in Thinking?' (1786), Kant responds to sceptical attacks upon reason which prefigure much of today's postmodern, neo-pragmatist, or sometimes cynical cant. Concerned about imposition of state censorship (censorship was a problem, e.g., for Humboldt's liberalism in 1792[7]), Kant highlights the close interdependence of thinking with public communication (GS 8:144). These close links are constitutive: Whatever cognitive capacities are innately ours, we only develop and learn to use through education—both formal and informal—by others who provide information, skills, methods, practice, and critical assessment (cf. Herman 2007, 130–53). To 'communication' belong all publications and social sources of information, including one's education, without which one cannot at all become a competent thinker or agent. Kant stressed that thinking cogently (mit welcher Richtigkeit; 'how accurately') requires more than merely thinking: for us fallible, limited human cognizers, distinguishing between genuinely cogent and merely apparently cogent thinking is vital, and requires communicating with others. Communicating with others is required to assess whether our thoughts, as we happen to have formulated and integrated them into judgments which we affirm or deny, are formulated and integrated by us as they ought to form a proper, accurate, and rationally justifiable judgment (KdrV A261–3/B317–19).

Whereas Kant's modal universalizability stresses the positive requirement to judge and to act only on the basis of principles and sufficient justifying grounds which can be addressed to and adopted by all others, Hegel highlights the complementary requirement that we must each listen to and seriously consider the principles, grounds, justifications, and conclusions others provide us. In 'The Animal Kingdom of the Spirit and Humbug, or the matter at hand' (Das geistige Tierreich und der Betrug, oder die Sache selbst; GW 9:216–28/§§397–417), Hegel draws the devastating reductio ad absurdum within the intellectual realm (specifically the literary realm of self-styled romantic geniuses), parallel to Hobbes' state of nature. Hegel's 'spiritual' parallel skewers Romantic—though likewise cynical or egoistic—self-infatuation which prompts individuals to declare that whatever most concerns him or herself is the most important concern for any and everyone, while consequently neglecting their comparable, equally (un)justified declarations. No communication, no significant expression can possibly be made under such presumptions. Accuracy and cogency are the first casualties of this verbal melee, just as Kant anticipated. Public reason requires much more than divulging one's thinking, including one's justifying reasons, publicly. Public reason

---

[7] Humboldt's Limits of State Action (1851) was composed in 1792; see the editor's introduction (v–viii) about problems posed by censors in Berlin.

requires justifying one's assessment on grounds, evidence, and principles which *all* others can understand, assess, adopt, and use consistently in thought and in action—including consistently with one's own thoughts, judgments, and actions on that occasion, and on all such occasions. This does not require that others in fact do so; it requires that one's own reasons, reasoning, judgments, and justifications are such that they *can* do so, and that we and they *do* pay attention to others' reasons and reasoning. That is the operative modality in Kant's and in Hegel's analysis of this social *conditio sine qua non* of rational justification (in non-formal, substantive domains). This *conditio sine qua non* does not (in many cases) itself *suffice* for rational justification, but typically it suffices to rule out inaccurate, poorly reasoned, or self-serving judgments or rationalizations. That is quite a lot from a universalizability test! Once those defective judgments are discarded, we can then assess the accuracy and cogency of the evidence, analysis, principles, and reasoning purporting to justify credible judgments on the matter at hand.

Conceptual Analysis versus *Conceptual Explication*. It is highly significant that Kant (*KdrV* A727–31/B755–9) and Carnap (1950, 1–18) both distinguish between conceptual analysis and conceptual explication, in the same way, in these same terms, for very much the same reasons, and to very much the same effect. Conceptual analysis aims to provide necessary and sufficient conditions for the use of a concept or principle. These strong modal claims can be satisfied in only two kinds of case: Within purely formal domains, or with regard to arbitrarily constructed concepts. However, in any substantive domain—whether within philosophy proper, or regarding either morals or empirical knowledge—we are unable to ascertain the completeness of any purported conceptual analysis. Kant and Carnap both stress that conceptual explication is inherently partial (incomplete) and aims to improve upon the explicated term or phrase, in order better to facilitate inquiry within the original context of usage. The (purported) method of conceptual analysis confronts the paradox of analysis undiluted: How can any mere analysis of a concept be both informative and yet also be recognized to be adequate or correct? Either we understand the concept in question, and so can determine the completeness and accuracy of its analysis, which accordingly is uninformative; or the analysis of the concept is informative, but we lack any adequate basis for determining its accuracy and completeness. The best responses to this paradox all replace conceptual analysis with conceptual explication—if implicitly and so not in these terms (cf. Hare 1960). Kant and Carnap both rightly insist that in all non-formal domains we must be methodologically cautious and claim only partially to explicate key concepts or principles, sufficient for the purposes of present inquiry, where the adequacy of any conceptual explication must be assessed within possible contexts of its actual use, *not* in merely imagined contexts of its (allegedly) possible use!

The fundamental connections of Hegel's philosophy to Kant's are not metaphysical, they are instead *methodological*. Having demonstrated by strictly internal critique that Transcendental Idealism is untenable, Hegel sought to revamp Kant's Critical account of justifiable rational judgment, both in theoretical and in moral philosophy

(Westphal 2009b). Hegel adopted Kant's key distinction between conceptual analysis and conceptual explication; he adopted Kant's fallibilism about rational justification, both within philosophical methodology, and in any philosophical account of empirical knowledge or moral philosophy. Hegel adopted and vigorously developed Kant's rudiments of a social and historical account of rational justification within non-formal domains; and he adopted and independently justified Kant's insightful semantics of singular, specifically *cognitive* reference (Westphal 2014). In sum, Hegel was the first, and is still one of the very most sophisticated pragmatic realists (Westphal 2015a, 2015b).

Because conceptual analysis only provides better knowledge of classificatory content (conceptual 'intension' or linguistic 'meaning'), whereas solving any substantive philosophical perplexity requires instead conceptual explication, *within* actual contexts of use, responsible philosophy must be both systematic and historical, because (as J.L. Austin and Wilfrid Sellars also realized[8]) the relevant issues are so easily obscured or distorted by incautious formulation; even if we reformulate our issues in the formal mode of speech, we must carefully consider how the many and the wise have discussed and formulated these issues, in order better to understand and assess our own and others' formulations presently, and in the future. This, Hegel recognized, is central to the pragmatic, social, and historical character of reconsidering, refining, improving, and, so far as we are now able, justifying our locutions, principles, and accounts of any substantive issue we address (Westphal 2010–11).

Fallibilist accounts of rational justification are fundamentally historical and social, yet such accounts *can*, Hegel recognized, justify realism about the objects of empirical knowledge and strict objectivity about basic moral norms. In all non-formal, substantive domains, rational justification is in principle fallibilist (Westphal 2013b, 2016c). According to any tenable fallibilism, a classification, judgment, claim, or statement is justified so long and insofar as: (1) it is more adequate to its tasks than any alternative statement, (2) it is adequate to its designated range of use or phenomena, and (3) it remains adequate to its domain(s) as its use is renewed upon new, relevant occasions, which may include changed circumstances, information, or context. These results Hegel demonstrates in the *Phenomenology of Spirit* (Westphal 2009a); he develops his systematic philosophy in detailed critical consideration of relevant empirical phenomena in history and in the natural and social sciences (political economy). In all of these regards, Hegel further developed Kant's account of the discriminatory character of all identifying judgments (within substantive domains): Apprehending what something *is* requires comprehending how it could be otherwise, together with how it *ought* to be.

Realizing Hegel's concepts. The final methodological preliminary is an important terminological observation: Hegel adopted a key term and issue from Kant and from Tetens. Tetens (1775, 48, cf. 60–1, 80–1) coined this usage: to 'realize' (*realisieren*) a

---

[8] Sellars states this outright; Austin's student, Graham Bird, told me recently that Austin advised wide-ranging study of philosophy and allied disciplines. This attitude and practice undergirds the cogency and focus of Austin's philosophical assays, qualities ever more rare in today's overspecialized philosophical scene.

concept is to show that some actual instances of it can be located and identified by us. This task is crucial to show that any *a priori* concepts we might possess, we can accurately and justifiedly *use* in actual or humanly possible judgments *about* relevant particular instances we have located, identified, and individuated. Hegel uses this term *in exactly this sense* throughout his corpus (Westphal 2015a, 2015b, 2016d); it is central to his pragmatic realism.[9]

Hegel's methods and results are speculative, not in the current sense of empirically unfounded fantasies, but in the original, etymological sense of seeing into how things are. Hegel was the first who understood that in non-formal domains, rational justification is inherently fallible, *and* that this fallibility is consistent with, and ultimately justifies, realism about the objects of empirical knowledge, and strict objectivity about basic moral norms. Central to Hegel's methods and results is his insight that comprehending what something is, what it can be, and what it ought to be, are mutually interdependent, integral cognitive achievements.

13.3. Some Normative Fundamentals

Hegel's functionalist moral philosophy. Hegel's analysis of social practices and institutions is deeply functional, in ways which allow us to argue that a form of institution he did not consider may equally well, or perhaps better, fulfil the function(s) Hegel ascribed to those historical institutions he considered.[10]

Sittlichkeit and practical anthropology. The normativity of Hegel's practical philosophy is underwritten by the principles and methods he adopts from Kant's *Metaphysics of Morals*. Hegel's account of *Sittlichkeit* or 'ethical life'—that is, Part III of his *Outlines*—provides (in effect) the 'practical anthropology' Kant acknowledged is required to apply his *a priori* 'metaphysical principles' of morals to the human condition, and to us within it, which Kant had relegated to an unwritten 'appendix' to his *Metaphysics of Morals*. Both Kant and Hegel are ardent republicans (note the lower case 'r'), at a more fundamental methodological level than any other practical philosophy, for both recognize that no action can be morally justified if sufficient justifying reasons for that action cannot be provided to *all* affected parties, such that they can consistently adopt the same principle and reasons in thought or in action, consistent with one's own thought and action on that occasion (and all other relevant such occasions).

Natural Law Constructivism. In this regard, both Kant and Hegel join Rousseau in following Hume's innovative response to Hobbes' fundamental social coordination problems. Concerns about human motives (greed or malice) are tertiary to the two

---

[9] Hegel's usage and its derivation from Tetens and Kant has been widely neglected (*e.g.*, by Sans 2004), which leads to the presumption that Hegel's concepts and principles are supposed to 'realize' themselves into determinate existence *and* sequence out of (*ab initio*) absolutely nothing. (I do not say Hegel uses the term '*realisiren*' only in this sense; he also uses it in two other senses, but context makes clear which sense is relevant.)

[10] On Hegel's functionalism, see deVries (1991).

most fundamental points Hobbes makes with his analysis of the non-governmental state of nature. First: Simple, innocent (non-malicious) *ignorance* of what belongs to whom suffices—under conditions of some population density, Rousseau added—to generate total mutual interference. Second: Any solution to this fundamental coordination problem must in principle be *public*, so that everyone can *know* what belongs to whom, so that each and all *can* act accordingly. Reconsidering Hobbes' two key points, Hume recognized that a natural law theory can identify and justify strictly objective basic moral norms, while prescinding altogether from issues about moral realism and human motivation. Hume observed:

Though the rules of justice be artificial, they are not arbitrary. Nor is the expression improper to call them Laws of Nature; if by natural we understand what is common to any species, or even if we confine it to mean what is inseparable from the species.   (*T* 3.2.1.19)

Hume was the first to recognize that the most basic laws of justice can literally be artificial, our artefacts, and yet *not* be arbitrary, because certain basic principles and practices constituting justice are utterly non-optional for us very finite, mutually interdependent beings. Thus drawing the fangs of Socrates' question to Euthyphro (*Euthyphro* 10de), Hume articulated and argued for the most basic principles and practices required to solve Hobbes' central coordination problem. These elementary 'rules of justice', Hume showed, include publicly acknowledged principles and titles to acquire, possess, use, and exchange things and promised actions, together with sufficient social institutions to make known these principles and titles, to monitor compliance with them, and to make proper and no more than sufficient redress of infractions (Westphal 2016a, esp. §§4–11, 44).

However, Hume neglected issues about political legitimacy, and most issues of normative justification. Rousseau recognized that the *conditio sine qua non* of legitimate social and political principles and institutions is to proscribe injustice by instituting this further principle: No one is entitled to acquire the kind or extent of power or wealth so as to command unilaterally the decision of another person to do one's bidding (Neuhouser 2000, 55–81; Westphal 2013c). This is Rousseau's Independence Requirement, familiar today as the requirement of 'non-domination'.

Objectivity and practical anthropology. Implicit though central to Hume's, Rousseau's, and Kant's Natural Law Constructivism is this insight into developing a sound moral constructivism, which articulates the core principles of a natural law theory, though without invoking any version of moral realism: Rather than appeal to subjective 'basic elements' typical of contemporary moral constructivisms, they instead appeal to objective facts about our very finite form of semi-rational embodied agency, and about our basic circumstances of action here on Earth. Appeal to such objective, physiological, anthropological, and geographical facts about our finite form of agency is central to Kant's 'practical anthropology'. These are, broadly speaking, anthropological facts, *not* 'moral facts' (whatever those might be), yet they are *morally relevant* facts, because there is so much each of us can do either to exploit, respect, or minister to them. That is one key insight developed by Natural Law Constructivism. The second is the universality requirement of Kant's Critical methodology. The third is Rousseau's *conditio sine qua non* for the legitimacy of any social arrangements: To respect in theory and in practice the moral and civil independence and liberty of *each* and hence *every* member of society (Westphal 2013c). These three principles form the methodological core of 'Natural Law Constructivism' (Westphal 2016a). Taken together, they suffice to identify and to justify normatively the most basic principles and practices of morality. Kant adopted outright and further elaborated Rousseau's independence requirement (*MdS* 6:257–8); its violation is proscribed by Kant's universalizability test.

Practical anthropology, Sittlichkeit and the structure of moral philosophy. An important difference between Hegel's and Kant's moral philosophies is this: Kant regarded the scope of his Critical *Metaphysics of Morals* to concern the fundamental *a priori* principles of justice and virtue. Kant recognized throughout his moral philosophy that these principles, by themselves, do not specify any specific moral injunctions. Specifying any of our duties also requires a 'practical anthropology' which specifies basic features of our finite form of rational agency and very general conditions of our action. Kant regarded this practical anthropology as a 'proper appendix' to his *Metaphysics of Morals* (*TL* §45, *GS* 6:469.8–12), not an integral part of it, despite the fact that his *Metaphysics of Morals* 'must' often consider the specific nature of human beings (*MdS*, Einl. §II; *GS* 6:216–7) and must be applied to specific cases (*TL* §45, *GS* 6:464).

Hegel's infamous charge of 'empty formalism' against 'the moral point of view' in fact restates Kant's own view of his *a priori* principles of morals, in abstraction from practical anthropology. Directly in this connection, after extolling Kant's analysis of freedom as autonomy of the will and as the sole and proper basis of moral law (*Rph* §§133, 135R, cf. §4), Hegel takes it upon himself to *rebut* the threat of 'empty formalism' and to *preserve* and to further develop Kant's moral principles by developing his very detailed practical anthropology (as it were), titled '*Sittlichkeit*' or 'ethical life' (Westphal 2009c).

The social and historical realization of freedom. In Hegel's moral philosophy the key concept to be 'realized' is the concept of freedom (cf. *Rph* §§5–7, 127–8, 141). In this connection Hegel exploits an important feature of customs and the development of customary social practices, including economic practices (by which 'custom' was transmuted into 'customer') namely: Customs are not merely habitual, but are intelligent activities (cf. Ferguson 1787; Tönnies 1909; 1961). When aggregated across groups, customs often have important unintended consequences for such social phenomena as the distribution and division of labour, land use, law, regulations, privileges, differential advantages, and the common wealth, be it weal or woe of individuals, families, or the commonwealth (i.e. *res publica*). Not only are these activities often intelligent, they also typically serve to specify and to realize individual freedom to act, including individual innovations. The development and the individual adoption of social customs literally *customizes* whatever needs, ends, desires, or motives we have due simply to our human psychophysiology. Social custom thus marks, Hegel stresses, a decisive advance in human freedom, both collectively and individually (§§174, 175, 185, 187R, 193, 194 & R).

'Realizing' freedom in individual action must be understood both in Tetens's and in our common-sense senses. Whenever we consider how to act, we avail ourselves of conceptual and material resources, together with a variety of procedures, permissions, entitlements, and prohibitions. All of these are socially constituted, as is our knowledge and understanding of these provisions and how and when to use them (or not). Unlike social determinists and holists, however, Hegel recognized that individuals and the group(s) to which they belong are mutually *inter*dependent for their existence and characteristics. Social practices exist only in and through individuals who participate in, perpetuate, or *modify* them as occasion, need, and inventiveness allow and require (Hegel 1994b). Hegel's social ontology may be called 'moderate collectivism'.[11]

The centrality of social practices, including the economy, to Hegel's moral philosophy may suggest that he espouses either historicist relativism or communitarianism. Neither is correct: Hegel's moral philosophy combines these issues about free individual action, social custom, *and* the principles of Natural Law Constructivism (Westphal 2007). This is why Hegel's book is a normative theory of justice, a philosophy of law—both moral law and jurisprudence, which integrates both natural law and political science, as advertised in his subtitle: *oder Naturrecht und Staatswissenschaft im Grundrisse.* In Hegel's uniquely powerful combination of these resources, public reason is central, precisely because its exercise is decentralized (Westphal 2016b). The core principles of right action identified and justified by Natural Law Constructivism are human necessities and trans-social standards of justice, yet they can be satisfied, specified, and institutionalized in a wide range of social practices, suited to the geographical, historical, and technological conditions of a society.

13.4. Hegel's Reformist Principles in Practice

The conditio sine qua non of social and political legitimacy. Kant built Rousseau's Independence Requirement into the core of his theory of justice as the sole innate right to freedom (*MdS* 6:257–8), but then subverted its republican implications by distinguishing passive from active citizens, where the latter are male property owners (*RL* §46 + Remark). In a brilliant inversion of the traditional property requirement for suffrage (voting rights), Hegel argued instead that, because freedom of action requires disposing over at least some goods, every adult is entitled to some property.

---

[11] Hegel's social ontology must be borne in mind to understand properly his contrasting two approaches to normative social theory (*Rph* §156Z); though his brief formulation may suggest otherwise, Hegel does not contrast radical social holism to radical atomic individualism. Rawls (2000, 362) mistakes Hegel's view by assimilating Hegel's contrast to a familiar though mistaken dichotomy. On Hegel's social ontology, see Westphal (2003, §§32–7).

The *conditio sine qua non* of political legitimacy and social justice according to Hegel, like Rousseau and Kant, is the requirement of moral, civil, and financial independence (*Rph* §§124R, 230, 241–2, 244–5). Because modern nation states with their commercial economies occupy contiguous bounded territories, and have undermined and replaced subsistence production by families (*Rph* §§181, 217, 241–2), they are obligated to secure and facilitate for each and every citizen the opportunity to obtain sufficient livelihood *and* social recognition as citizens in good standing (*Rph* §§241, 244, cf. §§238Z, 244Z).

Hegel stresses that poverty is not only an economic, but also a social status. Those least well off economically within society must nevertheless be *in society*, not merely within its territory, *as* recognized, contributing members of society—citizens in good standing. Hegel's minimum for good standing is expressly relative within each society (*Rph* §244), rather than to some bare subsistence minimum. Whether an economy achieves Pareto optimality simply does not settle (because it does not address) whether those least well off in that economy are, or are not, contributing members of society in good standing, insofar as they are morally, civilly, and financially independent to the extent that in practice as well as in theory they are at liberty to agree to cooperate with others, or not, as they choose. The statistical fact that some individuals may abuse such liberty is no ground for denying to anyone these basic opportunities to attain and to retain good standing as a citizen. Once the territory is closed and access to self-subsistence denied, societies owe to all members the rights, opportunities, and privileges, as well as the responsibilities, of citizenship.

About moral, civil, and financial security, and the good standing of each citizen, Hegel was crystal clear: Poverty is an injustice to one class (*Klasse*) committed by another (*Rph* §§243–5), and must be rectified. He partially addressed though did not solve this problem; yet his reference to Scotland's blue shirts (*Rph* §245R) is significant (Waszek 1984). Note, however, that Hegel's principles and institutions lend themselves very well to J.M. Keynes' policy of government expansion of public works during economic contraction (and contraction of public works during economic expansion). This is a significant regard in which Hegel's principles and institutions afford social and moral progress.

These views were institutionalized by Johan Vilhelm Snellman (1806–1881), an Hegelian central to founding and developing modern Finland. His liberal, moderately collective republicanism is fundamental to Finnish politics, society, and culture, and typifies the ardently republican political and social policies and practices of Nordic and Scandinavian republics. Snellman's statue sits before the entrance to the National Bank of Finland (yes, the bank!); his portrait graced the 500 maarka banknote until Finland adopted the euro (1999). The Scandinavian and Nordic countries are splendid examples that justice—including far higher levels of social justice—can be achieved, consistently with an excellent standard of living and ample rewards for enterprising, responsible entrepreneurs. They are also splendid empirical examples of Schultz's (2001) theoretical demonstration that economic efficiency can only be achieved within moral constraints—a welcome corroboration of the classical understanding of political economy as a moral science, not merely a human but a normative science (cf. Ferguson 1787; Devas 1901).

Corporations, law, and liberty. Hegel's moderate collectivism undergirds his advocacy of his version of Montesquieu's and de Tocqueville's 'corporative individualism' (George 1922)—a view shared by T.H. Green (1883) and by Dewey (1922, 1930). Information transmitted *via* markets is important, but only concerns select features of economic production, consumption, and distribution. Production, consumption, and distribution also produce non-market benefits and burdens, including employment patterns; household weal or woe for employees, employers, and managers at all levels; and also waste, habitat destruction, pollution, and human dislocation as labour distributions and production technologies change. Liberal forms of moderate collectivism recognize the vital roles of proper government, law, and non-governmental agencies within civil society to monitor, facilitate, ameliorate, or correct good or ill effects of economic activities, as classical Scottish political economists—including Smith (Rothschild and Sen 2006)—recognized.

Legitimate positive (statute) law codifies and protects those social practices, especially economic practices, required to facilitate and protect individual security, freedom of action, and prospects of earning one's livelihood (*Rph* §§209–12, 218, 219; cf. §§187R, 249). Hegel's Administration of Justice (*Rechtspflege*) is charged with monitoring the effectiveness of statute law and proposing revised legislation as needed to better serve and protect individual freedom and prospects of welfare through successful, legitimate individual actions (*Rph* §§298, 299R). Hegel expressly adopts and further develops Montesquieu's view that positive laws are justified on the basis of their systematic interconnection within present social circumstances (*Rph* §§3R, 212), adding that promulgating codified law contributes to informing people about the structure of their social context of action, so that they may deliberate, decide, and act accordingly (§§132R, 209, 211R, 215; cf. 228R). Hence law must be codified and publicized in the national language (§216) and judicial proceedings must be public (§§224, 228R). All of these are institutional contributions to progress regarding how and how well our legal code and institutions serve justice, individual liberty, and prosperity, especially insofar as these are necessary for revising the law as social conditions change (*Rph* §298).

This holds too for constitutional law. As a bulwark against partisan meddling, Hegel insisted that the constitution ought to be *regarded* as permanent (*Rph* §273R). Yet he well knew that, even when so regarded, a people can in practice revise its legal, social, and political institutions to achieve significant and progressive constitutional reform over generations (*Rph* §§273R, 298 + Z; cf. Hegel 1817; Jamme 1986). This accords fully with Hegel's fallibilist, pragmatic realism (see Section 13.3), and underscores one of the virtues of Natural Law Constructivism (see Section 13.3).

Ethnicity, religion, and individual rights. Hegel insisted that citizenship is a human right, regardless of religion, ethnicity, or national origin (*Rph* §209R); in this Hegel was ahead of his time. Hegel has been faulted for not listing basic rights (Lübbe-Wolff 1986). Hegel did not list them all together in one paragraph, easily spotted by the censors, but he identified and argued strongly in favour of fundamental civil rights and freedoms of person, belief, property, profession, and trade (*Rph* §§35, 36, 38, 41–9, 57, 62R, 66, 206, 207, 209R, 252, 270R)—each considered in its proper systematic place, all of which accord with, and are justified by, Hegel's republican principles of Natural Law Constructivism.

While Hegel expressly repudiated the anti-Semitism common even to his liberal contemporaries, he shared their sexism. Though Hegel recognized women could acquire education (*Rph* §166Z), he did not transcend traditional patriarchy. Apparently, Émile du Châtalet (who translated Newton's very difficult *Principia* into French; 1756, 2nd ed. 1759), Olympe de Gouges (1791) and Anne Louise Germaine de Staël-Holstein ('Madame de Staël') appeared to Hegel too exceptional to occasion his reconsideration, though the contrast between Antigone (*Rph* §166R) and the subsequent advent of personal individuality through Christianity (*Rph* §185) provides sufficient basis for reconsidering women's rational agency and gender equality (cf. Hoy 2009). If we now understand that, and how, women are other and much more than half-men, Hegel's account of the family can be suitably revised, based fundamentally as it is on deep love and commitment between two adults, to the well-functioning of their joint household and to their children's upbringing, education, and well-being. At least we know Hegel was a devoted husband and father, and included his illegitimate first son, Karl, in the family. As for slavery—in 1821 still legal practice in the USA (*Rph* §270R n.2)—Hegel condemned it as an illegitimate abomination (*Rph* §57R).[12]

Hegel's rejection of open democratic plebiscite has drawn the undue ire of liberals. Hegel's objections to such electoral procedures presciently foresee all the weaknesses which have come to infect, e.g. the electoral process in the USA. Hegel's rejection of such procedures is not merely consistent with his staunch republicanism, it is required and justified by it. Hayek is correct that markets are systems of communication, but Hegel and the Scottish political economists are correct that markets are very imperfect communication channels, even within the socially restricted range of information they treat as relevant. Production, consumption, and distribution also produce non-market benefits and burdens, including employment patterns; household weal or woe for employees, employers, and managers at all levels; as also waste, habitat destruction, pollution, and human dislocation as labour distributions and production technologies change. Hegel's corporate system of representation is designed to underscore and make manifest the joint interests— and the joint achievements—of labour and management throughout a republic's economy (cf. Heiman 1971). The virtues of Hegel's system of representation are underscored by considering two problems (§§4.4, 4.5).

---

[12] Regarding Hegel's interest in the Haitian revolution, see Buck-Morss (2009), but cf. Hofheimer (2001).

Factory production and political education. In concluding the first Book of his *Inquiry into the Nature and Causes of the Wealth of Nations*, Smith observed the following about industrialized factory labour:

> Though the interest of the labourer is strictly connected with that of the society, he is incapable either of comprehending that interest or of understanding its connection with his own. His condition leaves him no time to receive the necessary information, and his education and habits are commonly such as to render him unfit to judge even though he was fully informed.
>
> (Smith 1784, 1:11; 1811, 2:396)

In his early work, *The Limits of State Action* (1792, published posthumously), Wilhelm von Humboldt wondered:

> When will the man arise to do for legislation what Rousseau did for education, and draw our attention from mere external, physical results, to the inner enculturation of mankind?
>
> (Humboldt 1851, 80; *GS* (1903), 1:162; (1969), 68; tr. Burrow, emended)

Both Smith's and Humboldt's concerns about the relations between the division of labour, culture, and enculturation (*Bildung*) attracted widespread intellectual interest in the German lands (Pascal 1962).

Although industrialization developed in Germany after his passing, Hegel and his contemporaries were very well informed about industrialization from the English model and from Scottish political economy, which expressly forms a major basis of Hegel's *Philosophical Outlines of Justice* (*Rph* §189R).[13] Hegel's unequivocal advocacy of Rousseau's Independence Condition requires restructuring labour so that workers can obtain 'the necessary information … education and habits', as Smith says, required to understand and assess political matters. The central aim of Hegel's corporate system of representation is *educative*. In addition to incorporated cities, towns, churches, or hospitals, there is to be one corporation for each branch of the economy which includes both management and labour. Hegel expects representatives to be chosen by corporate membership due to their expertise and capabilities, exhibited within corporation affairs. These representatives enter the lower chamber of Hegel's Estates Assembly. Hegel expects corporate representatives to the Estates Assembly to function, centrally, as conduits of information in both directions, from their membership *via* the Assembly to the rest of society (including government and economy), and from the rest of society back to their membership.

This arrangement for political representation first puts the legal and civil services of government, performed on behalf of the *res publica*, under the purview of all citizens. This is central to achieving individual autonomy within a complex commercial society. Hegel's system of political representation is expressly designed to insure that wealthy

---

[13] Hegel mentions Smith, Say, and Riccardo (§189R); Chamely (1963, 1965, 1967a, 1967b) demonstrates Hegel's study of Steuart's work. On Hegel's knowledge and use of Scottish political economy, see Waszek (1988); Plant (1973, 57ff.) first brought Chamely's work to my notice. See also Plant (1984).

entrepreneurs can be recognized within society for their contributions to general welfare—the *common*wealth—and to insure that they recognize that their own wealth is but their share within the commonwealth (cf. Plant 1980, Walton 1984). Precisely because the economy, law, and public regulation must be closely and carefully integrated, political representation is to insure that all sectors of society and all branches of the economy are represented within public political deliberations—and conversely that every citizen is represented politically.

The failure in principle of systems of district representation to include *all* segments of society and the economy undergirds Hegel's chief objection to open plebiscites:

The idea that those communities which are already present in the circles [of civil society] can be split up again into a collection of individuals as soon as they enter the sphere of politics—*i.e.* the sphere of the *highest concrete universality*—involves separating civil and political life from each other and leaves political life hanging, so to speak, in the air; for its basis is then merely the abstract individuality of arbitrary will and opinion, and is thus grounded only on contingency rather than on a foundation which is *stable* and *legitimate* in and for itself. (*Rph* §303R)

Since 1821 we have learnt all too much about how and how easily open plebiscites can be manipulated by the most vocal, aggressive, or sly factions (cf. Herman and Chomsky 1988). Hegel's system of representation guards against that, and provides unprecedented channels for regularizing the transmission, assessment, and use of vital economic, political, and social information. Hegel's system of political representation is designed to maximize and to regularize both transparency and accountability. His system can easily be made fully democratic by introducing universal suffrage via corporate membership, once it has achieved its first principal objective: Political education and participation of *all* citizens. Uneducated electors are demagogues' playthings; let 'liberal' democrats do better before criticizing Hegel's ardently republican proposals.

Lohnarbeiter. Hegel notes one group of men lacking corporation membership: Day labourers (*Lohnarbeiter*; *Rph* §252R). Since Hegel bases political representation on corporate membership, day labourers lack political representation. Thus they are not integrated into Hegel's society. That is a significant omission, but its significance is easily inflated, and the omission is not hard to remedy.

Bernard Cullen (1988, 23) contends that corporate membership in Hegel's view is quite restricted, since it excludes day labourers, who do not work under contract, and includes only guild masters. He disputes Knox's (and Nisbet's) rendering of Hegel's '*Meister*' as 'master of a craft'. He takes Hegel's term instead to be a direct appropriation of Smith's 'master', that is, capitalist employer. Cullen confuses and overstates the issue. Smith contrasts 'master' with 'men', as between an employer or entrepreneur and wage labourers. Smith's own usage is uncommon; he adapts an honorific term from feudalism to describe more favourably the new, widely detested capitalist. Hegel's analysis of corporate membership and functions is designed to modify fundamentally the economic categories initially established in the commercial 'system of needs'. Smith's 'masters' are capitalists who typically believed in unregulated markets and opposed the sorts of regulation and association paradigmatic of Hegelian corporate membership.

In his analysis of poverty and corporate membership, Hegel's main concern is not the contrast between the two economic classes of employers and employees, but rather the contrast between '*Meister*' and '*Arme*' (poor) or '*Pöbel*' (rabble). Hegel's '*Meister*', who enjoy corporate membership, are merely required to have a stable income derived from their craft or profession (§§252R, 253). Meeting that requirement does not require being master of a *guild*, nor owner of a factory! Knox's and Nisbet's translation is accurate. On the other hand, Smith's contrast term 'men' (employees) corresponds not at all to Hegel's contrasting terms, '*Pöbel*' or '*Arme*', especially in view of Hegel's lectures of 1824–5 (Ilting 4:608) distinguishing between '*Proletarier*', '*Arme*', and '*Pöbel*'. Hegel's whole concern is to *avoid* allowing workers to decline into a rabble. Appealing to Smith's 'master' confuses rather than clarifies Hegel's terms, and Cullen merely asserts his conviction to the contrary.

Cullen (1988, 32) contends that the 'logic of Hegel's analysis is inescapable: those who work for wages are deemed ineligible for corporate membership, and they are thereby excluded from political participation in the Assembly of Estates'. Hegel deems casual day labourers to be ineligible for corporate membership because they do not regularly derive their livelihood from one branch of industry. Thus they cannot be assumed to have stable interest in that industry, nor to share the interests of that industry over the course of their working lives. That kind of shared interest is the cornerstone of Hegel's corporate political representation. However, the implication of Hegel's Natural Law Constructivism is equally inescapable: Those who live in society can only be fully free and autonomous if they have (*inter alia*) political representation. Political representation is a fundamental republican right of *all* citizens. Omitting day labourers from representation is thus a major blemish for Hegel's political principles and proposals.

There are two straightforward solutions. One is to recognize what soon became established economic fact, that labourers typically work in the same industry, indeed in the same factory, on an ongoing basis. Once that regularity is established in an economy, then day labour is no longer so casual, and merits recognition as regular employment through labour contracts and, ultimately, through corporate membership and representation. The second measure addresses those who remain casual labourers, who frequently shift jobs and industries or who work on a daily or other brief, temporary basis. These workers deserve special attention, since one of Hegel's most fundamental principles is that people can be free only if they can regularly plan and reliably achieve their legitimate ends. Casual work is not, on the whole, a regular or reliable way of earning a living.[14] The proper Hegelian solution would be to establish a

---

[14] In view of Cullen's remarks it is important to observe that one owner of a four-storey house in the old town centre of Hann.Münden (Hannoverisch Münden) was a *Lohnarbeiter*. This may be exceptional, due in part to the exceptional economic circumstances of Hann.Münden (where three major rivers converge), but it suffices to caution against hasty assumptions about socio-economic standing and poverty. On the

government-sponsored agency to aid such workers by organizing and regularizing their job search and, wherever possible, to provide job training and placement in regular jobs. This agency would have to be government-sponsored, because those to whom it ministers don't have a commercial base to support their organization. This agency would also have to serve as a channel for their political representation, to insure that their interests are represented in the legislature, and to insure that insofar as possible, casual labourers are politically informed. Such social agencies are not merely possible in principle, in practice many such 'workfare' agencies now exist which could easily be adapted to Hegel's corporate system of representation.

13.5. Hegel's Progressive Politics in Practice

Hegel's first publication (1798) was a political treatise, translated anonymously from the French Swiss J.J. Cart, who had anonymously published 'Confidential Letters on the prior legal relations between *Pays de Vaud* and Bern', which Hegel annotated extensively. Hegel's translation was a deliberate attempt to expose obsolete feudal relations which still ruled Germanic lands. Hegel's Prefaces to the three editions of his philosophical *Encyclopaedia* (1817, 1822, 1831) become more emphatically religious. This has been taken as indicting Hegel's growing conservatism. To the contrary, Hegel did all he could as an author to outflank the rising religious conservatism, by using the same tactic as in his *Philosophical Outlines of Justice*, by demonstrating and using superior knowledge and more cogent interpretation of his opponent's chosen primary source materials: in the former case, Christian scripture, in the latter, Roman law. The Crown Prince, Friedrich Wilhelm III, greatly favoured the 'Historical School' of jurisprudence led by Carl von Savigny, also professor in Berlin. The key strategy of historical jurisprudence is to legitimate present law by deriving it from historical Roman law. Not only did Hegel highlight the genetic fallacy committed by this method, he pointed out that it actually *de*legitimates current law, because the circumstances which generated its Roman predecessor are long since vanished (*Rph* §3R). In the many (published) footnotes to his *Philosophical Outlines of Justice* Hegel fights a pitched battle against the Historical School, citing all sorts of quirks and absurdities with equal historical pedigree within Roman law to those provisions selectively favoured by that School. Hegel knew Roman law at least as well as his historicist adversaries.

Hegel advocated constitutional monarchy with a written constitution (*Rph* §273), very much a progressive stand on a burning issue of the day (Lübbe-Wolff 1981). Friedrich Wilhelm III repeatedly promised a written constitution, but only condescended to one after the 1848 revolts.[15] The last publication Hegel saw to print was his

---

other side of the ledger, while understandable, it is very regrettable that the former museum in Berlin-Mitte for the history of the working class movement is long since closed. It had much valuable detail about the labour and living conditions of working families in central Europe over several centuries.

[15] On these revolts, see Beck (1992), Böhme and Heidenreich (1999).

unsparing assessment of the English Reform Bill, published under his own name in the main government publicity organ, the *Allgemeine preußische Staats-Zeitung* (1831, Nr. 115–16, 118). In it Hegel grandly contrasts the juridical achievements of political and constitutional reform on the European continent to the hopelessly muddled confusion of merely positive (statutory, and to the extent they are unjustifiable, merely statutory) legal rights and privileges thwarting necessary political and constitutional reforms in England. The political and juridical conditions in England remained feudal—as they also did legally in contemporaneous Prussia. The Prussian crown did not miss the obvious parallel Hegel drew—and surely neither did Hegel's reading public; the Crown interdicted publication at mid-point. The remainder of Hegel's article was printed and circulated privately; the whole was published in 1835, in the first edition of his collected works (17.2:425–70)—a publication which itself was a serious political risk for the friends of the deceased who issued it (though the edition was published in Berlin, by Duncker und Humblot). Hegel had been called to Berlin by reformist ministers; throughout his career Hegel persistently and conscientiously did all he could to support liberal republican reform (cf. Drydyk 1986; D'Hondt 1968, 1986; Vieweg 2012).

Hegel had allowed his former student Gans to assume his lectures on natural law. Near the end of 1830, the crown prince alleged to Hegel in person that Gans was making 'the students into republicans', an utter 'scandal!' (Nicolin 1970, 437). If Hegel were upset with Gans about this, it could only have been because Gans had been incautious about republicanism and its public avowal.[16] In the Preface to his *Philosophical Outlines of Justice*, published after the infamous Carlsbad Decree against demagogic literature, Hegel played with the old adage about the impossibility of leaping over Rhodes, revising it to advocate dancing in the cross of the present (*Rph*, GW 14.1:15/21). This too was a political comment—directed against the other-worldly Rosicrucianism of (*inter alia*) the Prussian crown prince!

Following the same theme as his word-play on Rhodes and rose, in the next paragraph Hegel writes:

> It is a great obstinacy, the kind of obstinacy which does honour to human beings, that they are unwilling to acknowledge in their attitudes [*Gesinnung*] anything which has not been justified by thought—and this obstinacy is characteristic of the modem age, as well as being the distinctive principle of Protestantism. What Luther inaugurated as faith in feeling and in the testimony of the spirit is the same as what spirit, at a more mature stage of its development, endeavours to comprehend conceptually so as to free itself in the present and thus find itself therein.
>
> (*Rph*, GW 14.1: 16.12–19/22; tr. Nisbet, rev. *KRW*)

'Obstinacy' renders '*Eigensinn*', which literally means 'sense of oneself'—the kind of paradoxical etymology Hegel prized. Hegel committed himself publicly, persistently, and in print to the Enlightenment ideals of autonomy, freedom, and republican reform through rational insight *and* justification. This is central to Hegel's further development

---

[16]   On Gans, see Hofheimer (1995), Waszek (2006).

of Hume's, Rousseau's, and Kant's Natural Law Constructivism. Hegel's project of 'reconciliation' is not quietist (cf. Hardimon 1992, 1994). Hegel's focus upon comprehending the present is itself justified by his recognition that only by comprehending and conscientiously assessing the present can we correctly identify and enjoy our individual and collective achievements in matters moral, *and* also correctly identify those aspects of our individual and collective lives wherein we ought to and can improve morally, and how best to do so.

Some will object that issues of universal human rights and racial equality are now *passé*—either because now we're all egalitarians, or because the Enlightenment project failed. To the contrary, Hegel realized, the Enlightenment project is unfinished because unenlightened views, policies, and practices remain all too well entrenched. He turns from the economic analysis of civil society to the Administration of Justice by observing:

However, this sphere of relations [the mutual relations of needs and work], as *enculturation*, itself first brings justice into *existence*, as something *universally recognised, known* and *willed*, and through this being known and willed, [justice] is valid and objectively actual.

It belongs to education, to *thinking* as the individual's consciousness in the form of universality, that I am comprehended as a *universal* person, in which *all* are identical. The *human being [Mensch] counts in this way, because he is a human being*, not because he is a Jew, Catholic, Protestant, German, Italian *etc*. This consciousness, to which this *thought* is valid, is infinitely important, and is only defective if it is fixed as a *cosmopolitanism* that is contrasted to the concrete life of the polity [*Staatsleben*].   (Hegel *Rph* §209 + R; 1821, 207; tr. *KRW*)

In a published footnote, Hegel comments critically on contemporaneous slavery in the USA (*Rph* §270R, n.2; 1821, 263–5).

This issue is not merely of historical importance. Consider Alexander H. Stephens (1812–1883), constitutional lawyer, politician, and Vice President of the Confederate States of America. Slavery *was* expressly the 'cornerstone' of the Southern US and then the Confederate economy, and based on the empirical claim that whites are naturally superior to blacks. Stephens' infamous 'Cornerstone' speech in Savannah (Georgia) of 1861, he claims (1910, 172–5), was somewhat misreported and seriously misunderstood, but equally unequivocal is his speech in Richmond before the Virginia State Convention (23 April 1861).[17] On the title page of the first volume of his *Constitutional View of the Late War Between the States*, Stephens proclaims: 'Times change and men often change with them, but principles never!' Yes, nothing is so timely and decisive as the timeless principles of justice; equally decisive and timely is the rationality involved in and required for revisions of beliefs—even deeply held beliefs—in view of their critical scrutiny. Empirical and moral errors can be revised and corrected, though not by dogmatism and, most unfortunately, not by dogmatists. To suppose, as Confederates did, and as self-proclaimed 'Neo-Confederates' do today, that states' rights take

---

[17] Both speeches are reprinted in Cleveland (1866), 717–44.

precedence over federal (national) rights on any issue of fundamental human rights is to be unenlightened and anti-Enlightenment. It is bad enough for the health of one's own soul (to speak with Socrates) to be eternally in profound moral error, but the culpable errors of racism continue to have terrible consequences for all people whose lives are affected by racists: And these are all of us, in view of the enormous and not always salutary influence of the USA on the economic and political world today. These historical documents remain current due to such white racist organizations as 'Occidental Dissent', which quotes both of Stephens' speeches approvingly—in 2012, in connection with its self-proclaimed 'Confederate History Month'. On the masthead of its website (accessed 30 September 2015), Occidental Dissent proudly declares it is 'Pro-White, Pro-South, Pro-Independence'.[18] The notorious segregationist four-term governor of Alabama, George Wallace, late in life announced he was 'born again' to Christianity, recanted his error, apologized to African-American civil rights leaders, and, still in office, acted to compensate for his own years of racist administration by appointing as many blacks as he could to positions of political responsibility.[19] By the views of 'Neo-Confederates', Wallace became a race traitor. All of these documents, and many more like them, both historical and current, including the various confederate Declarations of Cause for Secession, can be found online with a modicum of diligence— as can relevant documentation of persisting US and also Germanic racism, which did not die with Jörg Haider.[20]

Hegel's Kantian, Rousseauian emphasis on everyone's moral and political equality remains progressive today, and not merely as a humanitarian sentiment: Hegel realized that Kant's analyses of the autonomy of rational, justificatory judgment both justifies and requires moral and political equality: universally. With that principle established, the rest of his moral and political analysis shows how to rectify his chauvinism.

13.6. Conclusion

It should surprise no one that so very much of Hegel's social philosophy lived on in Dewey's, whose likes we fortunately see again in Onora O'Neill and in Axel Honneth (2014). It is our obligation to discern what best to retain, and what best to change, as we move forward—at the very least, chronologically—from here. For far too long, obstinately pre-Kantian philosophical preconceptions, and ideological cant masquerading as liberal individualism in opposition to totalitarian collectivism, have impeded progress in philosophy as in justice, in theory and in practice.

---

[18] <http://www.occidentaldissent.com/2012/04/06/confederate-history-month-2012-mississippis-declaration-of-causes-of-secession/> (accessed 30 September 2015).

[19] See Carter (1995), esp. 236–7; Edwards et al. (2009), 80; Wallace (1963a), (1963b).

[20] On Haider see, e.g., Höbelt (2002); Goldmann et al. (1992). On the USA, see, e.g., the Library of the University of North Carolina at Chapel Hill's project, 'Documenting the South'; and The Southern Poverty Law Center: <https://www.splcenter.org/>.

James Reid (1932–2010) understood this, in theory and in practice. It is striking that Reid's Rectorial Address to the University of Glasgow, 'Alienation', identifies the pervasive alienation and sociopathy produced by major economic decisions affecting most people's lives being taken by corporate and financial chiefs, without equally pervasive purview and oversight:

Government by the people for the people becomes meaningless unless it includes major economic decision-making by the people for the people. This is not simply an economic matter. In essence it is an ethical and moral question, for whoever takes the important economic decisions in society *ipso facto* determines the social priorities of that society.

From the Olympian heights of an executive suite, in an atmosphere where your success is judged by the extent to which you can maximise profits, the overwhelming tendency must be to see people as units of production, as indices in your accountants' books.   (Reid 1972, 8)

This is exactly the bottom line of Hegel's critique of open democratic elections by district (*Rph* §303R). There was already ample empirical evidence for this conclusion in 1821. Hegel's corporate system of representation is an ardently republican alternative, which can easily be made fully democratic when society is sufficiently civilized. This chapter is dedicated to the memory of James 'Jimmy' Reid, and to continuing his tireless work for social justice and political inclusion of all competent adults.[21]

References

Beck, Hermann, 1992. 'State and Society in Pre-March Prussia: The Weavers' Uprising, the Bureaucracy, and the Association for the Welfare of Workers'. *Central European History* 25.3: 303–31.

Böhme, Klaus, and Bernd Heidenreich, eds, 1999. 'Einigkeit *und Recht und Freiheit'. Die Revolution von 1848/49 im Bundesland Hessen*. Opladen & Wiesbaden, Westdeutscher Verlag.

Buck-Morss, Susan, 2009. *Hegel, Haiti, and Universal History*. Pittsburgh, University of Pittsburgh Press.

Bunsen, Christian Carl Josias Freiherr von, 1868, 1869, 1871. *Aus seinen Briefen und nach eigener Erinnerung, geschildert von seiner Witwe*, durch neue Mittheilungen vermehrt von F. Nippold (Leipzig, Brockhaus), 3 vols.

Carnap, Rudolf, 1950. *Logical Foundations of Probability*. Chicago, University of Chicago Press.

Carter, Dan T., 1995. *The Politics of Rage: George Wallace, the Origins of the New Conservatism, and the Transformation of American Politics*. Baton Rouge, Louisiana State University Press.

Chamely, Paul, 1963. *Economie politique chez Steuart et Hegel*. Paris, Dalloz.

Chamely, Paul, 1965. 'La Doctrine économique du Hegel et la conception Hegelienne du travail'. *Hegel-Studien* Beiheft 4: 147–59.

Chamely, Paul, 1967a. 'Les origines de la pensée économiue de Hegel'. *Hegel-Studien* 3: 225–61.

Chamely, Paul, 1967b. 'Notes de lecture relatives à Smith, Steuart et Hegel'. *Revue d'économie politique* 77.6: 857–78.

---

[21] The present research was generously supported by the Boğaziçi Üniversitesi Research Fund (BAP; grant code: 9761).

Cleveland, Henry, 1866. *Alexander H. Stephens in Public and Private: With Letters and Speeches Before, During, and Since the War.* Philadelphia, National Publishing Company.

Cullen, Bernard, 1988. 'The Mediating Role of Estates and Corporations in Hegel's Theory of Political Representation'. In *Hegel Today* (Aldershot, Gower), 22–41.

Devas, Charles, 1901. *Political Economy*, 2nd rev. ed. London, Longmans, Green & Co.

deVries, Wilhelm, 1991. 'The Dialectic of Teleology'. *Philosophical Topics* 19.2: 51–70.

Dewey, John, 1922. *Human Nature and Conduct: An Introduction to Social Psychology.* New York, Holt & Co.

Dewey, John, 1930. *Individualism, Old and New.* New York, Minton, Balch & Co.

D'Hondt, Jacques, 1968. *Hegel en son temps: (Berlin, 1818–1831).* Paris, Éditions sociales; engl. tr. (1988).

D'Hondt, Jacques, 1986. *Hegel secret: recherches sur les sources cachées de la pensée de Hegel.* Paris, Presses universitaires de France.

D'Hondt, Jacques, 1988. J. Burbridge, tr., *Hegel in his Time: Berlin, 1818–1831.* Peterborough, Ont., Broadview.

Drydyk, Jay, 1986. 'Hegel's Politics: Liberal or Democratic?'. *Canadian Journal of Philosophy* 16.1: 99–122.

Edwards, George C. III, Martin P. Wattenberg, and Robert L. Lineberry, 2009. *Government in America: People, Politics, and Policy.* New York, Pearson Education.

Erickson, Paul, Judy L. Klein, Lorraine Daston, Rebecca Lemov, Thomas Sturm, and Michael D. Gordin, 2013. *How Reason Almost Lost Its Mind: The Strange Career of Cold War Rationality.* Chicago, University of Chicago Press.

Ferguson, Adam, 1787. *An Essay on the History of Civil Society*, 5th ed. London, Cadell; Edinburgh, Creech & Bell. Critical edition by F. Oz-Salzberger, Cambridge University Press, 1995.

George, William Henry, 1922. 'Montesquieu and De Tocqueville and Corporative Individualism'. *American Political Science Review* 16.1: 10–21.

Goldmann, Harald, Hannes Krall, and Klaus Ottomeyer, 1992. *Jörg Haider und sein Publikum: eine sozialpsychologische Untersuchung.* Klagenfurt, Drava.

Gouge, Olympe de, 1791. 'Déclaration des droits de la femme et de la citoyenne'. Paris; <http://www.philo5.com/Mes%20per%20cent20lectures/GougesOlympeDe-DeclarationDroitsFemme.htm>.

Green, Thomas Hill, 1883. A.C. Bradley, ed., *Prolegomena to Ethics*, 4th ed. Oxford, The Clarendon Press.

Hardimon, Michael, 1992. 'The Project of Reconciliation: Hegel's Social Philosophy'. *Philosophy and Public Affairs* 21.2: 165–95.

Hardimon, Michael, 1994. *Hegel's Social Philosophy: The Project of Reconciliation.* Cambridge, Cambridge University Press.

Hare, R.M., 1960. 'Philosophical Discoveries'. *Mind* 69.274: 145–62.

Hegel, G.W.F. [Anon.], 1798. 'Vertrauliche Briefe über das vormalige staatsrechtliche Verhältnis des Wadtlandes (Pays de Vaud) zur Stadt Bern. Eine völlige Aufdeckung der ehemaligen Oligarchie des Standes Bern. Aus dem Französischen eines verstorbenen Schweizers [Jean Jacques Cart] übersetzt und mit Anmerkungen versehen'. Frankfurt am Main, Jäger; in: *GW 3*.

Hegel, G.W.F., 1807. *Phänomenologie des Geistes.* Bamberg & Würzburg, Goephard; W. Bonsiepen & R. Heede, eds, in *GW* 9.

Hegel, G.W.F., 1817. 'Verhandlungen in der Versammlung der Landstände des Königreichs Württemberg im Jahr 1815 und 1816. XXXIII Abteilungen'. *Heidelbergische Jahrbücher der Literatur* 10.66–68:1041–88, 10:73–77:1153–1232; rpt. in: *GW* 15; engl. tr. (1964), 246–94.

Hegel, G.W.F., 1821. *Grundlinien der Philosophie des Rechts oder Naturrecht und Staatswissenschaft im Grundrisse.* Berlin, Nicolai; abbreviated '*Rph*', cited by main sections (§) or by Hegel's published Remarks (§*n*R); *GW* 14.

Hegel, G.W.F., 1831. 'Über die englische Reformbill'. *Allgemeine preußische Staats-Zeitung*, 1831, Nr. 115–16, 118; second half printed and circulated privately. Published complete in G.W.F. Hegel (1832–45), vol. 17.2 (1835): 425–470; Engl. tr. in G.W.F. Hegel (1994a), 234–70.

Hegel, G.W.F., 1832–1845. *Georg Wilhelm Friedrich Hegel's Werke.* Vollständige Ausgabe durch einen Verein von Freunden des Verewigten (Berlin, Duncker und Humblot), 19 vols.

Hegel, G.W.F., 1964. T.M. Knox, tr., *Hegel's Political Writings.* Oxford, Clarendon Press.

Hegel, G.W.F., 1974. K.-H. Ilting, ed., *Vorlesungen über Rechtsphilosophie 1818–1831*, 6 vols. Stuttgart-Bad-Cannstadt, frommann-holzboog.

Hegel, G.W.F., 1986–2013. *Gesammelte Werke*, 31 vols. Deutsche Forschungsgemeinschaft, with the Hegel-Kommission der Rheinisch-Westfälischen Akademie der Wissenschaften and the Hegel-Archiv der Ruhr-Universität Bochum. Hamburg, Meiner; cited as '*GW*' by volume:page.line numbers. Individual works are indicated by their German initials. Volumes 23–31 contain lecture manuscripts or transcripts; these are cited as '*Vor.*' by volume:page numbers. These references are used in all recent, reliable translations.

Hegel, G.W.F., 1991. *Elements of the Philosophy of Right.* A. Wood, ed., H. B. Nisbet, tr., Cambridge, Cambridge University Press; abbreviated '*Rph*', cited by main sections (§), by Hegel's published Remarks (§*n*R) or very occasionally by lecture notes (§*n*Z) ('*Z*' for '*Zusatz*'); *GW* 14. Hegel, G.W.F., 1994a. *Political Writings.* L. Dickey, ed., H.B. Nisbet, tr. Cambridge, Cambridge University Press.

Hegel, G.W.F., 1994b. 'Community as the Basis of Free Individual Action'. Excerpts from Hegel (1807), K. R. Westphal, tr. and notes; in M. Daly, ed., *Communitarianism* (Belmont, CA: Wadsworth), 36–40.

Hegel, G.W.F., 2009. K. Worm, ed., *Hegels Werk im Kontext*, 5th Release. Berlin, InfoSoftWare.

Hegel, G.W.F., forthcoming. *The Phenomenology of Spirit*, T. Pinkard, tr. Draft bi-lingual translation in PDF format; cited by paragraph (¶) numbers correctly provided by the translator corresponding to *GW* 9.

Heiman, G., 1971. 'The Sources and Significance of Hegel's Corporate Doctrine'. In Z.A. Pelczynski, ed., *Hegel's Political Philosophy* (Cambridge: Cambridge University Press, 1971), 111–35.

Herman, Barbara, 2007. *Moral Literacy.* Cambridge, MA, Harvard University Press.

Herman, Edward, and Noam Chomsky, 1988. *Manufacturing Consent: The Political Economy of the Mass Media.* New York, Pantheon; 2nd ed. with new Introduction, 2002.

Höbelt, Lothar, 2002. *Jörg Haider and the Politics of Austria, 1986–2000.* West Lafayette, IN, Purdue University Press.

Hofheimer, Michael, 1995. *Eduard Gans and the Hegelian Philosophy of Law*. Dordrecht, Kluwer.

Hofheimer, Michael, 2001. 'Hegel, Race, Genocide'. *The Southern Journal of Philosophy* 39: 35–65.

Honneth, Axel, 2014. *Freedom's Right*. Cambridge, Polity.

Hoy, Jocelyn B., 2009. 'Hegel, Antigone, and Feminist Critique: The Spirit of Ancient Greece'. In K.R. Westphal, ed., *The Blackwell Guide to Hegel's Phenomenology of Spirit* (London, Blackwell), 172–89.

Humboldt, Wilhelm von, 1851. *Ideen zu einem Versuch, die Gränzen der Wirksamkiet des Staats zu Bestimmen*. Breslau, Trewendt; rpt. in Wilhelm von Humboldt (1903), 1:97–254; engl. tr. in *idem*. (1969).

Humboldt, Wilhelm von, 1903. A. Leitzmann, ed., *Wilhelm von Humboldts Gesammelte Schriften* (Berlin, Behr), vol. 1.

Humboldt, Wilhelm von, 1969. J. W. Burrow, tr., *The Limits of State Action*. London, Cambridge University Press.

Jamme, Christoph, 1986. 'Die Erziehung der Stände durch sich selbst: Hegels Konzeption der neuständisch-bürgerlichen Repräsentation in Heidelberg 1817/18'. In H.-C. Lucas and O. Pöggeler, eds, *Hegels Rechtsphilosophie im Zusammenhang der europäischen Verfassungsgeschichte* (Stuttgart-Bad Cannstatt, Frommann-Holzboog), 160–1.

Kant, Immanuel, 1798. *Die Metaphysik der Sitten*, in *GS* 6:205–493; cited as '*MdS*' (for its introductory materials) or by '§' of its first (*RL*) or second (*TL*) Parts: *Rechtslehre* (Doctrine of Justice) and *Tugendlehre* (Doctrine of Virtue).

Kant, Immanuel, 1902–. *Kants Gesammelte Schriften*. Königlich Preussische, now Berlin-Brandenburgische Akademie der Wissenschaften. Berlin, Reimer, now deGruyter; cited by the initials of Kant's titles and volume:page numbers.

Kant, Immanuel, 1999. *Practical Philosophy*. M.J. Gregor, tr., Cambridge, Cambridge University Press; cited by volume:page numbers of Kant's *Gesammelte Schriften* ('*GS*'), printed in the margins.

Kaufmann, Walter, 1951. 'The Hegel Myth and its Method'. *Philosophical Review* 60.4: 459–86.

Lübbe-Wolff, Gertrude, 1981. 'Hegels Staatsrecht als Stellungnahme im ersten preußischen Verfassungskampf'. *Zeitschrift für philosophische Forschung* 35: 476–501.

Lübbe-Wolff, Gertrude, 1986. 'Über das Fehlen von Grundrechten in Hegel's Rechtsphilosophie'. In H.-C. Lucas and O. Pöggeler, eds, *Hegels Rechtsphilosophie im Zusammenhang der europäischen Verfassungsgeschichte* (Stuttgart-Bad Cannstatt, Frommann-Holzboog), 421–46.

Marx, Karl, 1843. *Marx's Critique of Hegel's Philosophy of Right*. T. O'Malley, tr. Oxford Oxford University Press, 1970.

Neuhouser, Frederick, 2000. *The Foundations of Hegel's Social Theory*. Cambridge, MA, Harvard University Press.

Nicolin, Günter, 1970. *Hegel in Berichte seiner Zeitgenossen*. Hamburg, Meiner.

O'Neill, Onora, 1992. 'Vindicating Reason'. In Paul Guyer, ed., *The Cambridge Companion to Kant* (Cambridge, Cambridge University Press), 280–308.

O'Neill, Onora, 2004. 'Autonomy, Plurality and Public Reason'. In Natalie Brender and Larry Krasnoff, eds, *New Essays on the History of Autonomy* (Cambridge, Cambridge University Press), 181–94.

O'Neill, Onora, 2015. 'Autonomy and Public Reason in Kant'. In Mark Timmons and Robert Johnson, eds, *Reason, Value, and Respect: Kantian Themes from the Philosophy of Thomas E. Hill, Jr* (Oxford, Oxford University Press), 119–31.

Pascal, Roy, 1962. '"Bildung" and the Division of Labor'. In *German Studies: Presented to Walter Horace Bruford on His Retirement by His Pupils, Colleagues, and Friends* (London, Harrap), 14–28.

Plant, Raymond, 1973. *Hegel*. London, George Allen & Unwin.

Plant, Raymond, 1980. 'Economic and Social Integration in Hegel's Political Philosophy'. In D.P. Verene, ed., *Hegel's Social and Political Thought: The Philosophy of Objective Spirit* (Atlantic Highlands, Humanities), 59–90.

Plant, Raymond, 1984. 'Hegel on Identity and Legitimation'. In Z.A. Pelczynski, ed., *The State and Civil Society* (Cambridge, Cambridge University Press), 227–43.

Rawls, John, 2000. *Lectures on the History of Moral Philosophy*, ed. B. Herman. Cambridge, MA, Harvard University Press.

Reid, James, 1972. 'Alienation'. Rectorial Address to Glasgow University, 28 April 1972; Glasgow University Publications; <www.gla.ac.uk/media/media_167194_en.pdf>.

Reisch, George, 2005. *How the Cold War Transformed the Philosophy of Science*. Cambridge, Cambridge University Press.

Reisch, George, 2007. 'From "the Life of the Present" to the "Icy Slopes of Logic": Logical Empiricism, the Unity of Science Movement, and the Cold War'. In A. Richardson and T. Uebel, eds, *The Cambridge Companion to Logical Empiricism* (Cambridge, Cambridge University Press), 58–87.

Rothschild, Emma, and Amartya Sen, 2006. 'Adam Smith's Economics'. In K. Haakonssen, ed., *The Cambridge Companion to Adam Smith* (Cambridge, Cambridge University Press), 319–365.

Sans, Georg, 2004. *Die Realisierung des Begriffs. Eine Untersuchung zu Hegels Schlusslehre*. Berlin, Akademie Verlag (de Gruyter).

Schultz, Walter, 2001. *The Moral Conditions of Economic Efficiency*. Cambridge, Cambridge University Press.

Smith, Adam, 1784. *An Inquiry into the Nature and Causes of the Wealth of Nations*, 3rd ed. London, Strahan and Cadell; rpt. (1811), vols. 2–4.

Smith, Adam, 1811. D. Stewart, ed., *The Works of Adam Smith*, 5 vols. London, Cadell; Edinburgh, Davies and Creech.

Stephens, Alexander H., 1867–70. *A Constitutional View of the Late War Between the States*, 2 vols. Philadelphia, National Publishing Co.; Chicago and St Louis, Zeigler, McCurty & Co.

Stephens, Alexander H., 1910. M.L. Avary, ed., *Recollections of Alexander H. Stephens. His diary kept when a prisoner at Fort Warren, Boston Harbour, 1865; giving incidents and reflections of his prison life and some letters and reminiscences*. New York, Doubleday, Page & Company.

Stewart, Jon, ed., 1996. *The Hegel Myths and Legends*. Evanston, IL, Northwestern University Press.

Tetens, Johann N., 1775. *Über die allgemeine speculativische Philosophie*. Bützow and Wismar, Boedner.

Tönnies, Ferdinand, 1909. *Die Sitte*. Frankfurt am Main, Literarische Anstalt Rütten & Loening.

Tönnies, Ferdinand, 1961. A.F. Borenstein, tr., *Custom: An Essay on Social Codes*. Glencoe, IL, Free Press.

Vieweg, Klaus, 2012. *Das Denken der Freiheit. Hegels Grundlinien der Philosophie des Rechts*. München, Fink.

University of North Carolina at Chapel Hill Library: Documenting the South. <http://docsouth.unc.edu/%20index.html> (accessed 30 September 2015).

Wallace, George C., 1963a. Inaugural Address, delivered at the Capitol in Montgomery, Alabama, 14 January 1963; State of Alabama Archive (file name: 'Q20276-Q20290'; accessed: 4 October 2015): <http://digital.%20archives.alabama.gov/cdm/singleitem/collection/voices/id/2952/rec/6>.

Wallace, George C., 1963b. 'Schoolhouse Door Speech', 11 June 1963, blocking two black students from registering at the University of Alabama; State of Alabama Archive (accessed: 4 October 2015): <http://www.archives.%20state.al.us/govs_list/schooldoor.html>.

Walton, A.S., 1984. 'Economy, Utility, and Community in Hegel's Theory of Civil Society'. In Z.A. Pelczynski, ed., *The State and Civil Society* (Cambridge, Cambridge University Press), 244–61.

Waszek, Norbert, 1984. 'Hegels schottische Bettler'. *Hegel-Studien* 19: 311–16.

Waszek, Norbert, 1988. *The Scottish Enlightenment and Hegel's Account of 'Civil Society'*. Dordrecht, Kluwer.

Waszek, Norbert, 2006. 'Eduard Gans on Poverty and on the Constitutional Debate'. In D. Moggach, ed., *The New Hegelians: Politics and Philosophy in the Hegelian School* (Cambridge, Cambridge University Press), 24–49.

Westphal, Kenneth R., 1993. 'The Basic Context and Structure of Hegel's *Philosophy of Right*'. In F.C. Beiser, ed., *The Cambridge Companion to Hegel* (Cambridge, Cambridge University Press), 234–69.

Westphal, Kenneth R., 1998. 'Hegel's Solution to the Dilemma of the Criterion'. In J. Stewart, ed., *The Phenomenology of Spirit Reader: A Collection of Critical and Interpretive Essays* (Albany, SUNY Press), 76–91.

Westphal, Kenneth R., 2002. 'Hegel's Standards of Political Legitimacy'. *Jahrbuch für Recht und Ethik/Annual Review of Law and Ethics* 10: 307–20.

Westphal, Kenneth R., 2003. *Hegel's Epistemology: A Philosophical Introduction to the Phenomenology of Spirit*. Cambridge, MA, Hackett Publishing Co.

Westphal, Kenneth R., 2007. 'Normative Constructivism: Hegel's Radical Social Philosophy'. *SATS—Nordic Journal of Philosophy* 8.2: 7–41.

Westphal, Kenneth R., 2009a. 'Hegel's Phenomenological Method and Analysis of Consciousness'. In K. R. Westphal, ed., *The Blackwell Guide to Hegel's Phenomenology of Spirit* (Oxford, Wiley-Blackwell), 1–36.

Westphal, Kenneth R., 2009b. 'Does Kant's *Opus Postumum* Anticipate Hegel's Absolute Idealism?' In E.-O. Onnasch, ed., *Kants Philosophie der Natur. Ihre Entwicklung bis zum Opus postumum und Nachwirkung* (Berlin, deGruyter), 357–83.

Westphal, Kenneth R., 2009c. 'Kant, Hegel and Determining Our Duties'. In D. Knowles, ed., *G. W. F. Hegel* (Aldershot, Ashgate), 337–56.

Westphal, Kenneth R., 2010. 'Hegel'. In J. Skorupski, ed., *The Routledge Companion to Ethics* (London, Routledge), 168–80.

Westphal, Kenneth R., 2010–11. 'Analytic Philosophy and the Long Tail of *Scientia*: Hegel and the Historicity of Philosophy'. *The Owl of Minerva* 42.1–2: 1–18.

Westphal, Kenneth R., 2013a. 'Proof, Justification, Refutation'. In A. deLaurentiis and B. J. Edwards, eds, *The Bloomsbury Companion to Hegel* (London, Bloomsbury Publishing), 289–302.

Westphal, Kenneth R., 2013b. 'Rational Justification and Mutual Recognition in Substantive Domains'. *Dialogue: Canadian Journal of Philosophy/Revue canadienne de philosophie* 52: 1–40.

Westphal, Kenneth R., 2013c. 'Natural Law, Social Contract and Moral Objectivity: Rousseau's Natural Law Constructivism'. *Jurisprudence* 4.1: 48–75.

Westphal, Kenneth R., 2013d. 'Substantive Philosophy, Infallibilism and the Critique of Metaphysics: Hegel and the Historicity of Philosophical Reason'. In L. Herzog, ed., *Hegel's Thought in Europe: Currents, Cross-Currents and Undercurrents* (Basingstoke, Palgrave Macmillan), 192–220.

Westphal, Kenneth R., 2014. 'Hegel's Semantics of Singular Cognitive Reference, Newton's Methodological Rule Four and Scientific Realism Today'. *Philosophical Inquiries* 2.1: 9–65.

Westphal, Kenneth R., 2015a. 'Hegel's Pragmatic Critique and Reconstruction of Kant's System of Principles in the 1807 *Phenomenology of Spirit*'. In N. Gascoigne, guest ed., *Hegel & Pragmatism; Hegel Bulletin* 36.2: 159–86.

Westphal, Kenneth R., 2015b. 'Hegel's Pragmatic Critique and Reconstruction of Kant's System of Principles in the *Logic & Encyclopaedia*'. *Dialogue: Canadian Journal of Philosophy/Revue canadienne de philosophie* 54.2: 333–69.

Westphal, Kenneth R., 2016a. *How Hume and Kant Reconstruct Natural Law: Justifying Strict Objectivity without Debating Moral Realism*. Oxford, Clarendon Press.

Westphal, Kenneth R., 2016b. 'The Centrality of Public Reason in Hegel's Moral Philosophy'. In P.N. Turner and G. Gaus, eds, *Public Reason in the History of Political Philosophy: Classical Sources and Contemporary Commentaries* (London and New York, Routledge).

Westphal, Kenneth R., 2016c. 'Mind, Language and Behaviour: Kant's Critical Cautions *contra* Contemporary Internalism and Causal Naturalism'. In S. Babür, ed., *Method in Philosophy* (İstanbul: Yeditepe Üniversitesi Press).

Westphal, Kenneth R., 2016d. 'Cognitive Psychology, Intelligence and the Realisation of the Concept in Hegel's Anti-Cartesian Epistemology'. In S. Herrmann-Sinai and L. Ziglioli, eds, *Hegel's Philosophical Psychology* (New York and London, Routledge).

Wood, Allen, 1990. *Hegel's Ethical Theory*. Cambridge, Cambridge University Press.

Index

Allison, Henry 31, 149
Antigone 98, 265
Aquinas, Thomas 16, 189–91
Aristotle 6, 34, 36, 72–4, 76, 104, 158, 167–8

Beaney, Michael 27
Berlin, Isaiah 194, 253
Beiser, Frederick 30, 48, 50, 82–3, 161, 204
Boyle, Michael 150–1
Brandom, Robert 34
Brooks, Thom 1–2, 17–18, 23, 82, 161, 173, 183,
    188, 197, 200, 202–3, 209–10, 216–17, 220
Brudner, Alan 211–12
Butler, Judith 241, 242–3, 246, 250

Carnap, Rudolf 25–6, 29, 257
Cooper, David 202–4, 219
Cullen, Bernard 267–8

Davidson, Donald 151
Deligiorgi, Katerina 16–17, 168, 183, 194
Disley, Liz 20–1, 247

Fichte, Johann Gottlieb 4, 8–9, 13, 29–33, 37,
    42, 87–93, 100, 145, 194, 198
Findlay, J. N. 202, 213, 251

Gans, Eduard 124, 270
Geach, Peter 16, 185, 189–92
Goodfield, Eric Lee 82
Green, Thomas Hill 218, 220

Hardimon, Michael 45, 271
Hartmann, Klaus 45, 134, 183
Hegel, Georg Wilhelm Friedrich 1–279
Heidegger, Martin 26–7, 30
Honneth, Axel 36, 161, 183, 272
Houlgate, Stephen vii, 47, 82, 124, 165–6,
    169, 188, 199
Hume, David 22, 30, 33, 152, 156–7, 159,
    166, 259–60, 271

Ilting, Karl-Heinz 45, 125, 268
Inwood, Michael vii, 130, 161, 175, 179, 202

Kant, Immanuel 4–6, 8–9, 13, 16, 18, 22–3,
    28–33, 35, 37, 39, 42–3, 55, 67, 69–73, 78, 85,
    87–9, 91–2, 98, 104, 110, 112–13, 116, 136,
    142–3, 145–9, 152–7, 159–60, 161, 163, 167,

185–7, 194, 197–8, 203, 210–12, 217, 243–7,
    249, 252, 256–63, 271–2
Keynes, J. M. 83, 263
Knowles, Dudley 2, 204, 211, 213–14
Korsgaard, Christine 146, 156
Kreines, James 161

Longuenesse, Beatrice 156, 161, 167

Marcuse, Herbert 245
Marx, Karl 1, 7, 26, 30, 79–80, 85, 99, 244,
    246, 253
Moyar, Dean 68, 183, 243–4
Mure, R. G. R. 74, 77

Neuhouser, Frederick 3, 45, 183, 194,
    196–8, 260
Nietzsche, Friedrich 27, 32, 253
Nuzzo, Angelica 10–11, 103, 168

O'Connor, Brian vii, 168, 175, 217

Parekh, Bhikhu vii
Pelczynski, Z. A. 1–2, 202, 248
Peperzak, Adriaan 44
Pinkard, Terry 13–15, 28, 45, 72, 149, 153–4,
    177–8, 183
Pippin, Robert vii, 6–7, 28, 45, 67, 125, 146–7,
    151, 154, 156, 161, 163, 168, 178, 194–5, 246
Plant, Raymond 266–7
Popper, Karl 1, 253
Primoratz, Igor 202

Quante, Michael 83
Quine, W. V. O. 37

Redding, Paul 4–5, 30, 72–3, 83, 188
Reyburn, Hugh 44
Riedel, Manfred 44, 72
Ritter, Joachim 45, 72
Rorty, Richard 4, 25–31, 33, 40–3
Rosen, Michael vii, 62, 77
Ruda, Frank 175
Russell, Bertrand 1, 27, 86, 184

Sartre, Jean-Paul 26–7, 29–30, 241
Schelling, Friedrich 87, 89, 106, 253–4
Sedgwick, Sally 163
Sellars, Wilfried 26, 245, 258

Siep, Ludwig 125, 132–3, 167
Snellman, Johan Vilhelm 263
Socrates 74, 172, 176, 190–2, 229, 248,
    260, 272
Spinoza, Baruch 16, 162, 166, 168, 186
Stein, Sebastian 11, 15–16, 162, 166, 168–9,
    177, 200
Stern, Robert vii, 165, 244
Stillman, Peter G. 202, 213
Stone, Allison 175
Strawson, Peter 71

Taylor, Charles 45, 84, 185
Thompson, Kevin 5–6, 166–7

Vieweg, Klaus vii, 11–13, 77, 123, 124, 136, 161,
    175, 270
von Humboldt, Wilhelm 256, 266

Wallace, R. J. 144, 147–8, 151, 154–6
Westphal, Kenneth R. 21–3, 161, 169, 177–8,
    184–5, 195, 197–8, 254–5, 258–62
Williams, Bernard 35, 146, 183–4
Winfield, Richard Dien 19–20, 168, 175, 228,
    237–8, 239–40
Wittgenstein, Ludwig 26, 86
Wolff, Michael 49, 69–71, 125, 133–5
Wood, Allen W. 3, 7–9, 32, 45, 67, 84–5, 146,
    161, 178, 183, 197, 202–4, 210, 213, 249, 253